I'm so happy to be able to take a photo like this. It's a fusuma with the kanji for Fear on it. Cool, right? This was part of the set at an event called the Night Parade of a Hundred Demons Banquet. Next to it was a sakura tree. It wasn't thick enough for Rikuo or Gozumaru to climb, though! (*laughs*) I sure was happy to see the world of my work come to life!

—HIROSHI SHIIBASHI,
2011

HIROSHI SHIIBASHI debuted in BUSINESS JUMP magazine with *Aratama*. NURA: RISE OF THE YOKAI CLAN is his breakout hit. He was an assistant to manga artist Hirohiko Araki, the creator of *Jojo's Bizarre Adventure*. *Steel Ball Run* by Araki is one of his favorite manga.

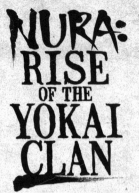

NURA: RISE OF THE YOKAI CLAN

NURA: RISE OF THE YOKAI CLAN
VOLUME 15
SHONEN JUMP Manga Edition

Story and Art by HIROSHI SHIIBASHI

Translation – John Werry
Touch-up Art and Lettering – Annaliese Christman
Graphics and Cover Design – Fawn Lau
Editor – Joel Enos, Megan Bates

Printed in the U.S.A.

Published by VIZ Media, LLC
P.O. Box 77010
San Francisco, CA 94107

10 9 8 7 6 5 4 3 2 1
First printing, June 2013

www.viz.com www.shonenjump.com

NURA: RISE OF THE YOKAI CLAN

15

FRAGMENTS OF THE PAST

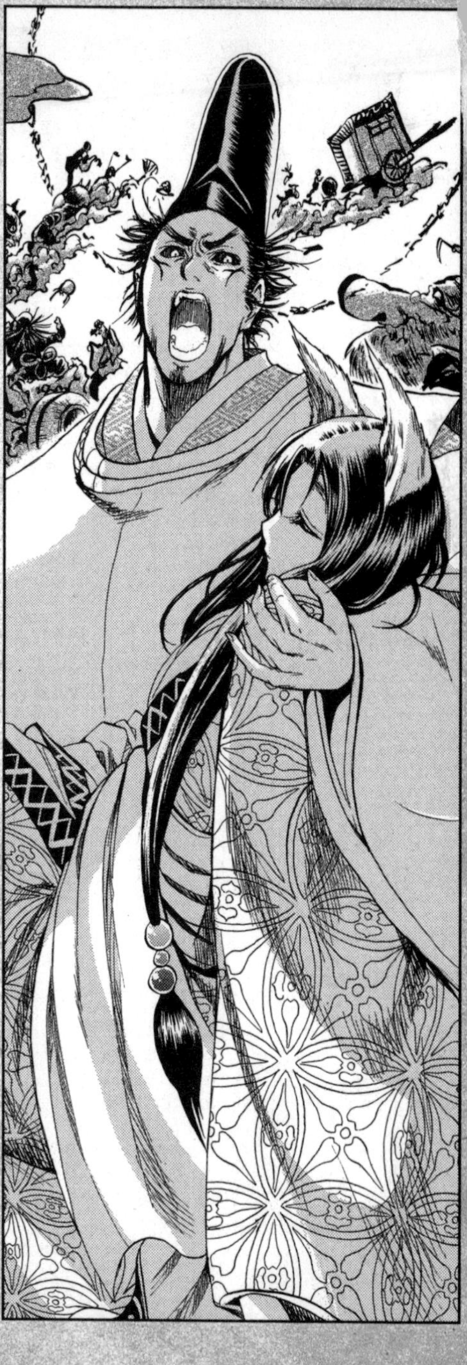

STORY AND ART BY
HIROSHI SHIIBASHI

CHARACTERS

NURARIHYON

Rikuo's grandfather and the Lord of Pandemonium. He intends to pass leadership of the Nura clan—a powerful yokai consortium—to Rikuo. He's a mischievous sort who enjoys slipping out of diners without paying his bill.

RIKUO NURA

Though he appears to be a human boy, he's actually the grandson of Nurarihyon, a yokai. His grandfather's blood makes him one-quarter yokai, and he transforms into a yokai at times.

KIYOTSUGU

Rikuo's classmate. He has adored yokai ever since Rikuo saved him in his yokai form, leading him to form the Kiyojuji Paranormal Patrol.

KANA IENAGA

Rikuo's classmate and a childhood friend. Even though she hates scary things, she's a member of the Kiyojuji Paranormal Patrol for some reason.

YUKI-ONNA

A yokai of the Nura clan who is in charge of looking after Rikuo. She disguises herself as a human and attends the same school as Rikuo to protect him from danger. When in human form, she goes by the name Tsurara Oikawa.

YURA KEIKAIN

Rikuo's classmate and a descendant of the Keikain family of onmyoji. She transferred into Ukiyoe Middle School to do field training in yokai exorcism. She has the power to control her shikigami and uses them to destroy yokai.

HAGOROMO-GITSUNE

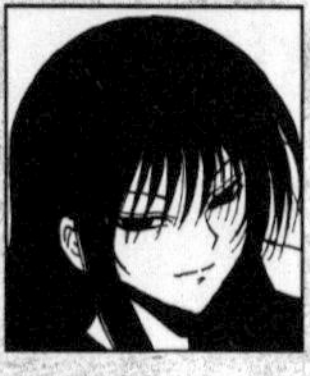

A great Kyoto yokai who has a fateful connection to both Nurarihyon and the Keikain family. She possesses humans and forces them to do evil things. She has returned to life after a 400-year absence.

KUROTABO

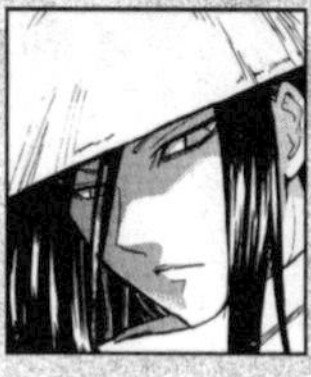

A Nura clan yokai, also known as the Father of Destruction. One of the clan's best warriors, he hides a healthy arsenal of lethal weapons under his priest's robe.

TSUCHIGUMO

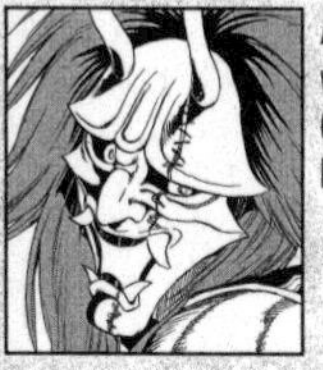

A rogue-minded Kyoto yokai who won't bow to Hagoromo-Gitsune. He's so powerful, he's known as an ayakashi to avoid.

KIDOMARU

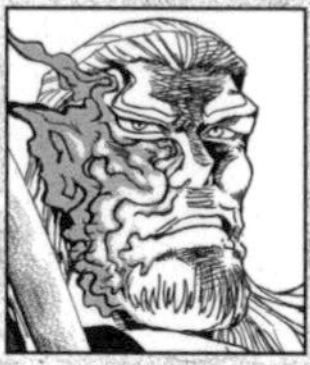

An executive of Kyoto yokai who's been serving Abe no Seimei since the Heian period. Hence, he strongly desires Nue's revival.

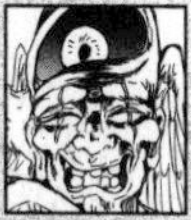

MINAGOROSHI-JIZO

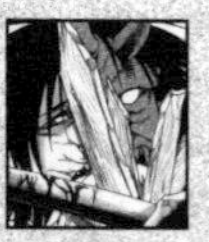

IBARAKI-DOJI

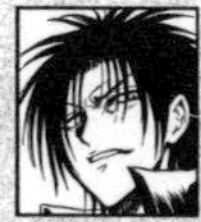

RYUJI

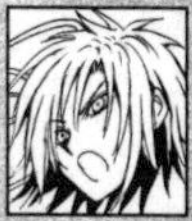

KUBINASHI

STORY SO FAR

Rikuo Nura is a seventh-grader at Ukiyoe Middle School. At a glance, he appears to be just another average, normal boy. But he's actually the grandson of the yokai Overlord Nurarihyon. He's also the Underboss of the powerful Nura clan. He spends his days as a human, despite the clan's hopes that he will someday become a great Overlord like his grandfather.

Itaku and others join the battle against Tsuchigumo! By doing an Equip attack move called Indigo Aster Scythe with Itaku, Rikuo cuts Tsuchigumo in half with a single blow—but still doesn't beat him! Tsuchigumo appears to have enjoyed this deadly fight. Before leaving, he tells Rikuo that Nue is actually the legendary onmyoji Abe no Seimei.

Meanwhile, Nurarihyon goes to Kyoto, where he has a fateful reunion with Hagoromo-Gitsune at the Pond of Nue, her spawning ground. Nurarihyon senses a strange and evil Fear coming from Nue in Hagoromo-Gitsune's womb and realizes with dismay that birth is near. He turns his sword on her, but the Kyoto yokai attack in large number and he barely escapes with his life.

Rikuo fights his way into Nijo Castle only to find Kidomaru blocking his way. Kidomaru withstands Rikuo's Equip with Tsurara, but then Kurotabo and others show up.

TABLE OF CONTENTS

NURA:RISE OF THE YOKAI CLAN

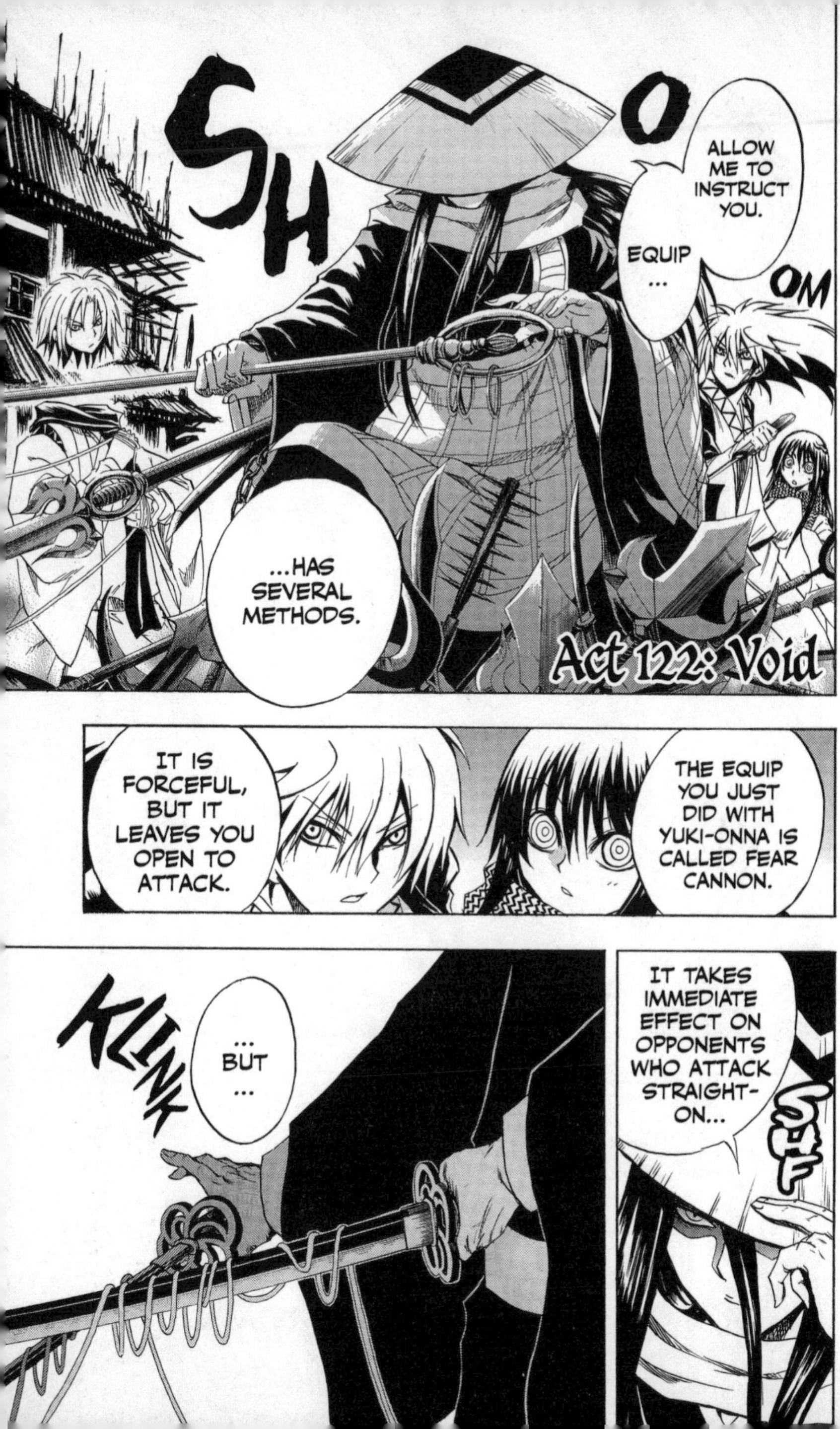
SH O OM
ALLOW ME TO INSTRUCT YOU.
EQUIP ...
...HAS SEVERAL METHODS.
Act 122: Void
THE EQUIP YOU JUST DID WITH YUKI-ONNA IS CALLED FEAR CANNON.
IT IS FORCEFUL, BUT IT LEAVES YOU OPEN TO ATTACK.
IT TAKES IMMEDIATE EFFECT ON OPPONENTS WHO ATTACK STRAIGHT-ON...
KLINK
... BUT ...

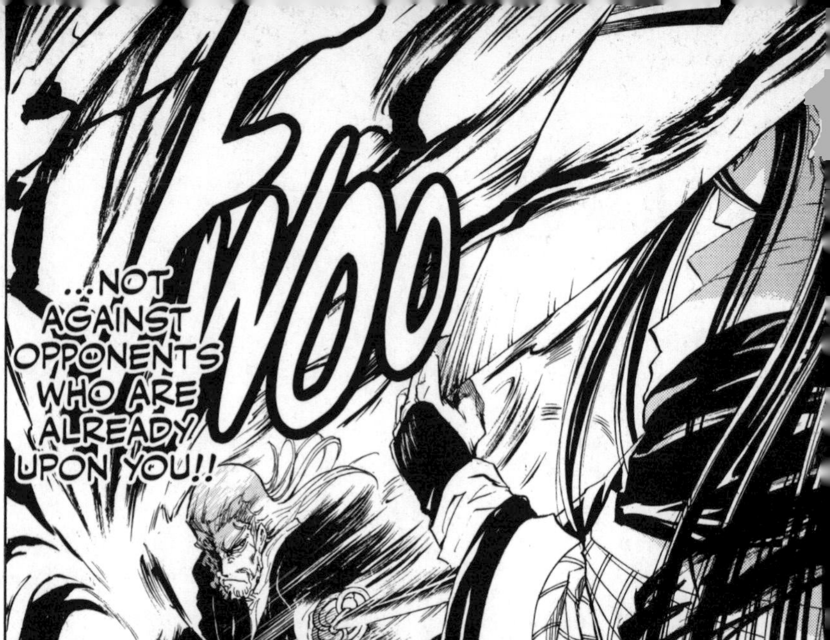
...NOT AGAINST OPPONENTS WHO ARE ALREADY UPON YOU!!
WHOOSH

Act 122: Void

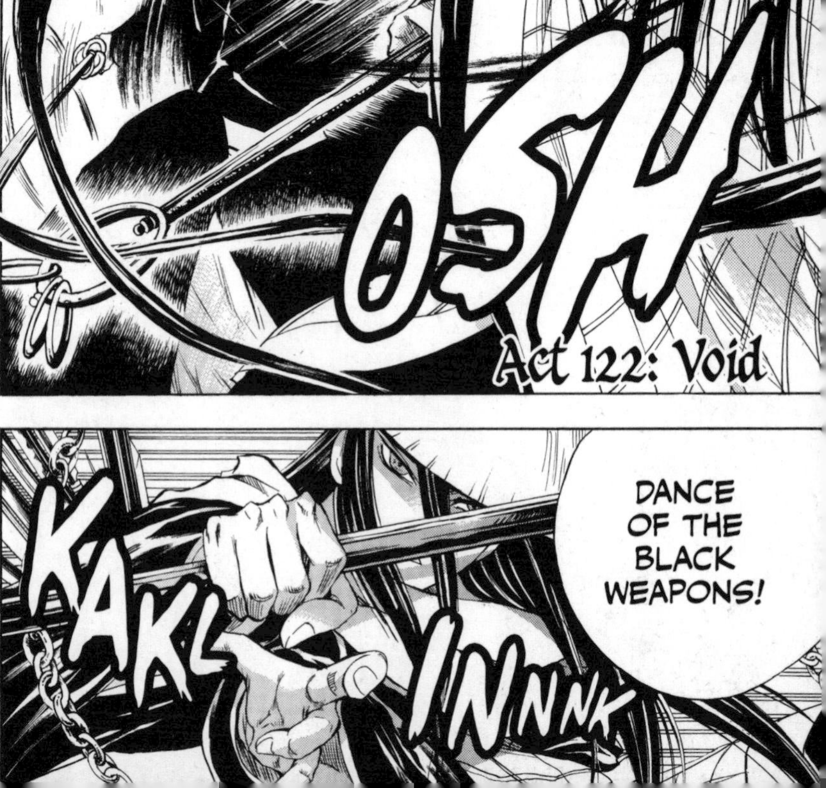
DANCE OF THE BLACK WEAPONS!
KAKLINNNK

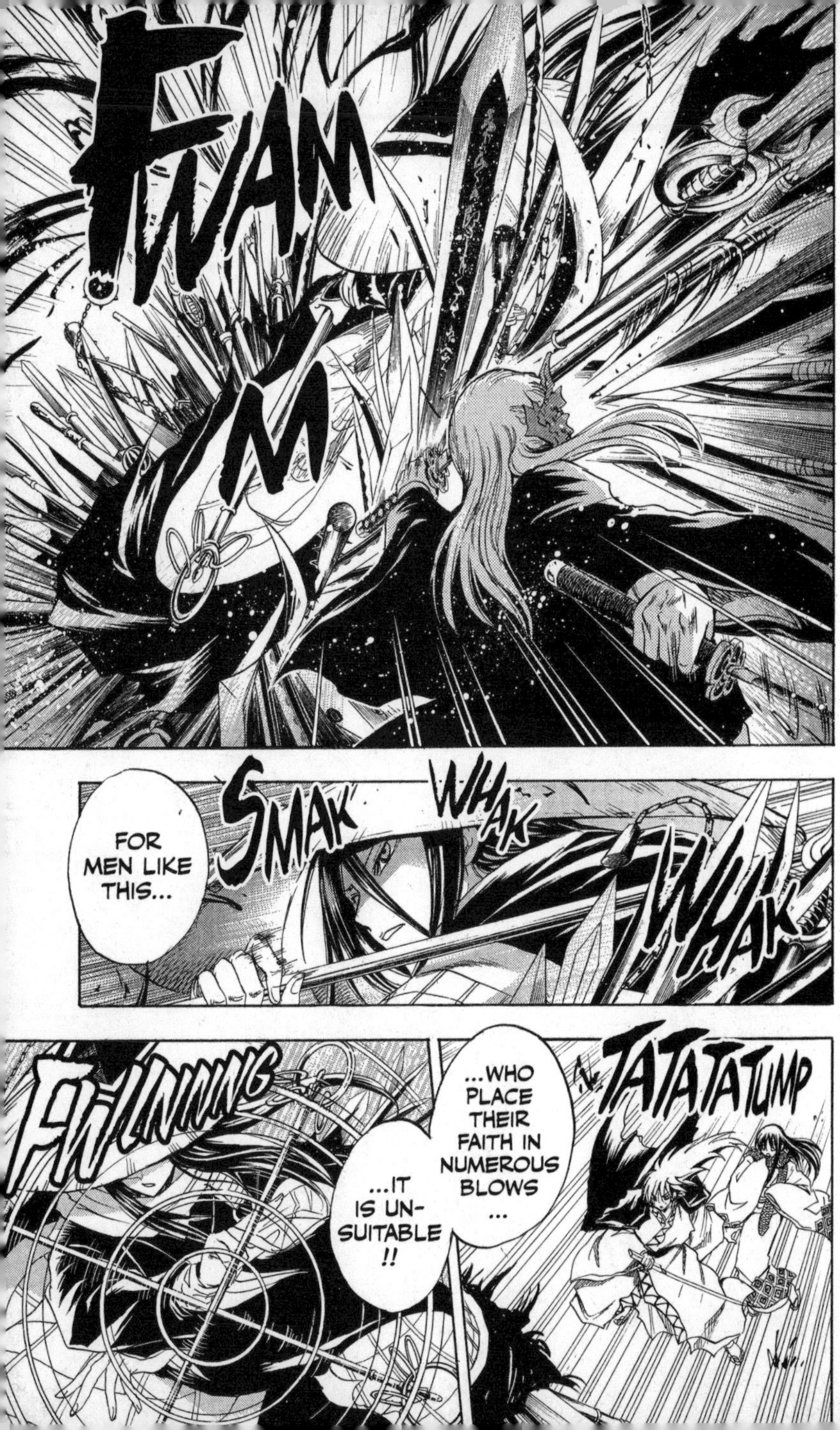
FWAMM
WHAK
WHAK
SMAK
FOR MEN LIKE THIS...
TATATATUMP
...WHO PLACE THEIR FAITH IN NUMEROUS BLOWS ...
...IT IS UN-SUITABLE !!
FWNNNNG

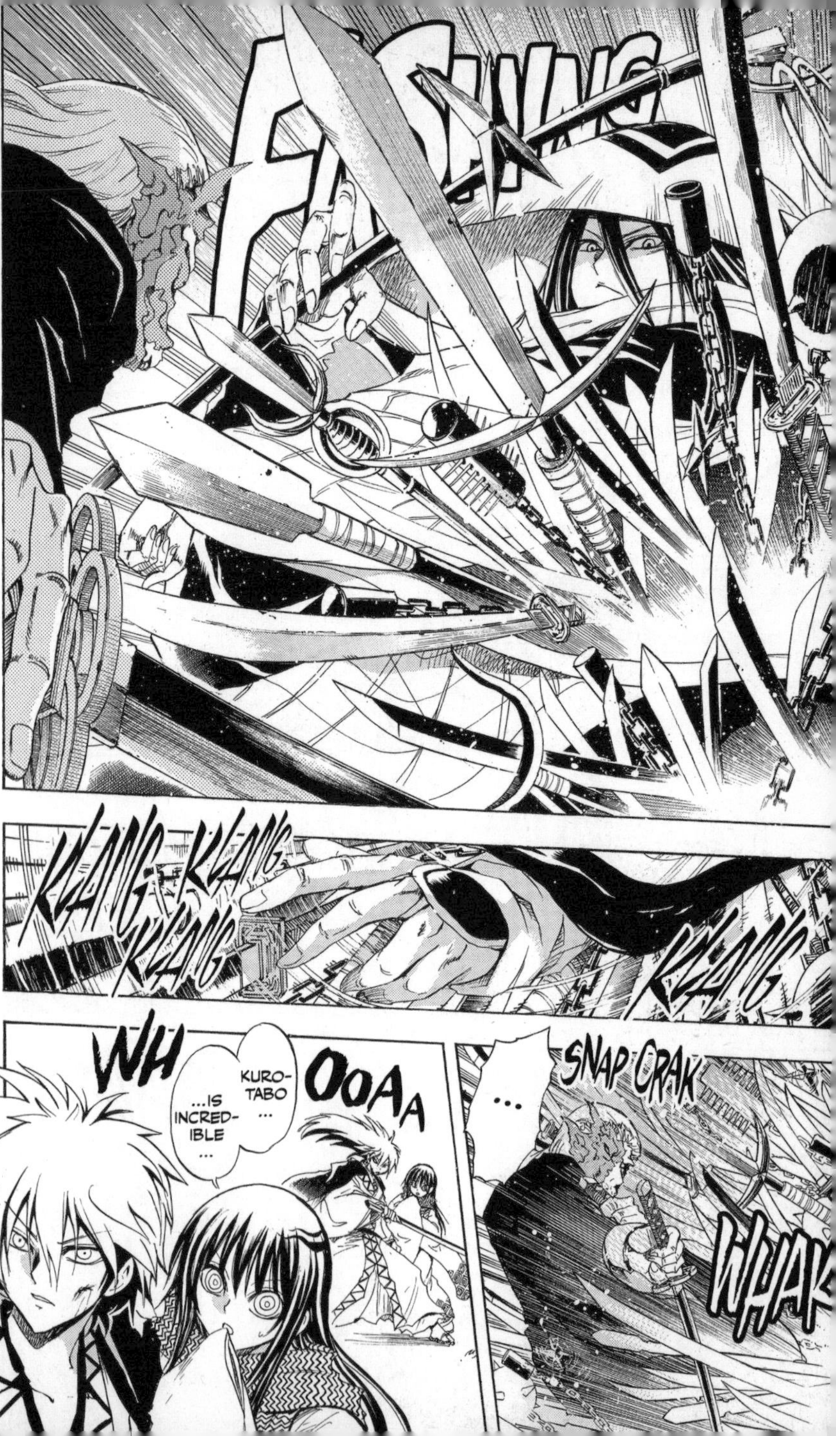
KLANG
KLANG KLANG KLANG
SNAP CRAK
...
WHAK
WHOOAA
KURO-TABO ...
...IS INCREDIBLE ...

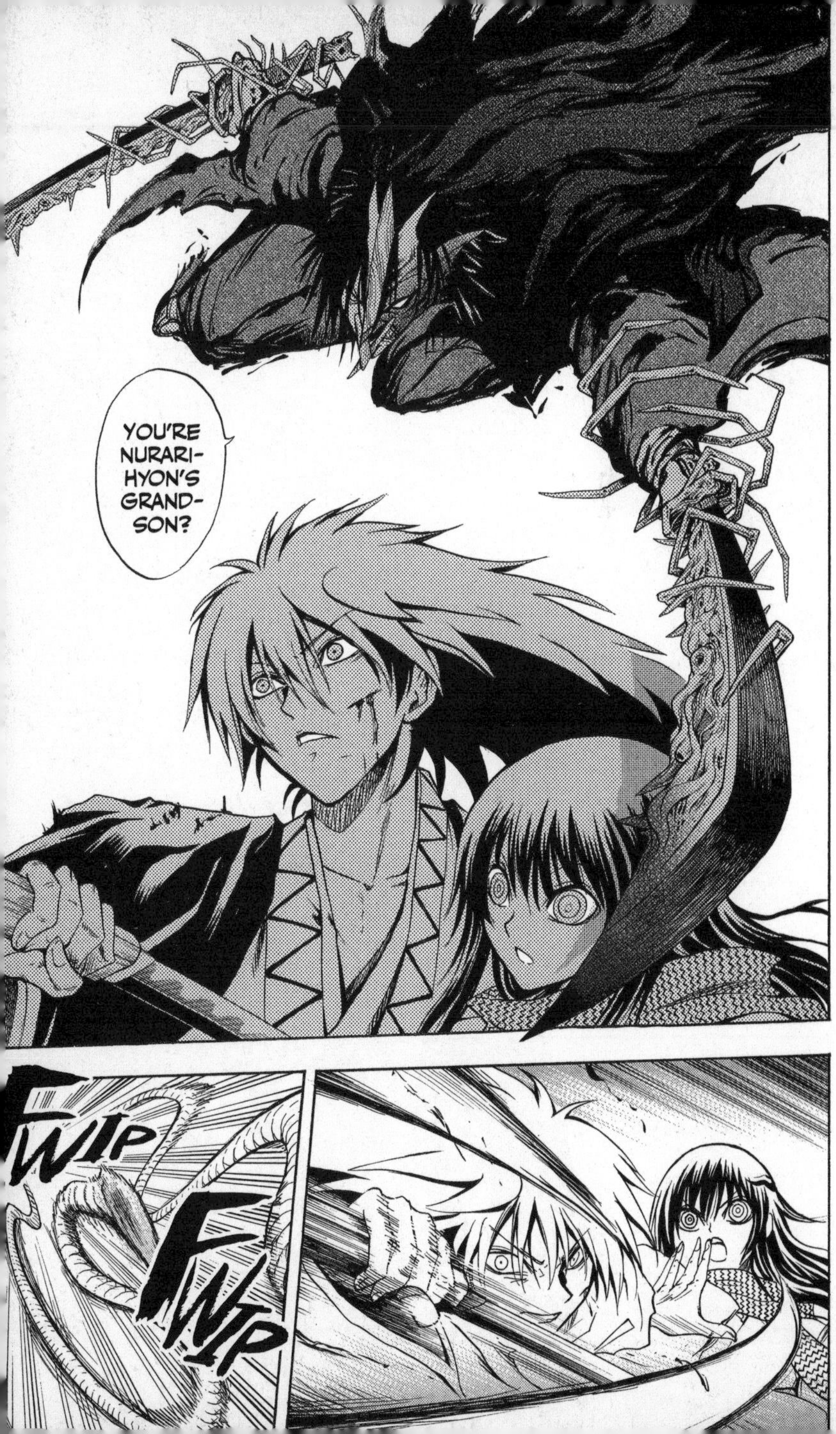
YOU'RE NURARI-HYON'S GRAND-SON?
FWIP
FWIP

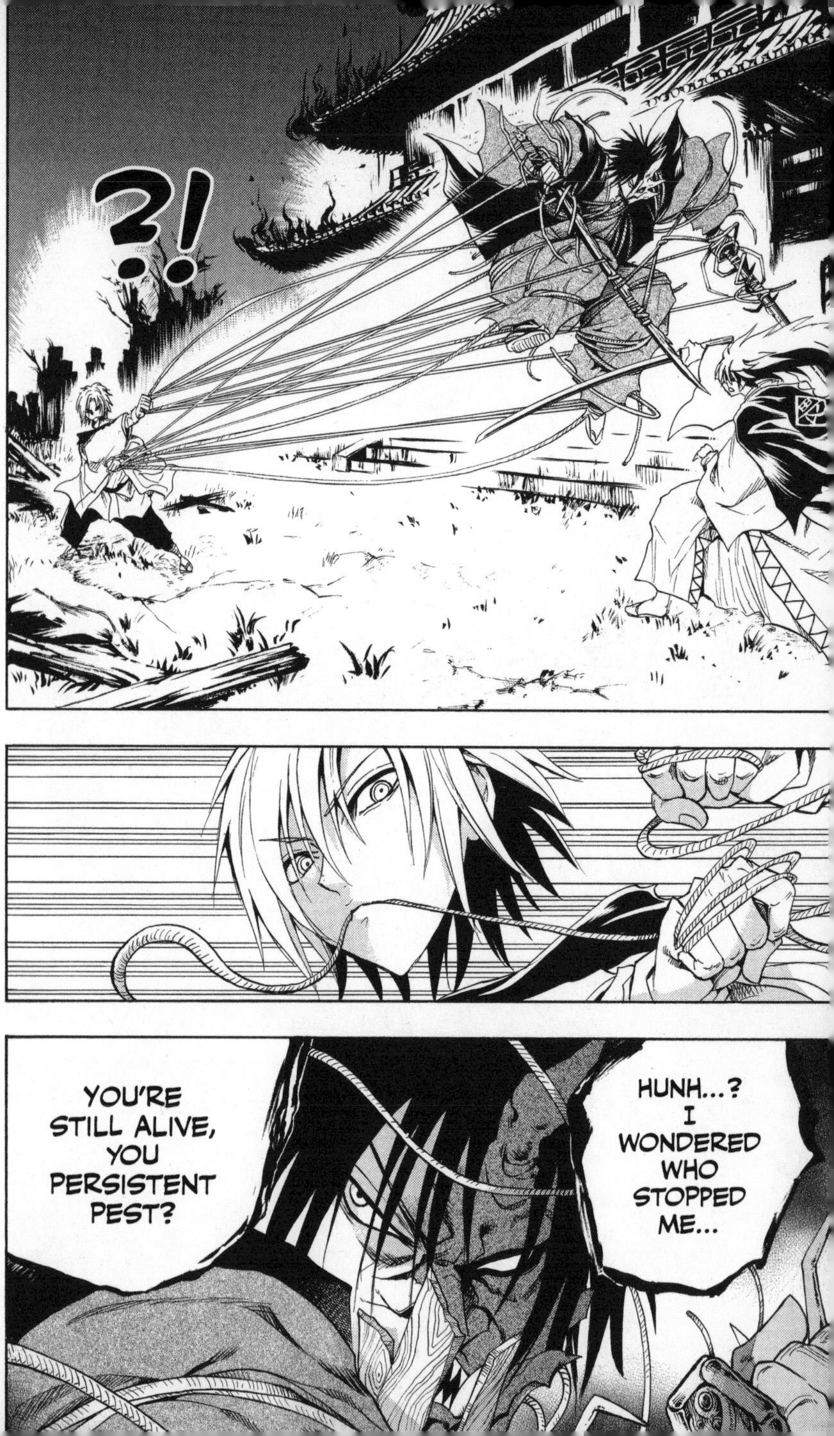
?!
HUNH...? I WONDERED WHO STOPPED ME...
YOU'RE STILL ALIVE, YOU PERSISTENT PEST?

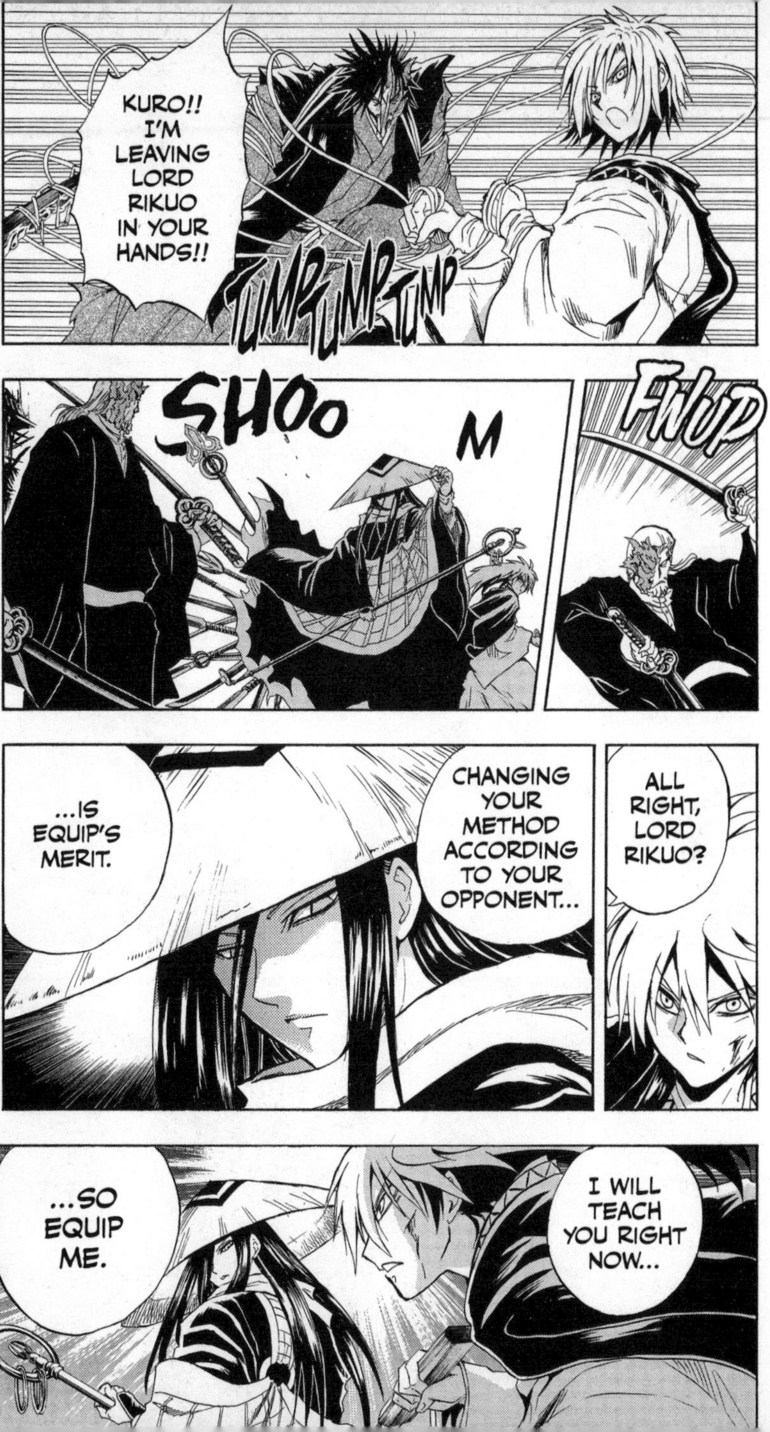
KURO!! I'M LEAVING LORD RIKUO IN YOUR HANDS!!
TUMP TUMP TUMP
FWUP
SHOOM
ALL RIGHT, LORD RIKUO?
CHANGING YOUR METHOD ACCORDING TO YOUR OPPONENT...
...IS EQUIP'S MERIT.
I WILL TEACH YOU RIGHT NOW...
...SO EQUIP ME.

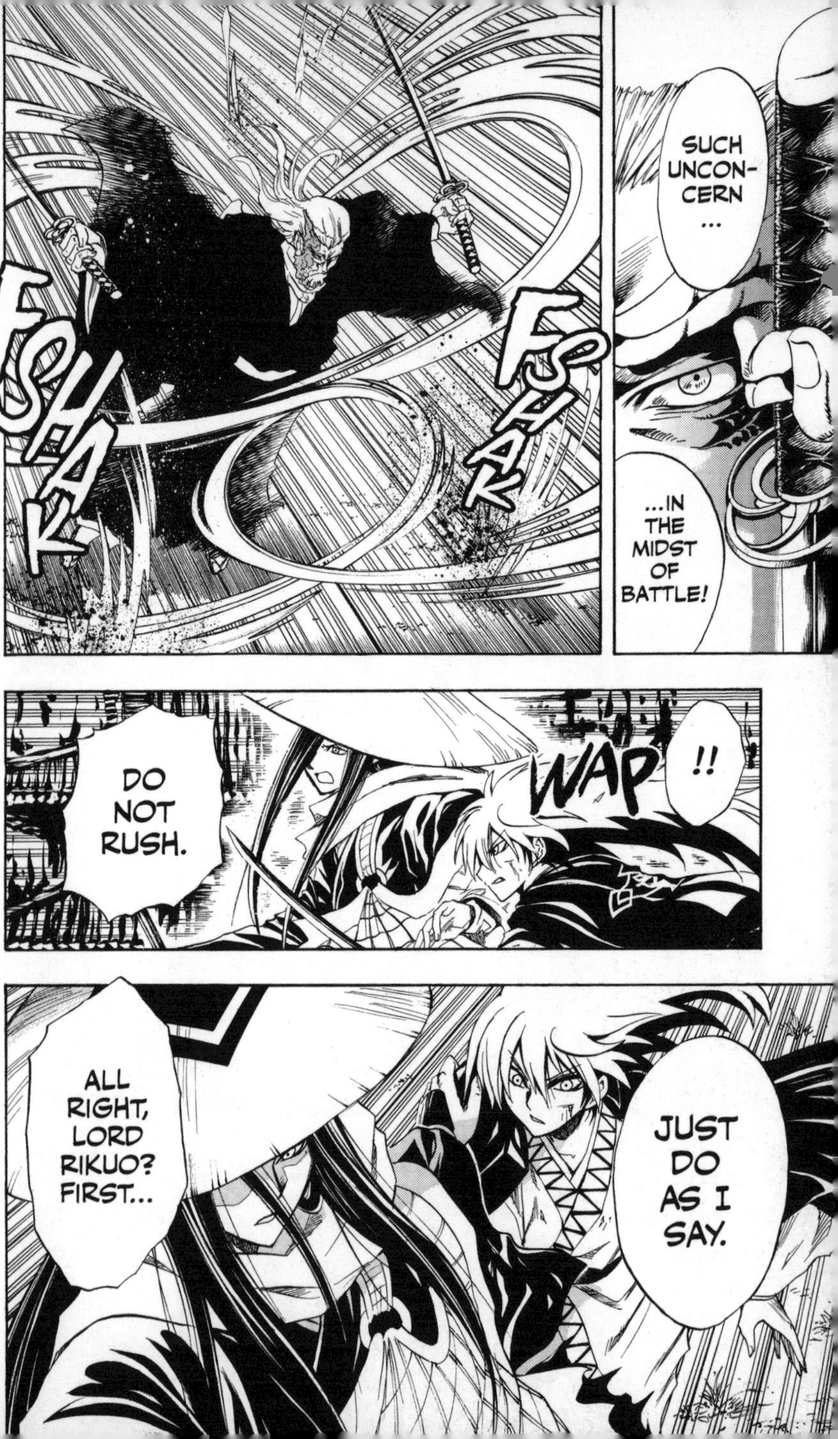
SUCH UNCONCERN ...
...IN THE MIDST OF BATTLE!
FSHAK
FSHAK
!!
WAP
DO NOT RUSH.
JUST DO AS I SAY.
ALL RIGHT, LORD RIKUO? FIRST...

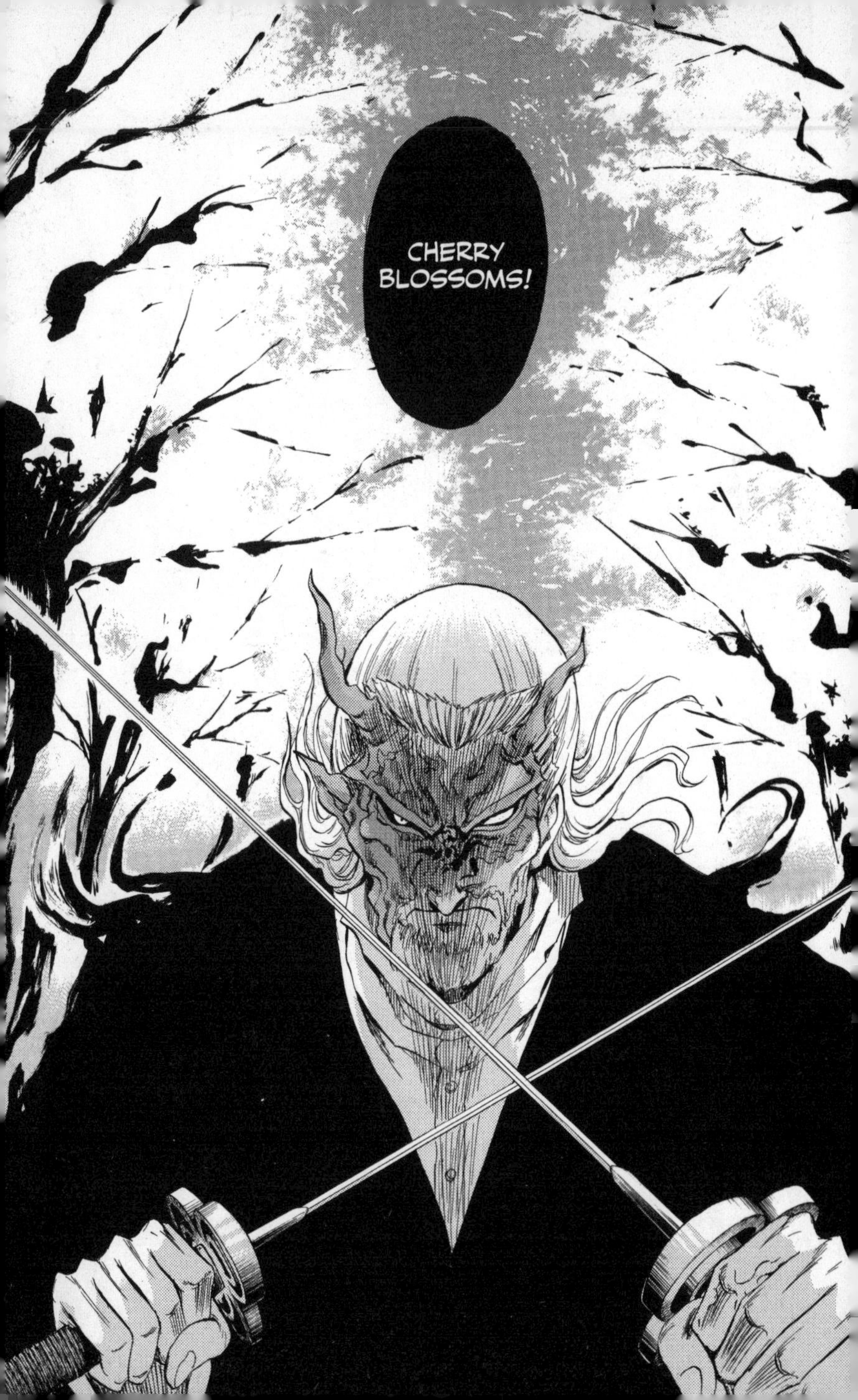
CHERRY BLOSSOMS!

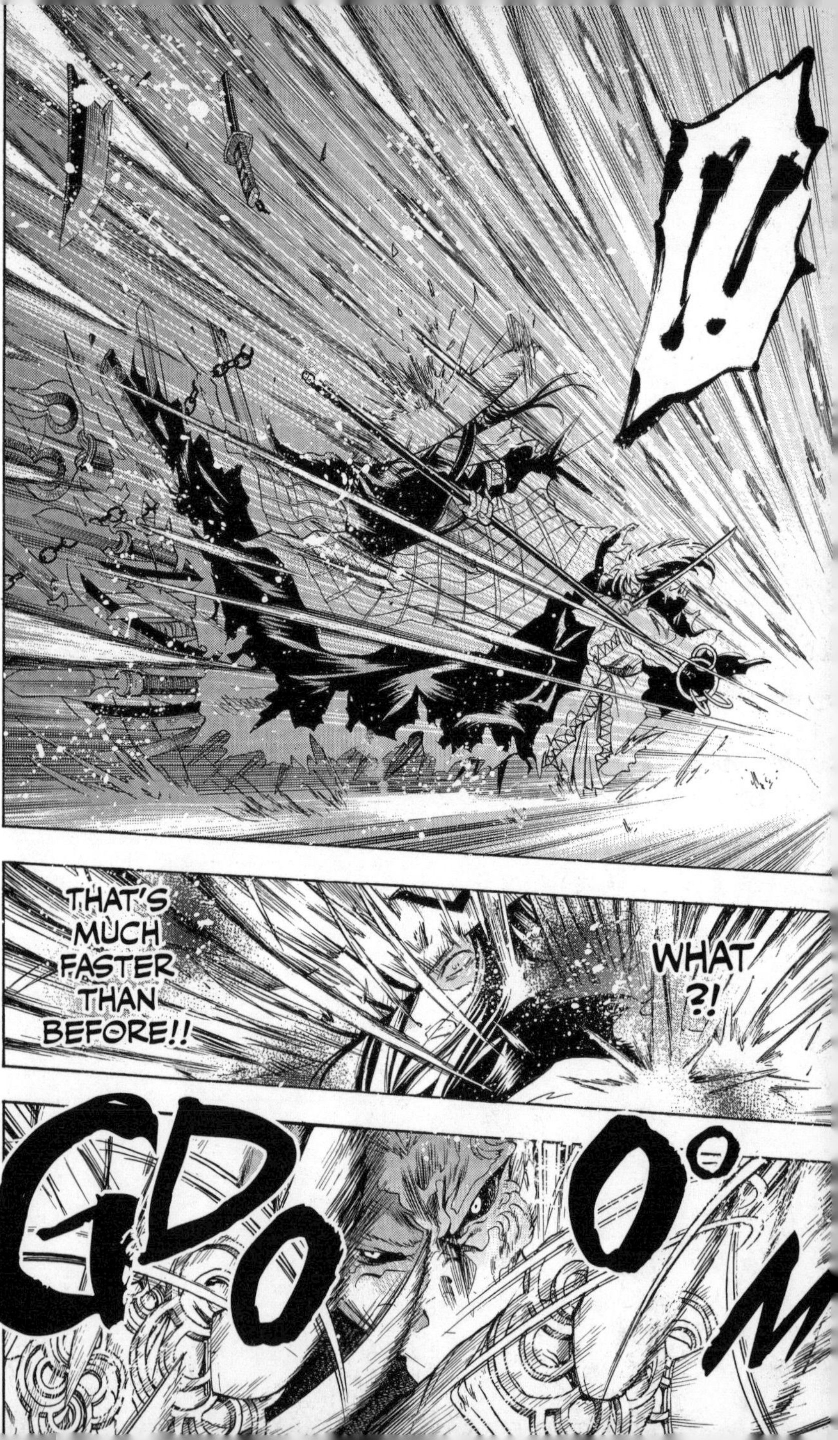
!!
WHAT ?!
THAT'S MUCH FASTER THAN BEFORE!!
GDOOOM

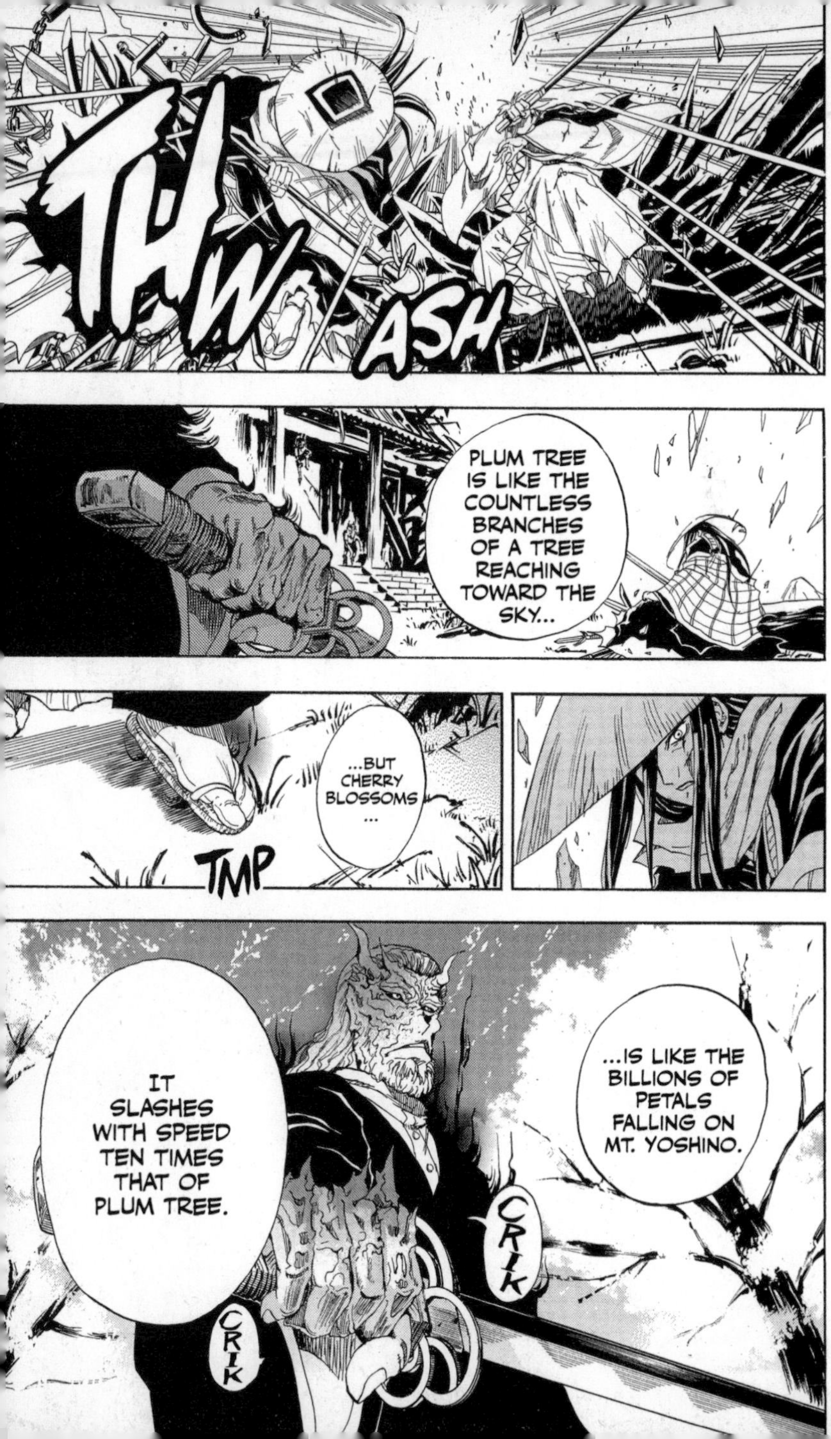
THWASH
PLUM TREE IS LIKE THE COUNTLESS BRANCHES OF A TREE REACHING TOWARD THE SKY...
...BUT CHERRY BLOSSOMS ...
TMP
...IS LIKE THE BILLIONS OF PETALS FALLING ON MT. YOSHINO.
IT SLASHES WITH SPEED TEN TIMES THAT OF PLUM TREE.
CRIK
CRIK

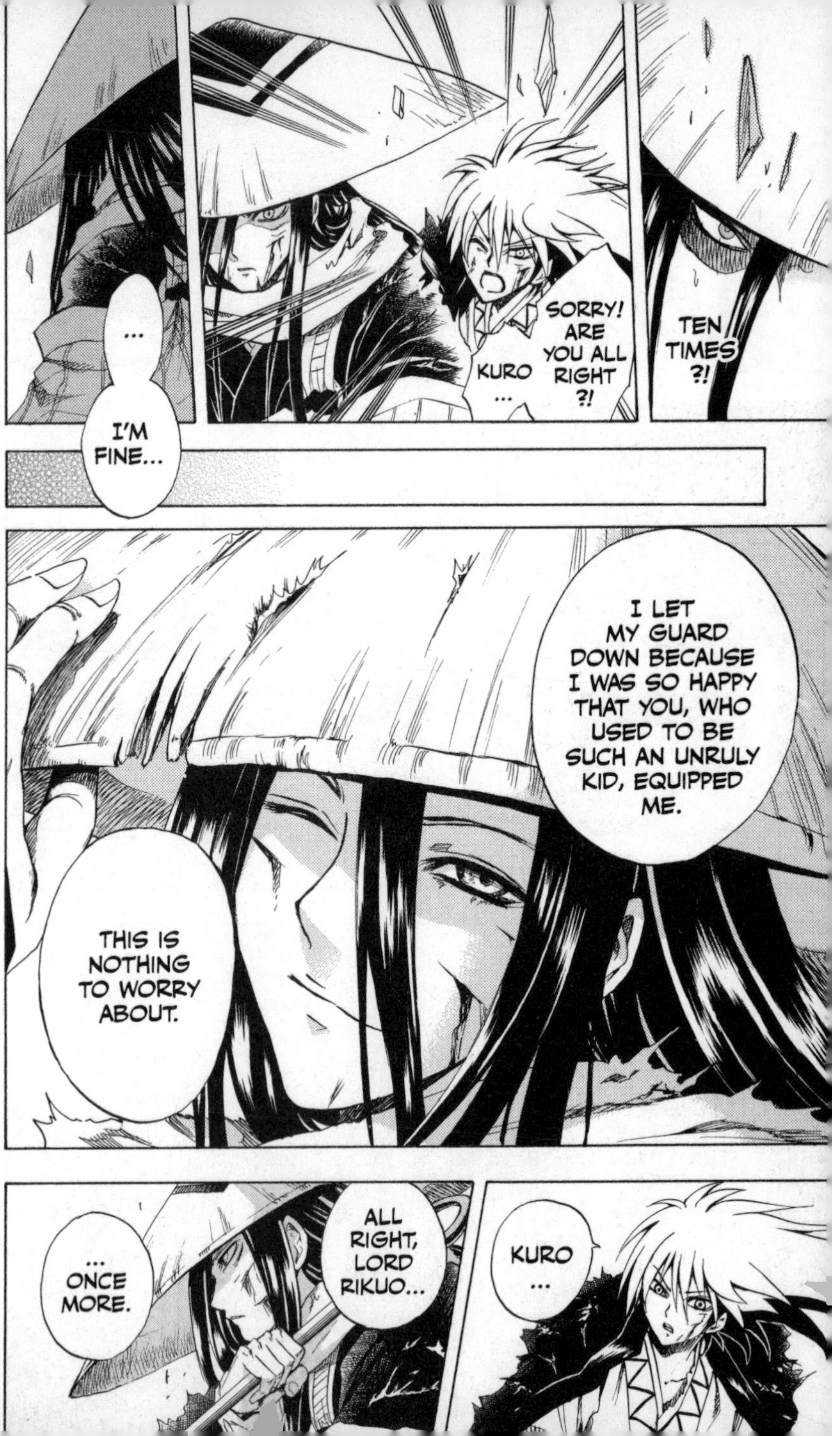
TEN TIMES ?!
SORRY! ARE YOU ALL RIGHT ?!
KURO ...
...
I'M FINE...
I LET MY GUARD DOWN BECAUSE I WAS SO HAPPY THAT YOU, WHO USED TO BE SUCH AN UNRULY KID, EQUIPPED ME.
THIS IS NOTHING TO WORRY ABOUT.
KURO ...
ALL RIGHT, LORD RIKUO...
... ONCE MORE.

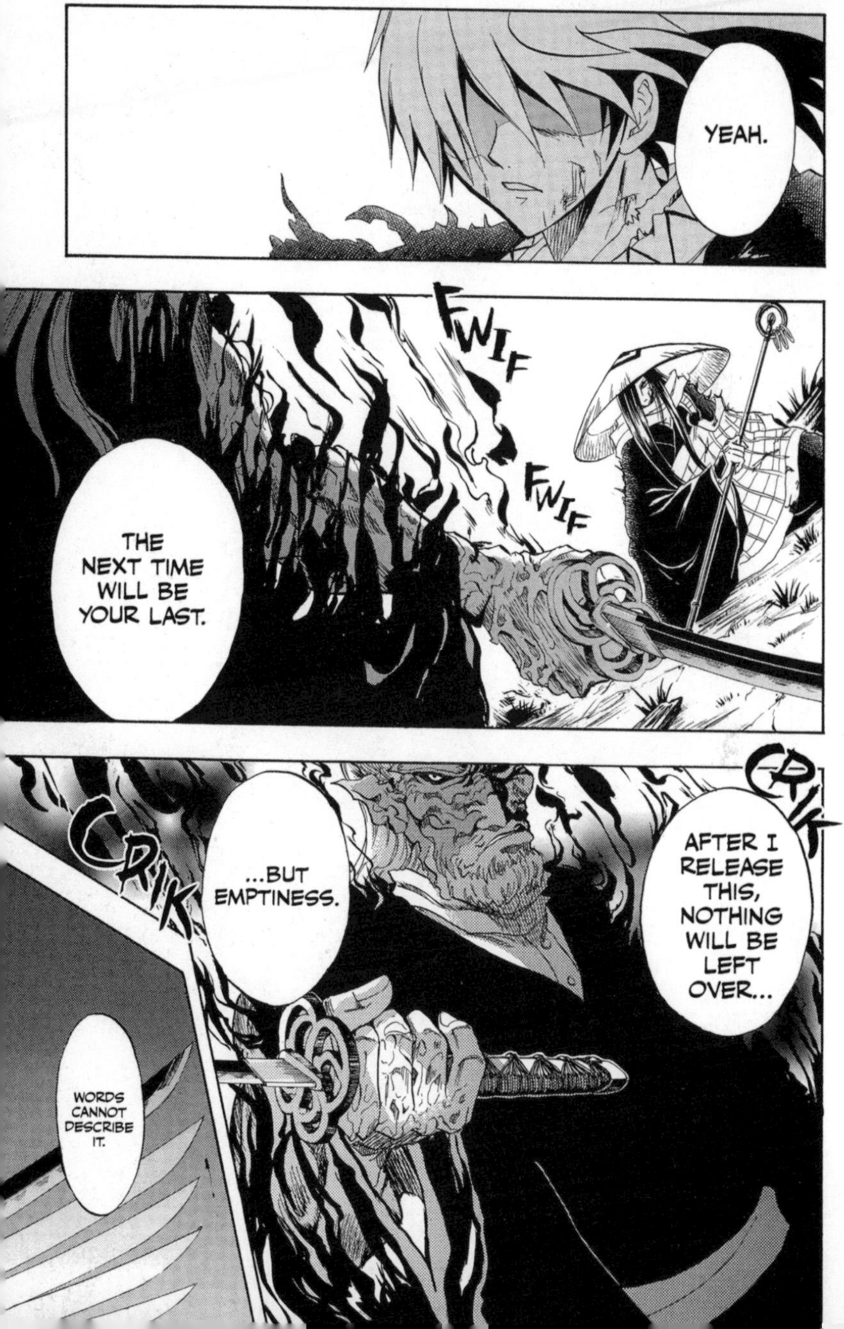
YEAH.
FWIF
FWIF
THE NEXT TIME WILL BE YOUR LAST.
CRIK
AFTER I RELEASE THIS, NOTHING WILL BE LEFT OVER...
...BUT EMPTINESS.
CRIK
WORDS CANNOT DESCRIBE IT.

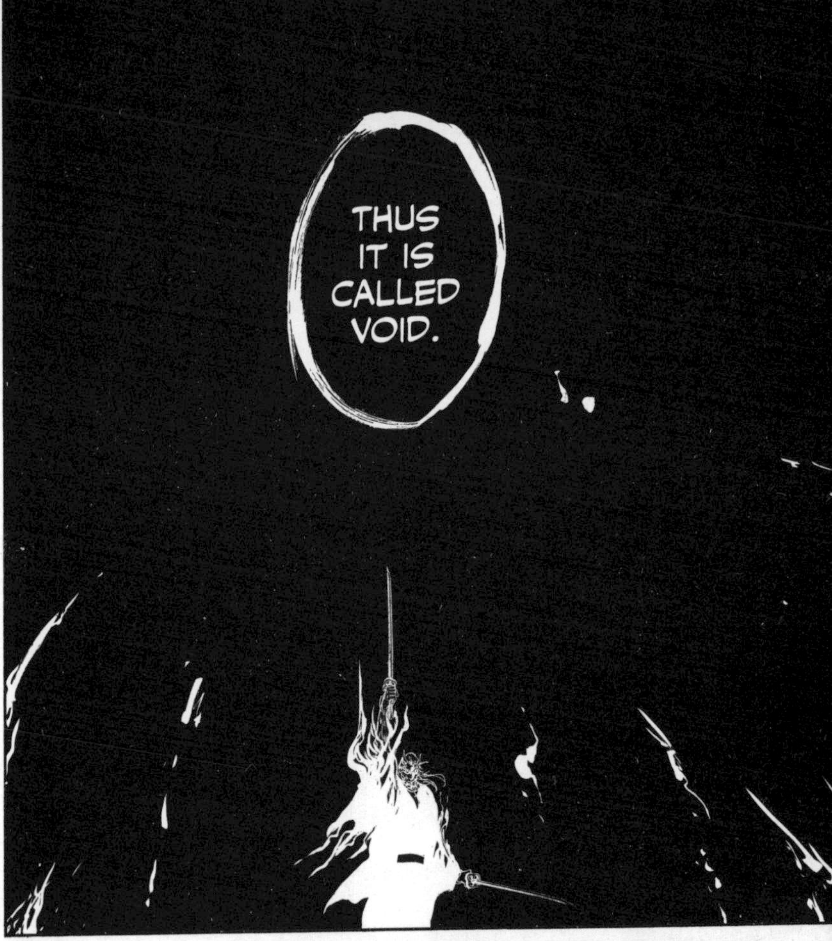
THUS IT IS CALLED VOID.

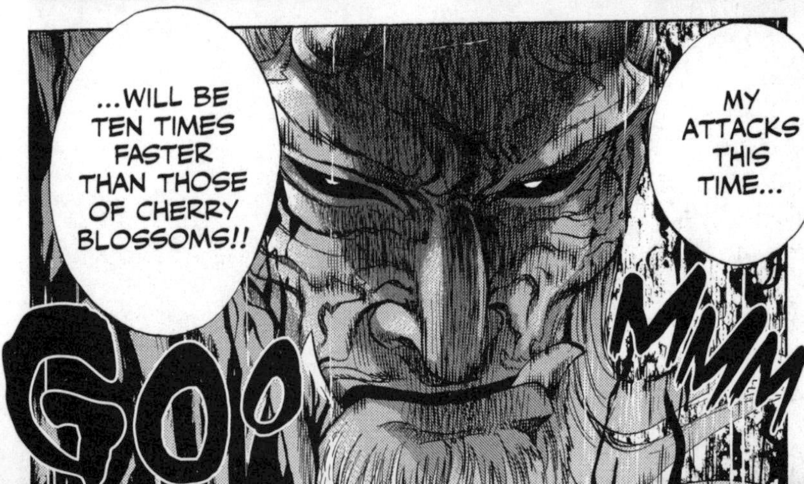
MY ATTACKS THIS TIME...
...WILL BE TEN TIMES FASTER THAN THOSE OF CHERRY BLOSSOMS!!
GOOMMM

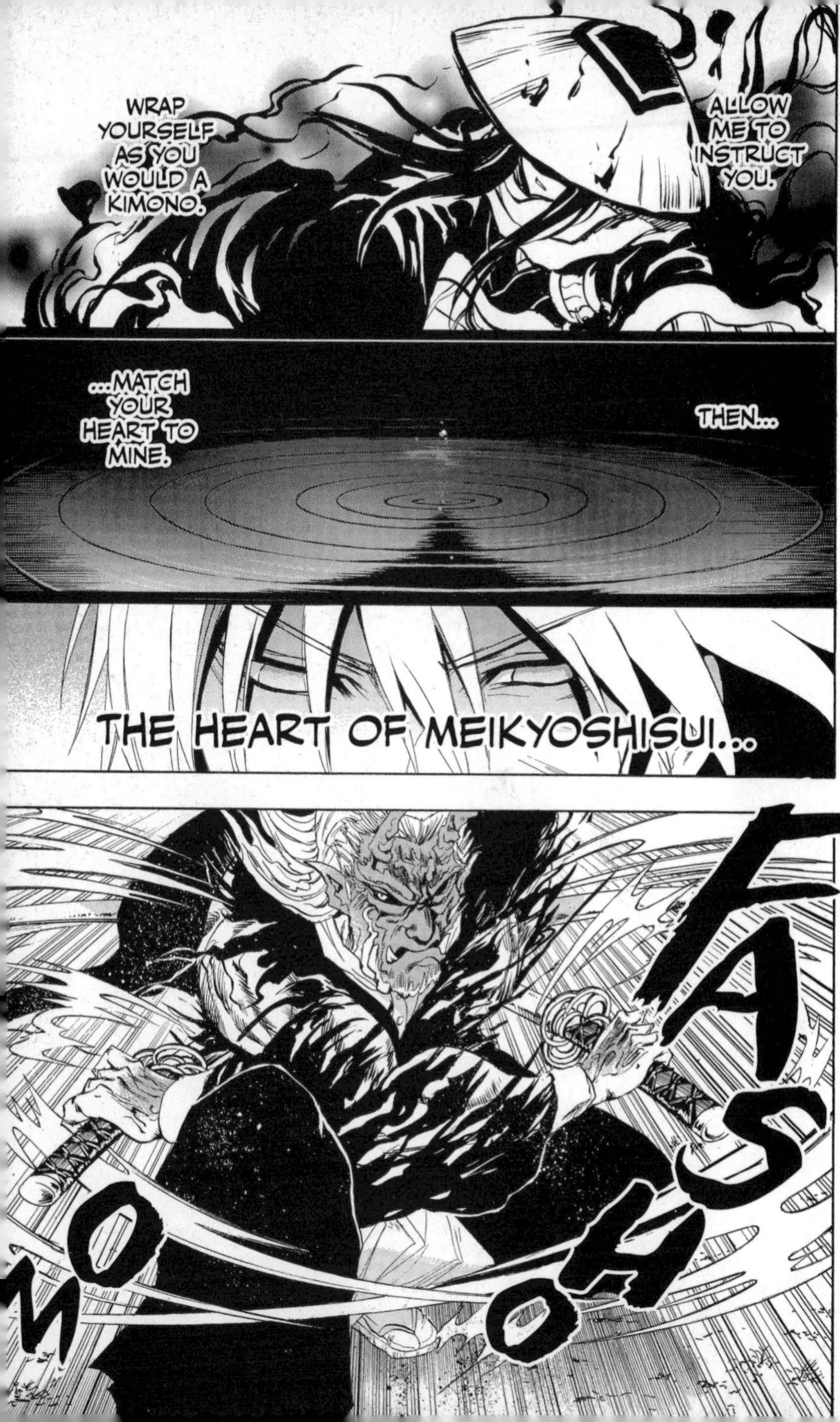
ALLOW ME TO INSTRUCT YOU.
WRAP YOURSELF AS YOU WOULD A KIMONO.
THEN...
...MATCH YOUR HEART TO MINE.
THE HEART OF MEIKYOSHISUI...
FASHOOM

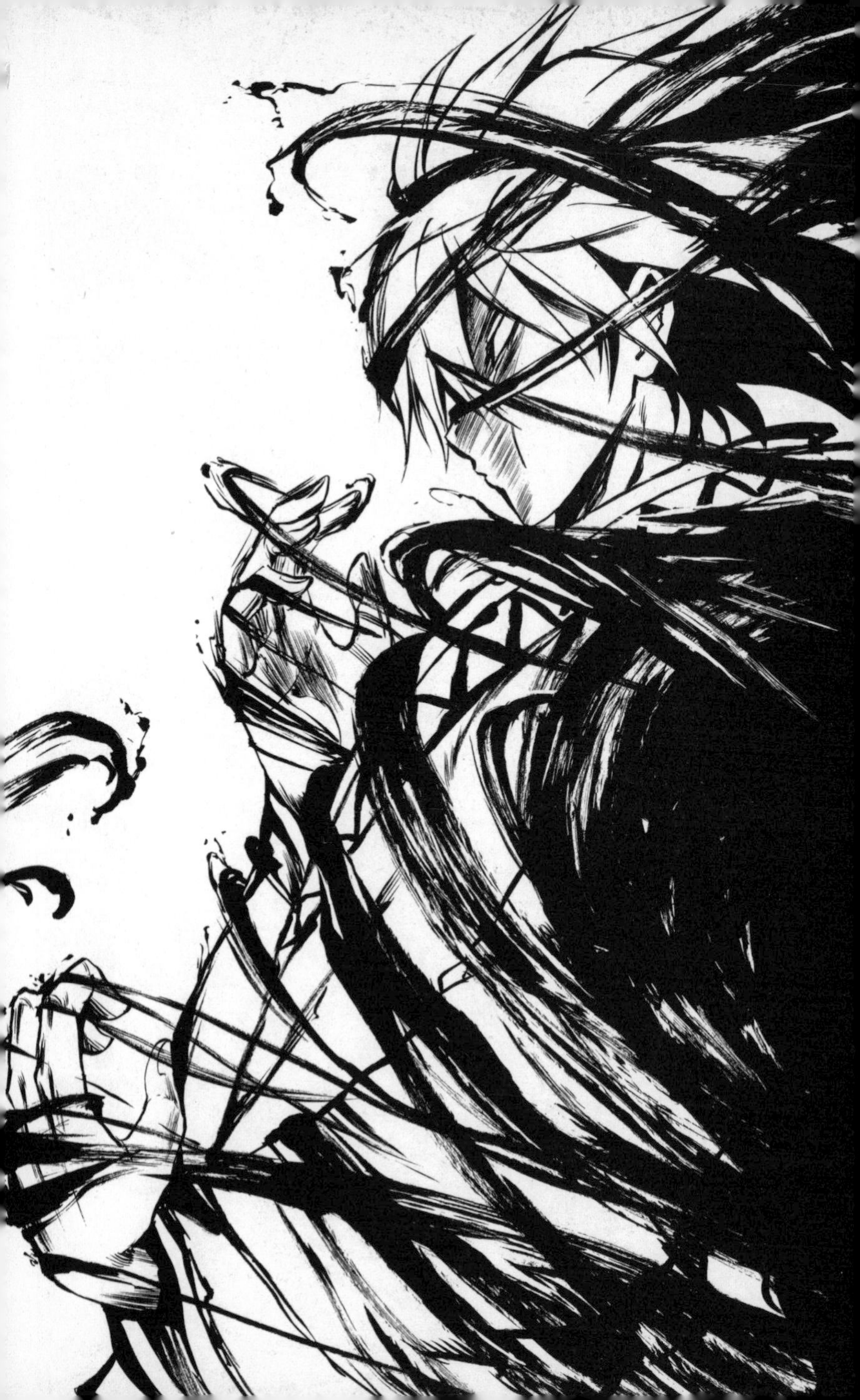

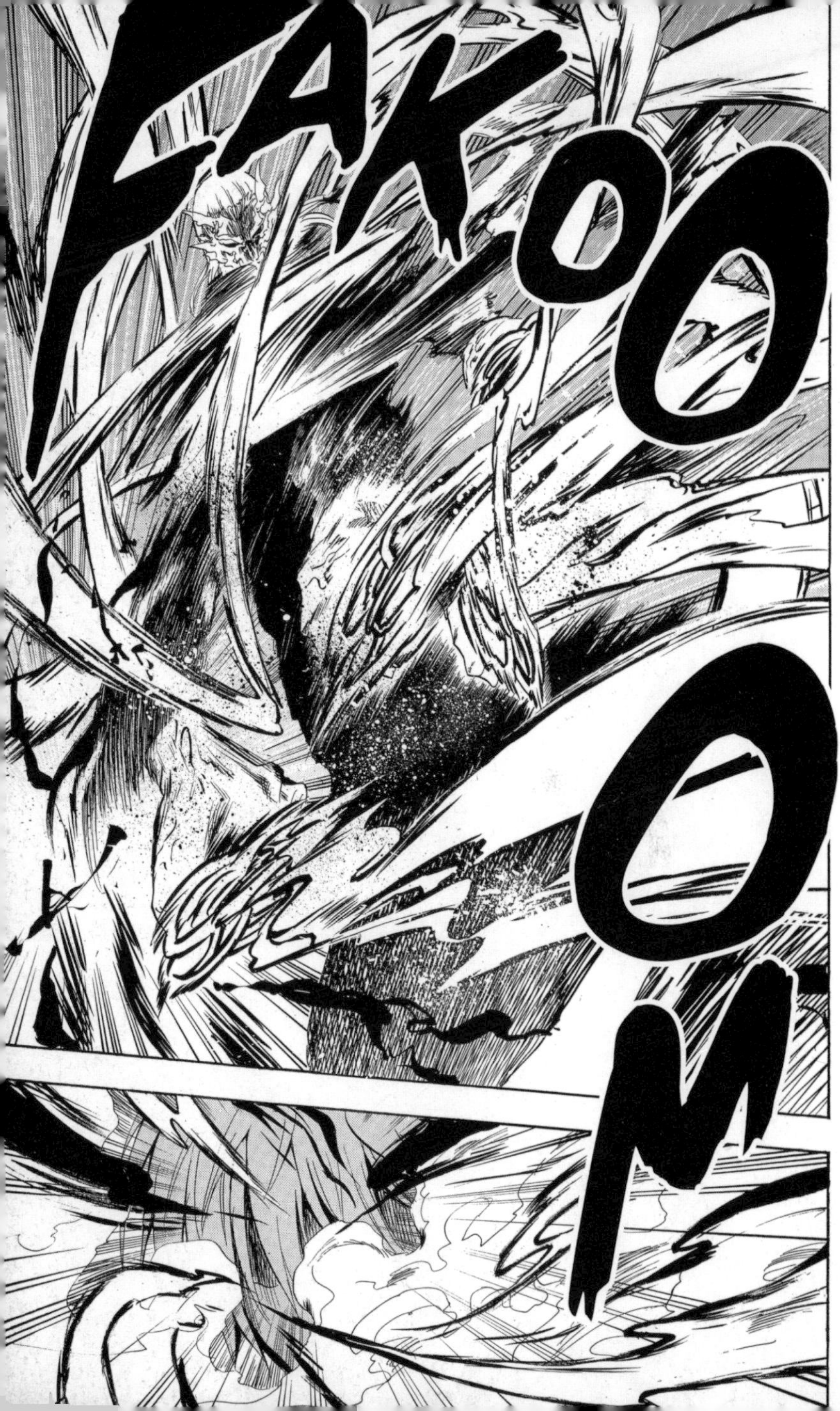
KAKOOOM

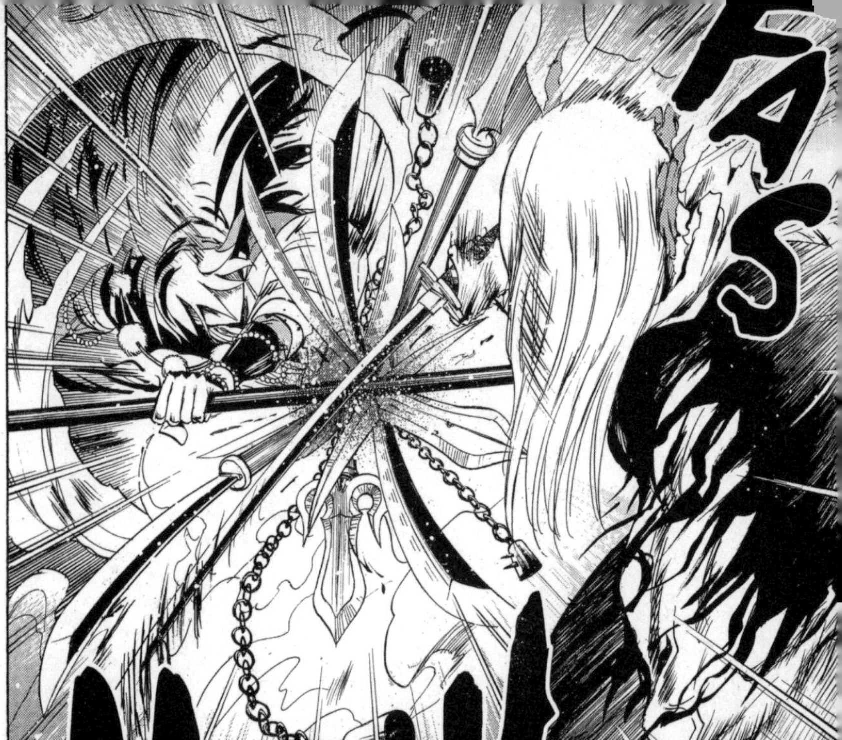
FÃS
MMÃH
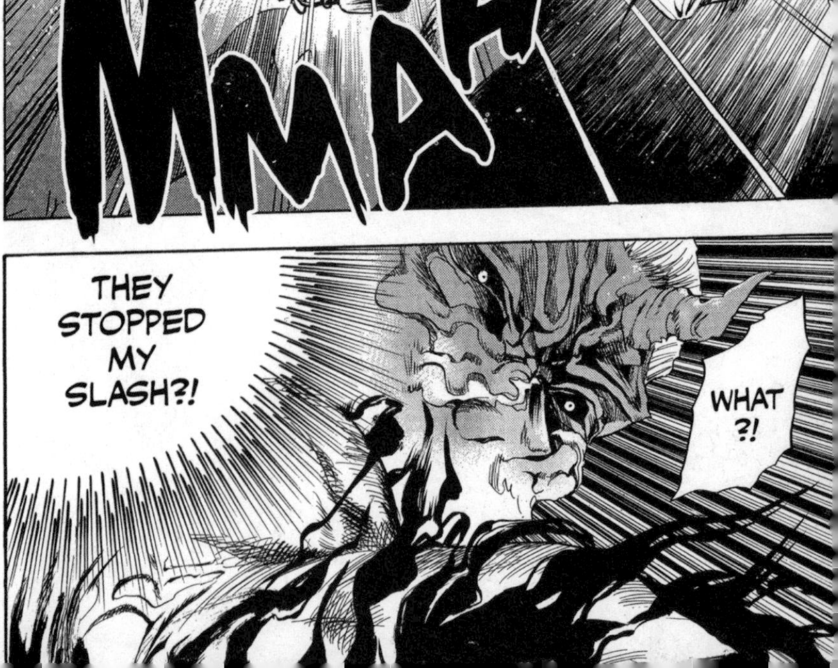
WHAT?!
THEY STOPPED MY SLASH?!

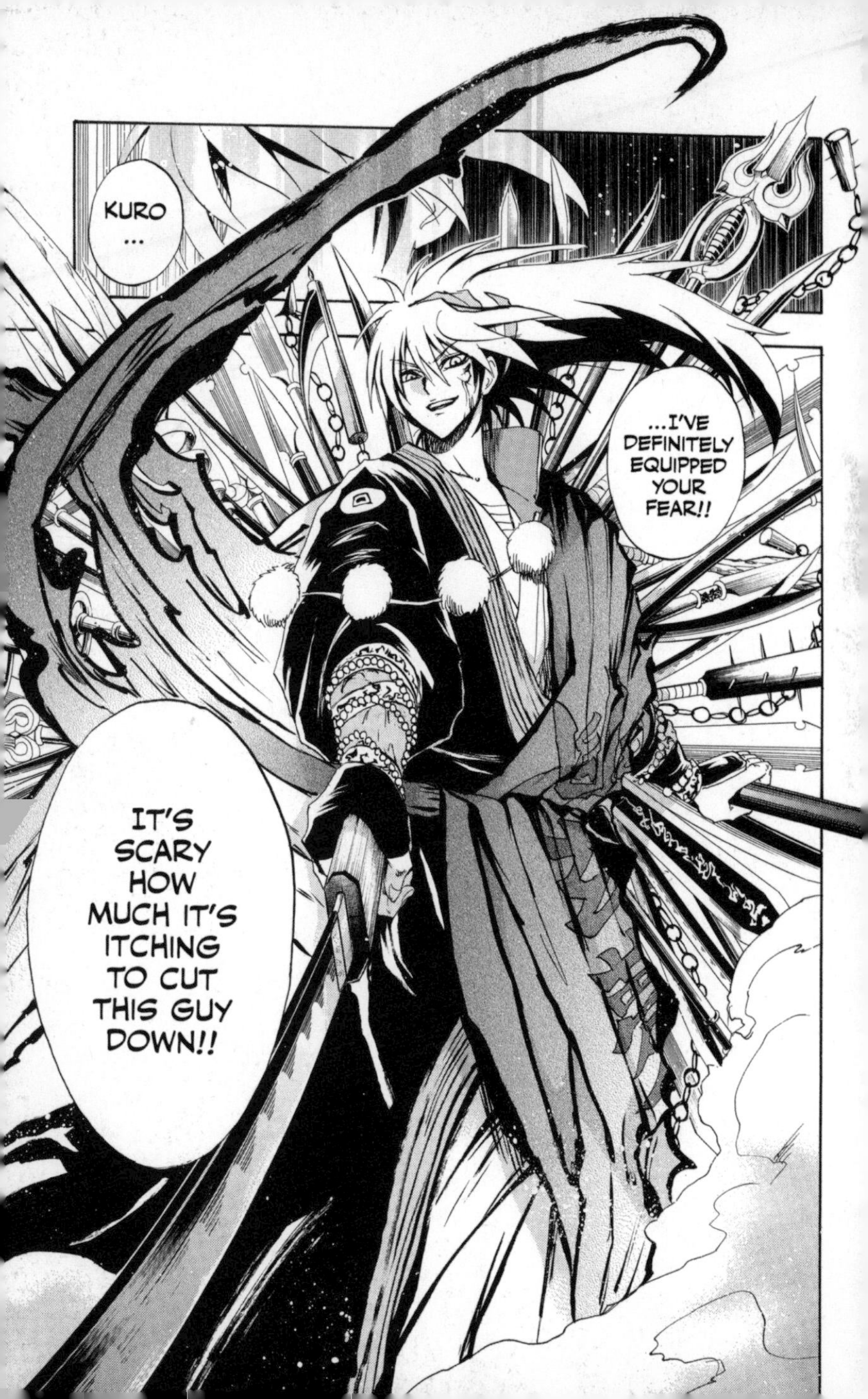
KURO ...
...I'VE DEFINITELY EQUIPPED YOUR FEAR!!
IT'S SCARY HOW MUCH IT'S ITCHING TO CUT THIS GUY DOWN!!

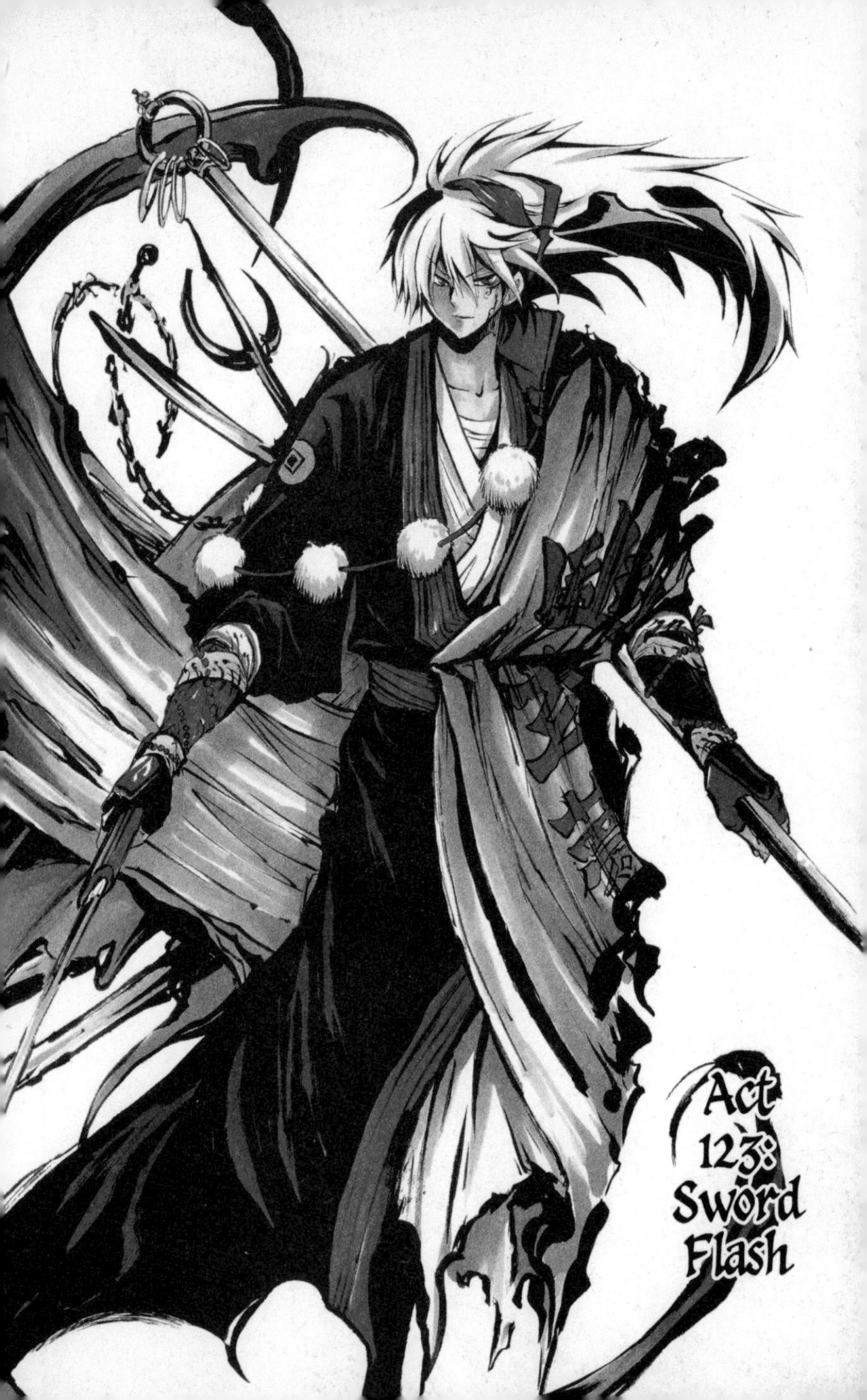
Act 123: Sword Flash

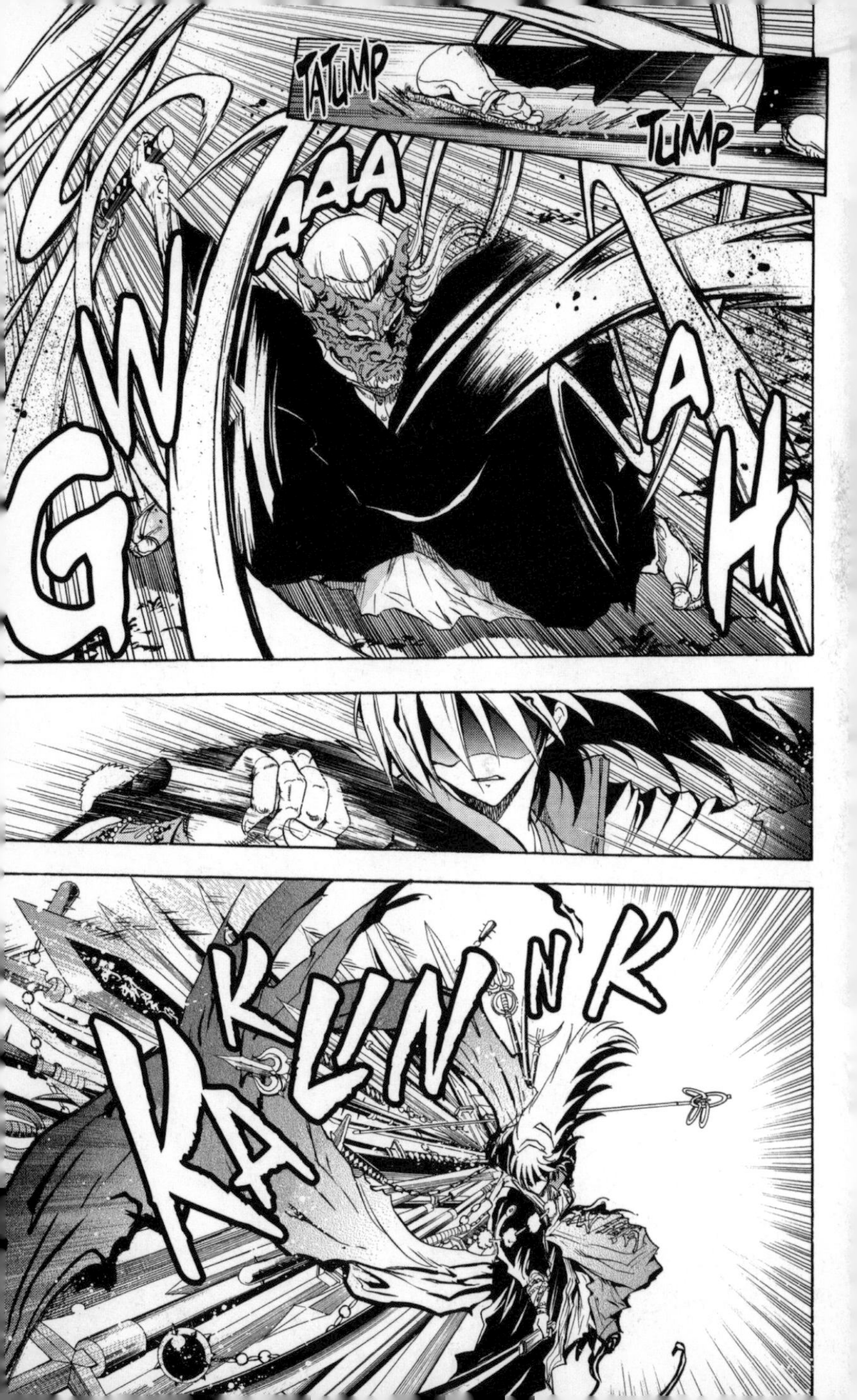
TATUMP
TUMP
GWAAA
AAH
KAKLINNK

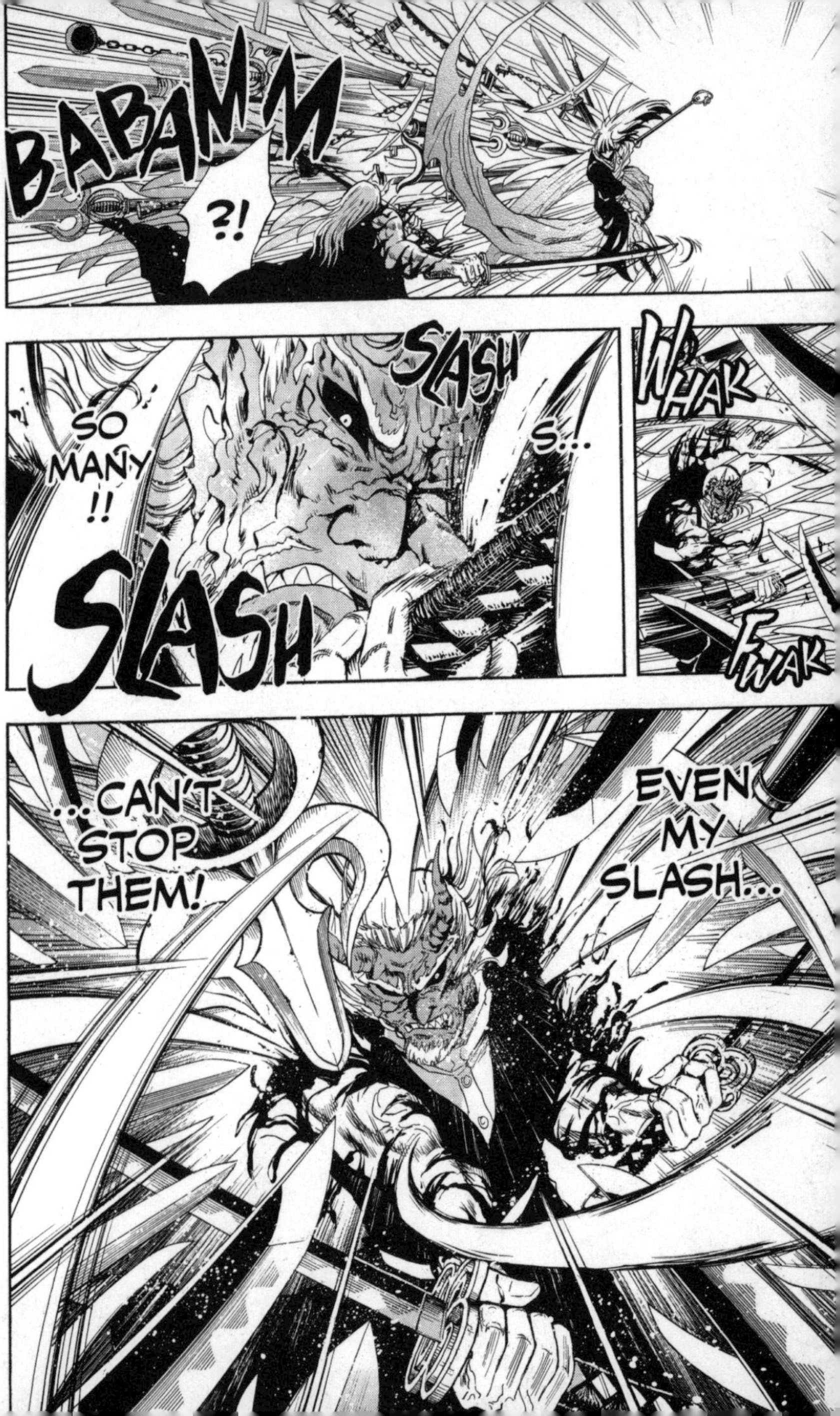
BABAMM
?!
WHAR
FWAR
SLASH
S...
SO MANY!!
SLASH
EVEN MY SLASH...
...CAN'T STOP THEM!

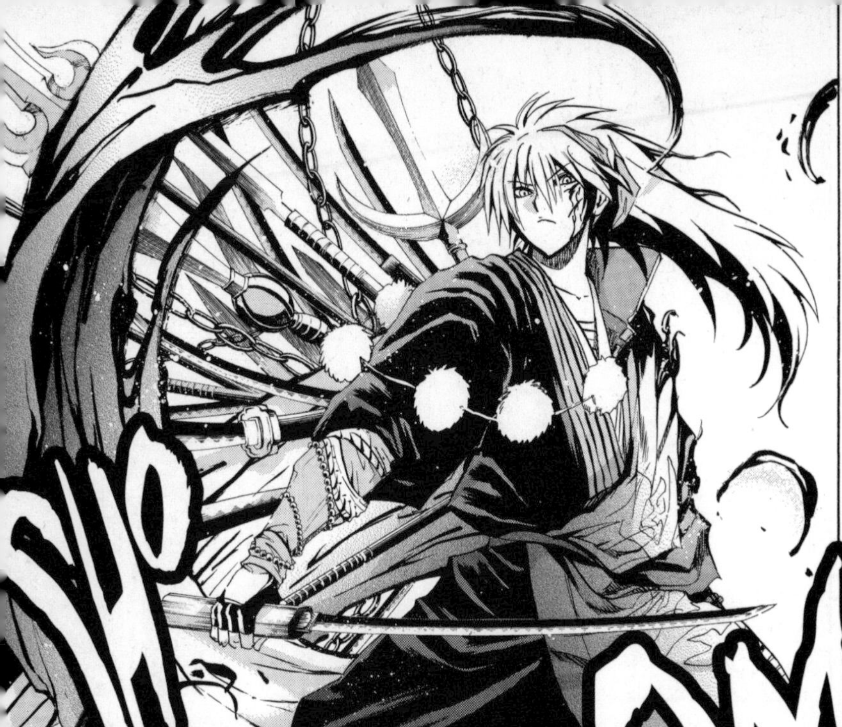

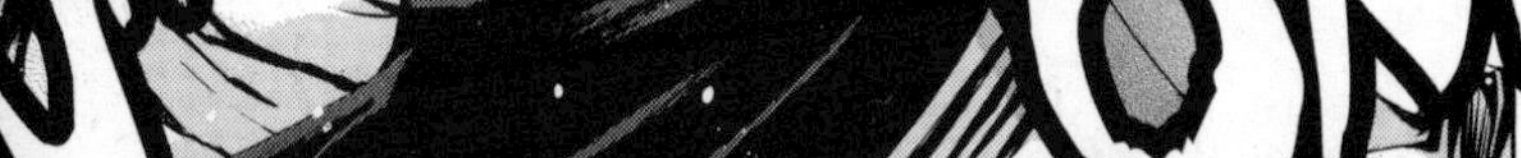
FWOO
HEH.

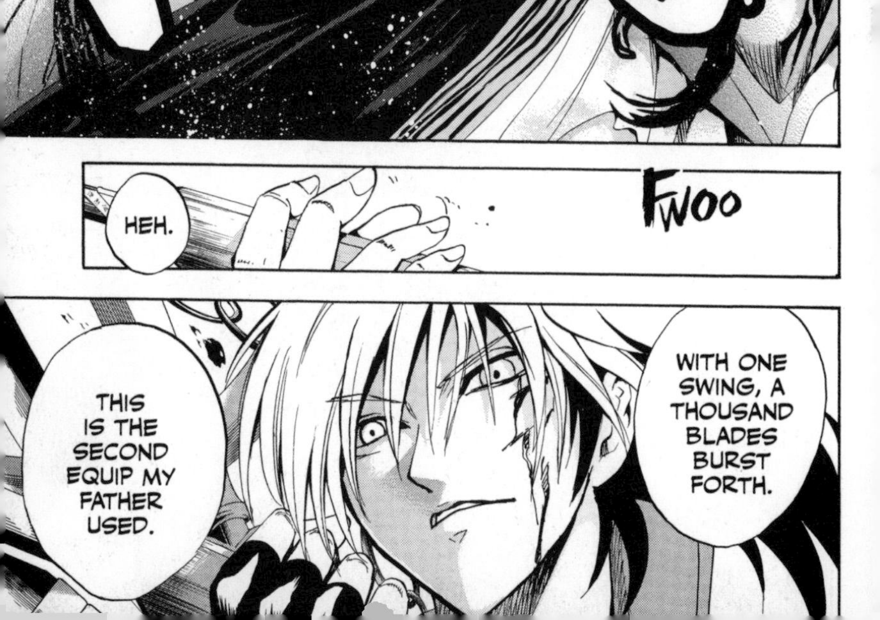
WITH ONE SWING, A THOUSAND BLADES BURST FORTH.
THIS IS THE SECOND EQUIP MY FATHER USED.

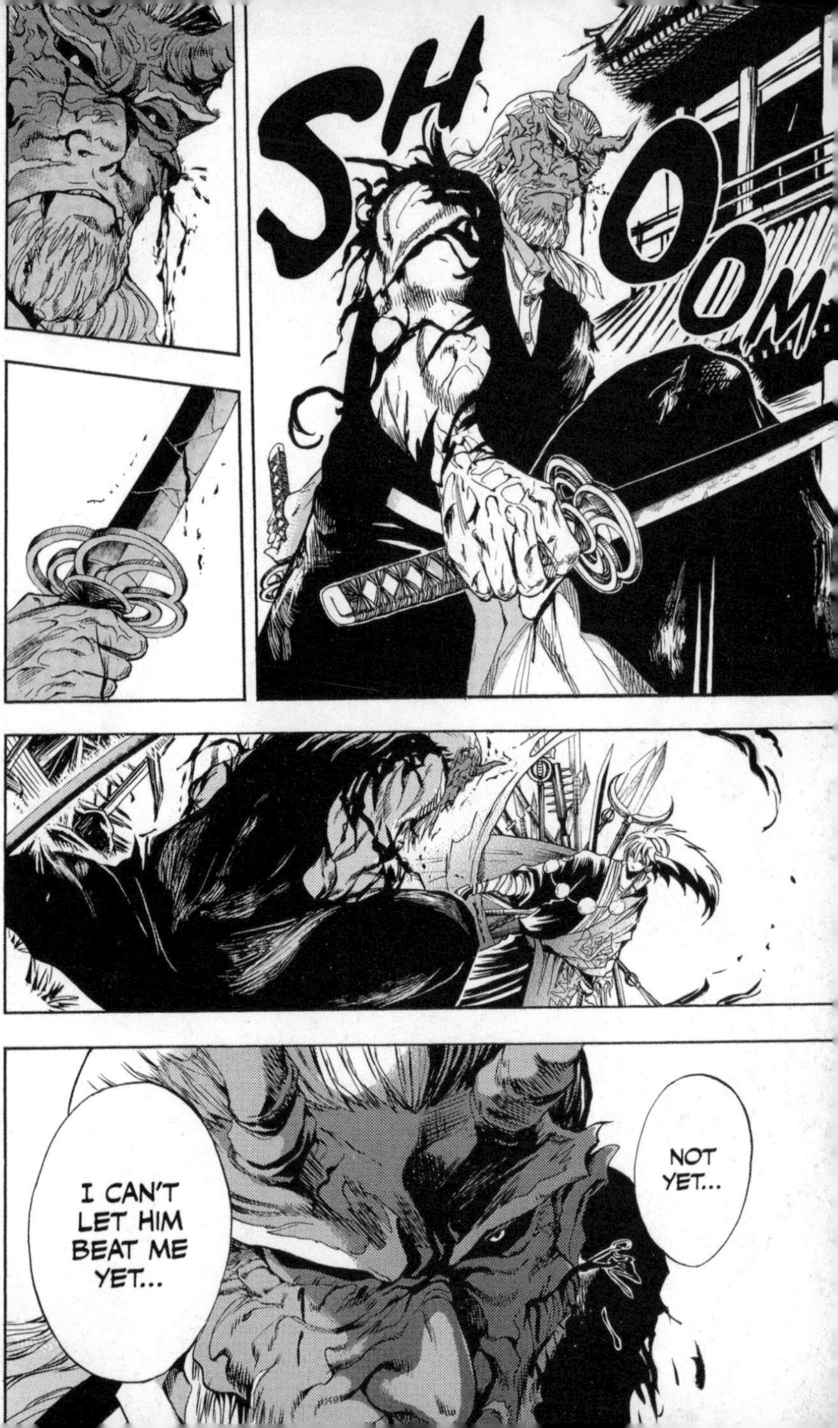
SHOOOM...
NOT YET...
I CAN'T LET HIM BEAT ME YET...

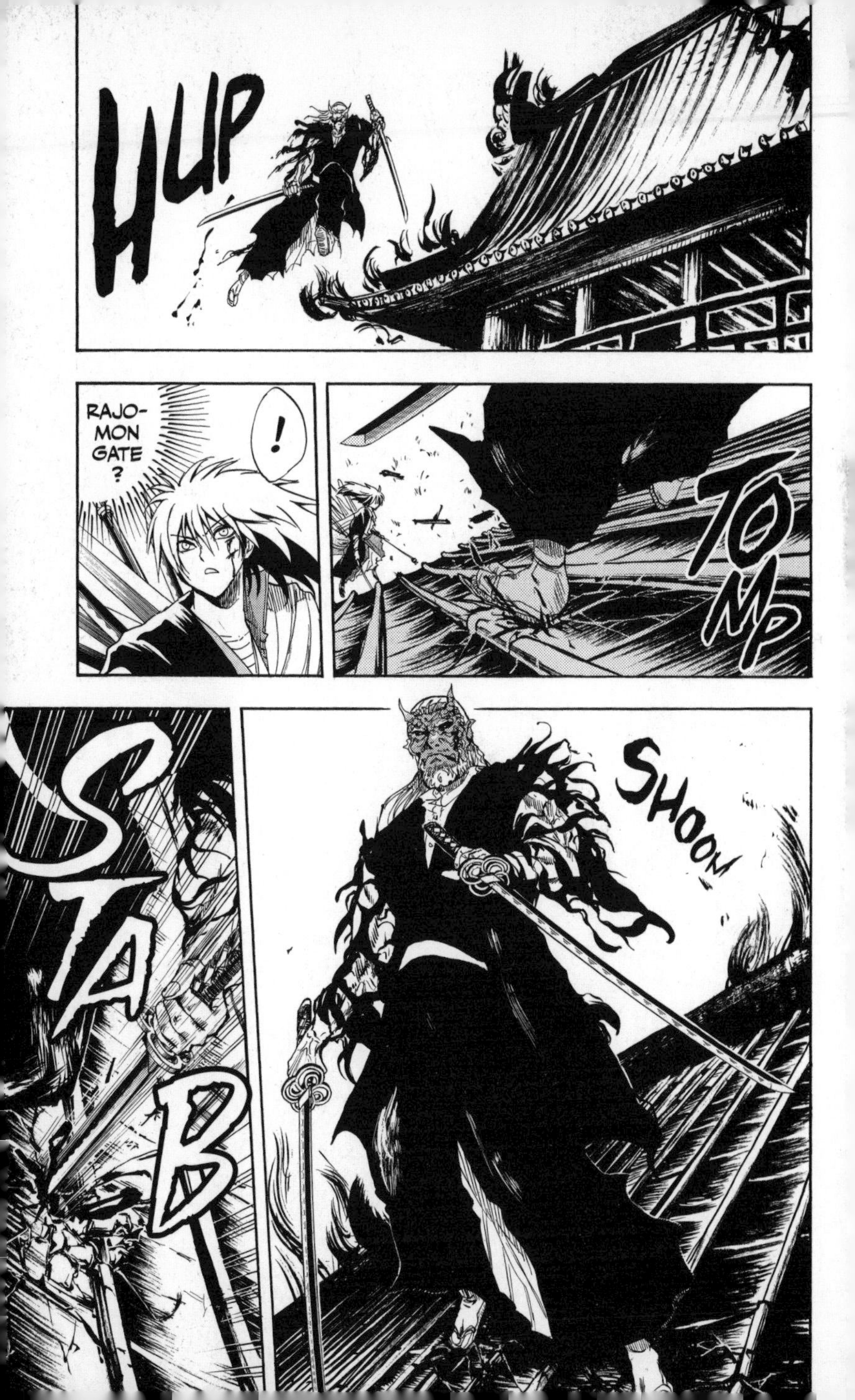
HUP
TOMP
!
RAJO-MON GATE ?
SHOOM
STAB

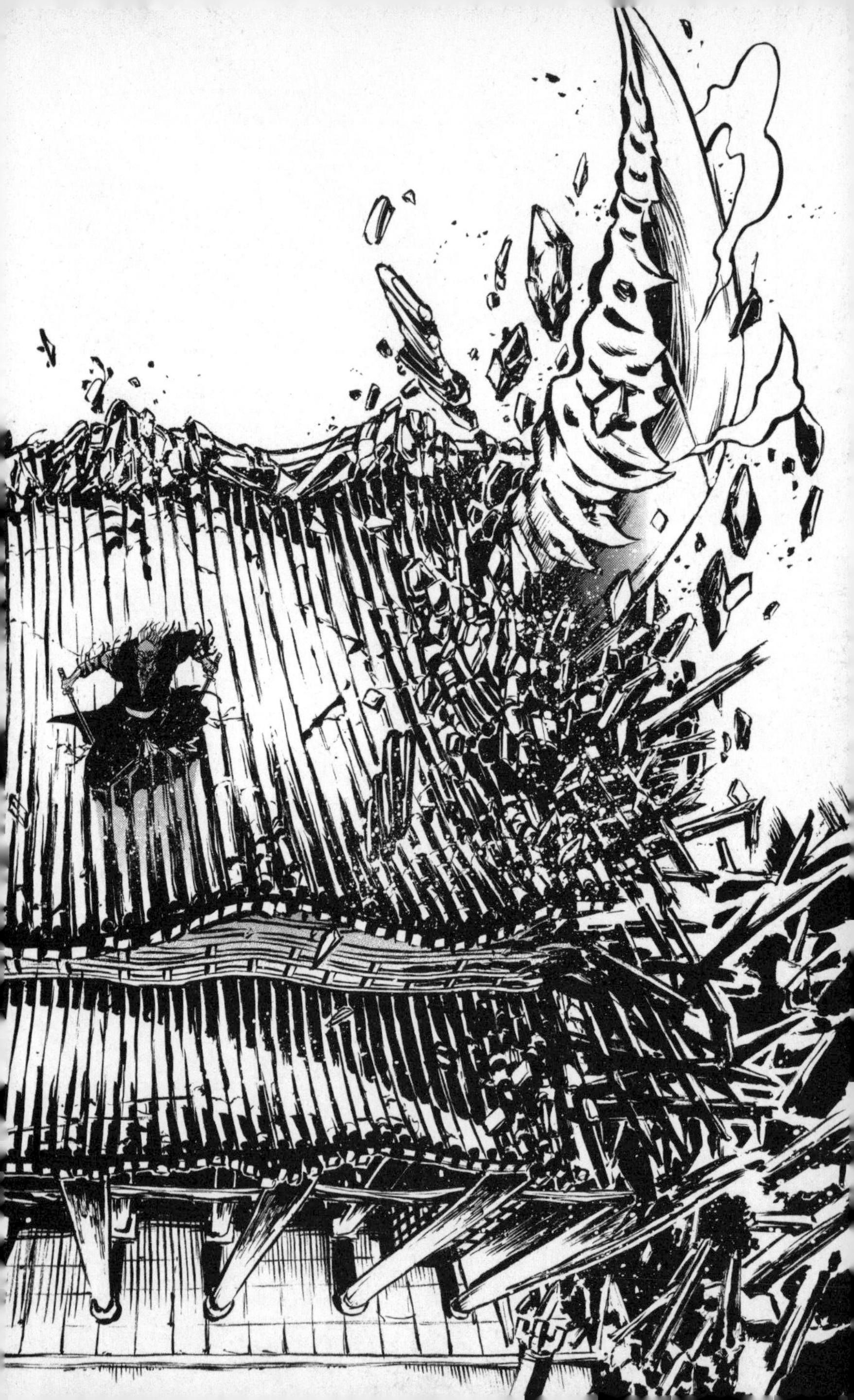

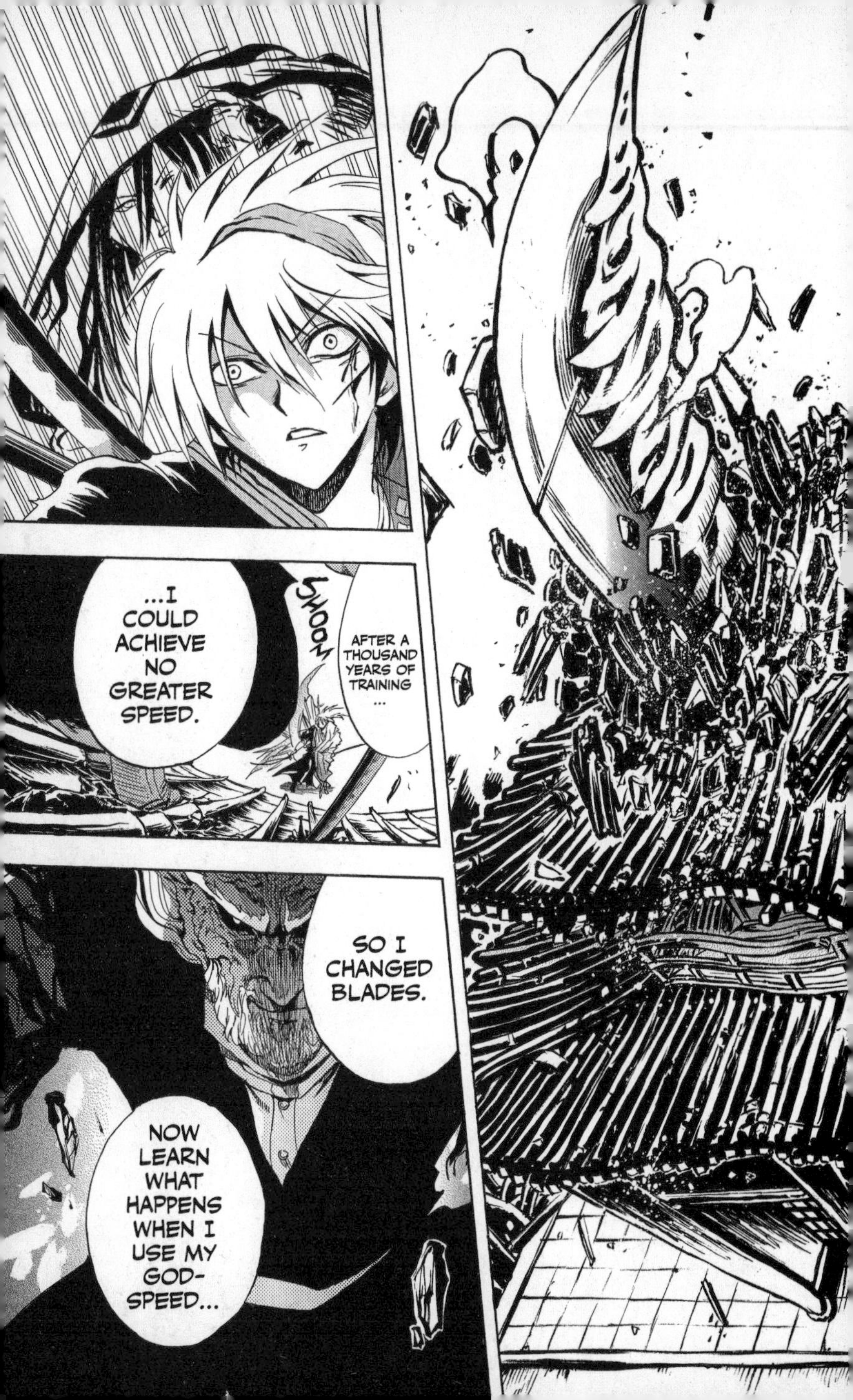
SHOOM
AFTER A THOUSAND YEARS OF TRAINING...
...I COULD ACHIEVE NO GREATER SPEED.
SO I CHANGED BLADES.
NOW LEARN WHAT HAPPENS WHEN I USE MY GOD-SPEED...

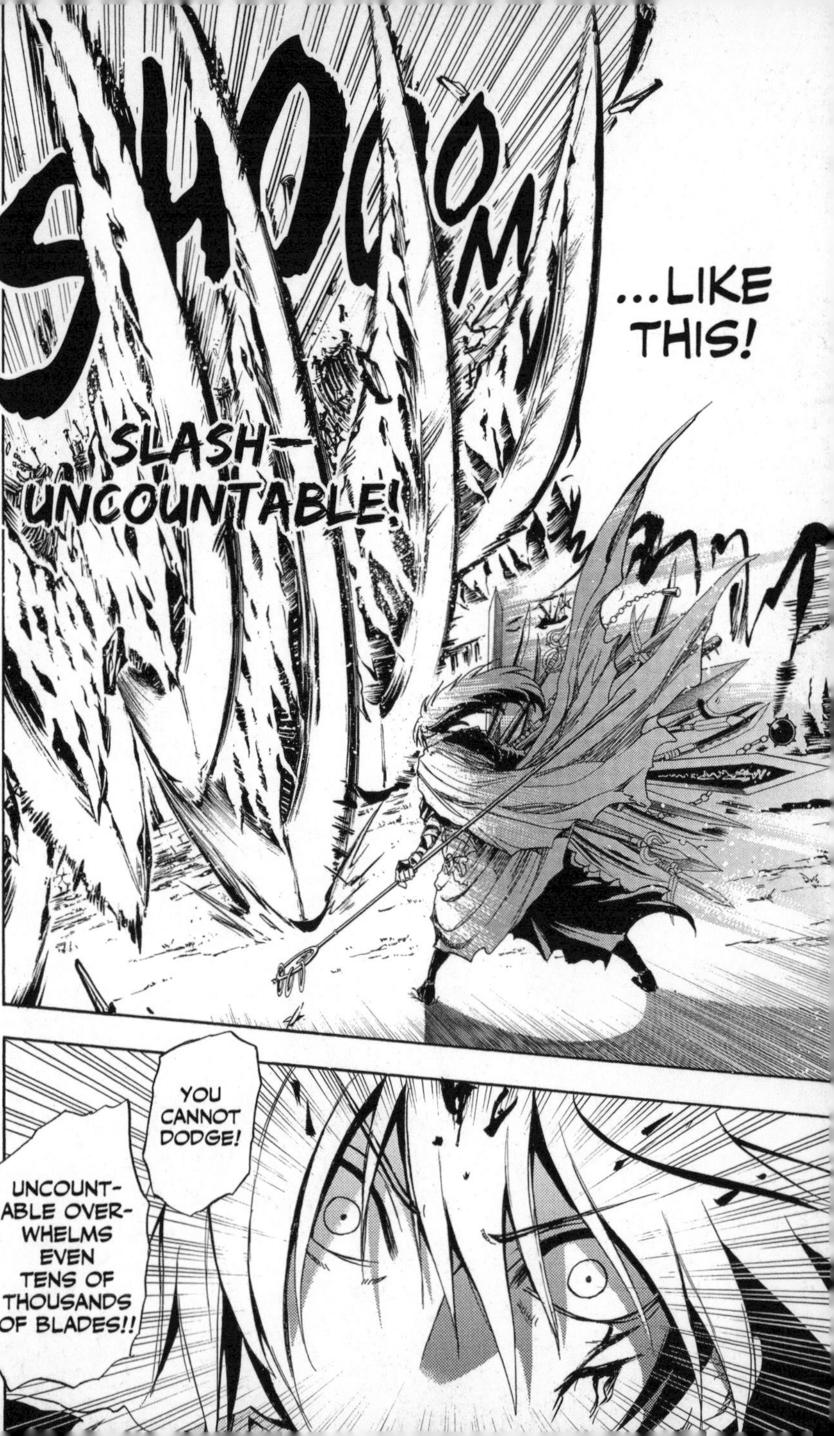
SHOOOM
...LIKE THIS!
SLASH-UNCOUNTABLE!
YOU CANNOT DODGE!
UNCOUNTABLE OVERWHELMS EVEN TENS OF THOUSANDS OF BLADES!!

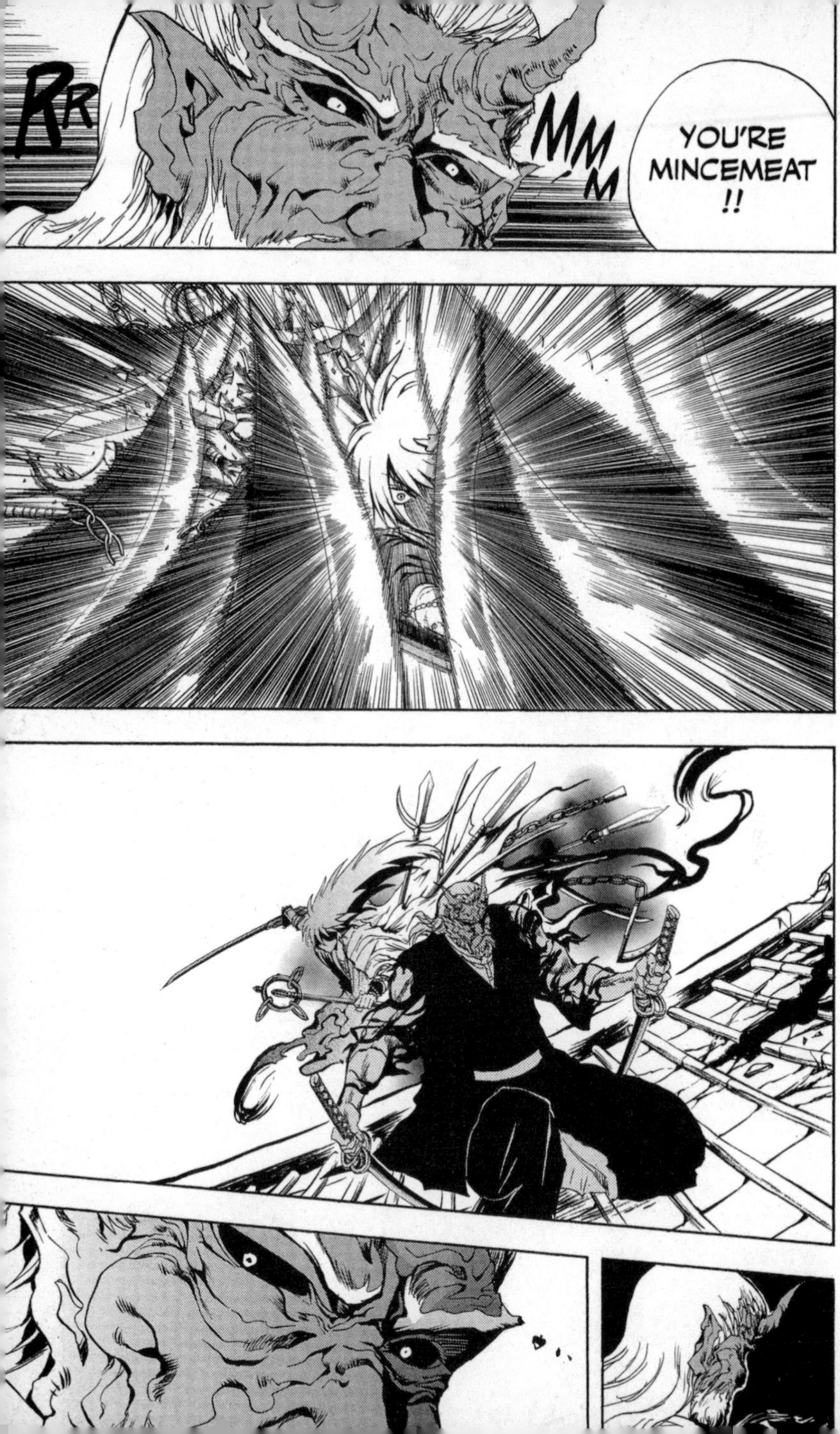
RRMMM
YOU'RE MINCEMEAT !!

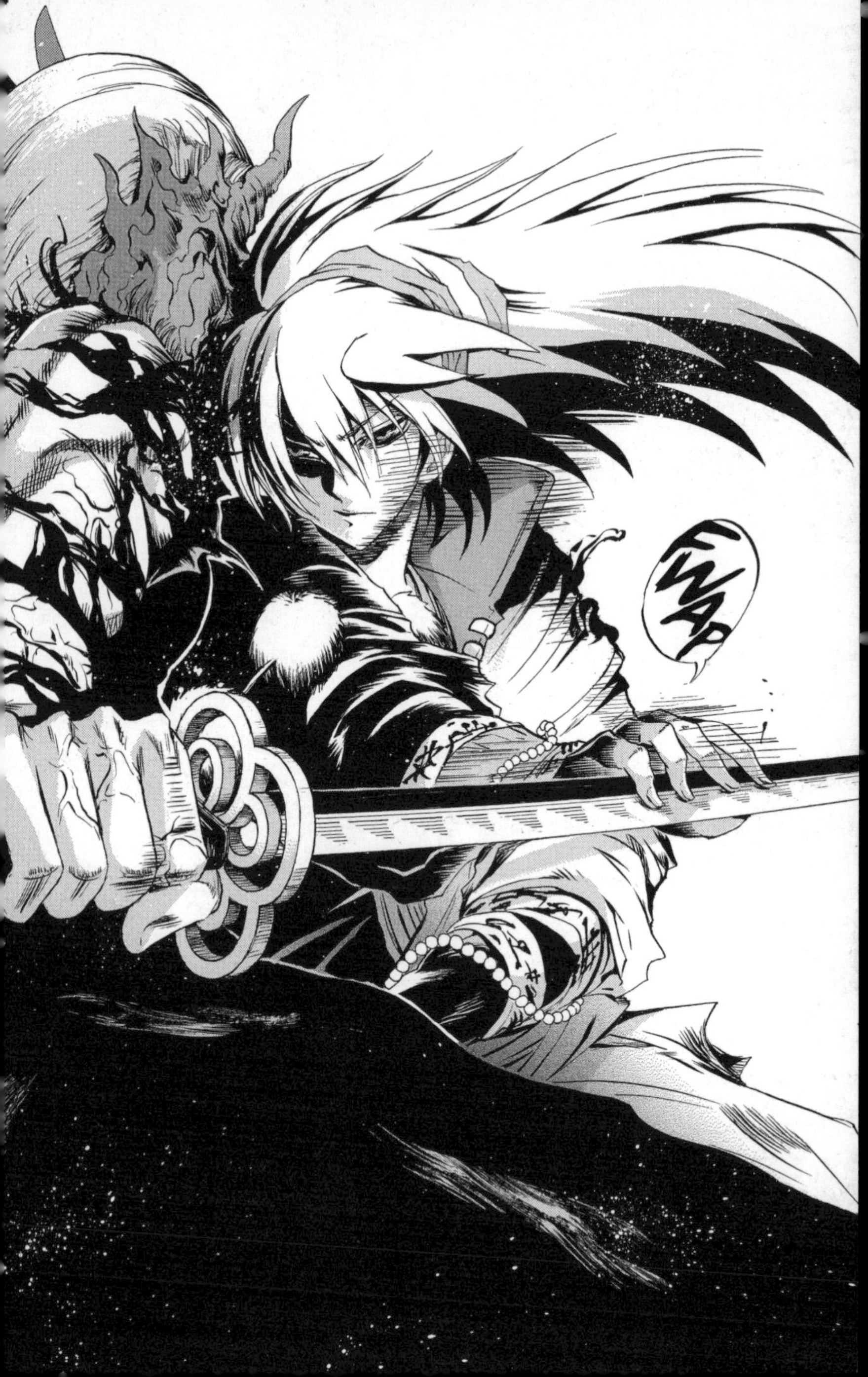
FWAP

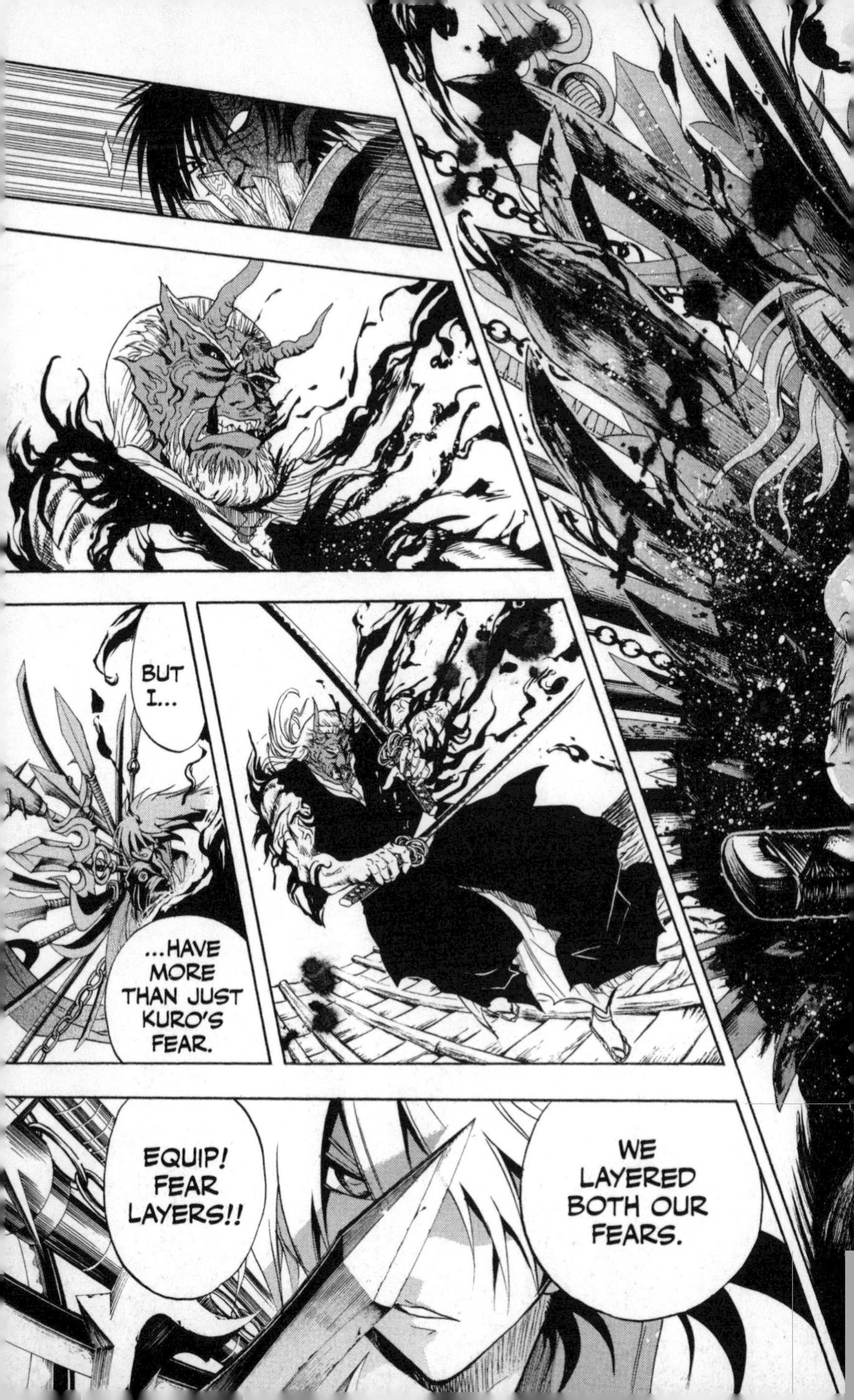
BUT I...
...HAVE MORE THAN JUST KURO'S FEAR.
WE LAYERED BOTH OUR FEARS.
EQUIP! FEAR LAYERS!!

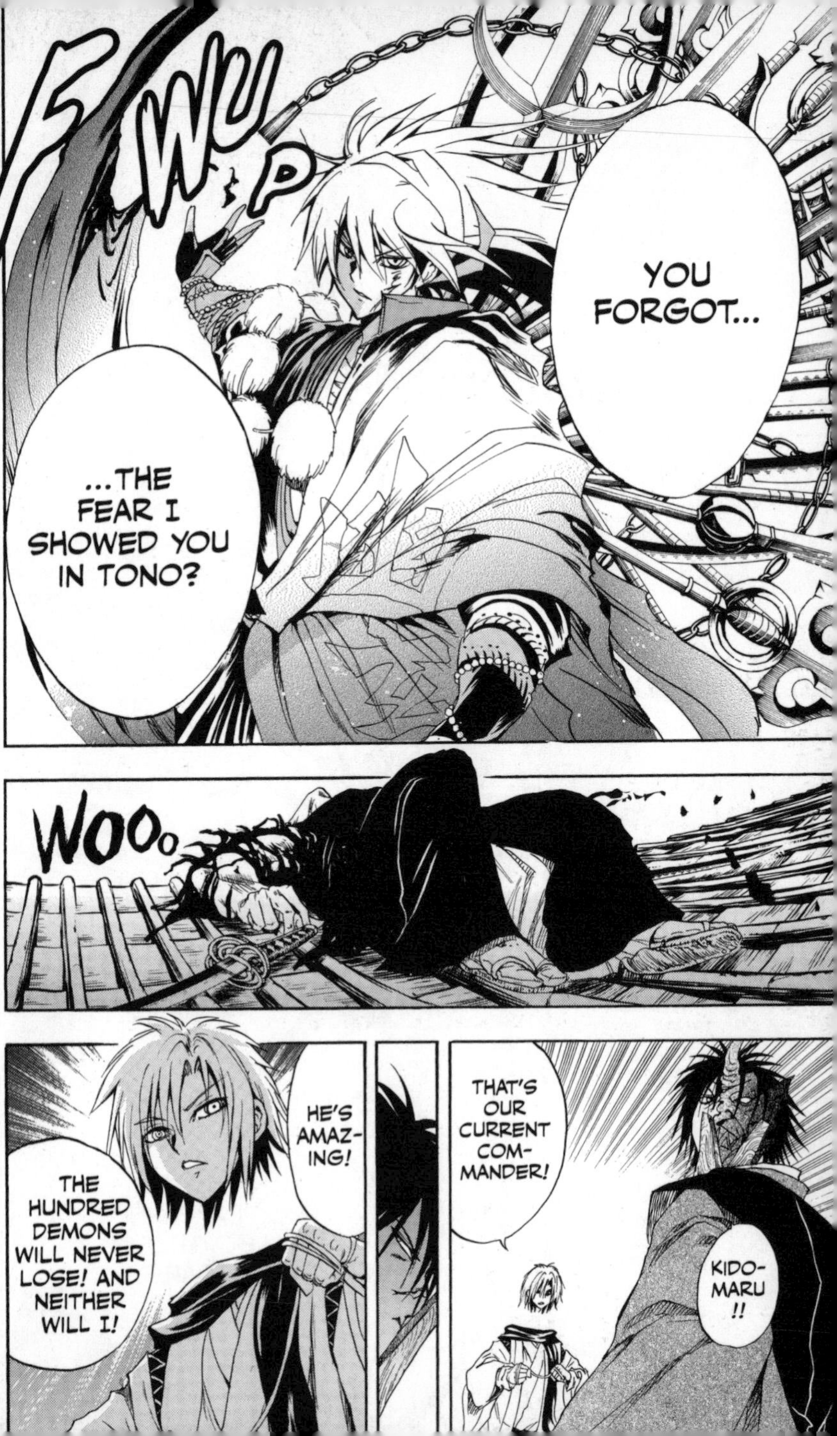
FWUP
YOU FORGOT...
...THE FEAR I SHOWED YOU IN TONO?
WOOo
THAT'S OUR CURRENT COM-MANDER!
KIDO-MARU!!
HE'S AMAZ-ING!
THE HUNDRED DEMONS WILL NEVER LOSE! AND NEITHER WILL I!

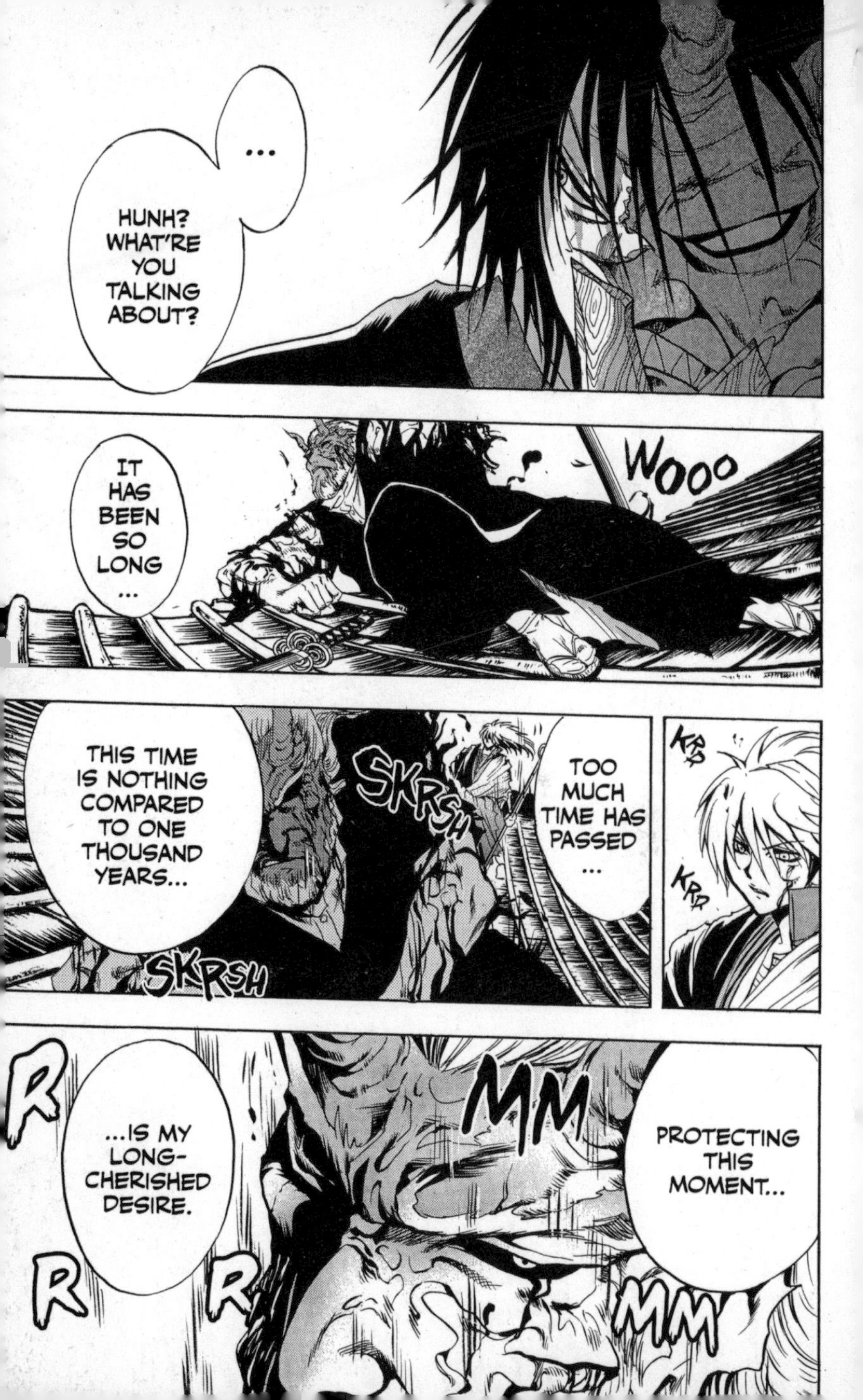
...
HUNH? WHAT'RE YOU TALKING ABOUT?
WOOO
IT HAS BEEN SO LONG...
KRR
KRR
TOO MUCH TIME HAS PASSED...
SKRSH
THIS TIME IS NOTHING COMPARED TO ONE THOUSAND YEARS...
SKRSH
PROTECTING THIS MOMENT...
MM
MM
...IS MY LONG-CHERISHED DESIRE.
R
R
R

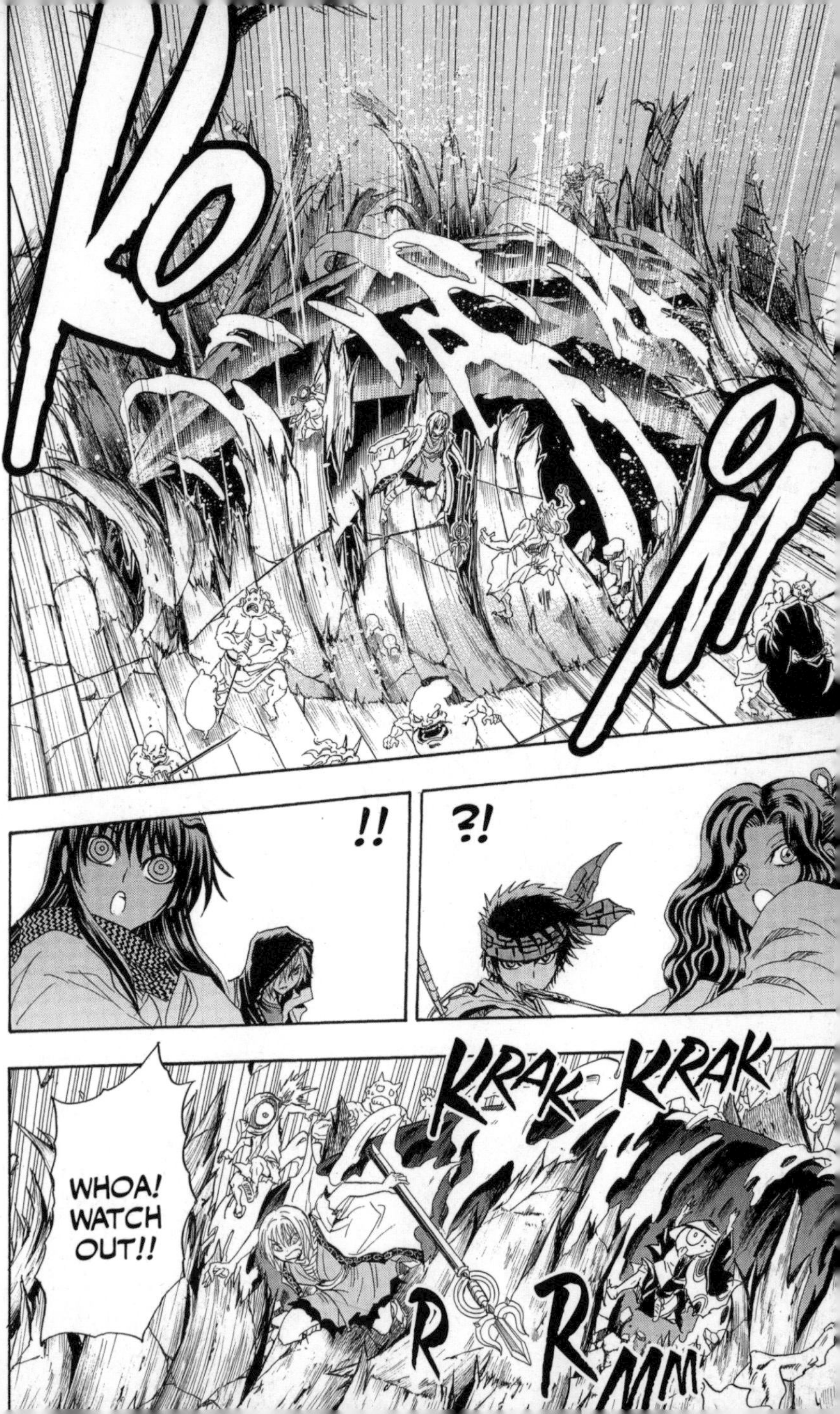
?!
!!
KRAK KRAK
WHOA! WATCH OUT!!
RRMM

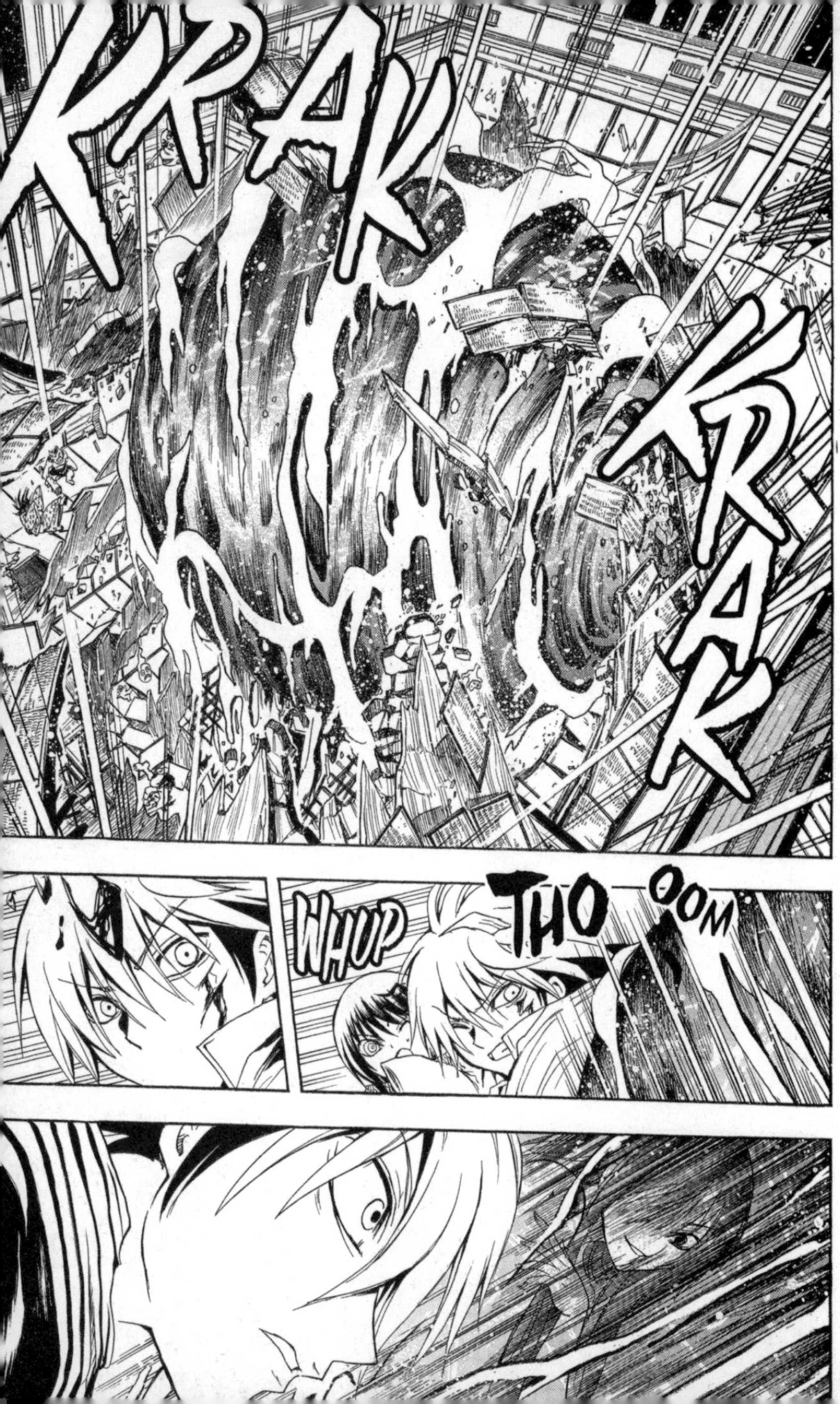
KRAK
KRAK
THOOOM
WHUP

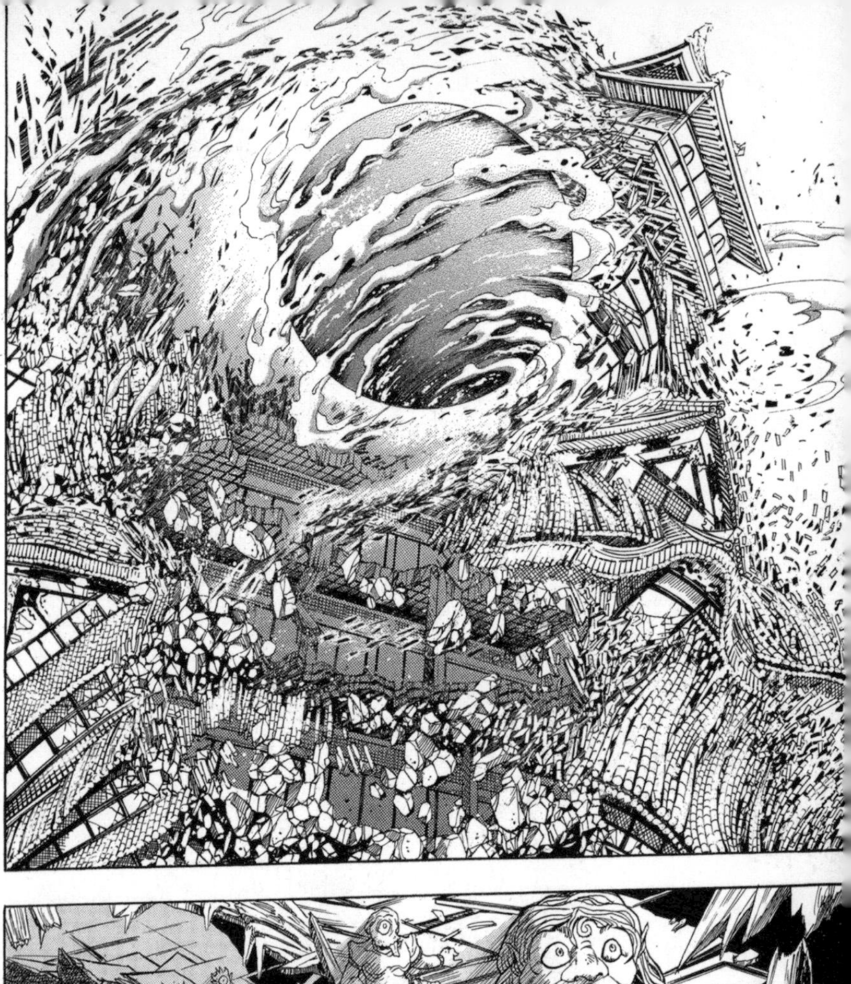

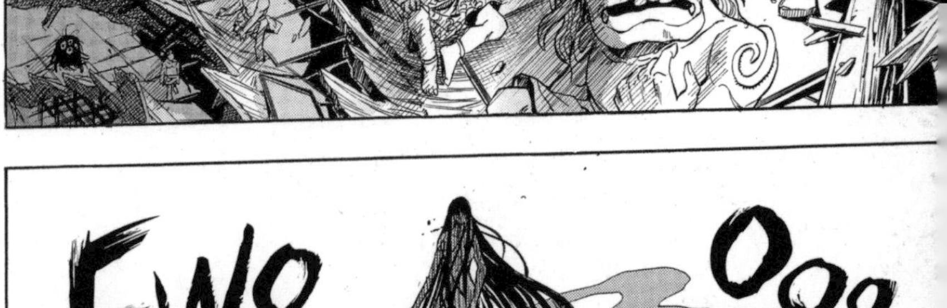

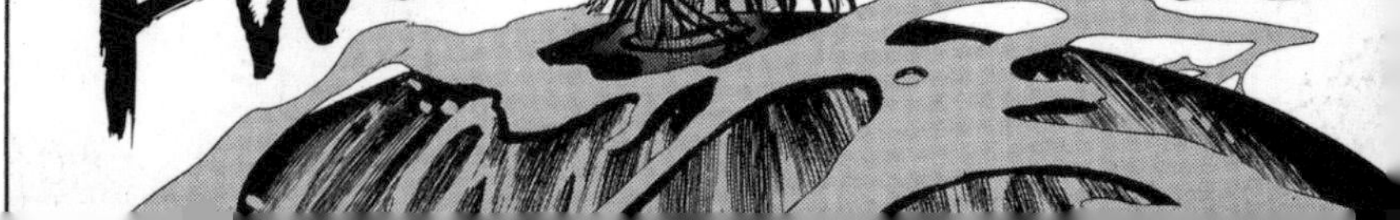
FWO Ooo

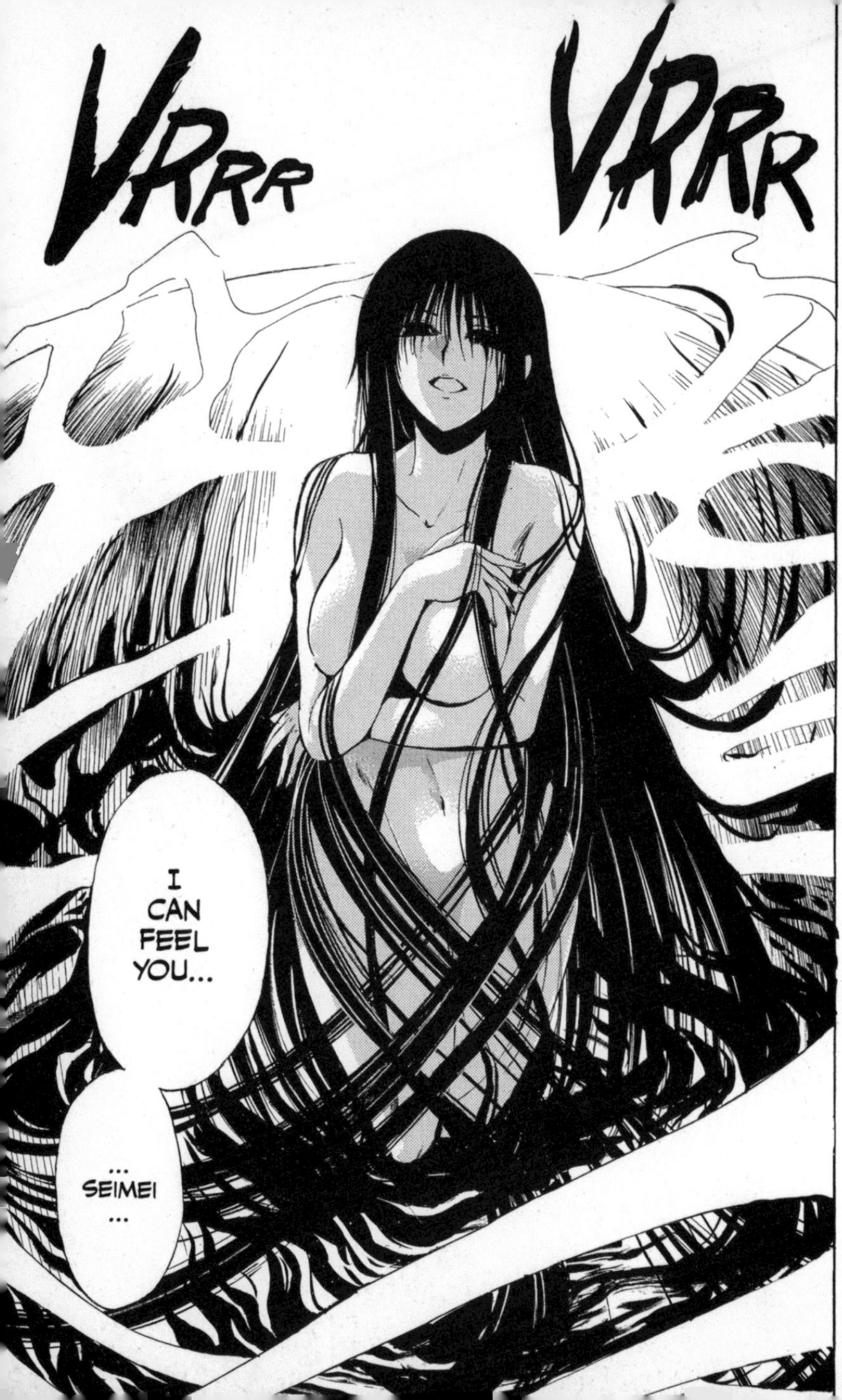
VRRR
VRRR
I CAN FEEL YOU...
...SEIMEI...

Godspeed Slash: Plum Tree is one thousand swords.

When I draw my sword and release a single slash of godspeed, it is called Camphor Tree.

(swords that cut through Rikuo's Fear in Tono) These are my two Slashes. I named them as such as they look like the branches of trees.

Uncountable and Cherry Blossoms are two developments.

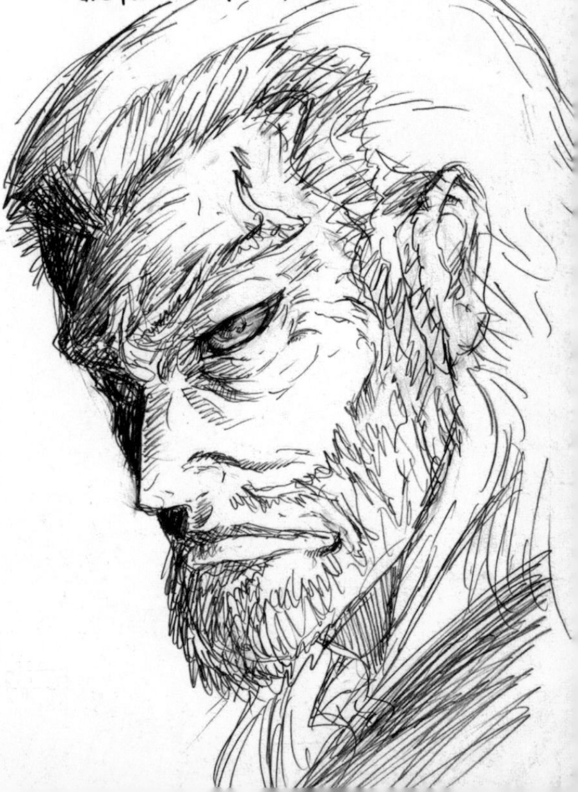

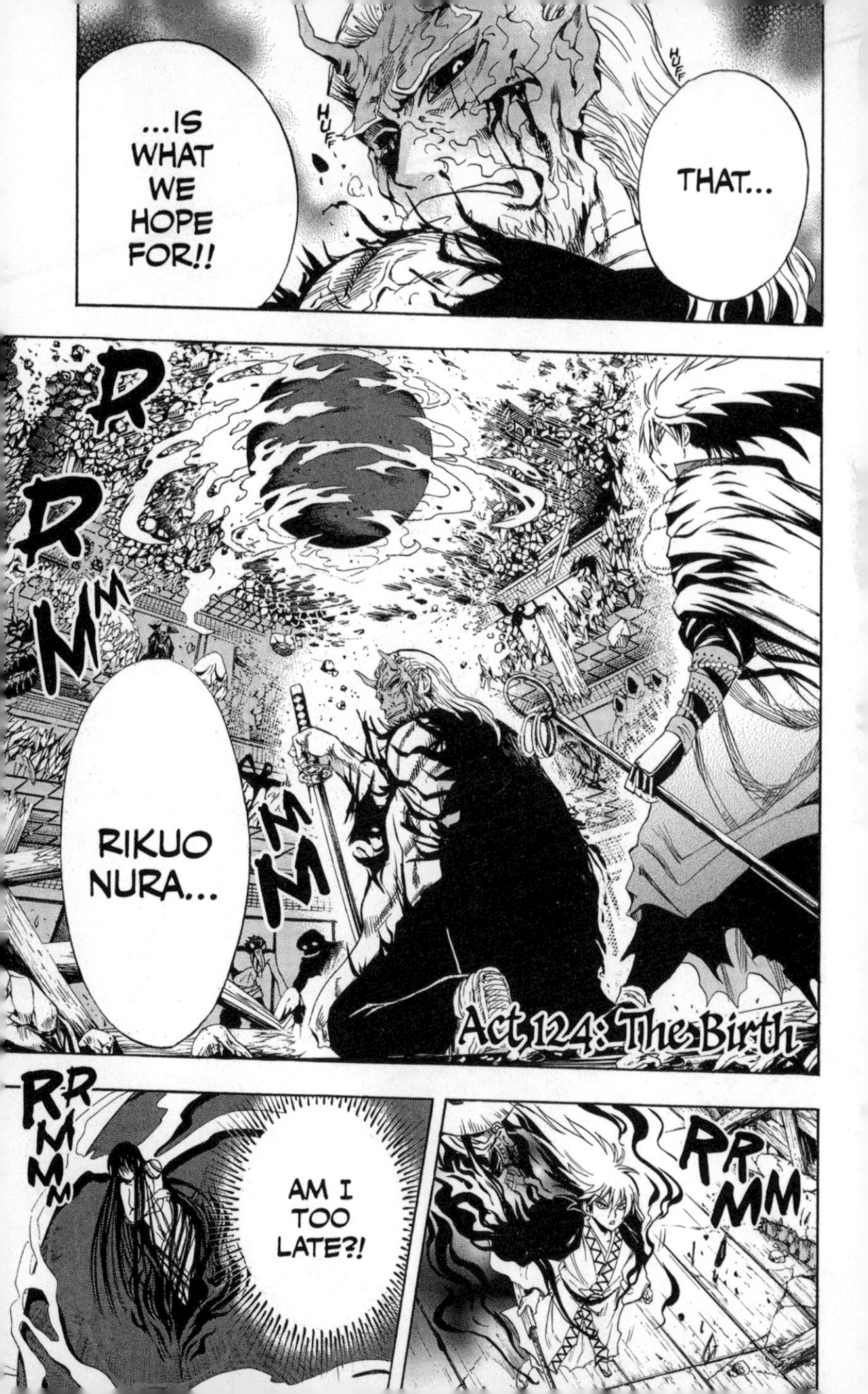
HUFF
THAT...
HUFF
...IS WHAT WE HOPE FOR!!
RRRMMM
RIKUO NURA...
MMM
Act 124: The Birth
RRMM
AM I TOO LATE?!
RRRMMMM

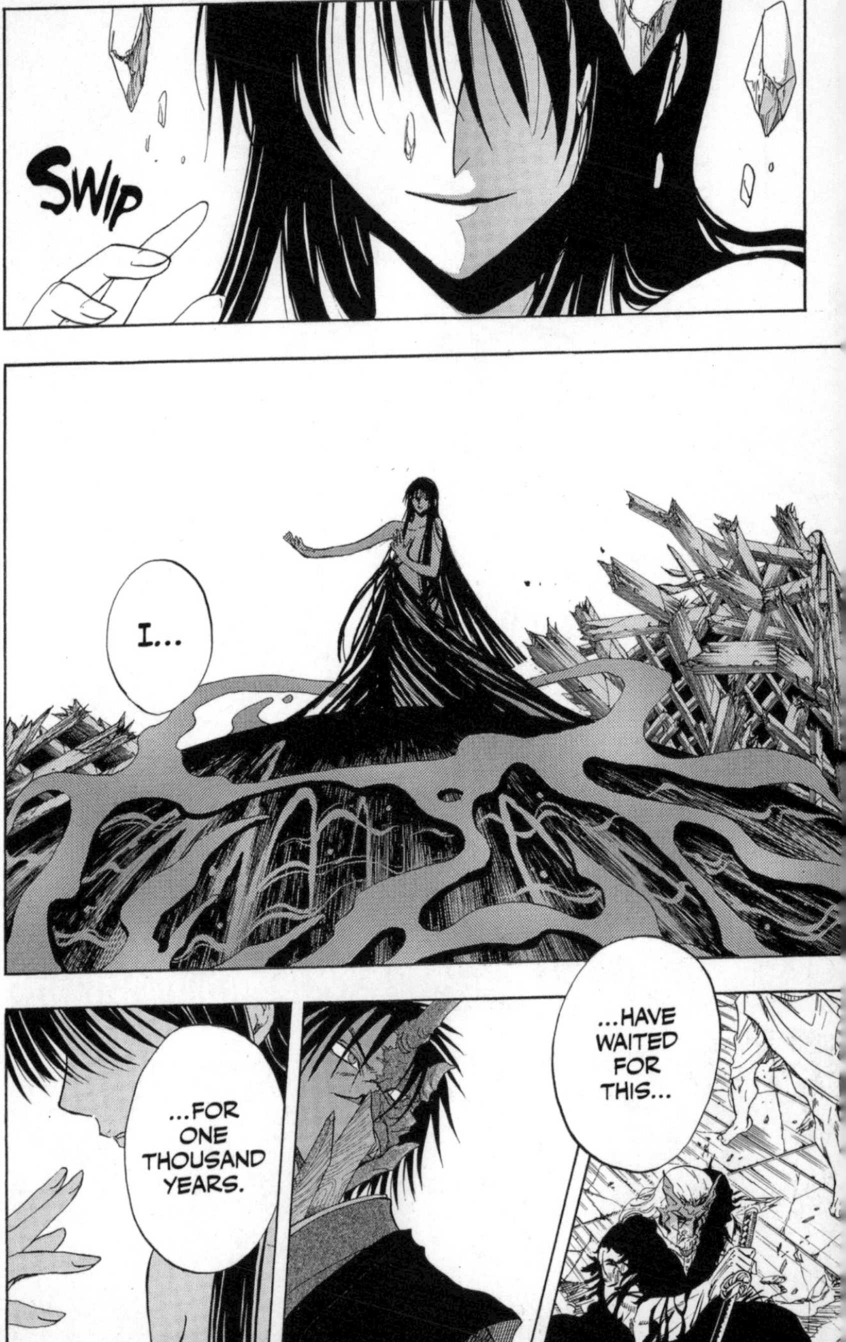
SWIP
I...
...HAVE WAITED FOR THIS...
...FOR ONE THOUSAND YEARS.

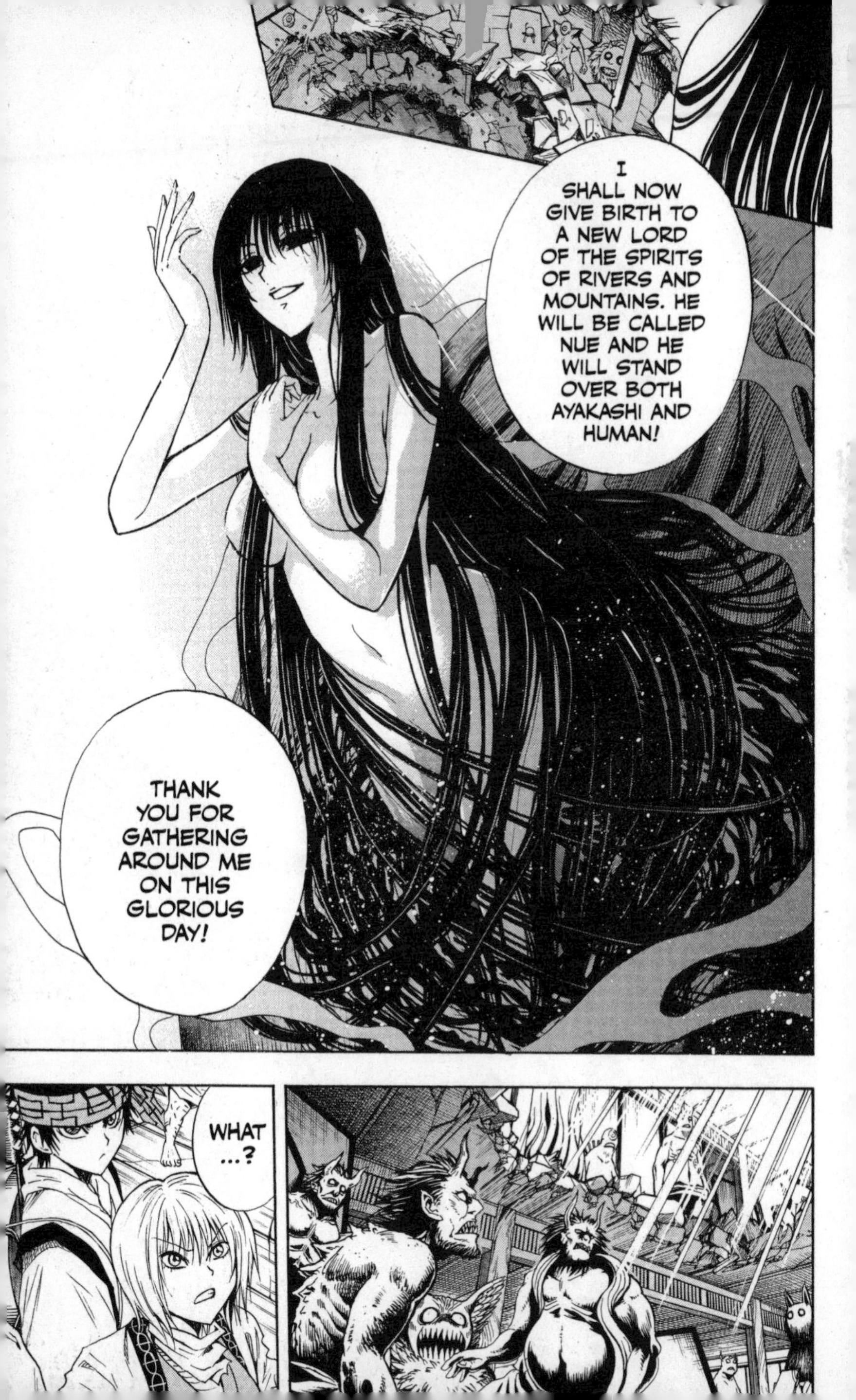
I SHALL NOW GIVE BIRTH TO A NEW LORD OF THE SPIRITS OF RIVERS AND MOUNTAINS. HE WILL BE CALLED NUE AND HE WILL STAND OVER BOTH AYAKASHI AND HUMAN!
THANK YOU FOR GATHERING AROUND ME ON THIS GLORIOUS DAY!
WHAT ...?

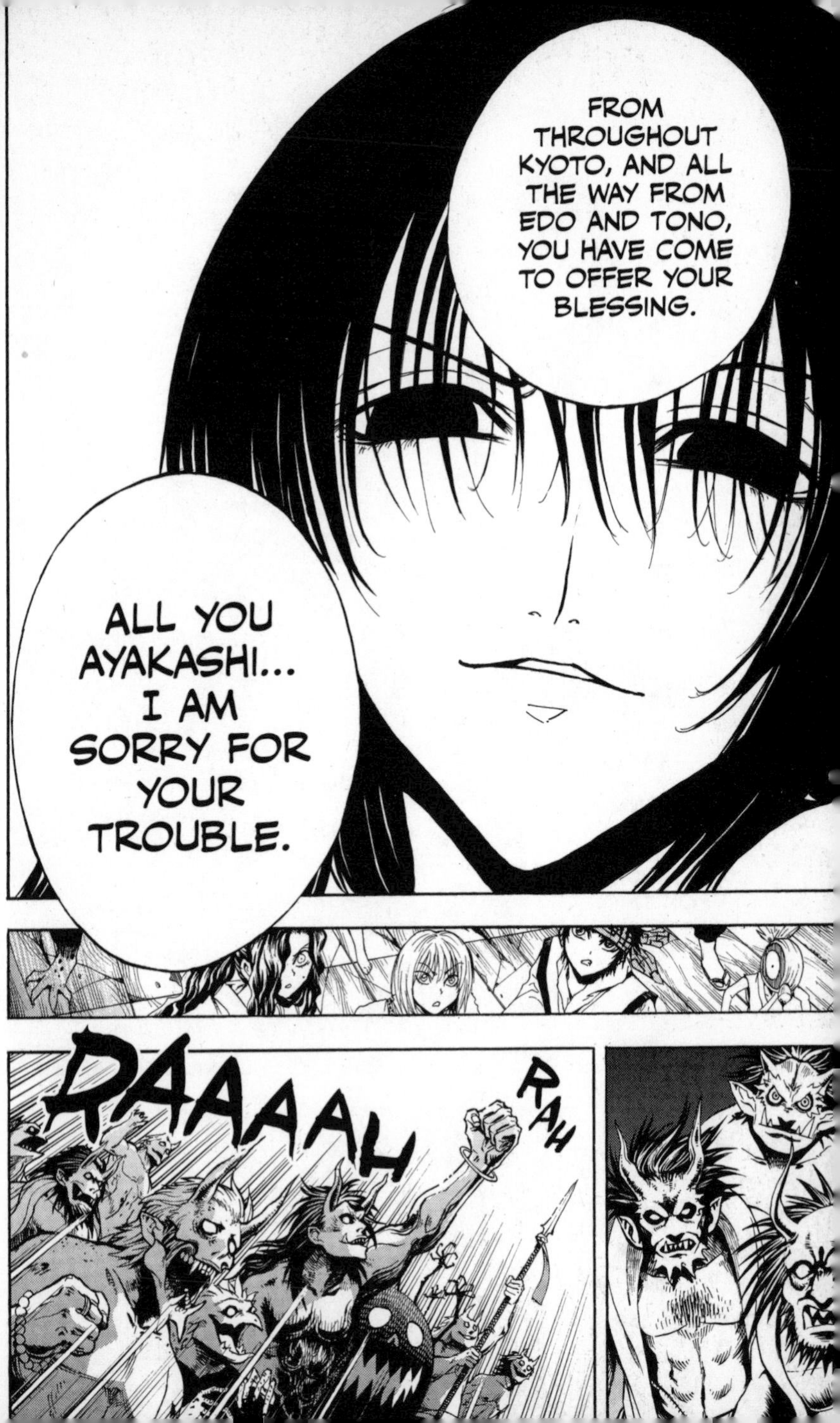
FROM THROUGHOUT KYOTO, AND ALL THE WAY FROM EDO AND TONO, YOU HAVE COME TO OFFER YOUR BLESSING.
ALL YOU AYAKASHI... I AM SORRY FOR YOUR TROUBLE.
RAH
RAAAAH

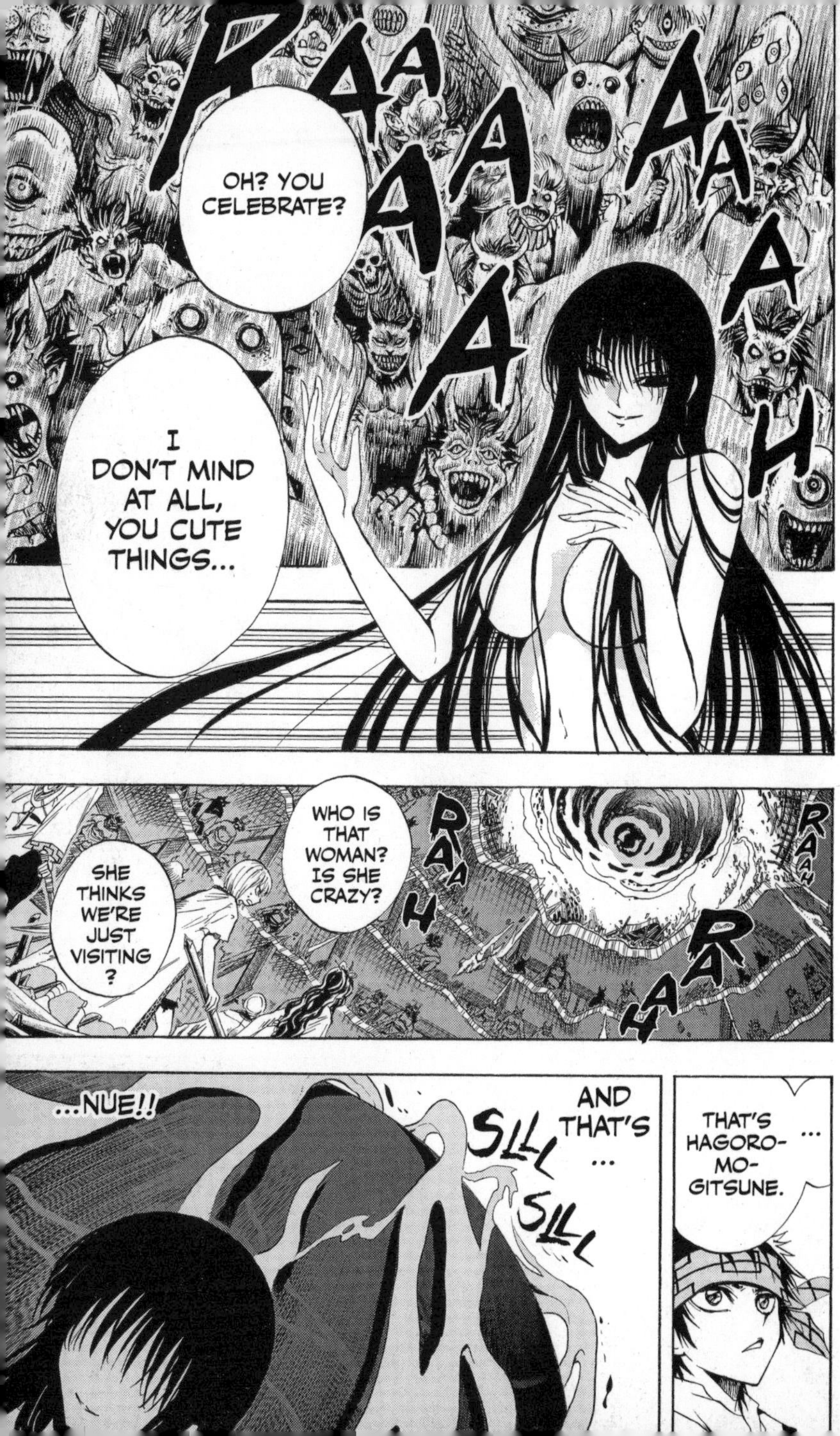
RAAAAAAAAAAH
OH? YOU CELEBRATE?
I DON'T MIND AT ALL, YOU CUTE THINGS...
RAAH
WHO IS THAT WOMAN? IS SHE CRAZY?
RAAAH
SHE THINKS WE'RE JUST VISITING?
RAAH
...
THAT'S HAGORO-MO-GITSUNE.
AND THAT'S ...
...NUE!!
SLLL
SLLL

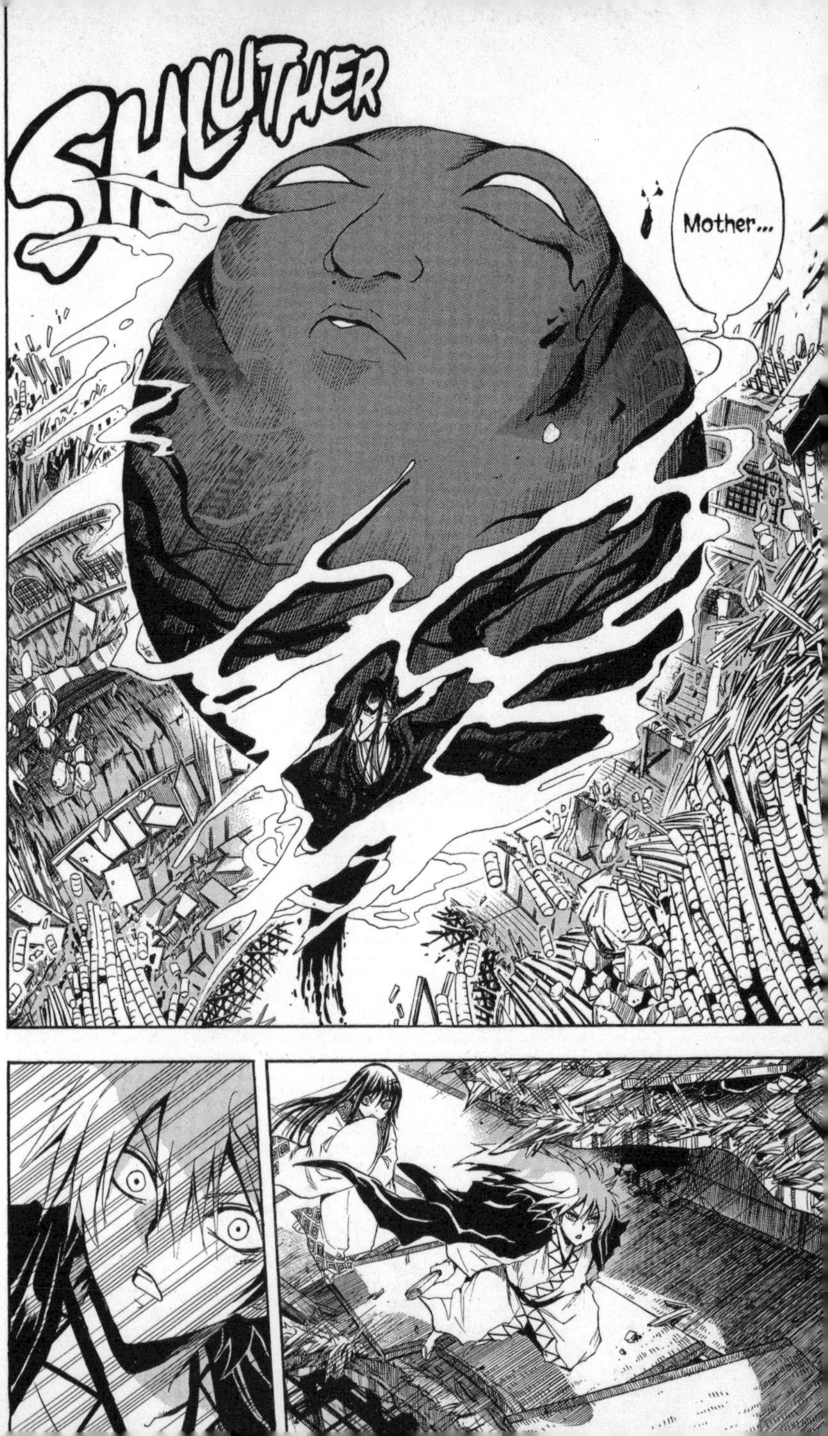
SHLUTHER
Mother...

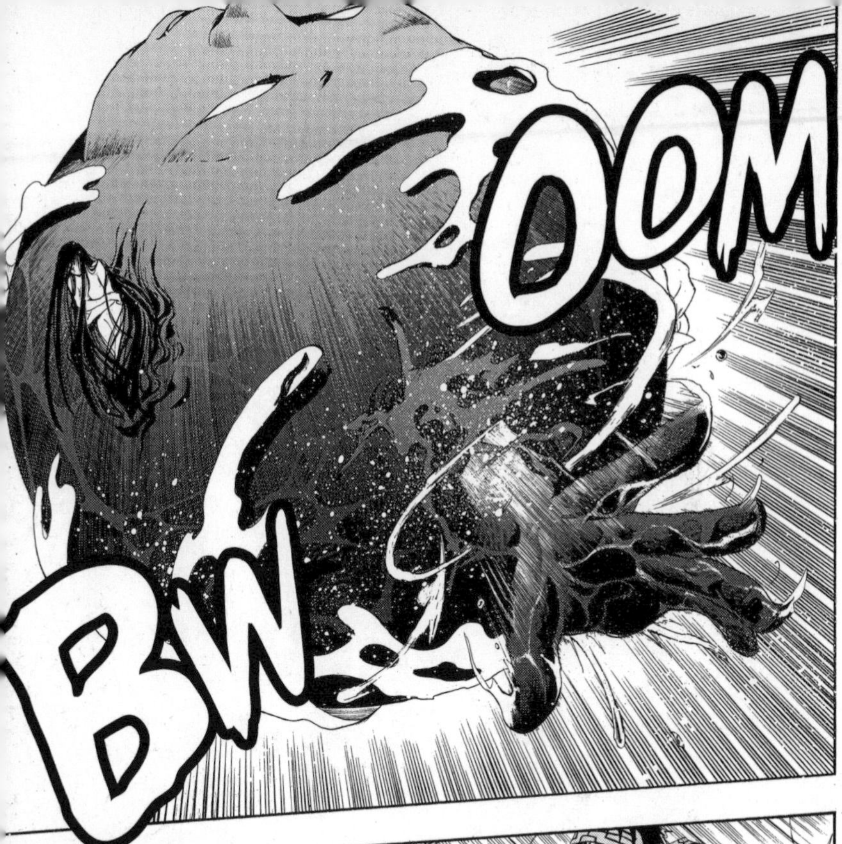
BW-OOM
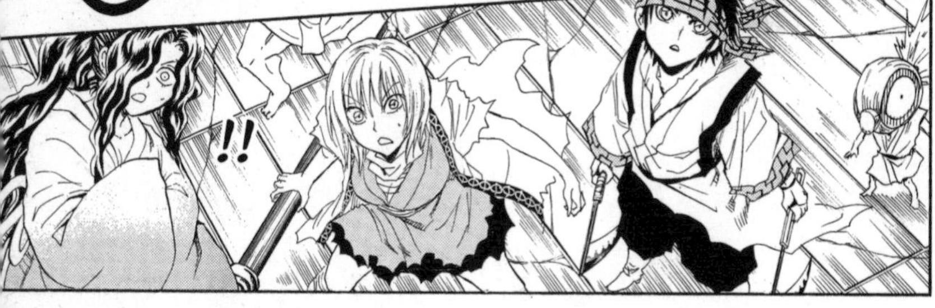
!!
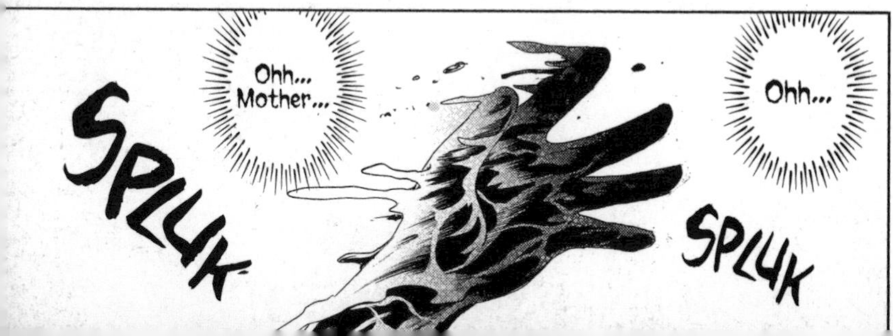
Ohh...
Ohh... Mother...
SPLUK
SPLUK

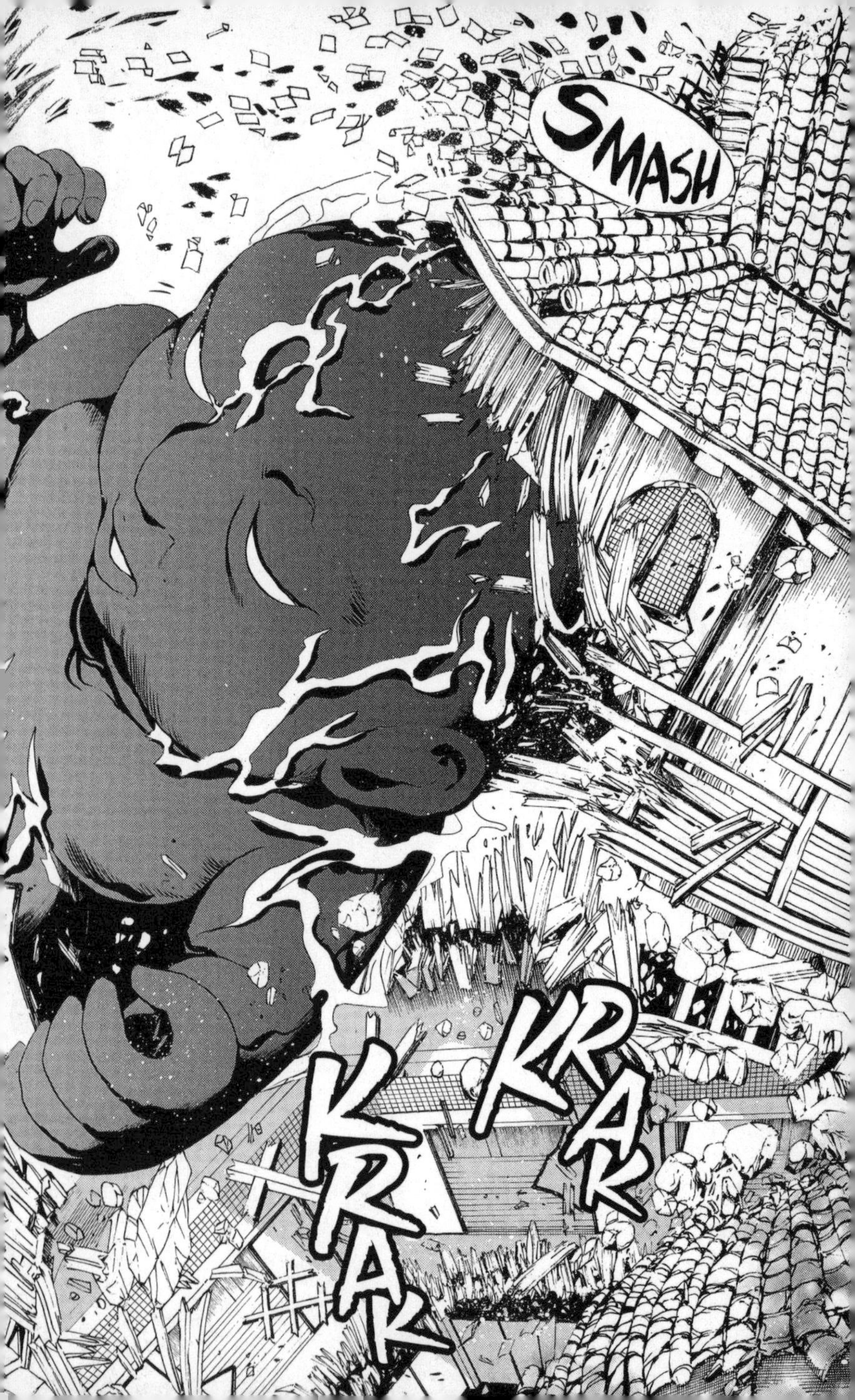
SMASH
KRAK
KRAK

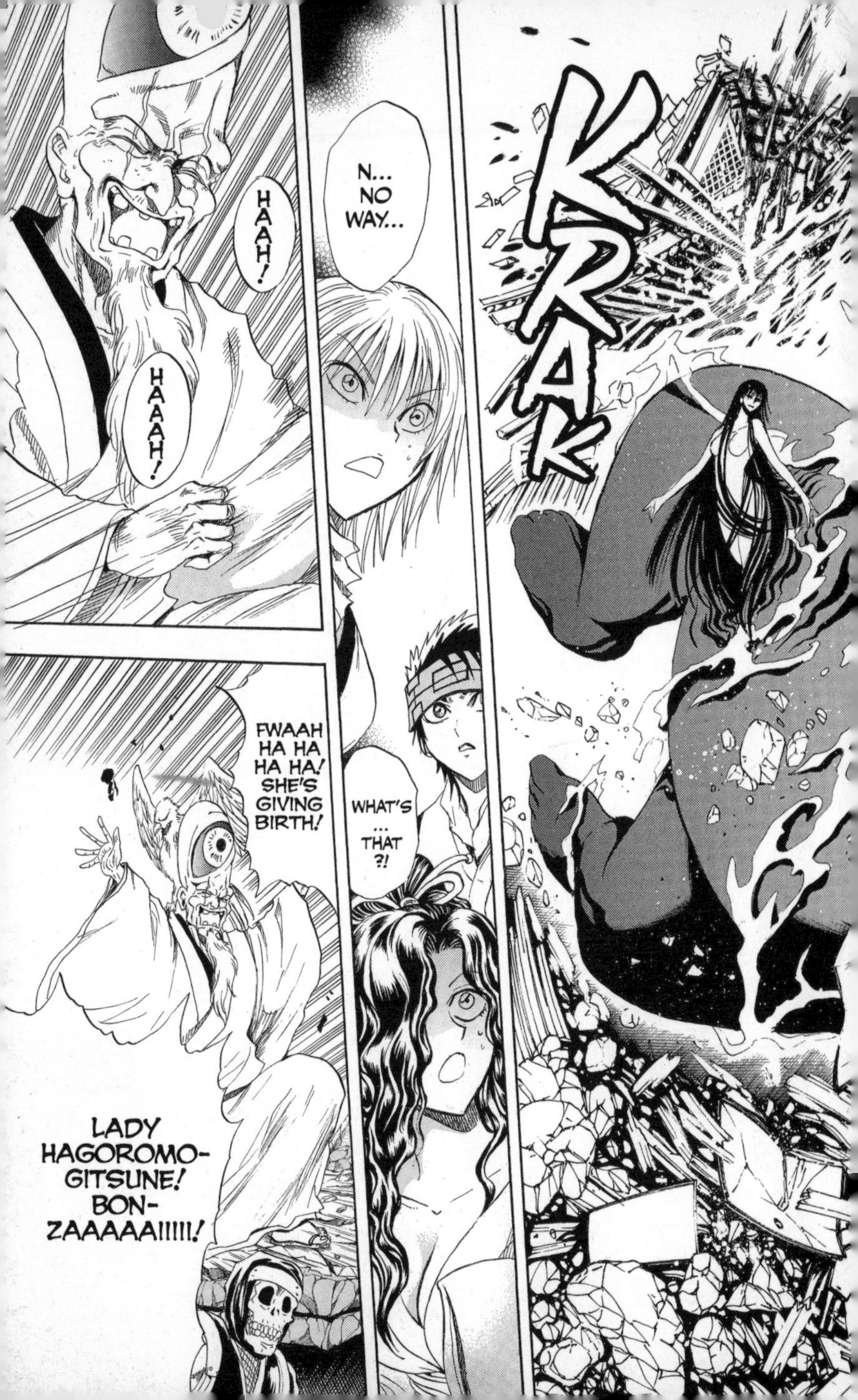
KRAK
N... NO WAY...
WHAT'S ... THAT?!
HAAAH!
HAAAAH!
FWAAH HA HA HA HA! SHE'S GIVING BIRTH!
LADY HAGOROMO-GITSUNE! BON-ZAAAAAI!!!!!!

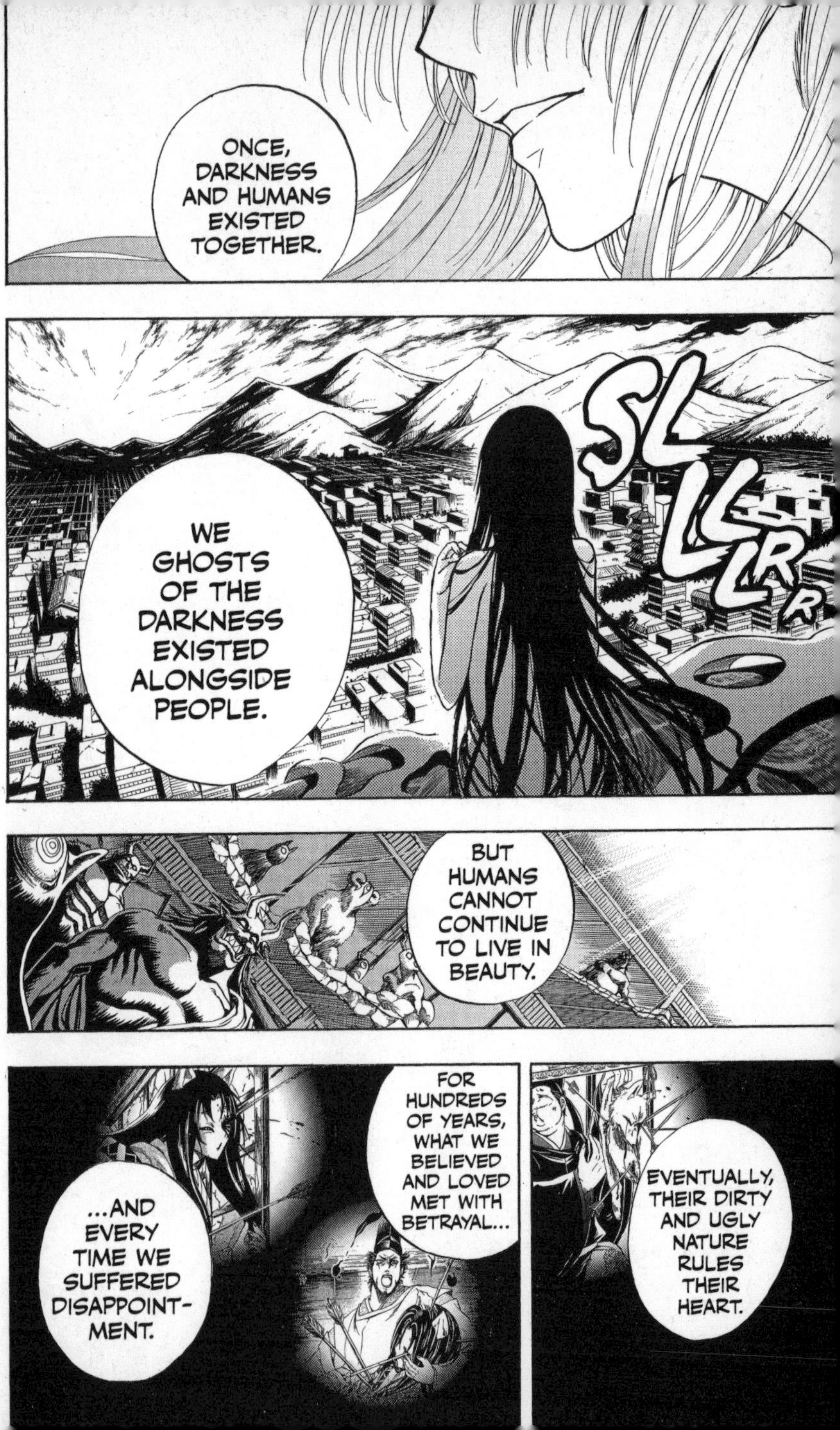
ONCE, DARKNESS AND HUMANS EXISTED TOGETHER.
SLLLRR
WE GHOSTS OF THE DARKNESS EXISTED ALONGSIDE PEOPLE.
BUT HUMANS CANNOT CONTINUE TO LIVE IN BEAUTY.
EVENTUALLY, THEIR DIRTY AND UGLY NATURE RULES THEIR HEART.
FOR HUNDREDS OF YEARS, WHAT WE BELIEVED AND LOVED MET WITH BETRAYAL...
...AND EVERY TIME WE SUFFERED DISAPPOINT-MENT.

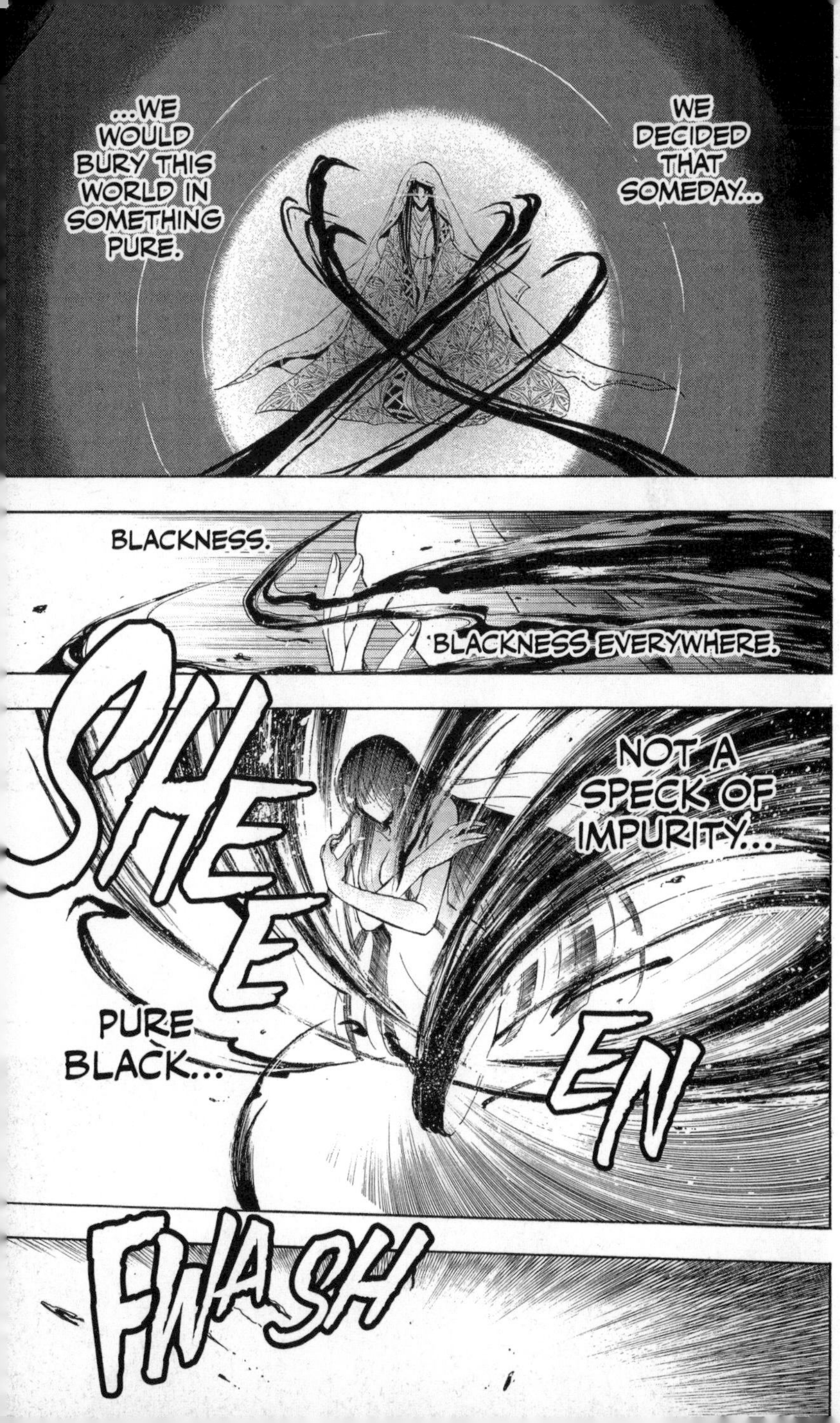
WE DECIDED THAT SOMEDAY...
...WE WOULD BURY THIS WORLD IN SOMETHING PURE.
BLACKNESS.
BLACKNESS EVERYWHERE.
NOT A SPECK OF IMPURITY...
SHEEEN
PURE BLACK...
FWASH

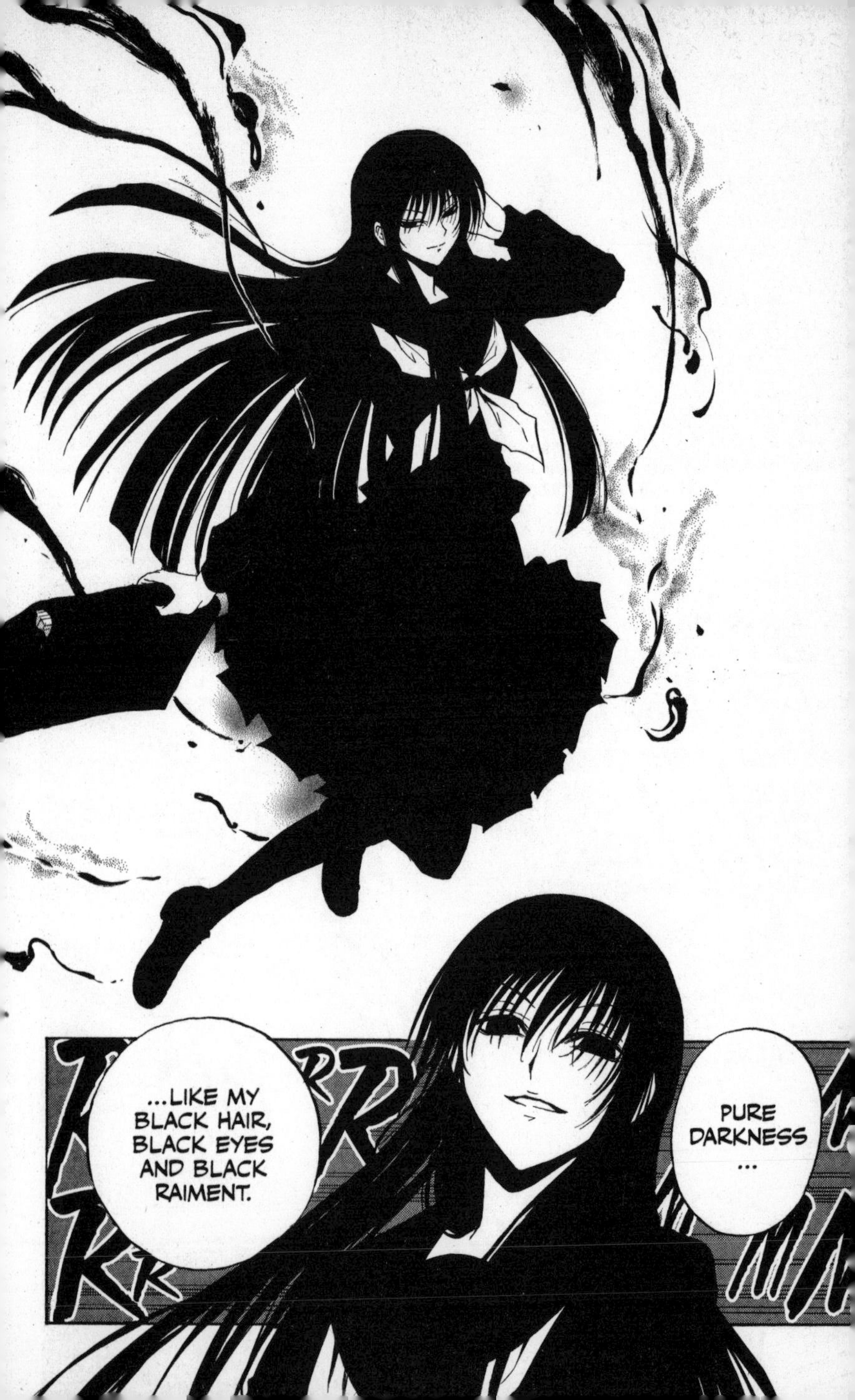
PURE DARKNESS ...
...LIKE MY BLACK HAIR, BLACK EYES AND BLACK RAIMENT.

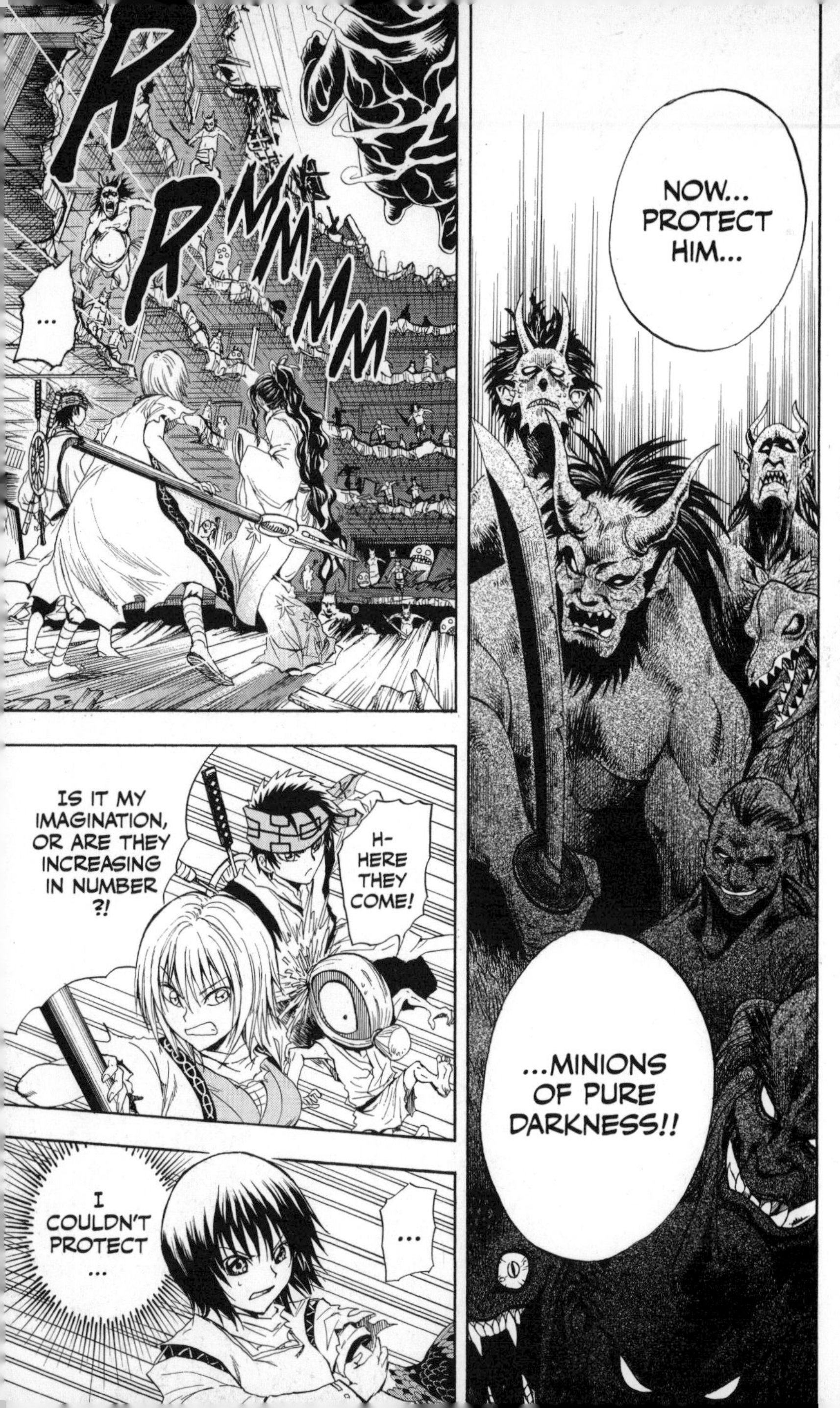
NOW... PROTECT HIM...
...MINIONS OF PURE DARKNESS!!
RRMMMMM
...
H- HERE THEY COME!
IS IT MY IMAGINATION, OR ARE THEY INCREASING IN NUMBER ?!
...
I COULDN'T PROTECT ...

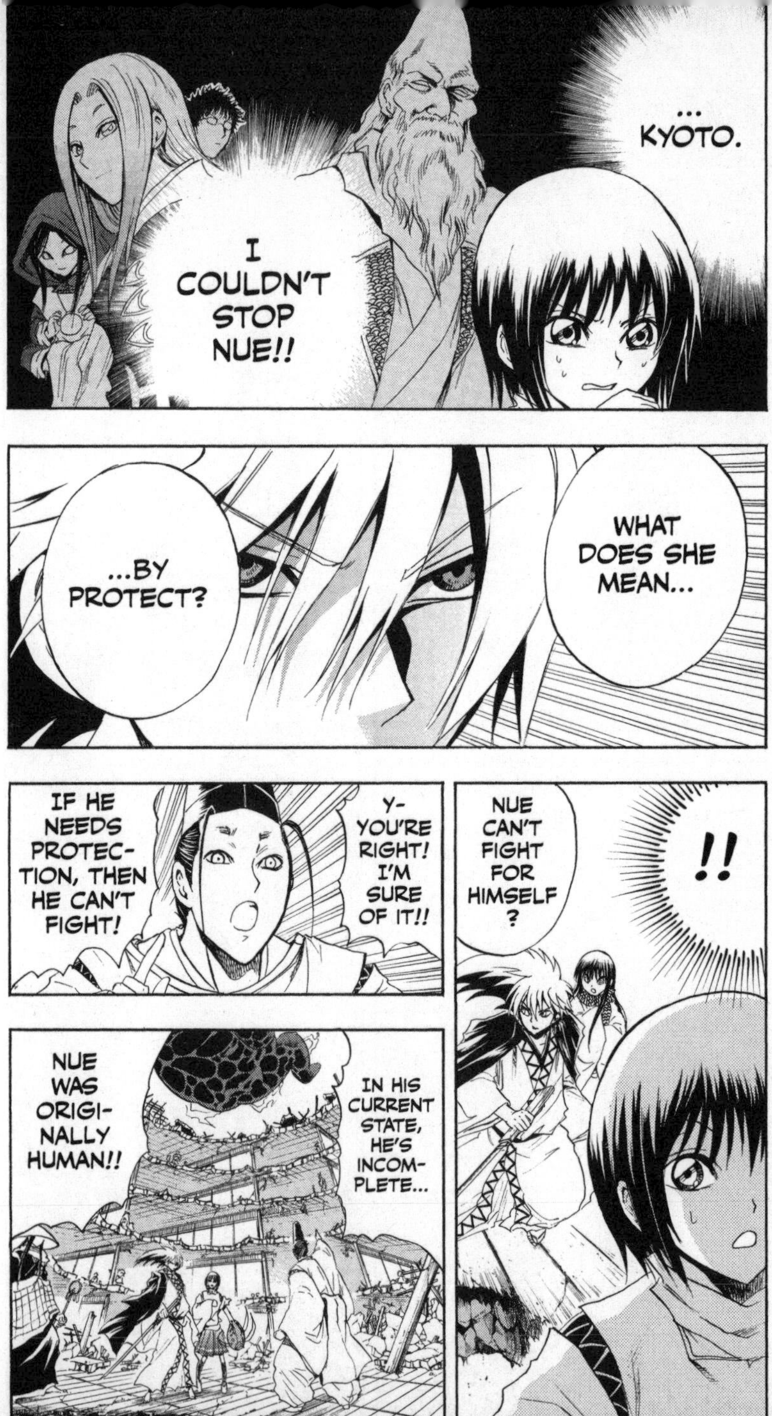
...KYOTO.
I COULDN'T STOP NUE!!
WHAT DOES SHE MEAN...
...BY PROTECT?
!!
NUE CAN'T FIGHT FOR HIMSELF?
IF HE NEEDS PROTECTION, THEN HE CAN'T FIGHT!
Y-YOU'RE RIGHT! I'M SURE OF IT!!
IN HIS CURRENT STATE, HE'S INCOMPLETE...
NUE WAS ORIGINALLY HUMAN!!

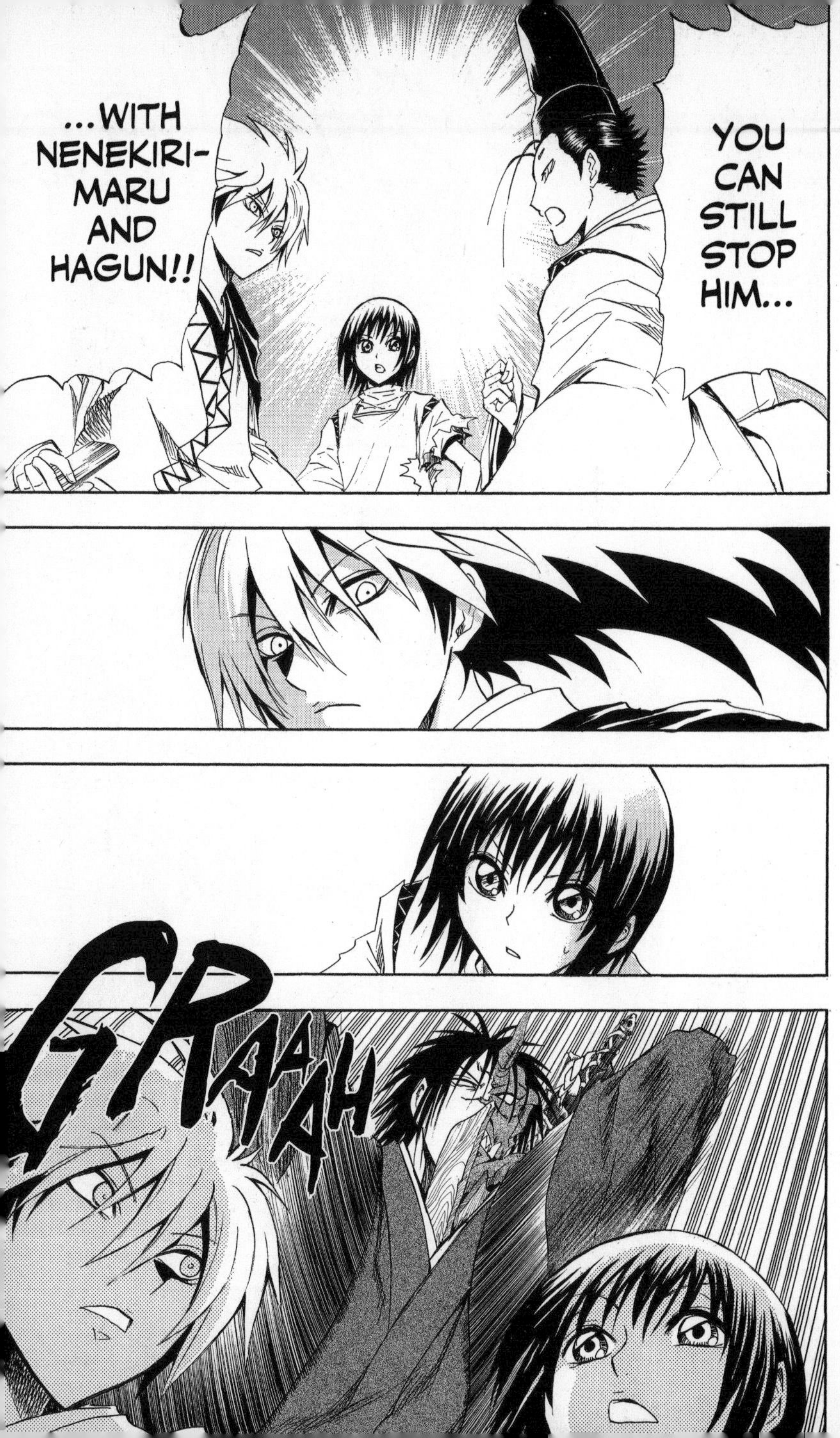
YOU CAN STILL STOP HIM...
...WITH NENEKIRI-MARU AND HAGUN!!
GRAAAH

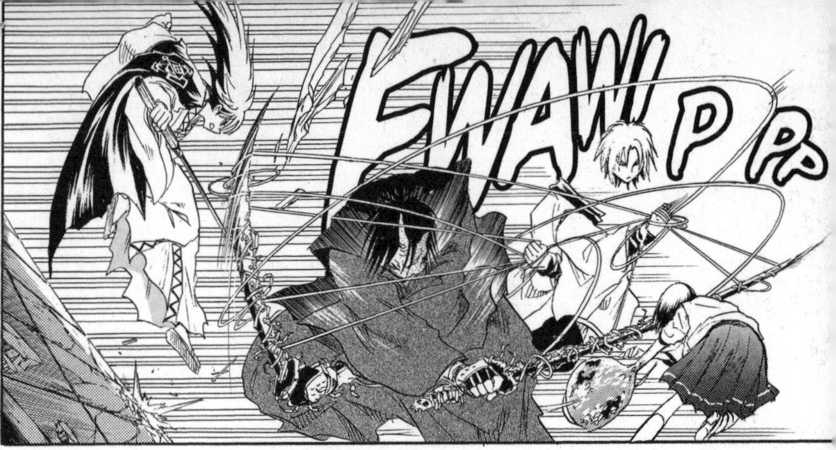
FWAWPPP

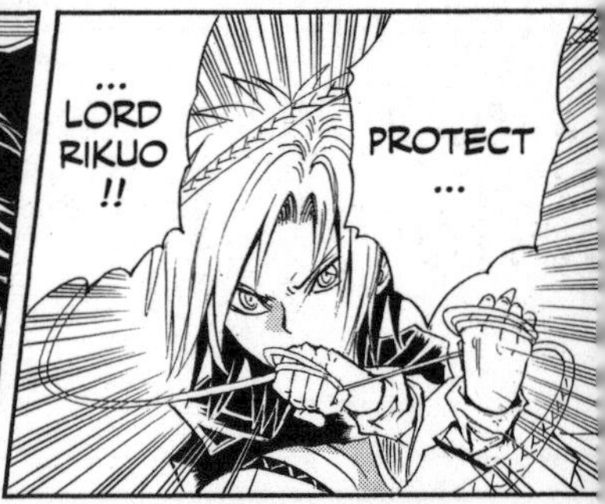
PROTECT
...
... LORD RIKUO !!

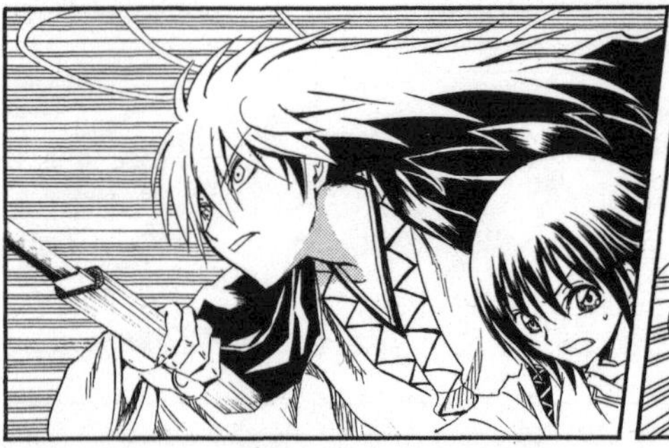

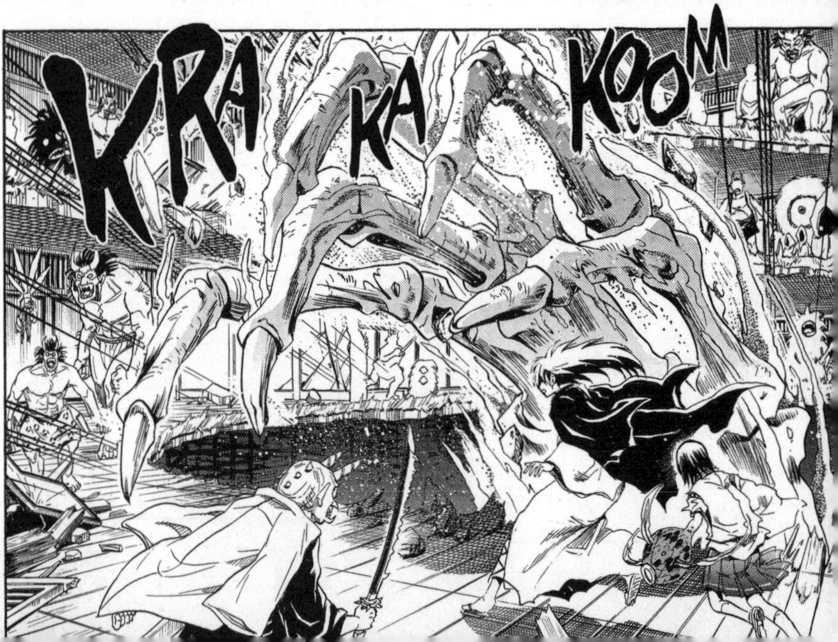
KRAKAKOOM

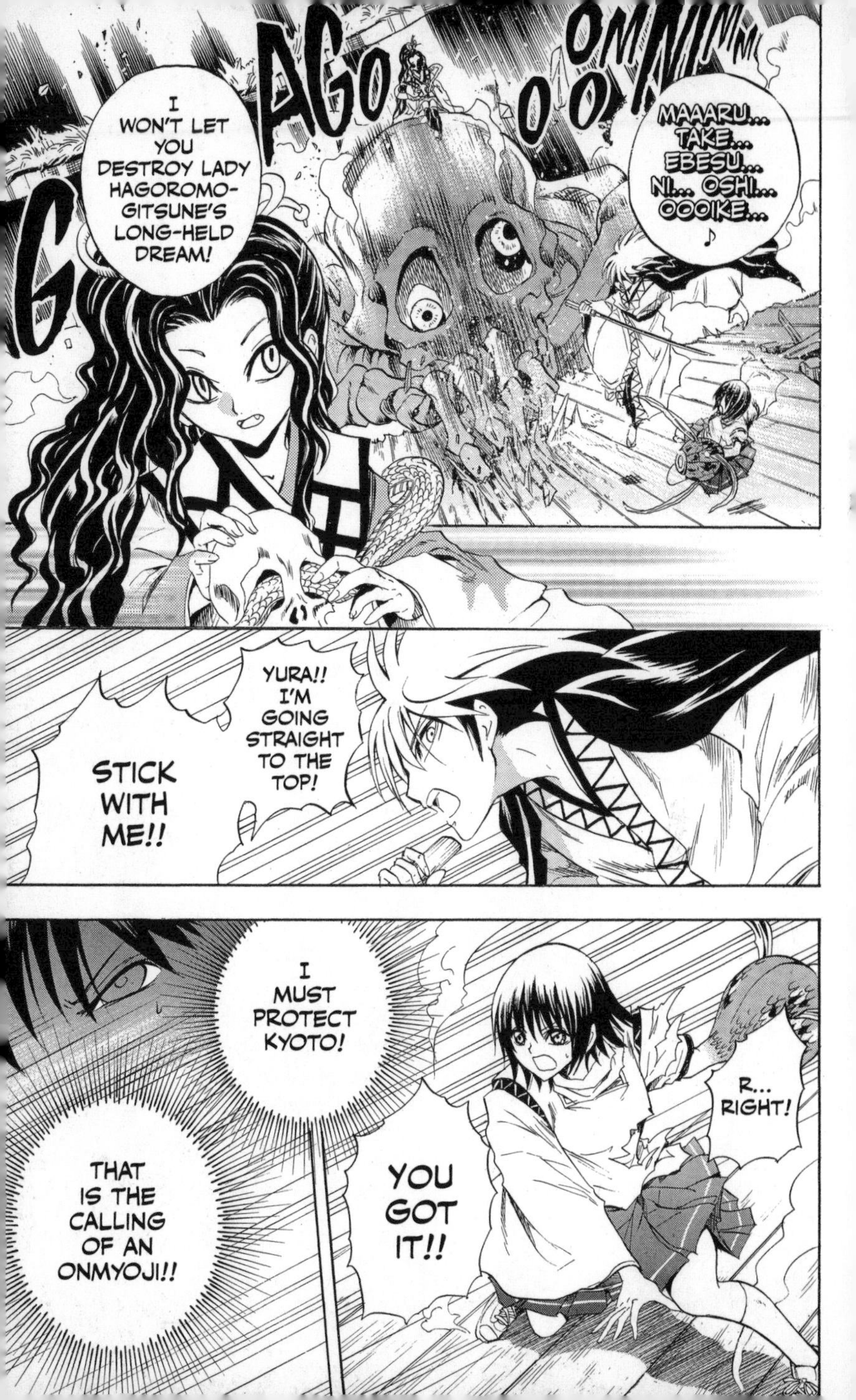
MAAARU... TAKE... EBESU... NI... OSHI... OOOIKE... ♪
I WON'T LET YOU DESTROY LADY HAGOROMO-GITSUNE'S LONG-HELD DREAM!
YURA!! I'M GOING STRAIGHT TO THE TOP!
STICK WITH ME!!
R... RIGHT!
YOU GOT IT!!
I MUST PROTECT KYOTO!
THAT IS THE CALLING OF AN ONMYOJI!!

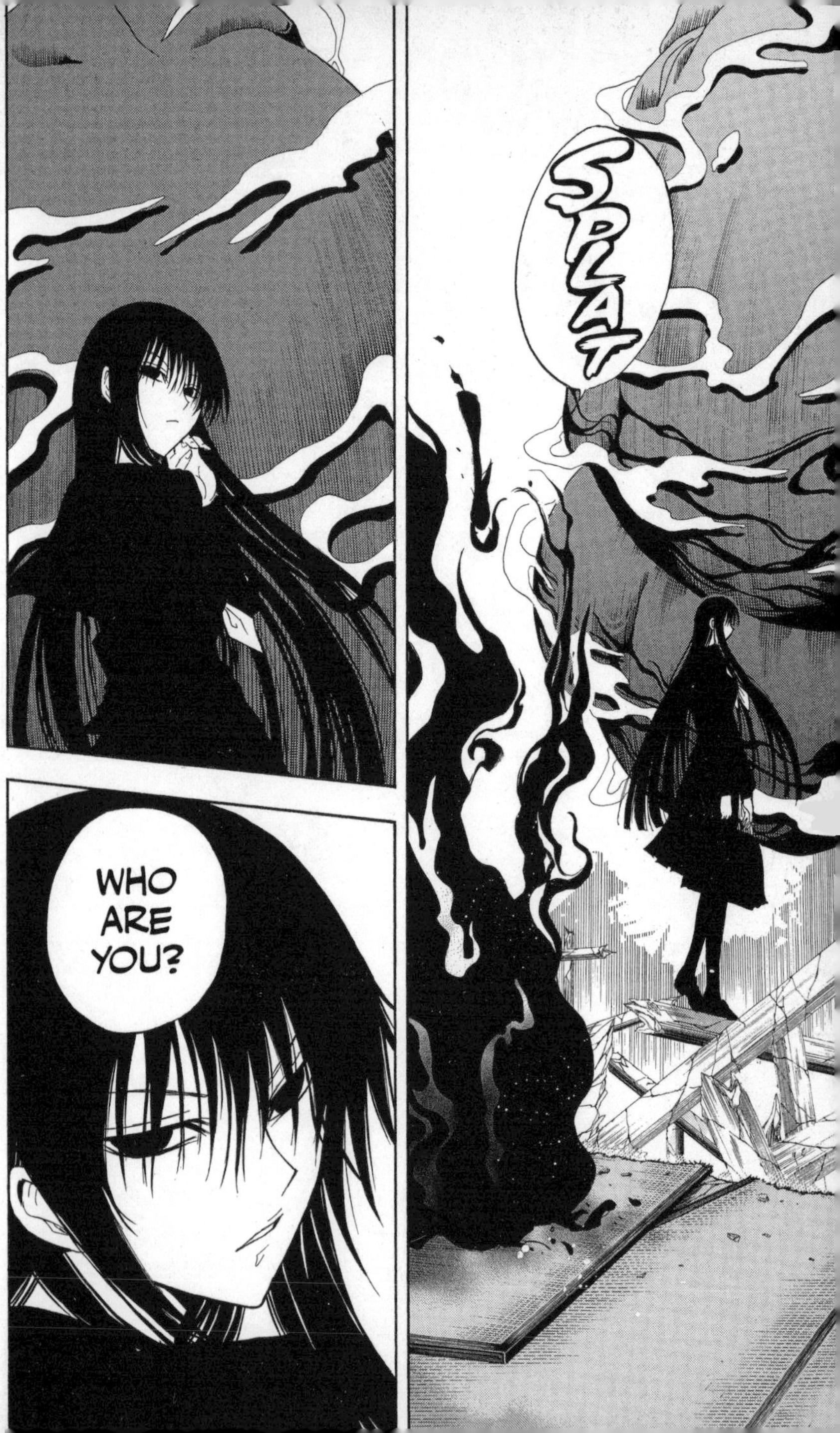
SPLAT
WHO ARE YOU?

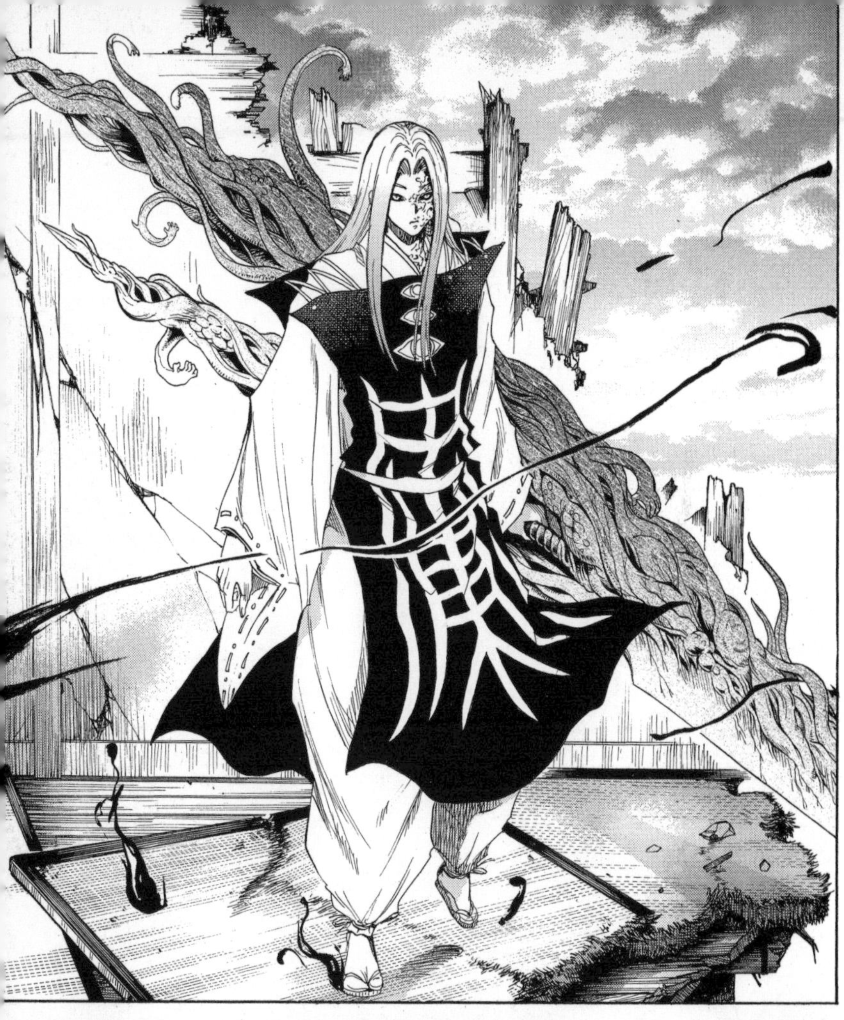

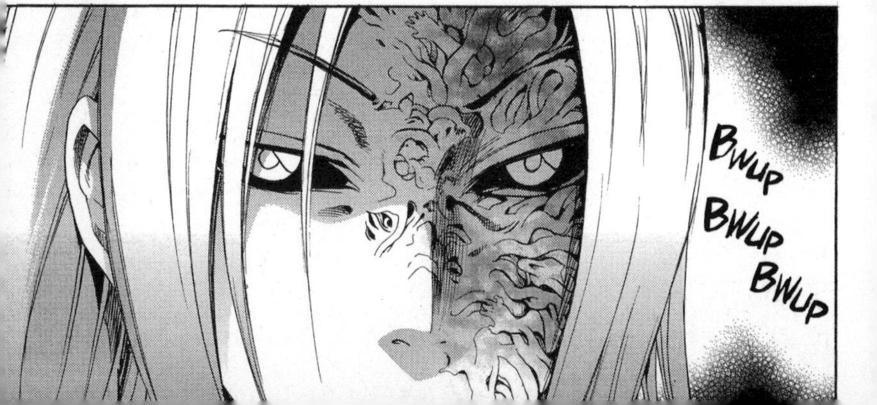
BWUP
BWUP
BWUP

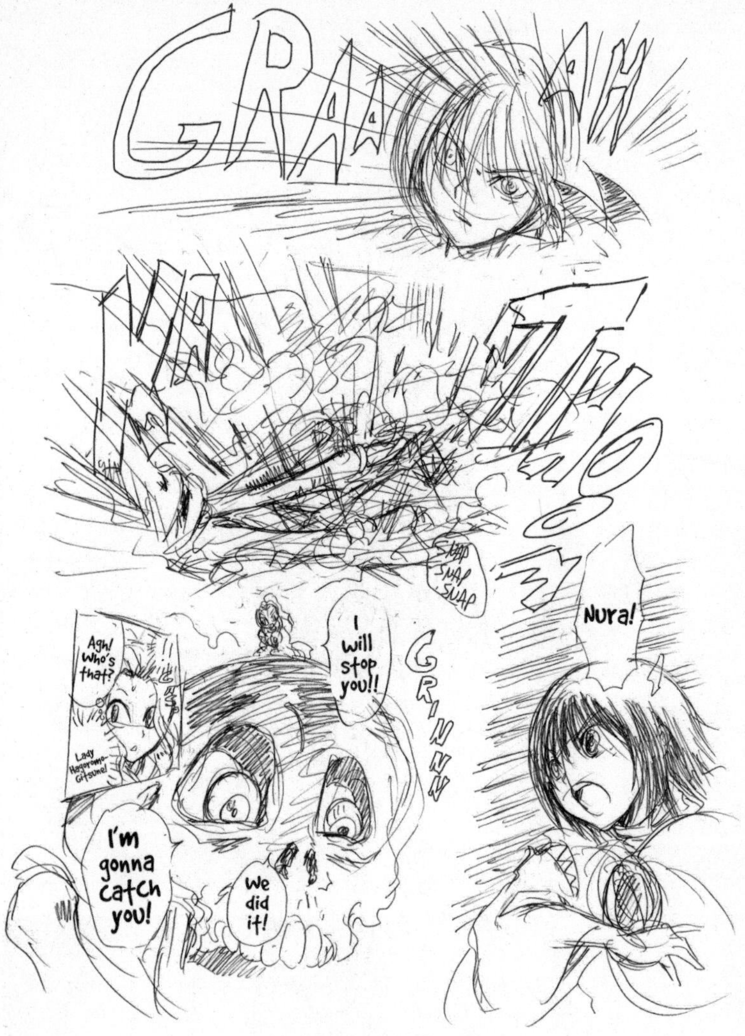
GRAAAAH
SNAP SNAP SNAP
Nura!
I will stop you!!
GRINNN
Agh! Who's that?
Lady Hagoromo-Gitsune!
I'm gonna catch you!
We did it!

Act 125: The Trap

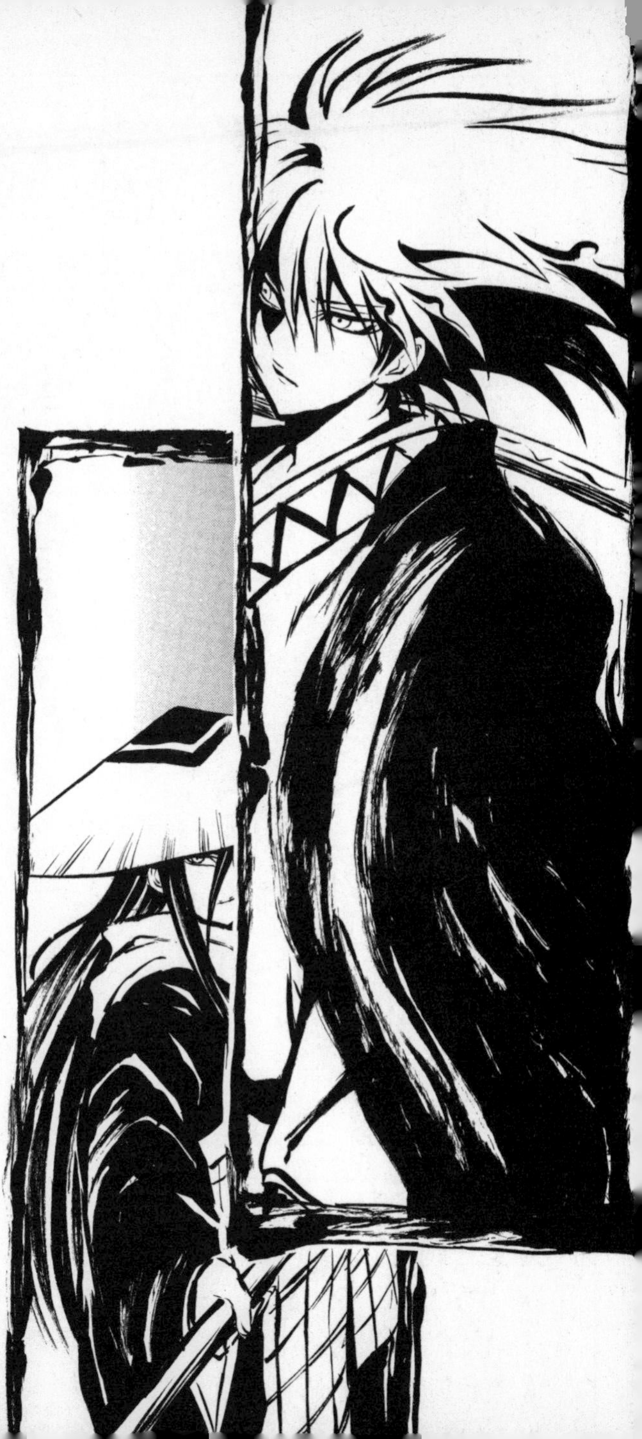

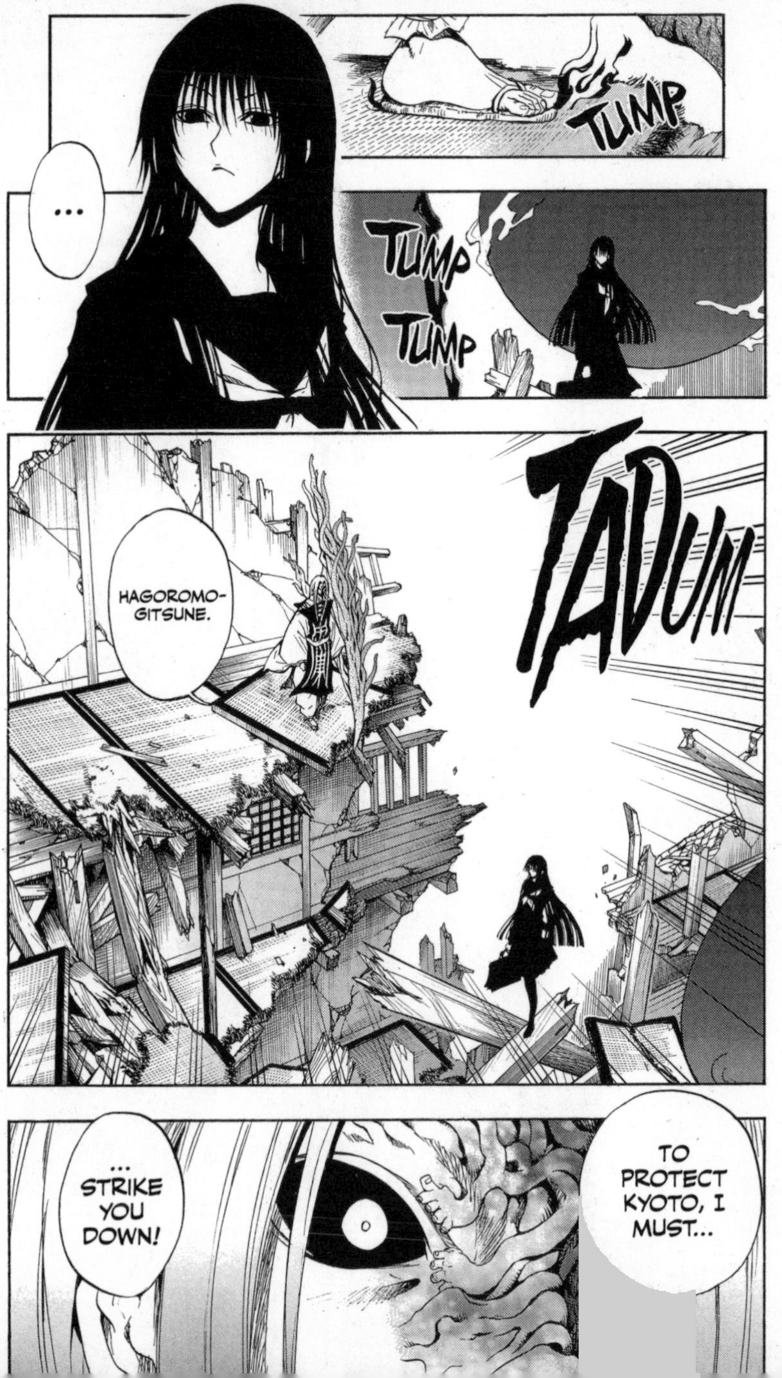
TUMP
TUMP
TUMP
...
TADUM
HAGOROMO-GITSUNE.
TO PROTECT KYOTO, I MUST...
... STRIKE YOU DOWN!

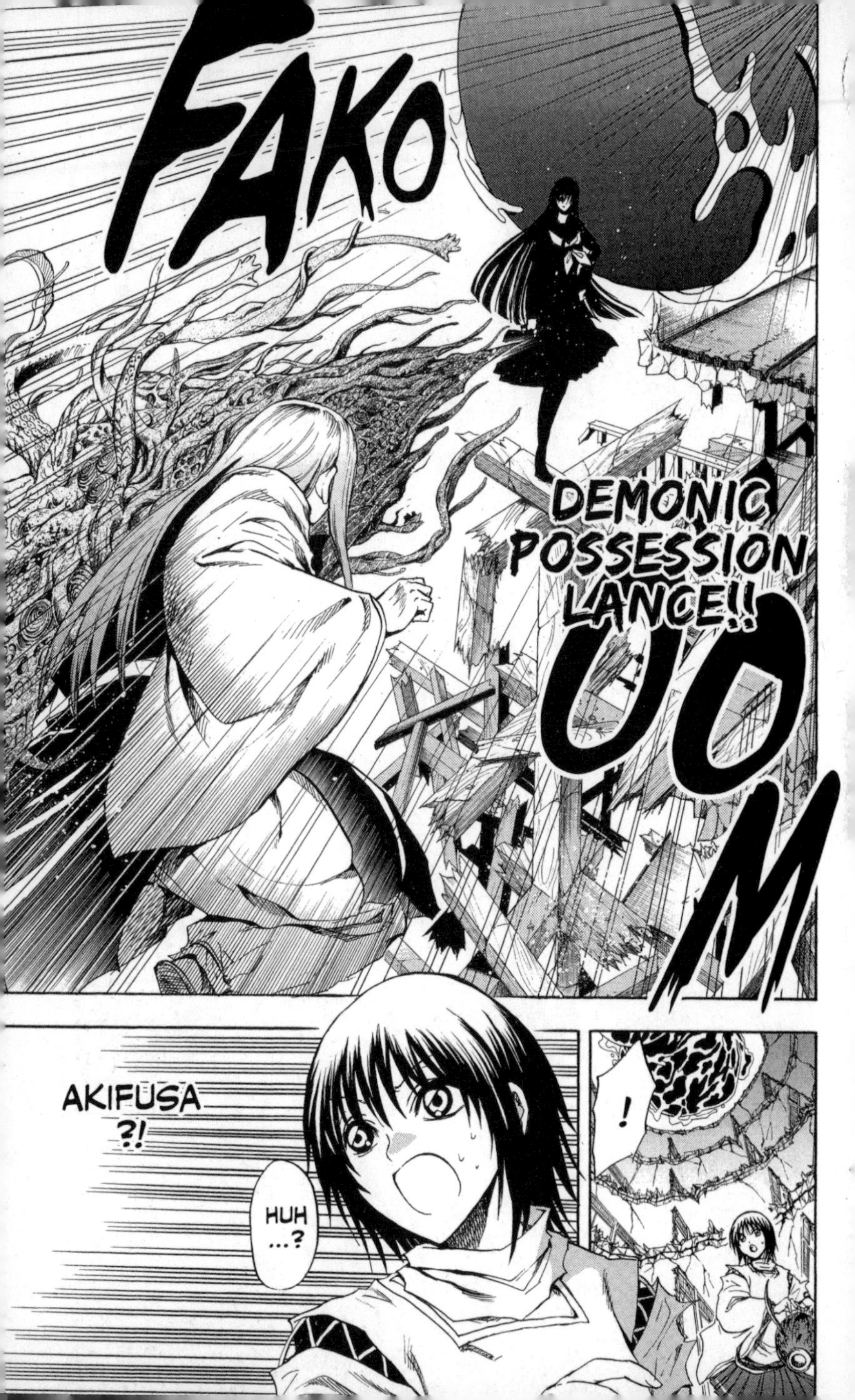
FAKO
DEMONIC POSSESSION LANCE!!
UOOM
!
AKIFUSA ?!
HUH ...?

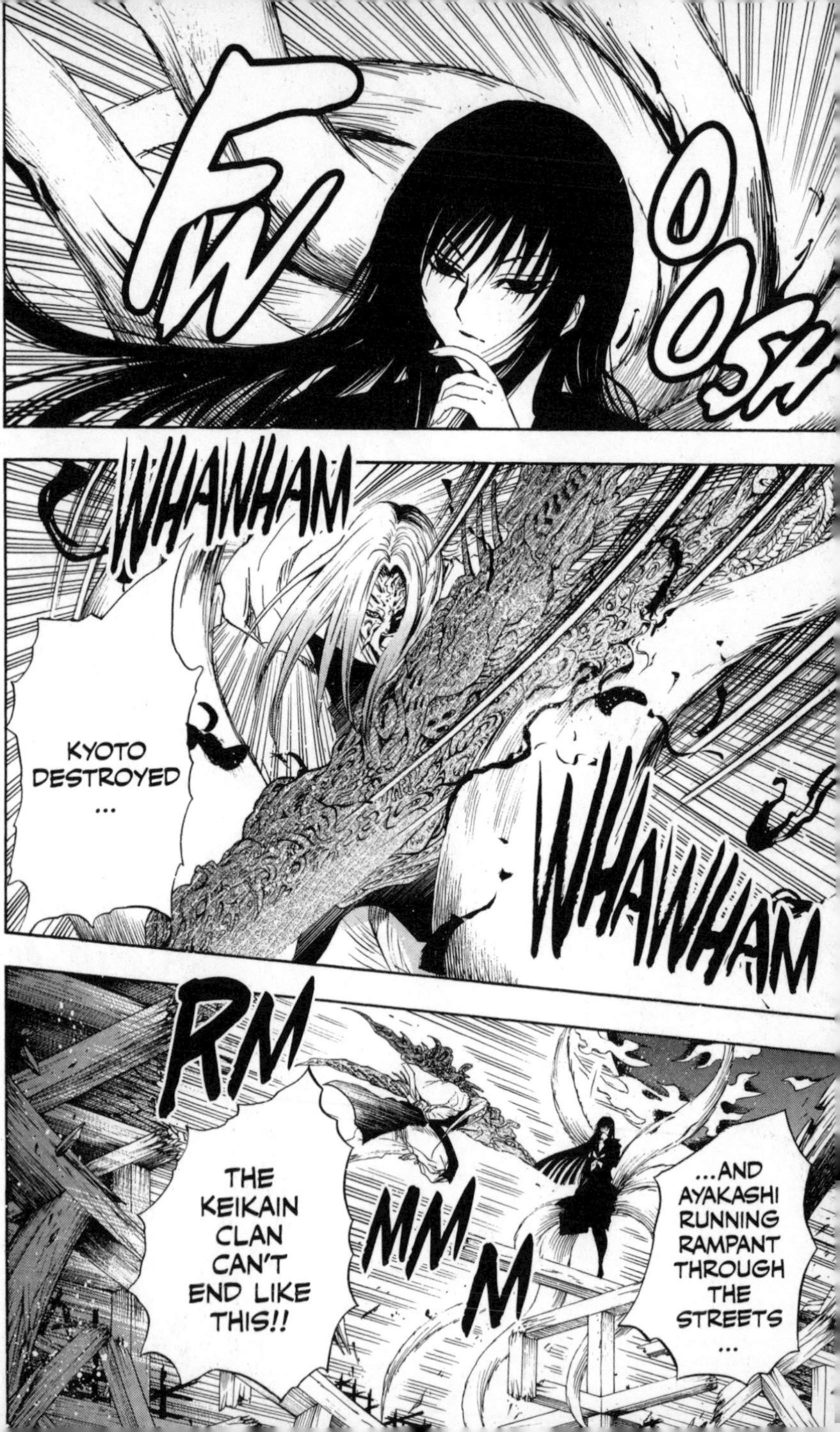
FWOOOSH
WHAWHAM
KYOTO DESTROYED ...
WHAWHAM
RM
...AND AYAKASHI RUNNING RAMPANT THROUGH THE STREETS ...
MMMM
THE KEIKAIN CLAN CAN'T END LIKE THIS!!

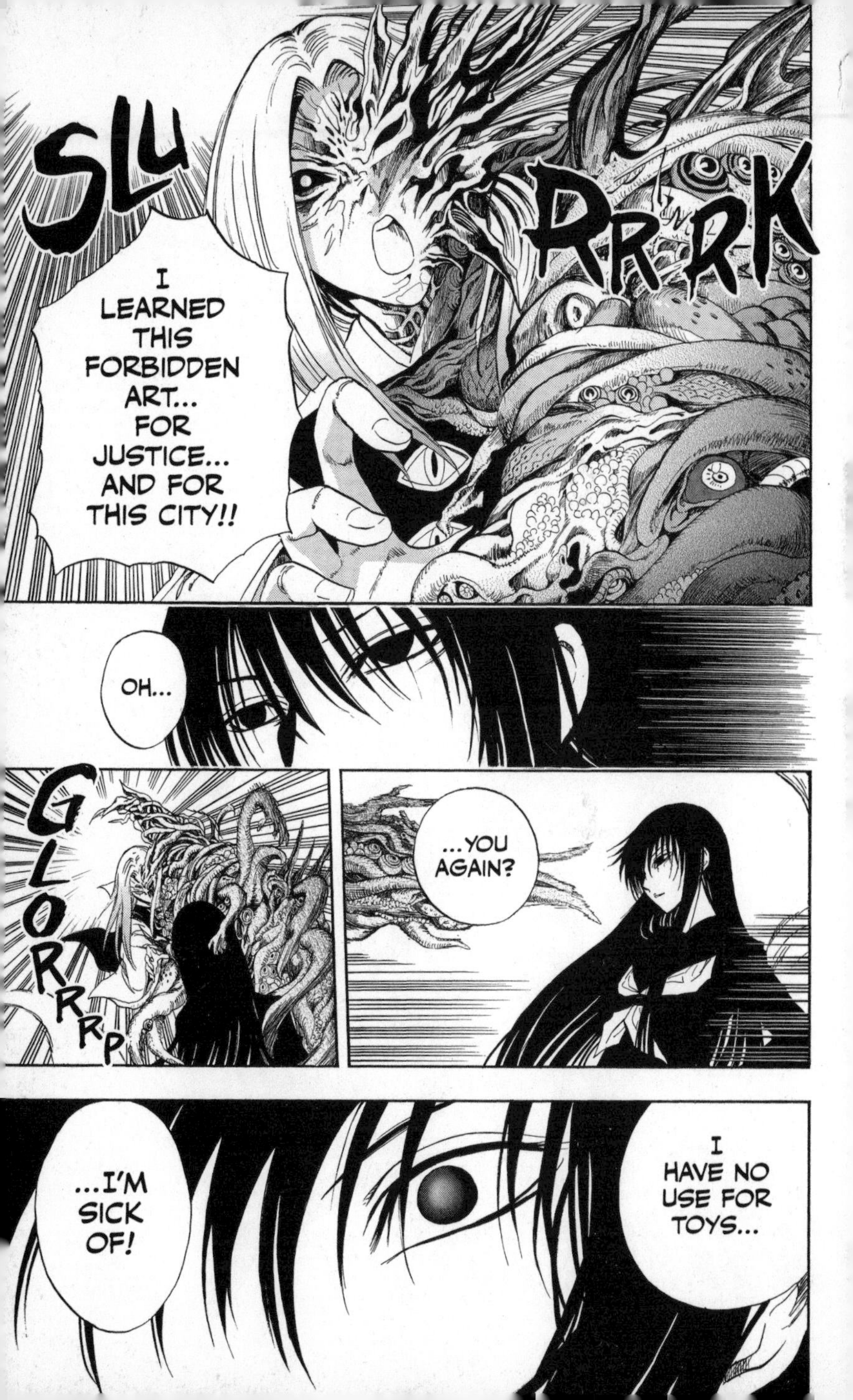
SLU
RRRK
I LEARNED THIS FORBIDDEN ART... FOR JUSTICE... AND FOR THIS CITY!!
OH...
...YOU AGAIN?
GLORRRRP
I HAVE NO USE FOR TOYS...
...I'M SICK OF!

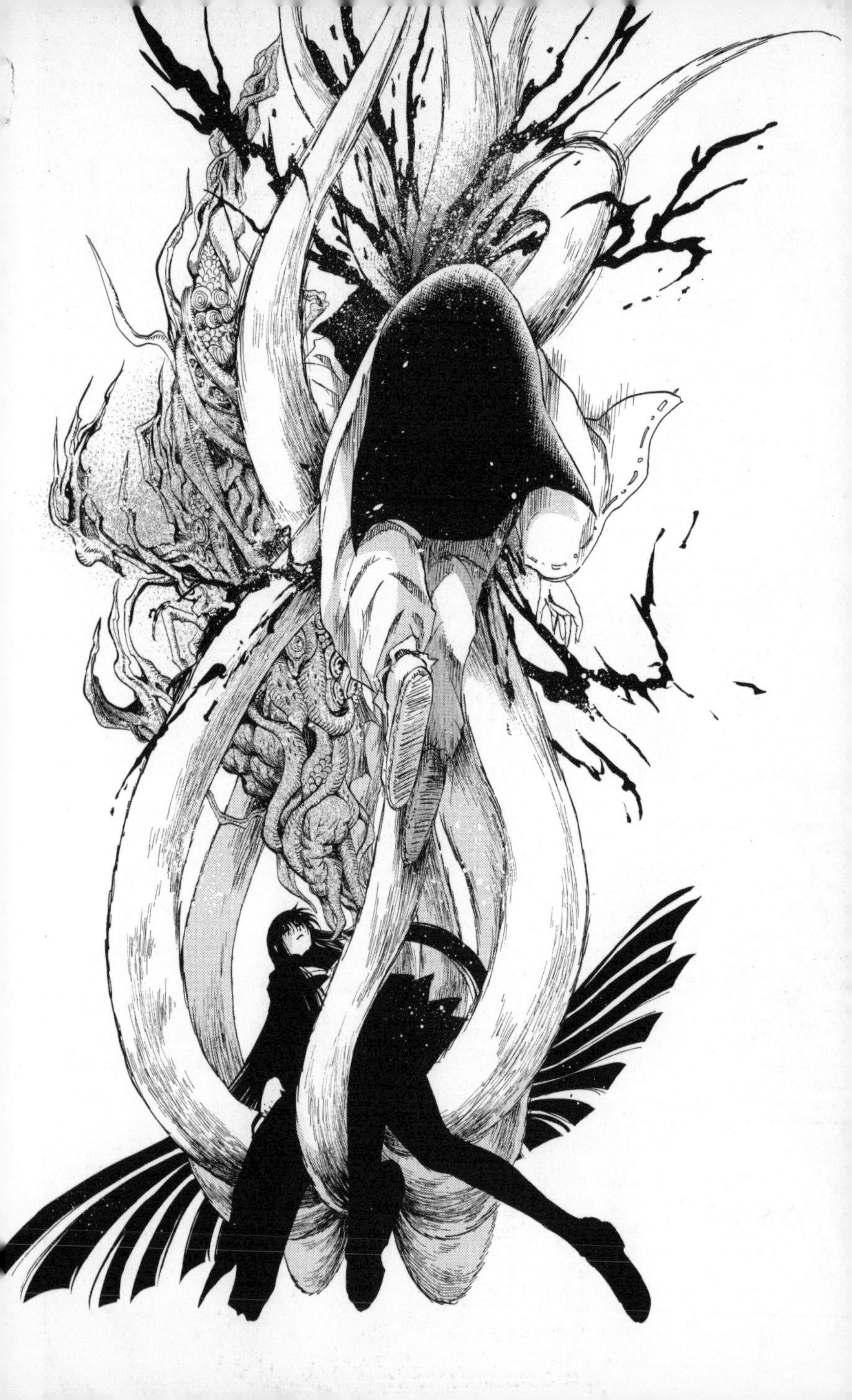

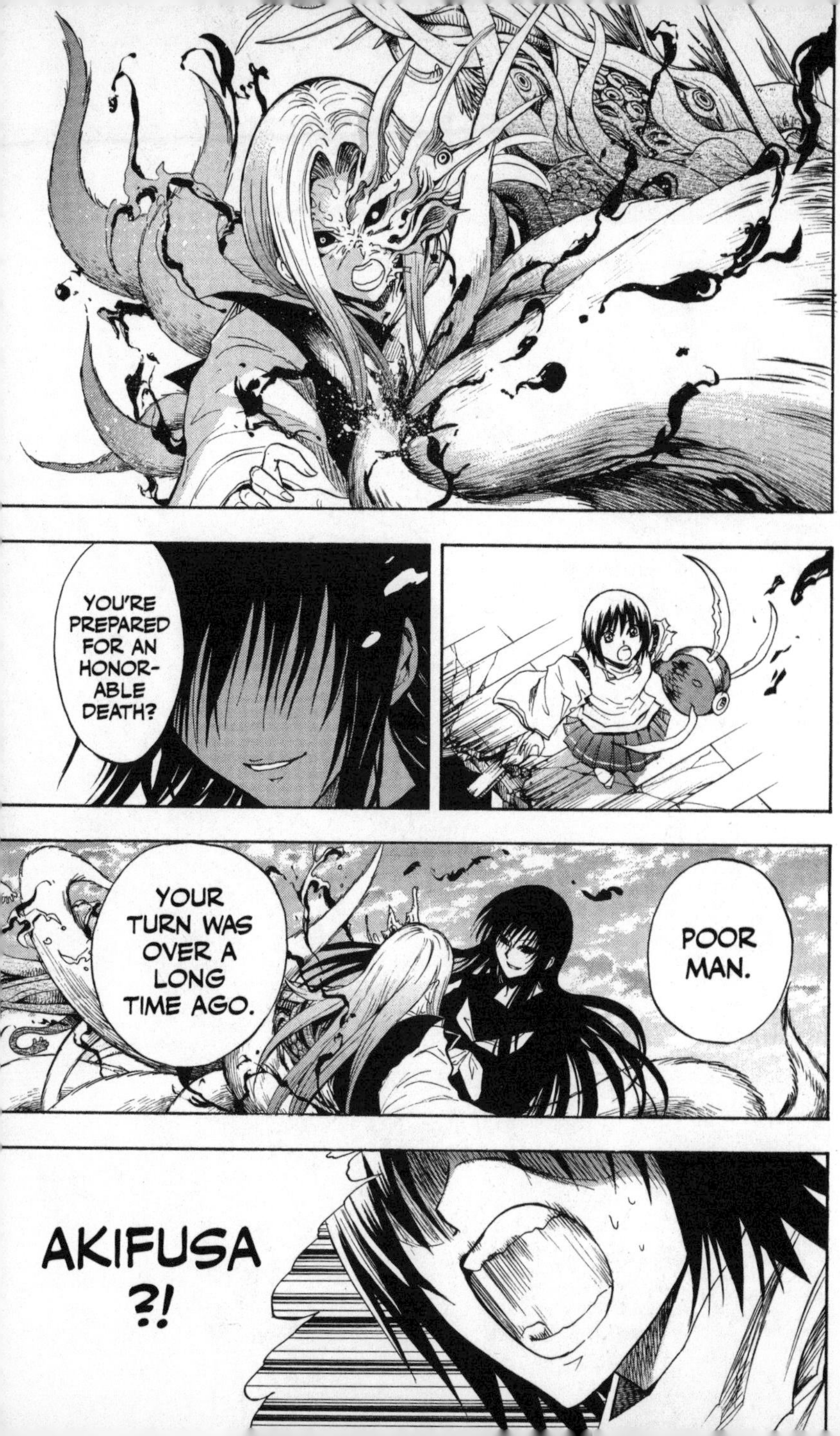
YOU'RE PREPARED FOR AN HONOR-ABLE DEATH?
POOR MAN.
YOUR TURN WAS OVER A LONG TIME AGO.
AKIFUSA ?!

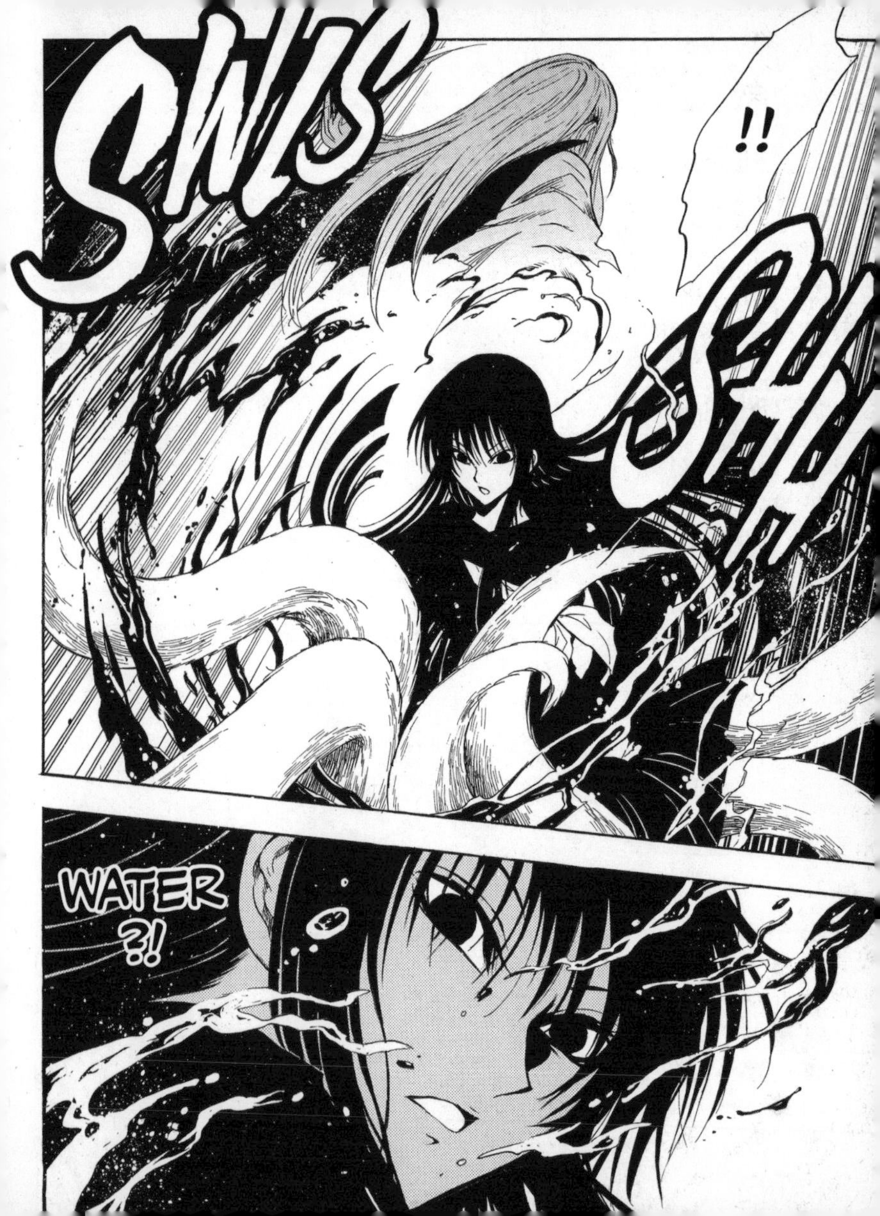
!!
SWIS
SHH
WATER ?!

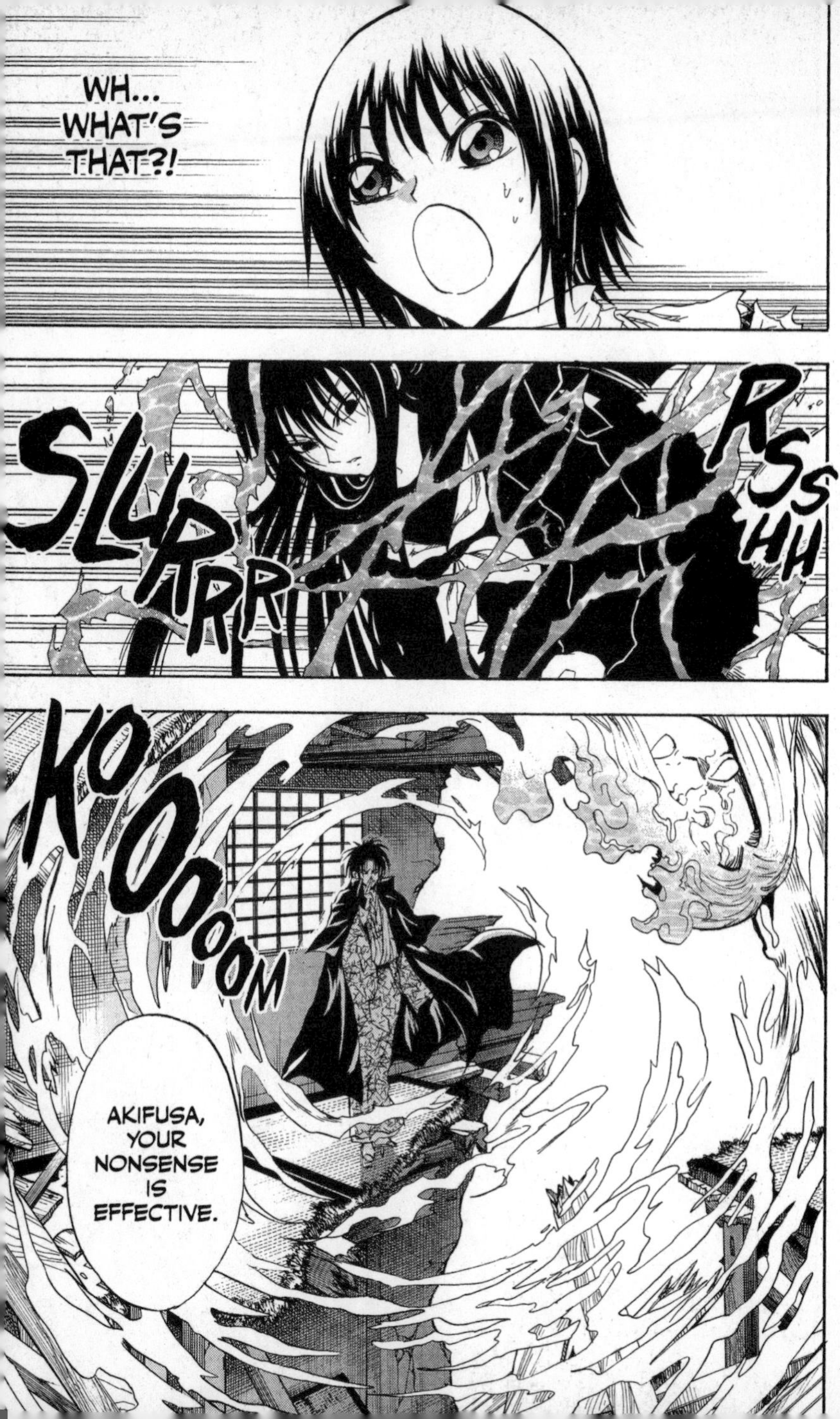
WH... WHAT'S THAT?!
RSSHH
SLURRR
KOOOOOOM
AKIFUSA, YOUR NONSENSE IS EFFECTIVE.

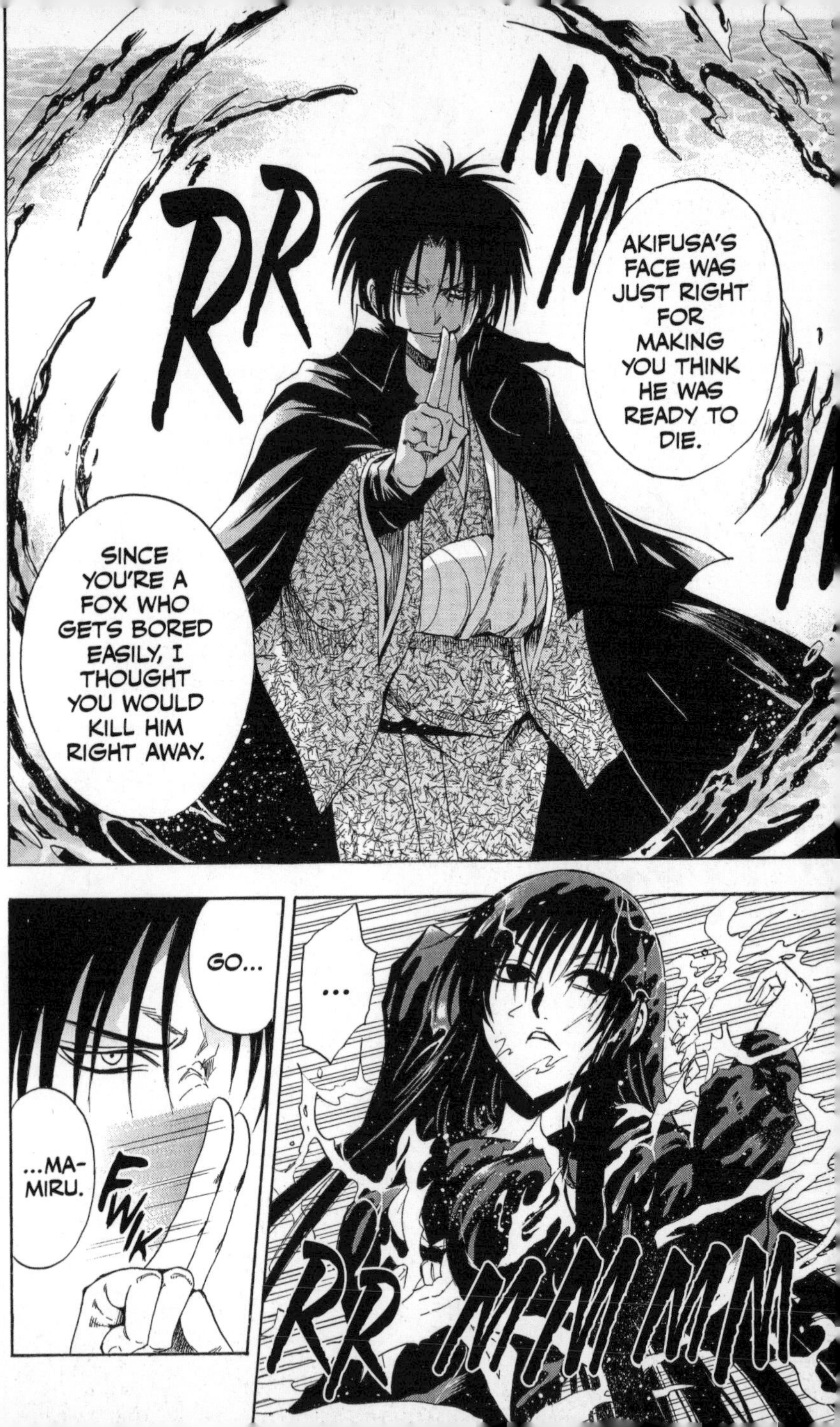
RRMMM
AKIFUSA'S FACE WAS JUST RIGHT FOR MAKING YOU THINK HE WAS READY TO DIE.
SINCE YOU'RE A FOX WHO GETS BORED EASILY, I THOUGHT YOU WOULD KILL HIM RIGHT AWAY.
...
RRMMMMMM
GO...
...MA-MIRU.
FWIK

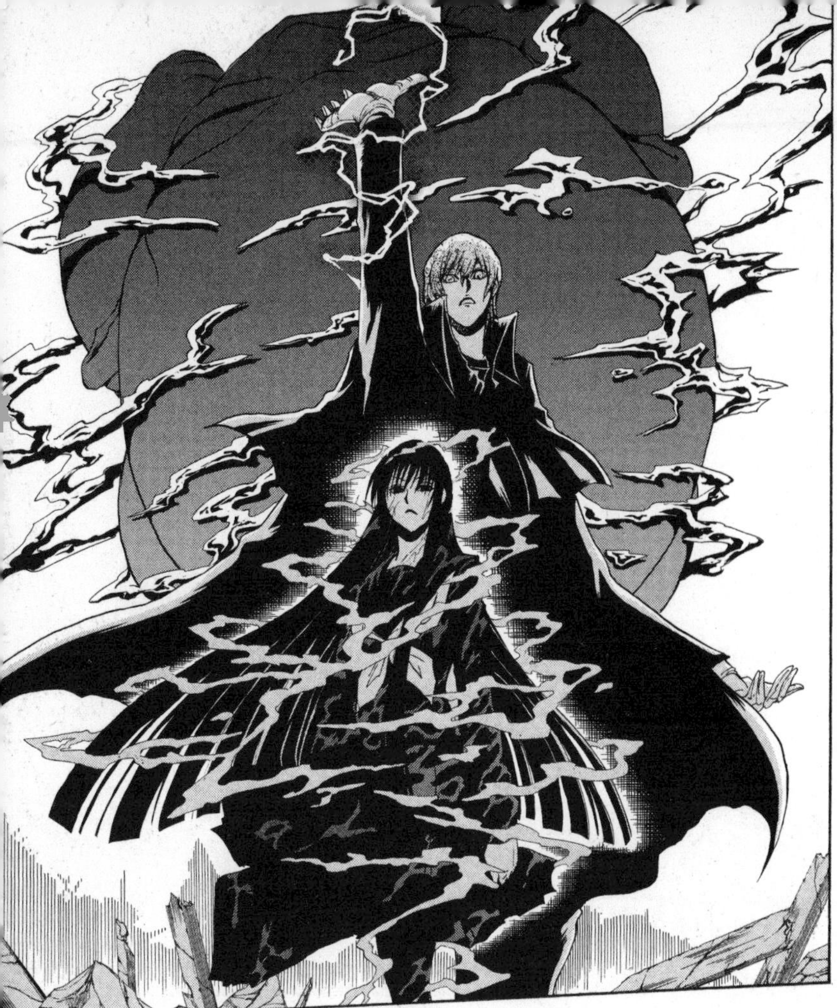

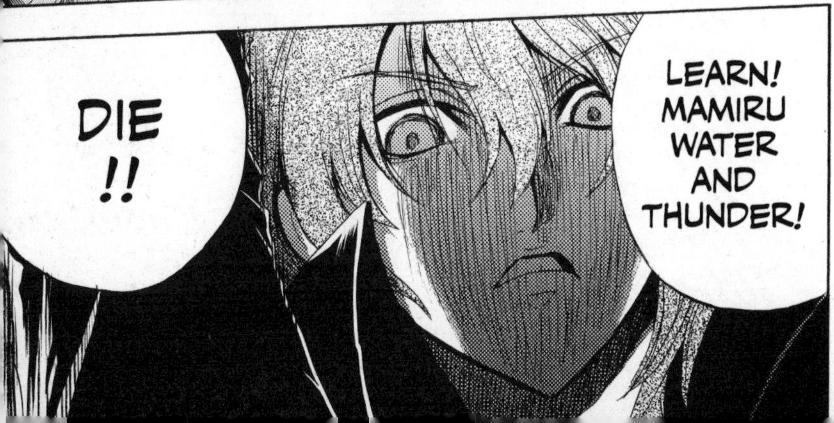
LEARN! MAMIRU WATER AND THUNDER!
DIE !!

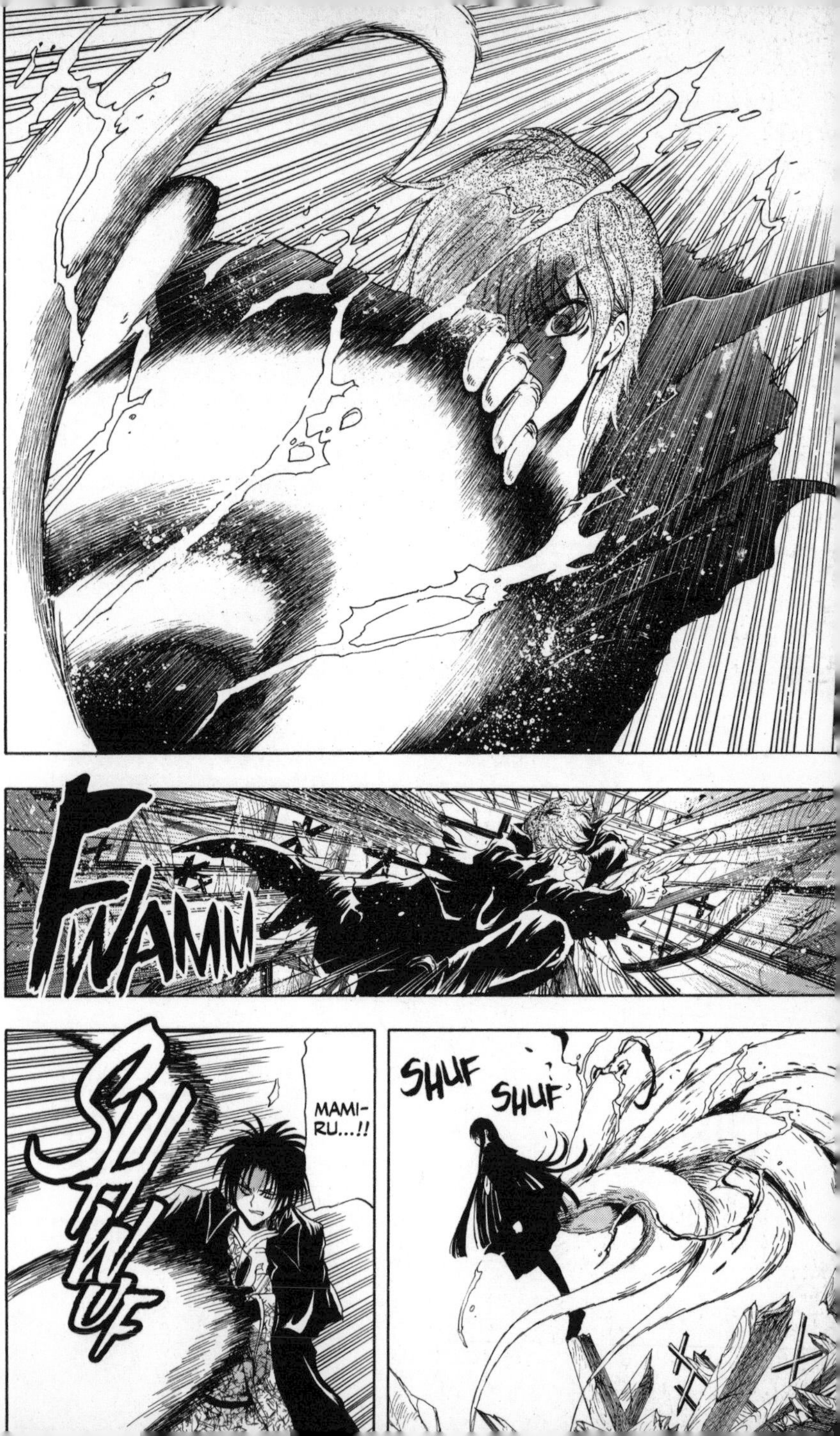
FWAMM
SHUF
SHUF
MAMI-
RU...!!
SHUF

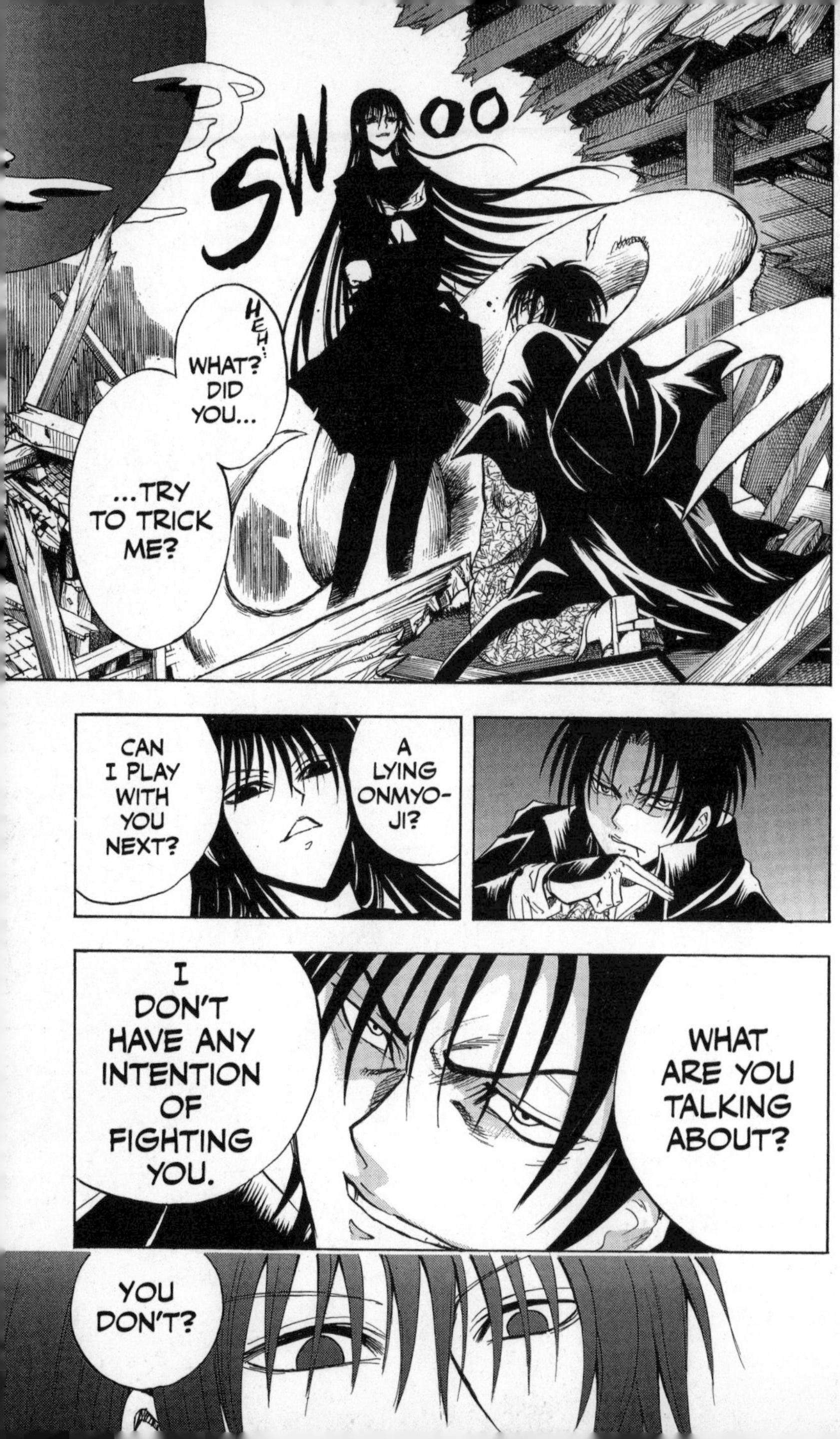
SWOOO
HEH
WHAT? DID YOU...
...TRY TO TRICK ME?
A LYING ONMYO-JI?
CAN I PLAY WITH YOU NEXT?
WHAT ARE YOU TALKING ABOUT?
I DON'T HAVE ANY INTENTION OF FIGHTING YOU.
YOU DON'T?

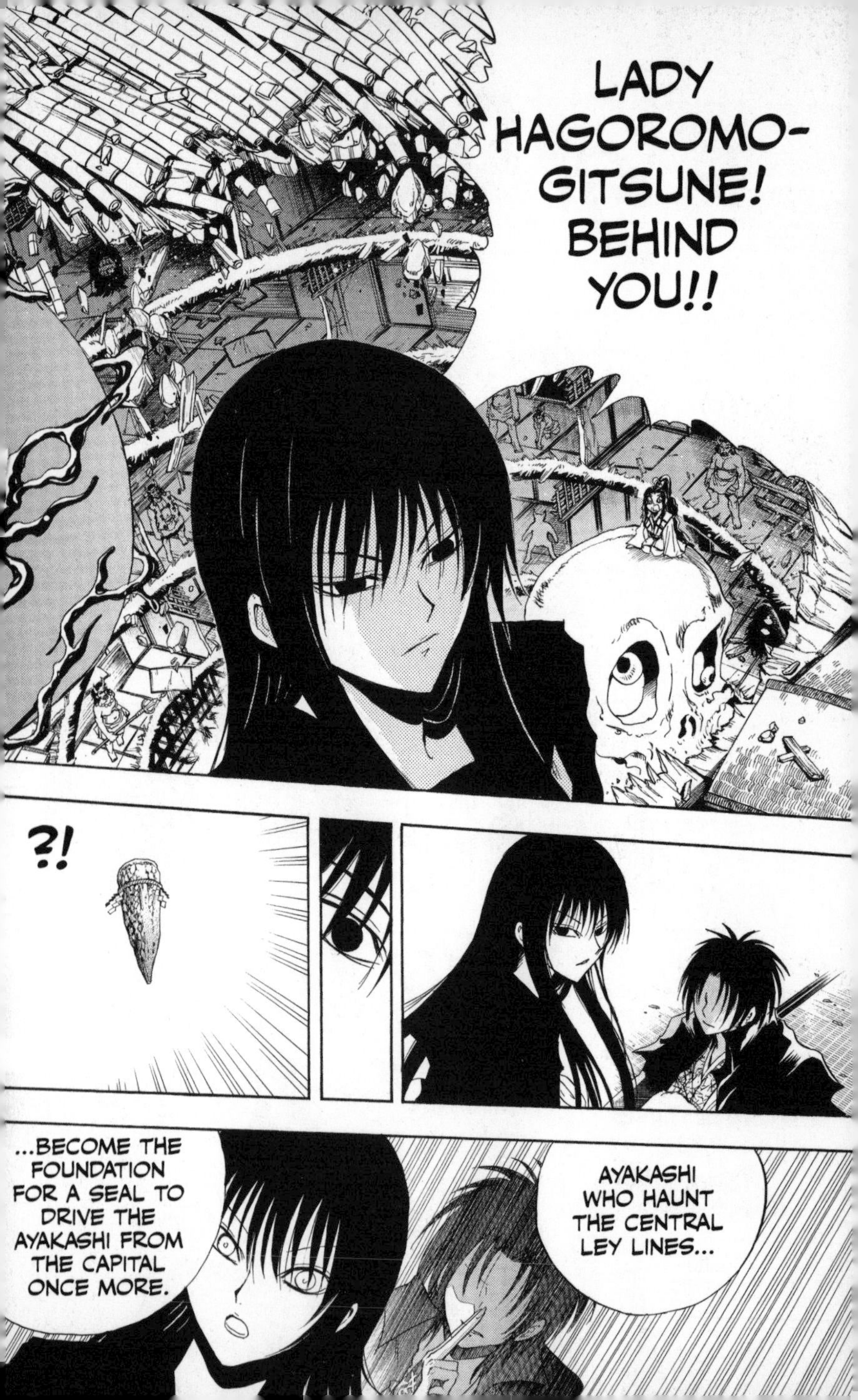
LADY HAGOROMO-GITSUNE! BEHIND YOU!!
?!
AYAKASHI WHO HAUNT THE CENTRAL LEY LINES...
...BECOME THE FOUNDATION FOR A SEAL TO DRIVE THE AYAKASHI FROM THE CAPITAL ONCE MORE.

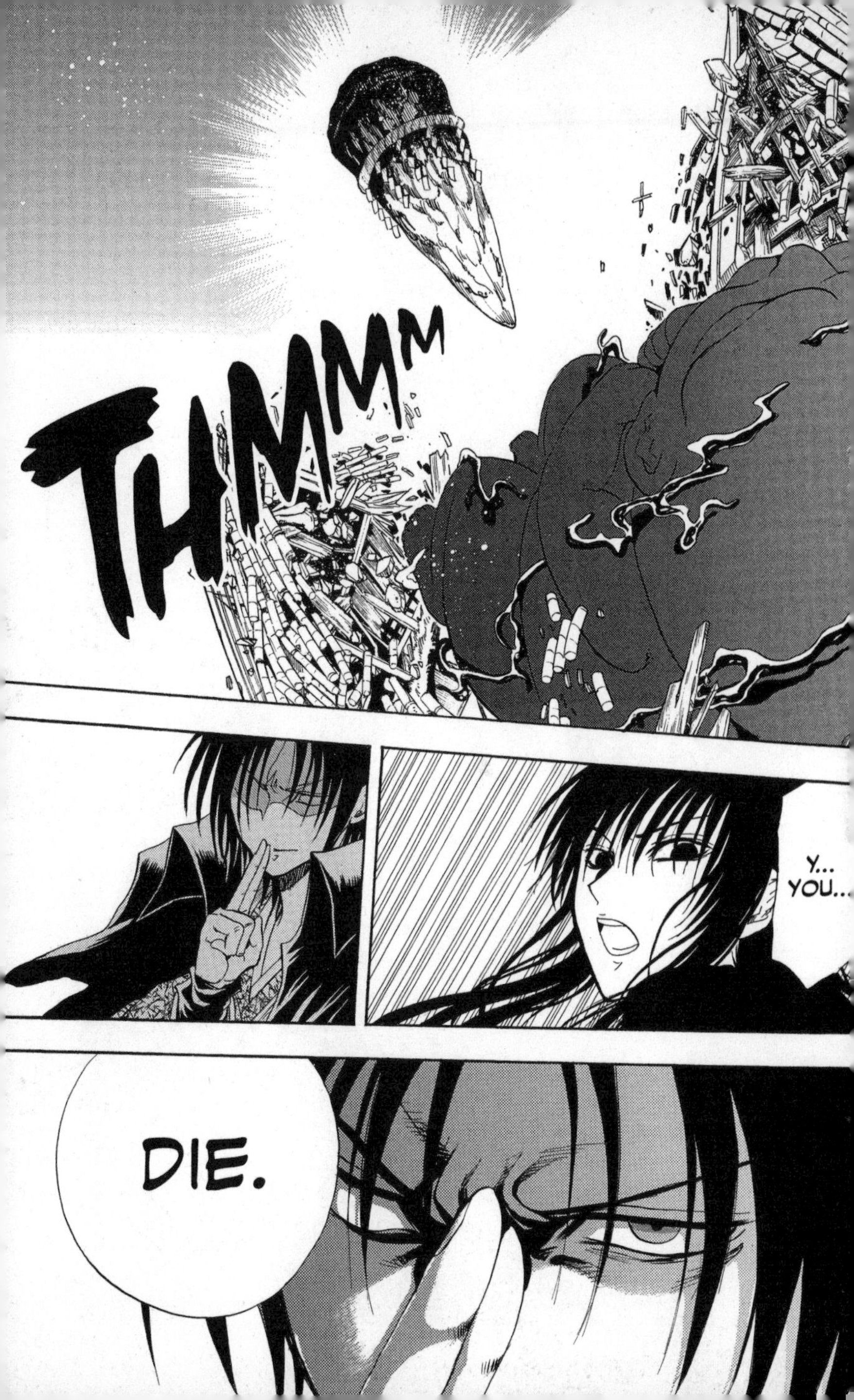
THMMM
Y... YOU...
DIE.

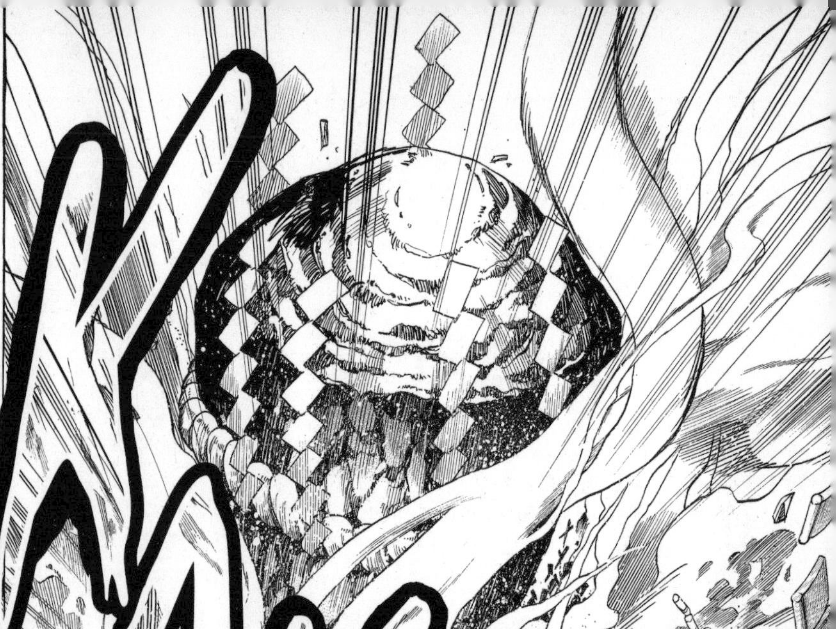
KA
KOOM
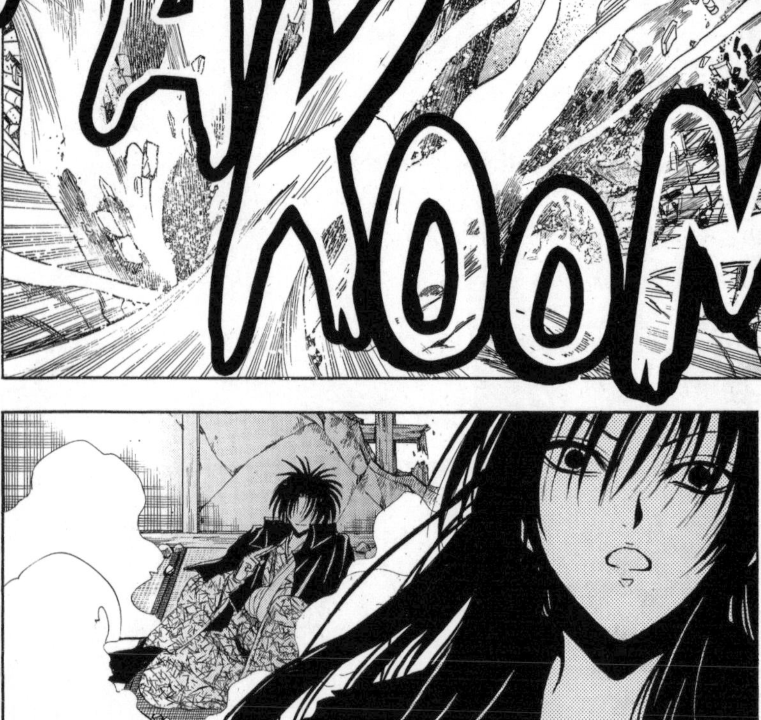

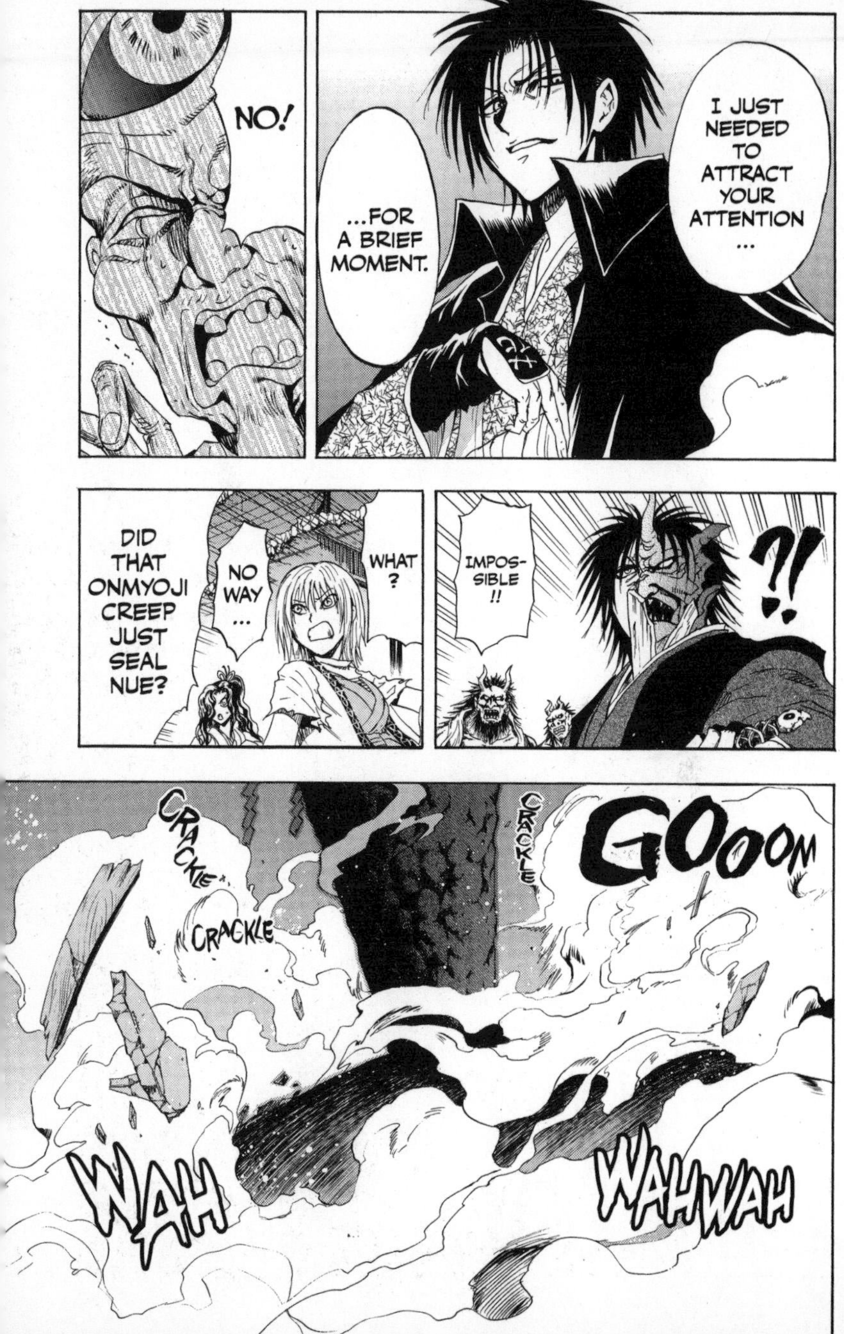
I JUST NEEDED TO ATTRACT YOUR ATTENTION ...
...FOR A BRIEF MOMENT.
NO!
IMPOS-SIBLE !!
?!
WHAT ?
NO WAY ...
DID THAT ONMYOJI CREEP JUST SEAL NUE?
GOOOM
CRACKLE
CRACKLE
CRACKLE
WAHWAH
WAH

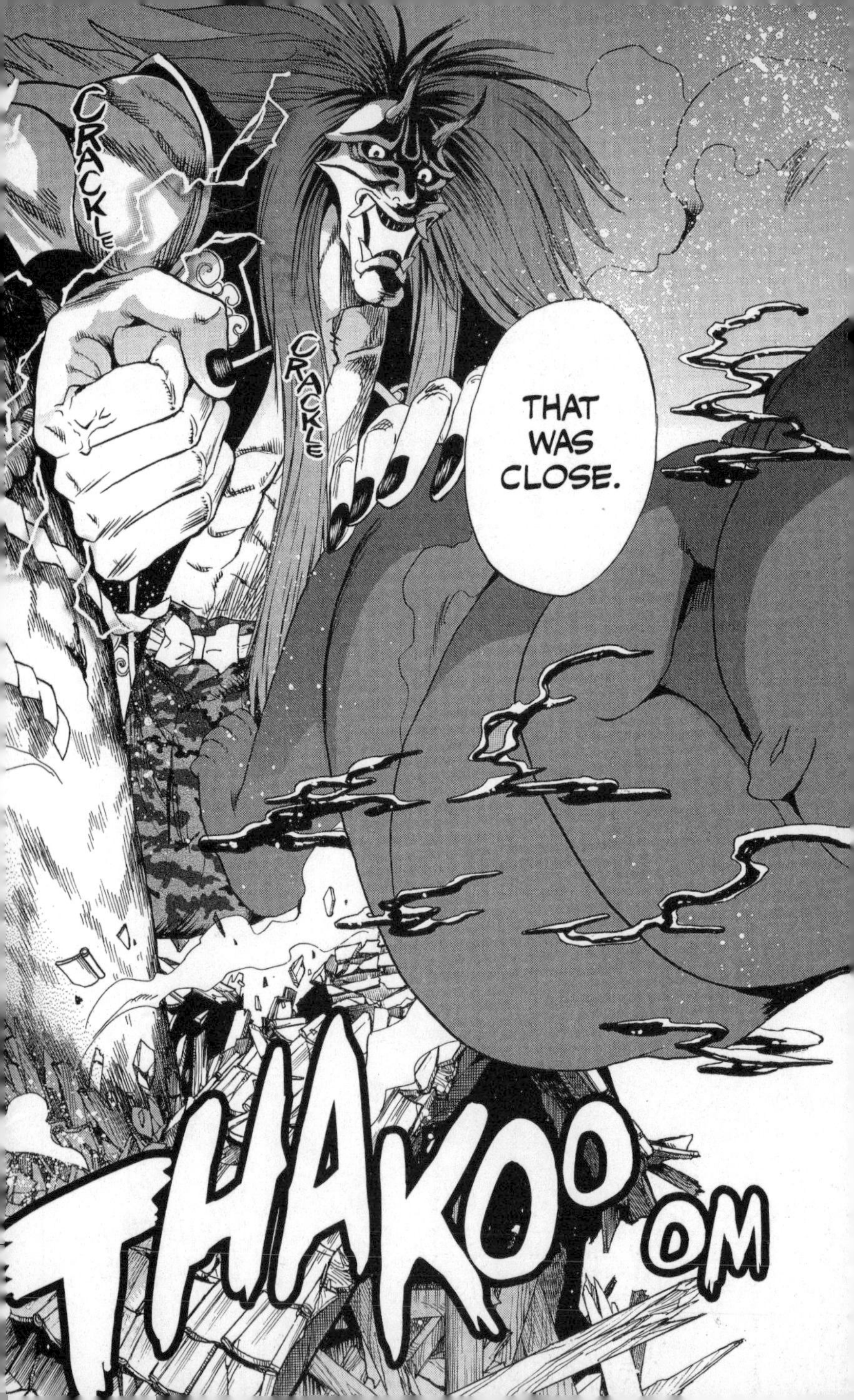
CRACKLE
CRACKLE
THAT WAS CLOSE.
THAKOOOM

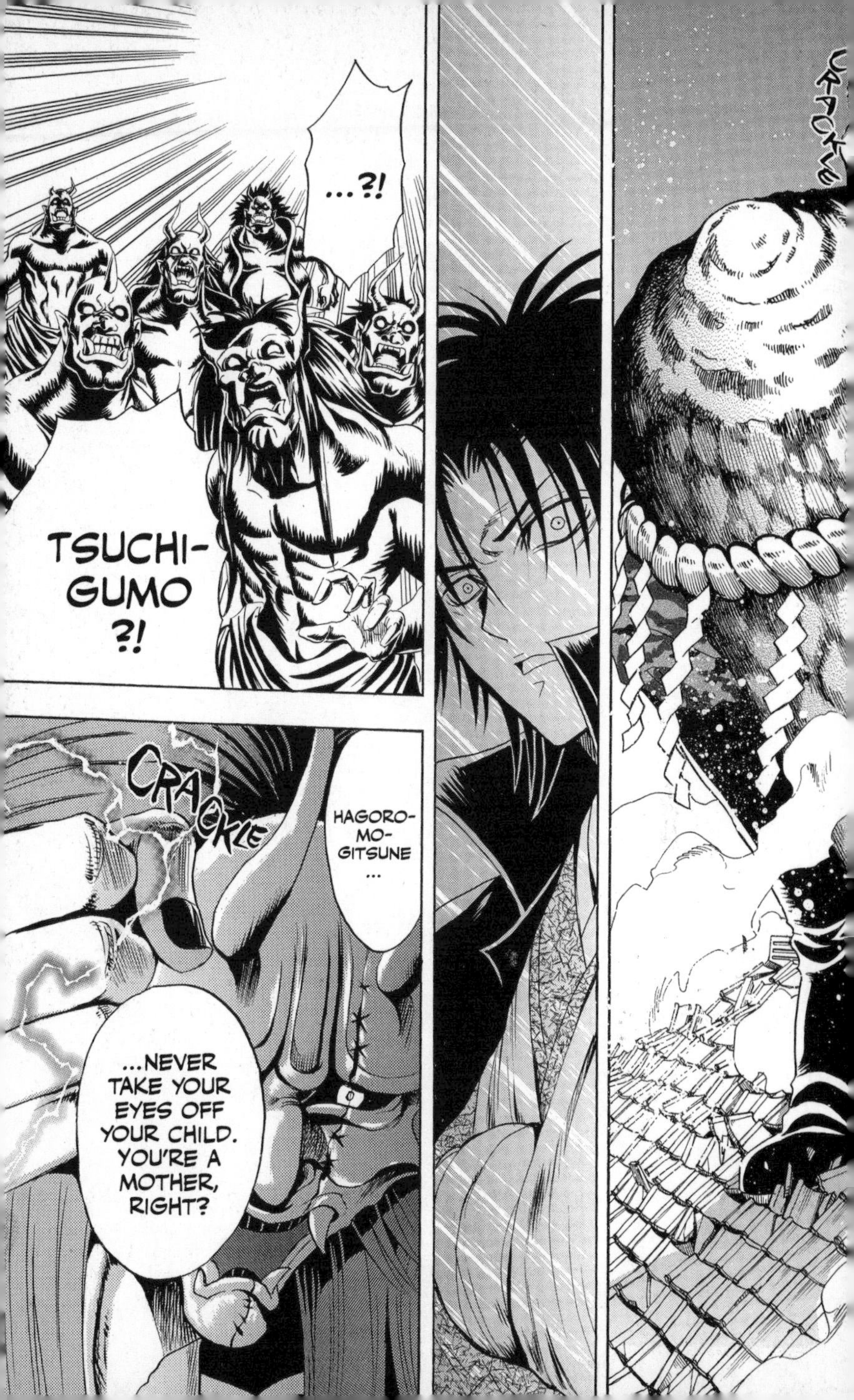
...?!
TSUCHI-GUMO ?!
CRACKLE
HAGORO-MO-GITSUNE ...
...NEVER TAKE YOUR EYES OFF YOUR CHILD. YOU'RE A MOTHER, RIGHT?

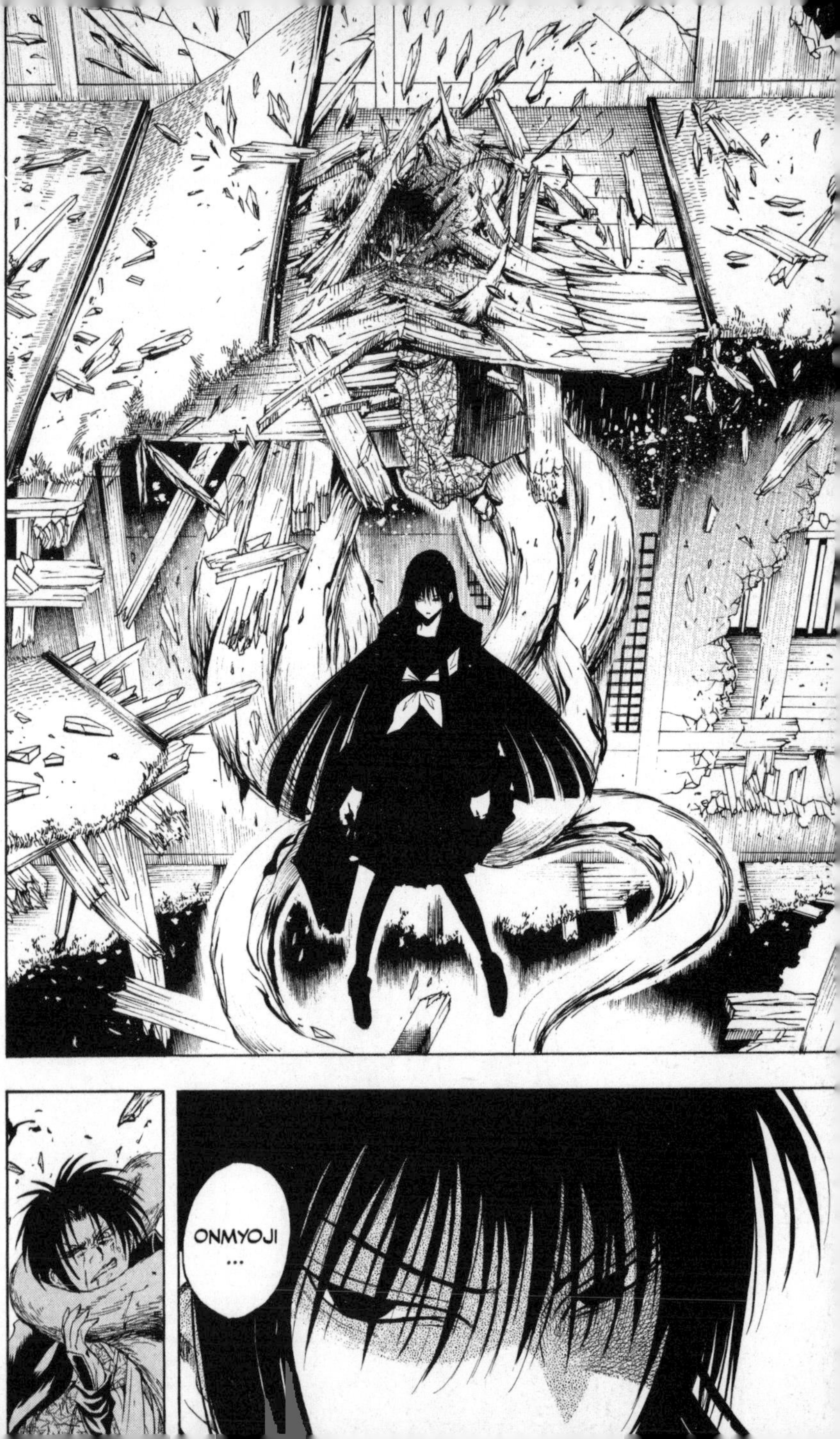
ONMYOJI
...

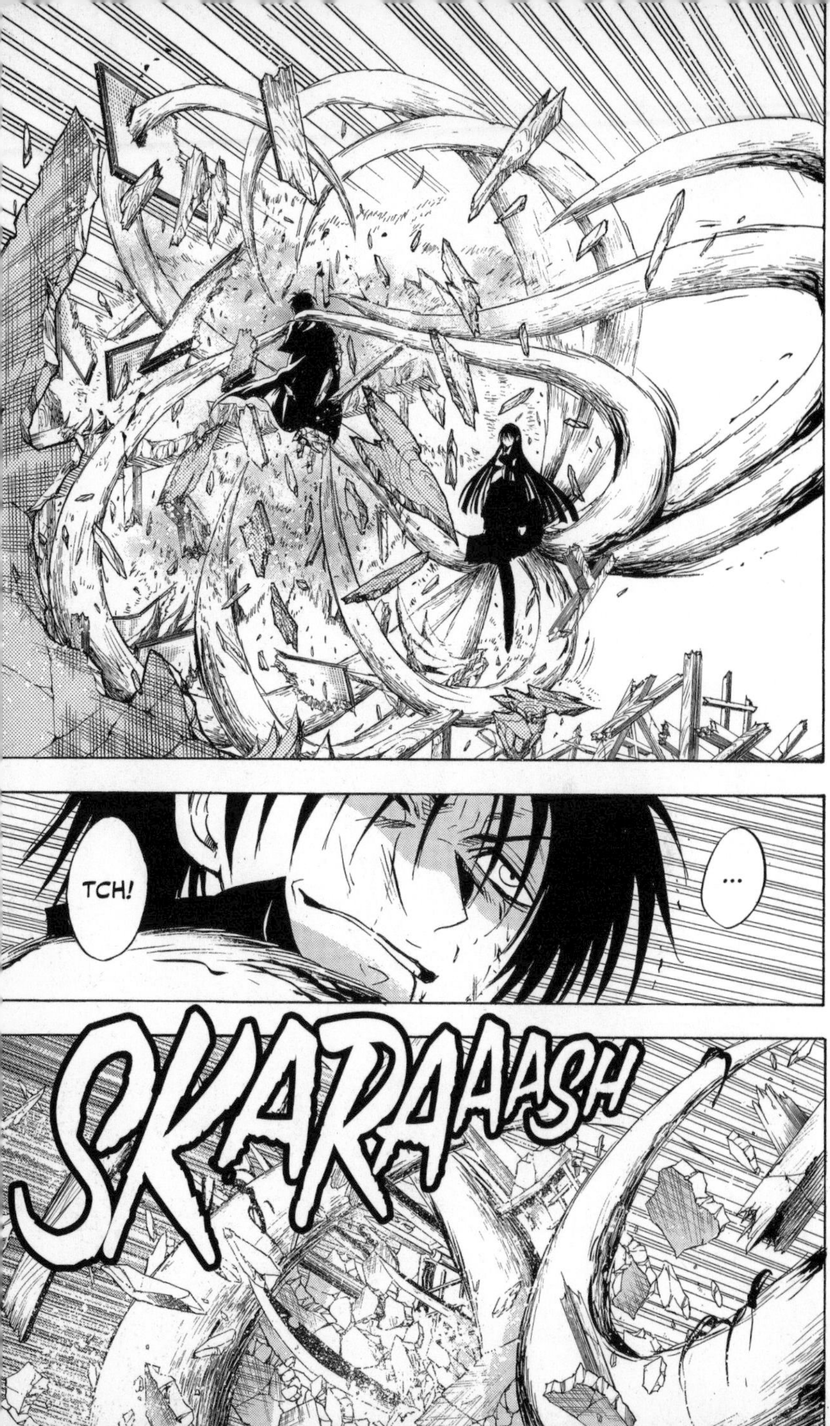
...
TCH!
SKARAAASH

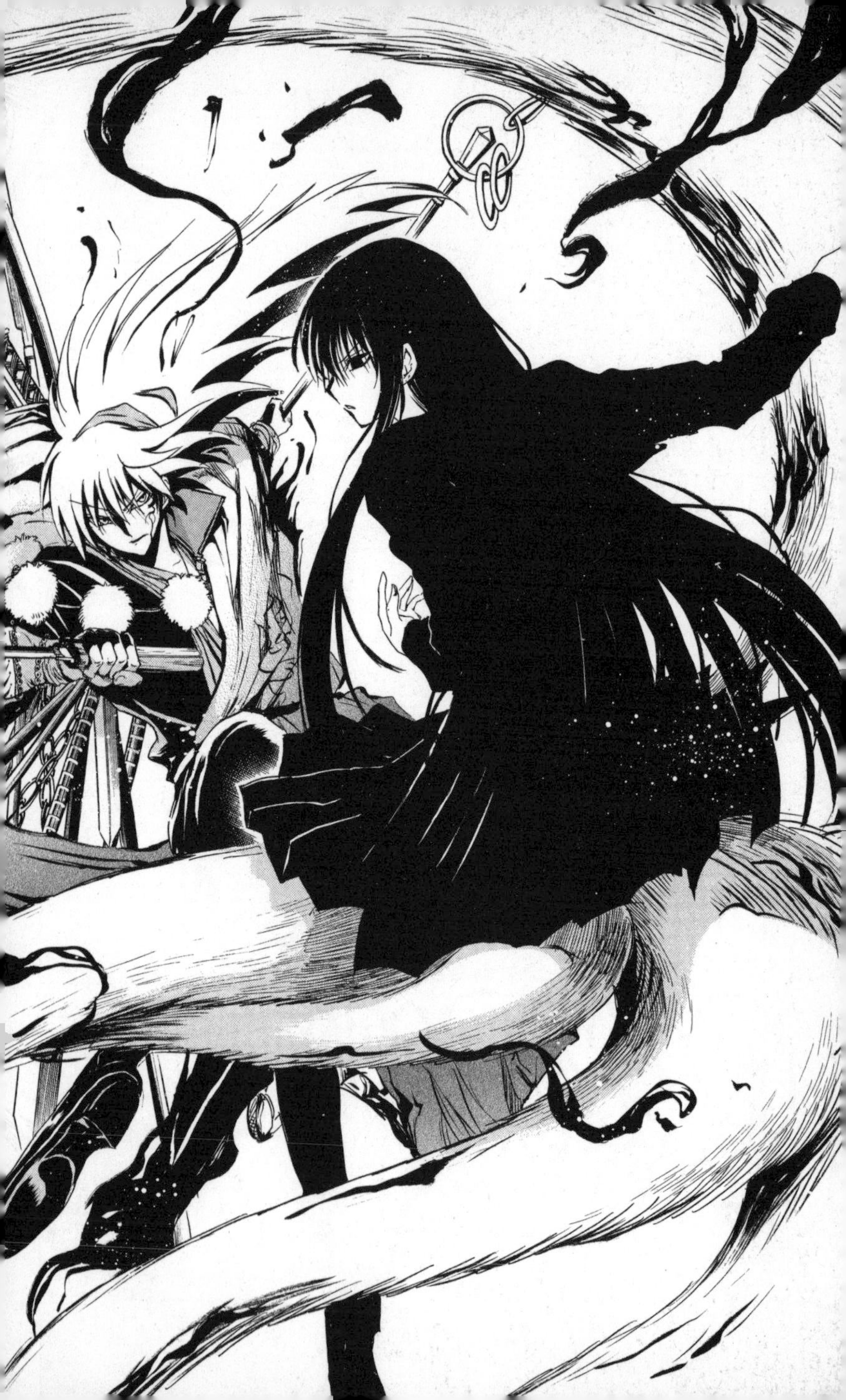

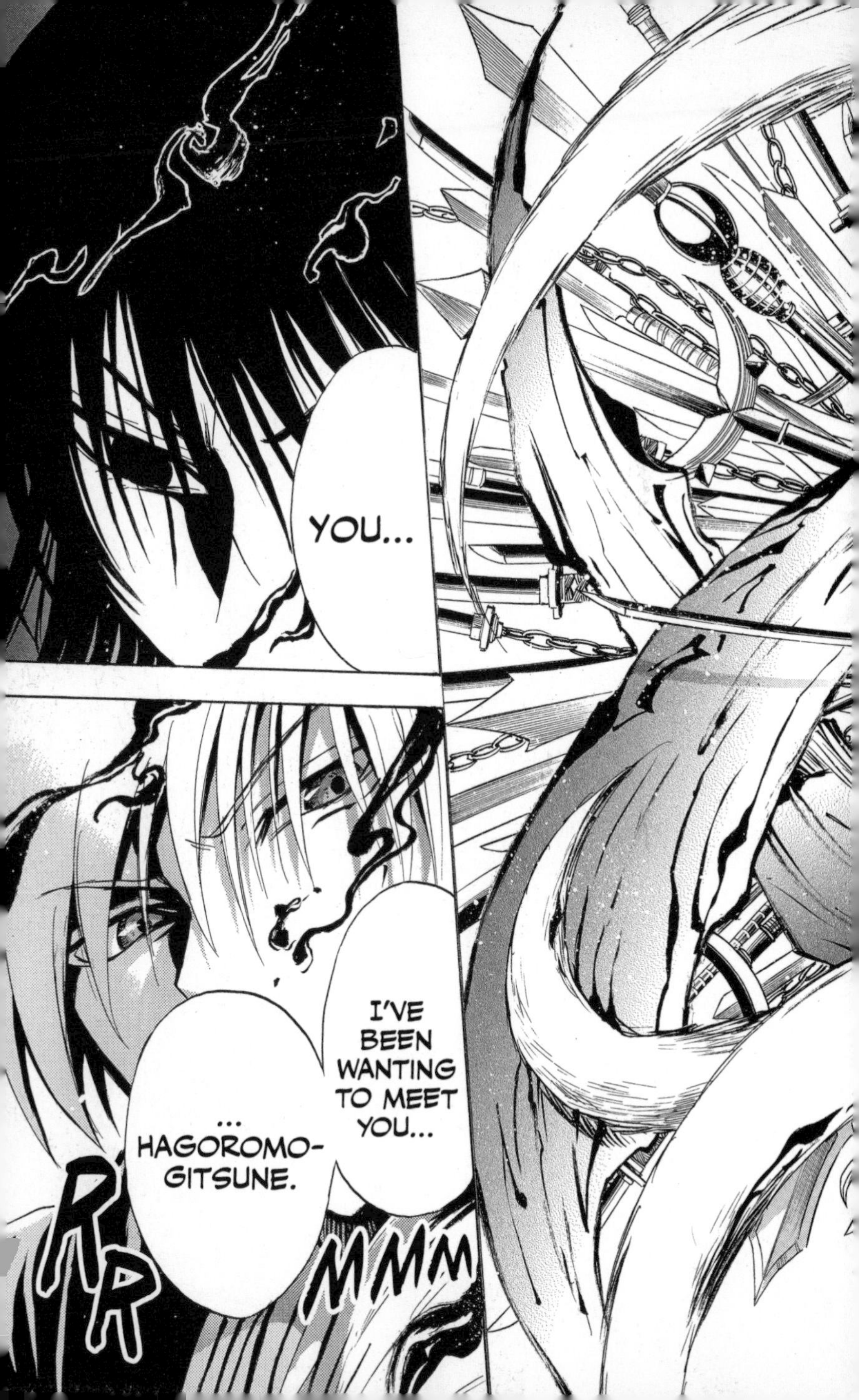
YOU...
I'VE BEEN WANTING TO MEET YOU...
... HAGOROMO-GITSUNE.
RRMMMM

NURA: RISE OF THE YOKAI CLAN

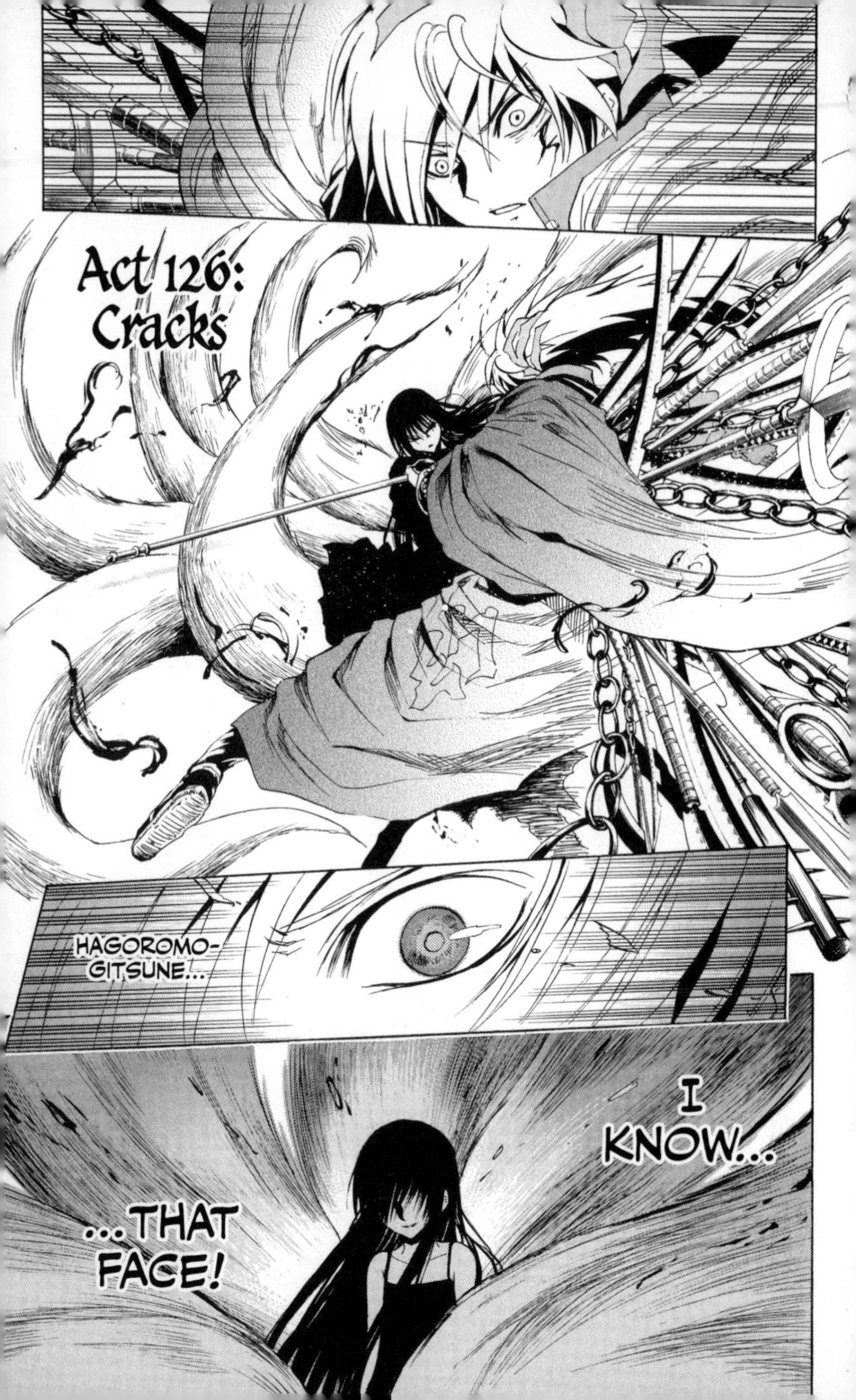
Act 126: Cracks
HAGOROMO-GITSUNE...
I KNOW...
...THAT FACE!

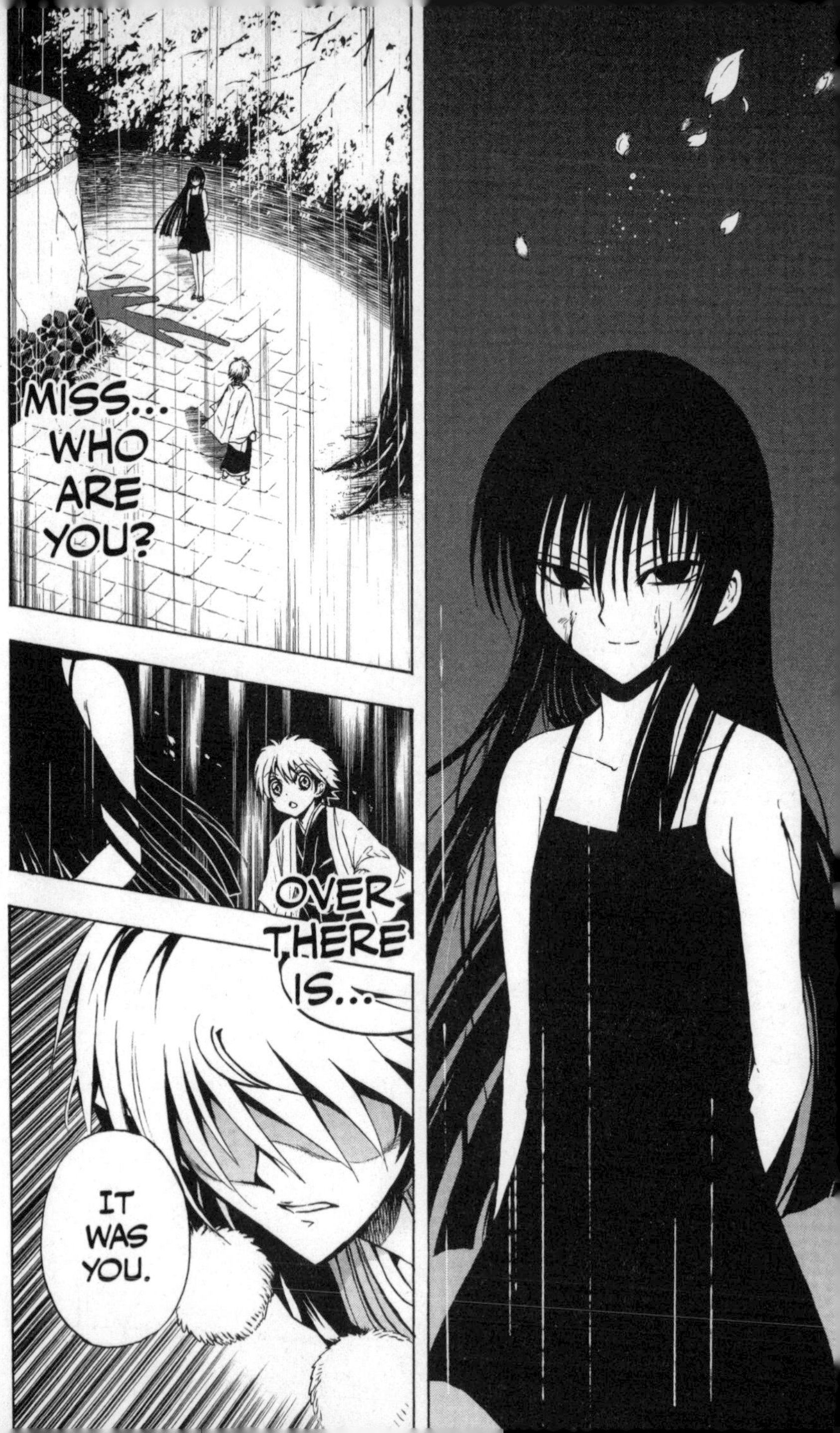
MISS... WHO ARE YOU?
OVER THERE IS...
IT WAS YOU.

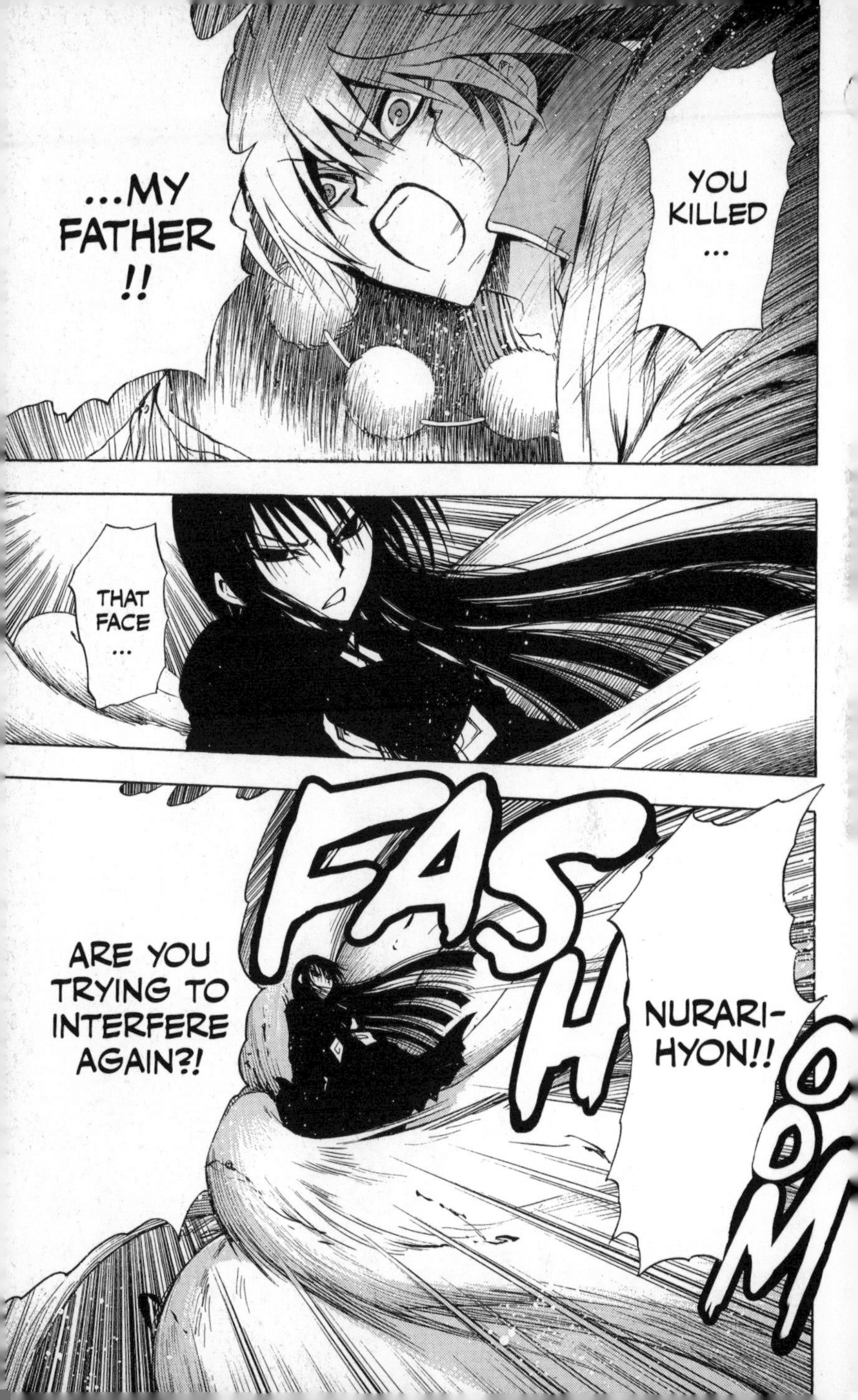
YOU KILLED ...
...MY FATHER !!
THAT FACE ...
NURARI-HYON!!
FASH
OOM
ARE YOU TRYING TO INTERFERE AGAIN?!

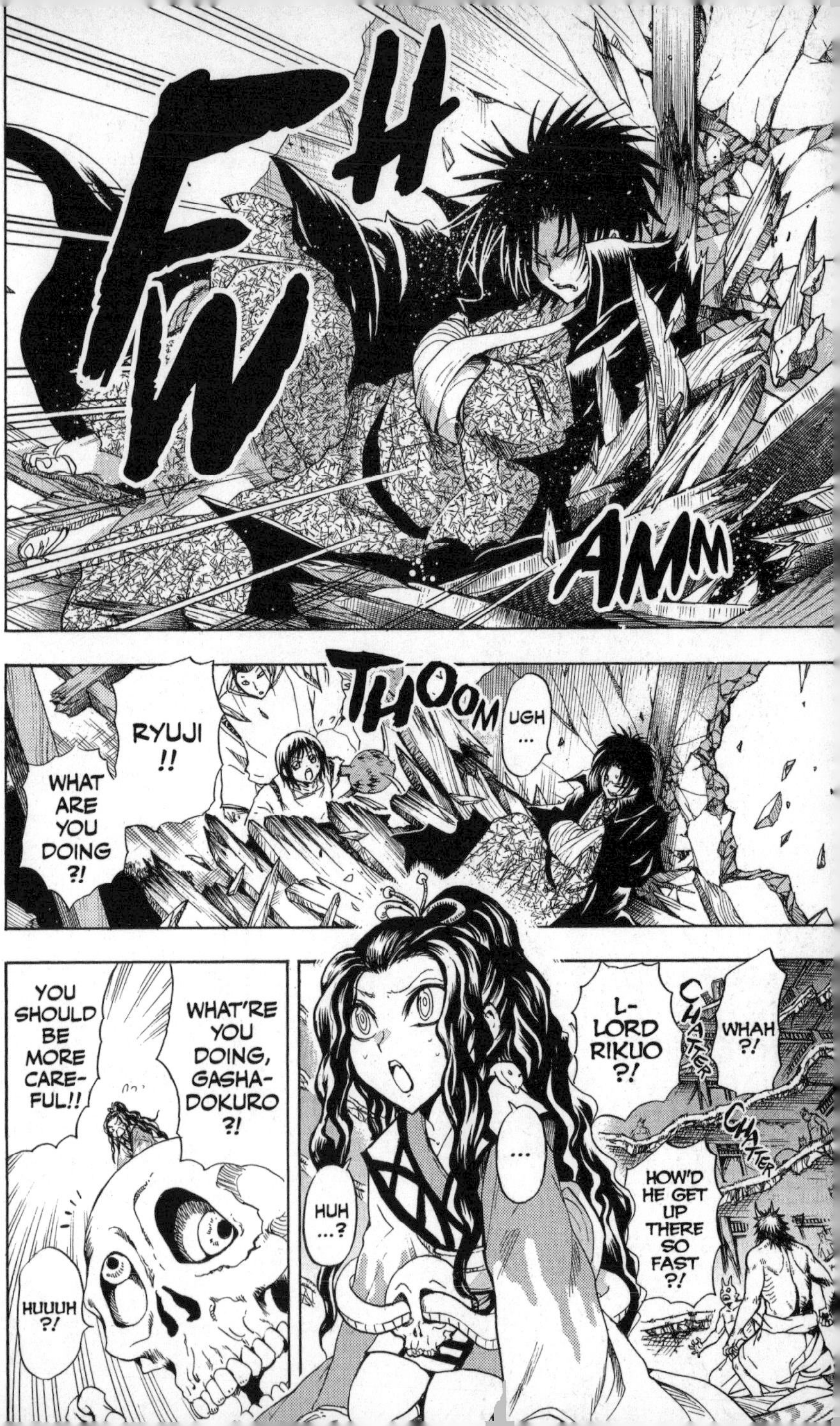
WHAMM
THOOM
UGH...
RYUJI!!
WHAT ARE YOU DOING?!
WHAH?!
L-LORD RIKUO?!
CHATTER
CHATTER
HOW'D HE GET UP THERE SO FAST?!
...
HUH...?
WHAT'RE YOU DOING, GASHA-DOKURO?!
YOU SHOULD BE MORE CARE-FUL!!
HUUUH?!

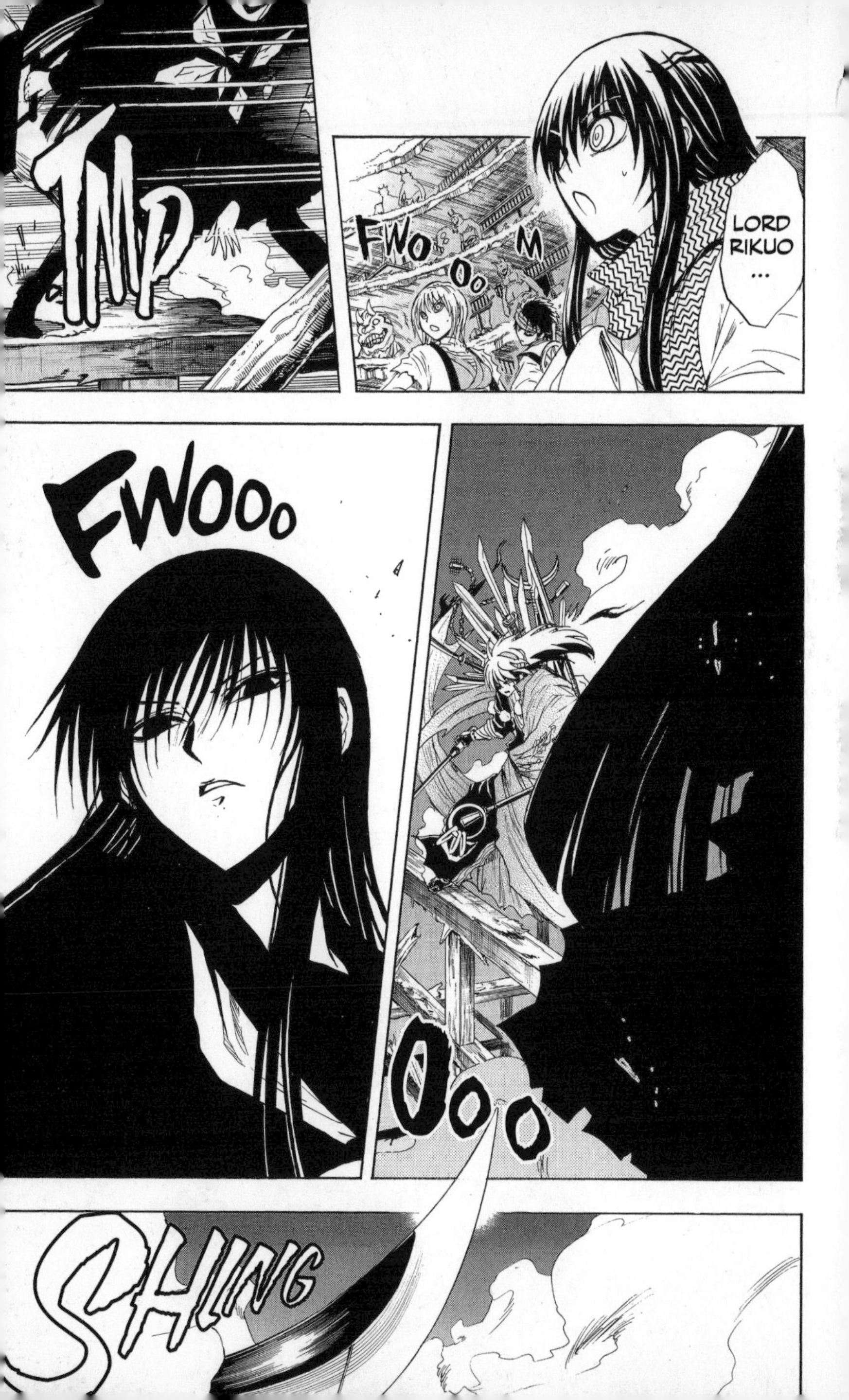
LORD RIKUO ...
FWOOOM
TMP
FWOOO
OOO
SHING

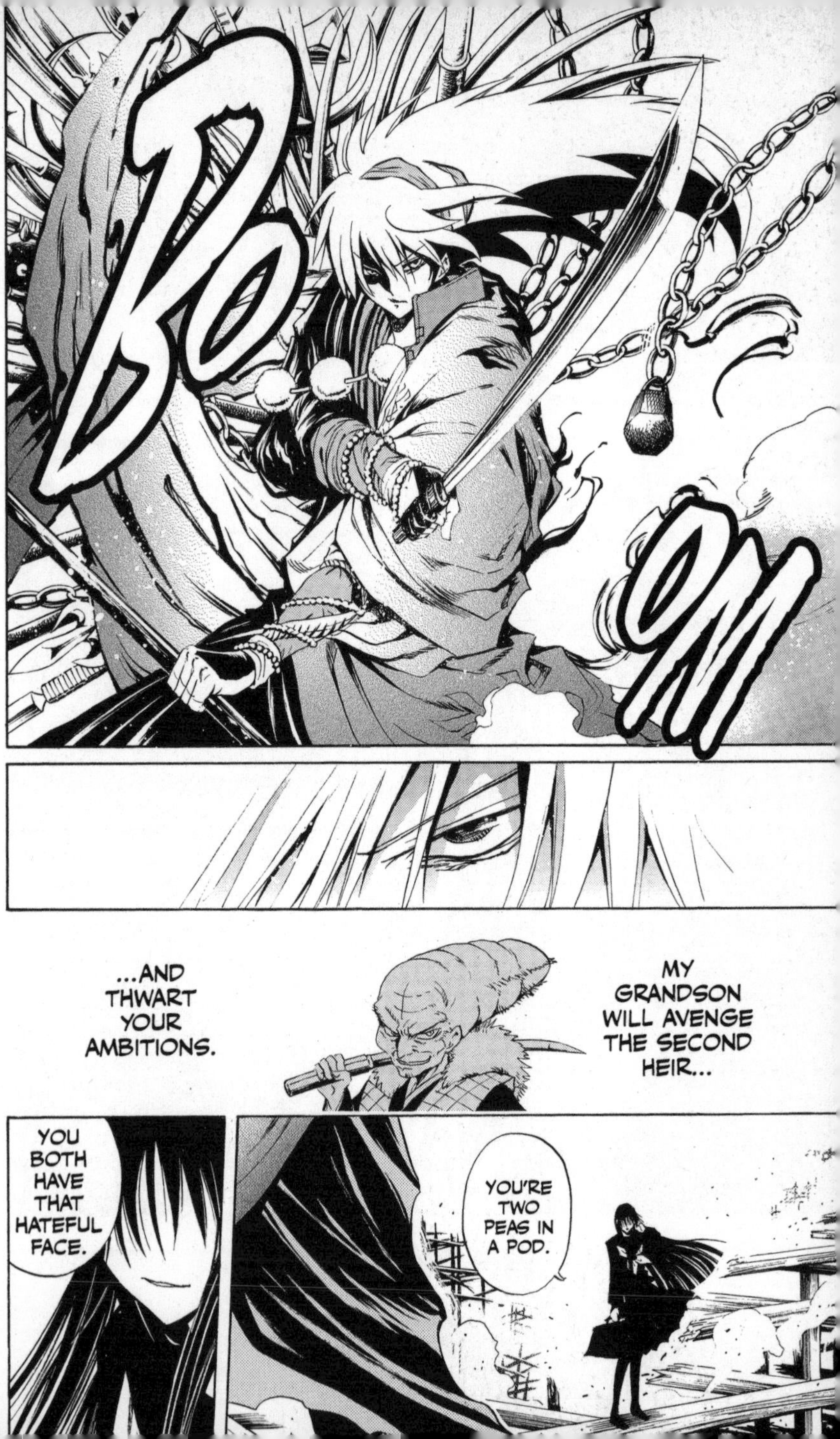
DO
OM
MY GRANDSON WILL AVENGE THE SECOND HEIR...
...AND THWART YOUR AMBITIONS.
YOU'RE TWO PEAS IN A POD.
YOU BOTH HAVE THAT HATEFUL FACE.

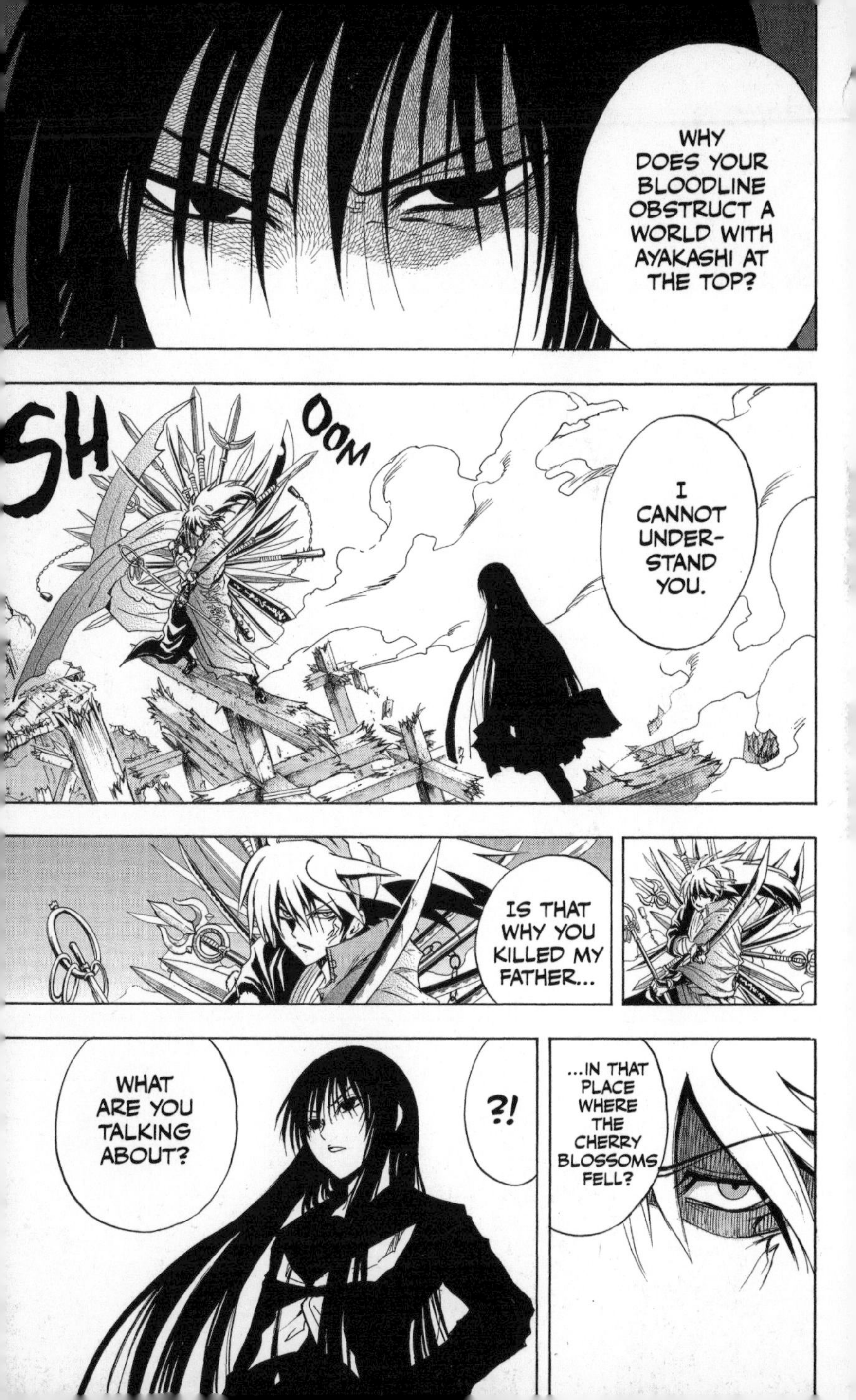
WHY DOES YOUR BLOODLINE OBSTRUCT A WORLD WITH AYAKASHI AT THE TOP?
SHOOM
I CANNOT UNDER-STAND YOU.
IS THAT WHY YOU KILLED MY FATHER...
...IN THAT PLACE WHERE THE CHERRY BLOSSOMS FELL?
?!
WHAT ARE YOU TALKING ABOUT?

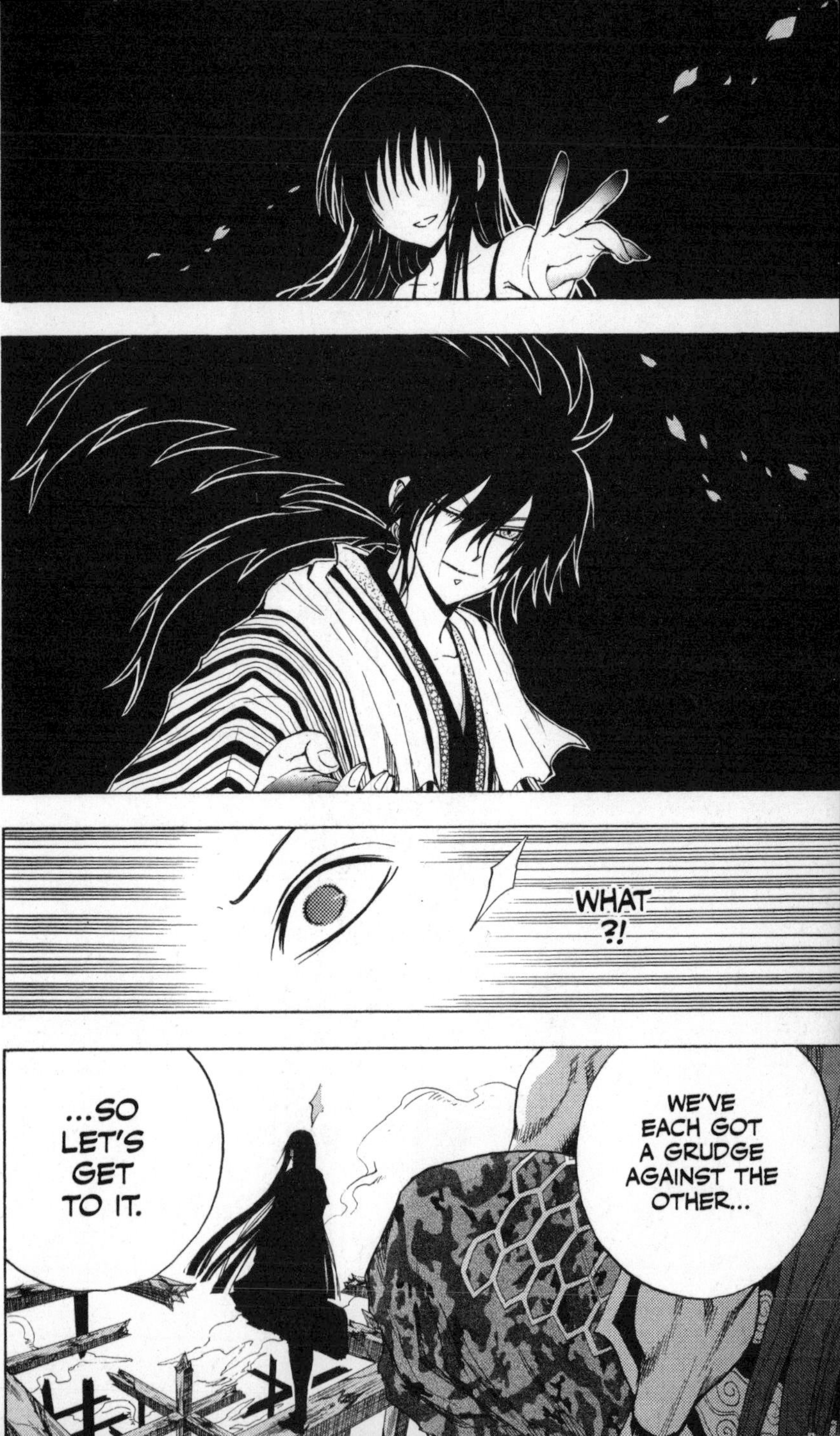
WHAT ?!
WE'VE EACH GOT A GRUDGE AGAINST THE OTHER...
...SO LET'S GET TO IT.

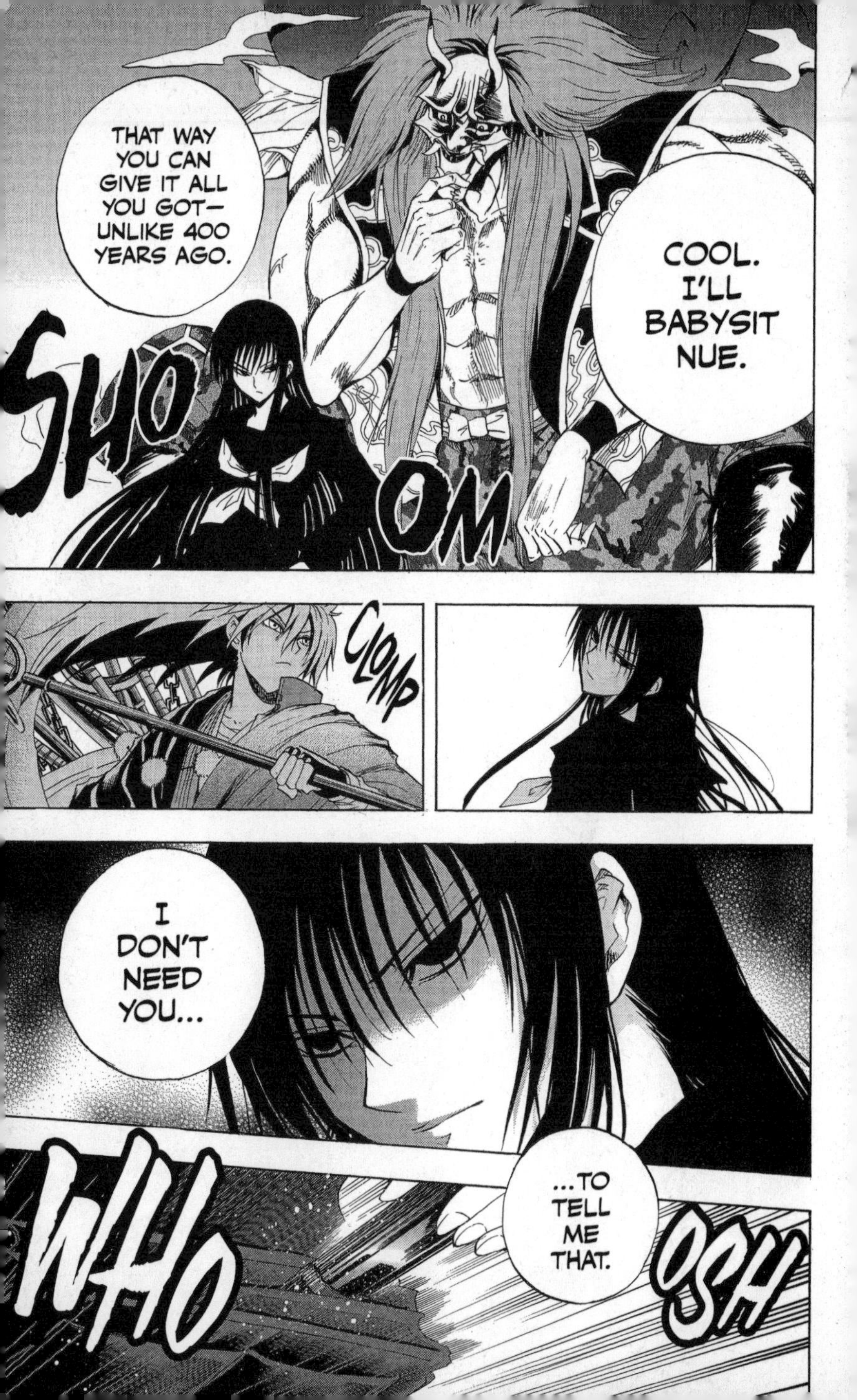
THAT WAY YOU CAN GIVE IT ALL YOU GOT—UNLIKE 400 YEARS AGO.
COOL. I'LL BABYSIT NUE.
SHOOM
CLOMP
I DON'T NEED YOU...
...TO TELL ME THAT.
WHOOSH

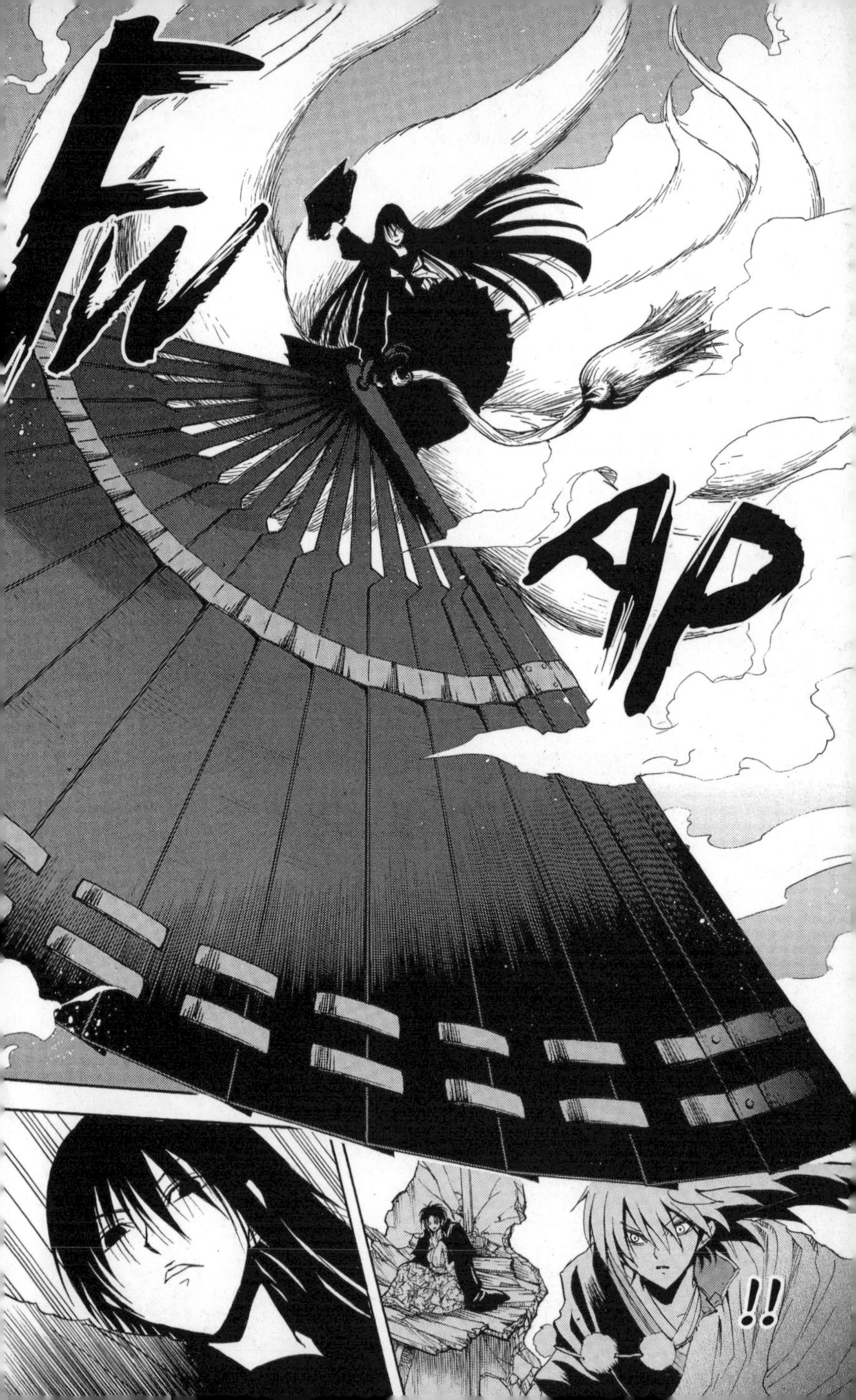
FWAP
!!

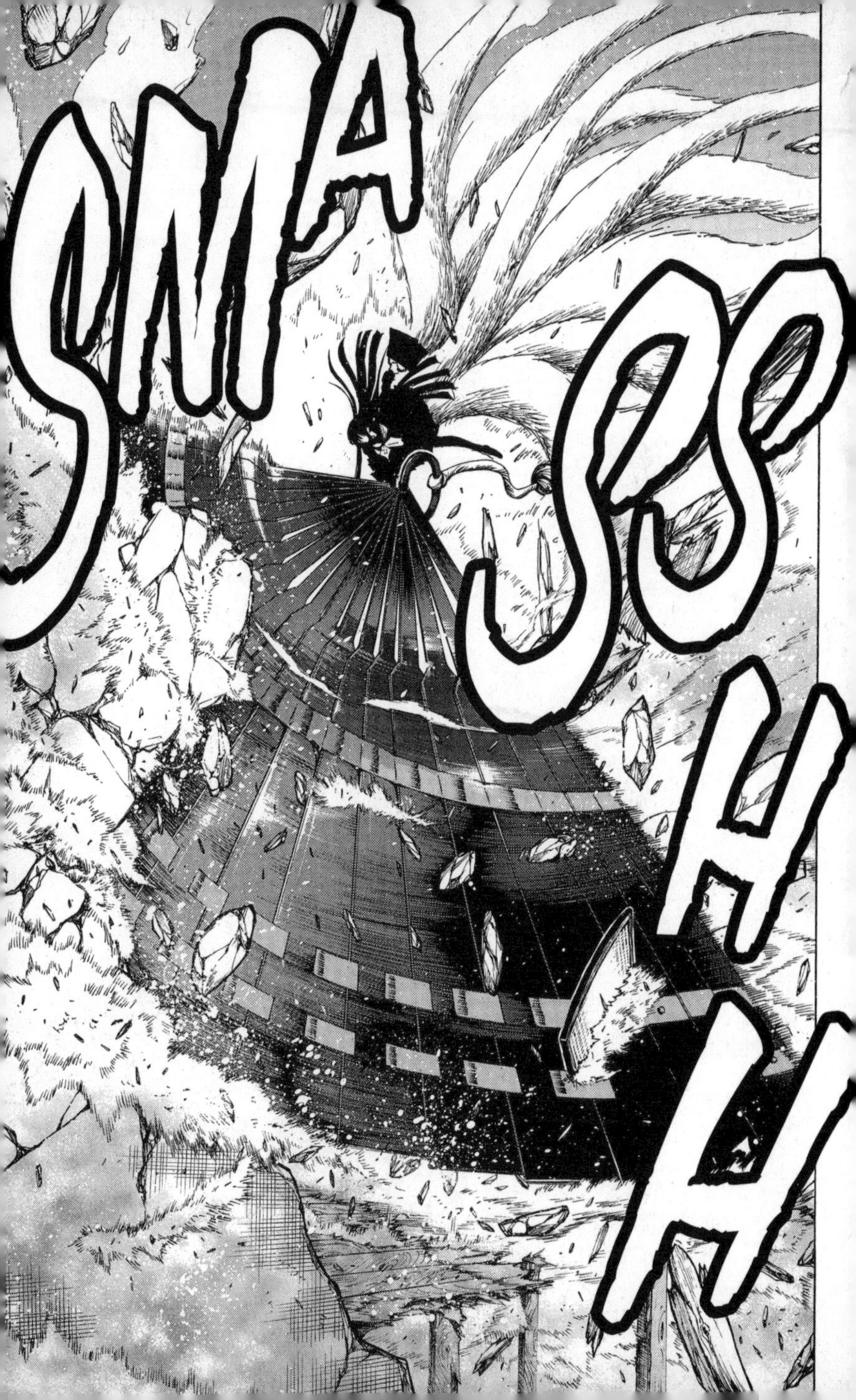
SMASHH

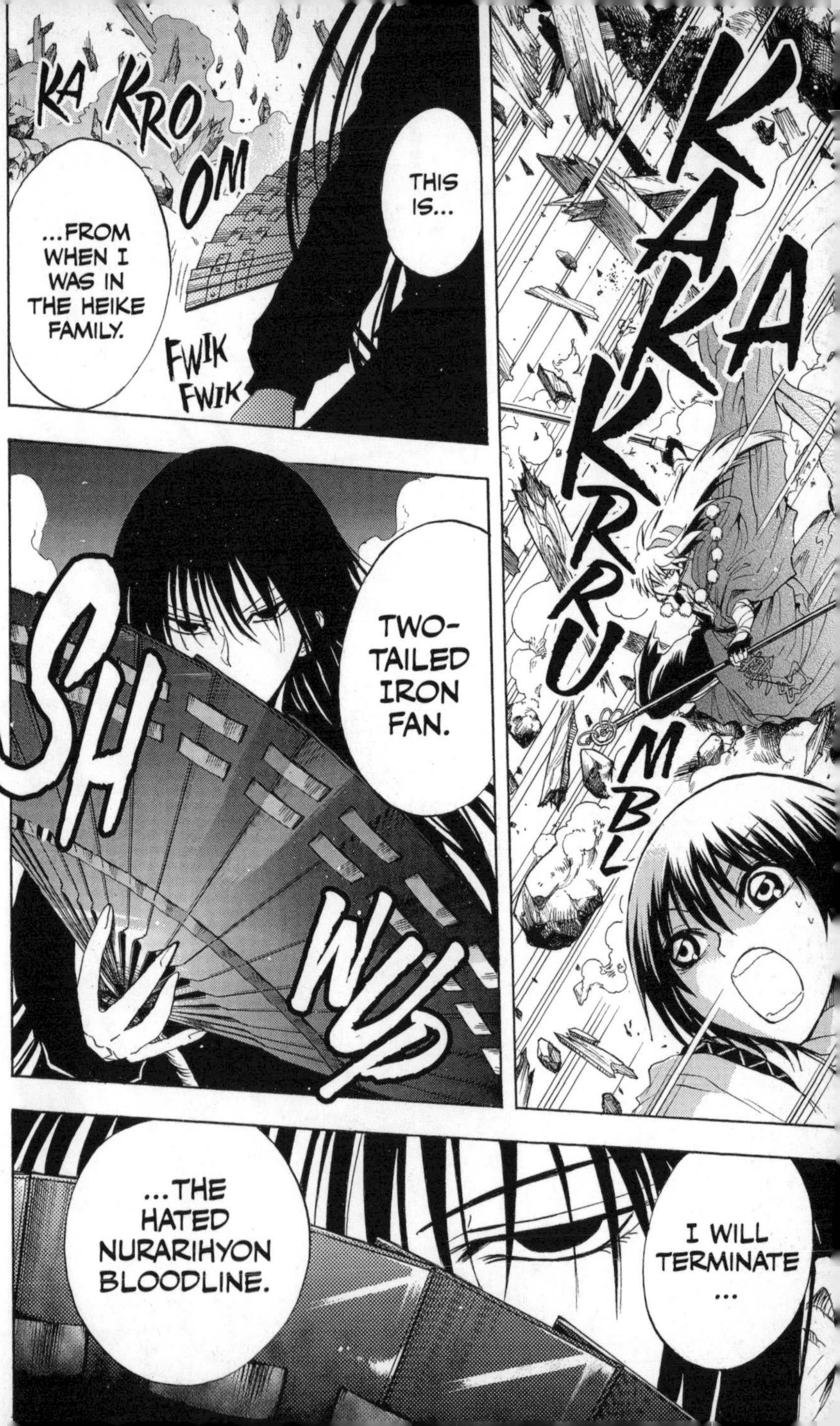
KAKAKRRUMBL
KA KRO OM
THIS IS...
...FROM WHEN I WAS IN THE HEIKE FAMILY.
FWIK FWIK
TWO-TAILED IRON FAN.
SH WUP
I WILL TERMINATE ...
...THE HATED NURARIHYON BLOODLINE.

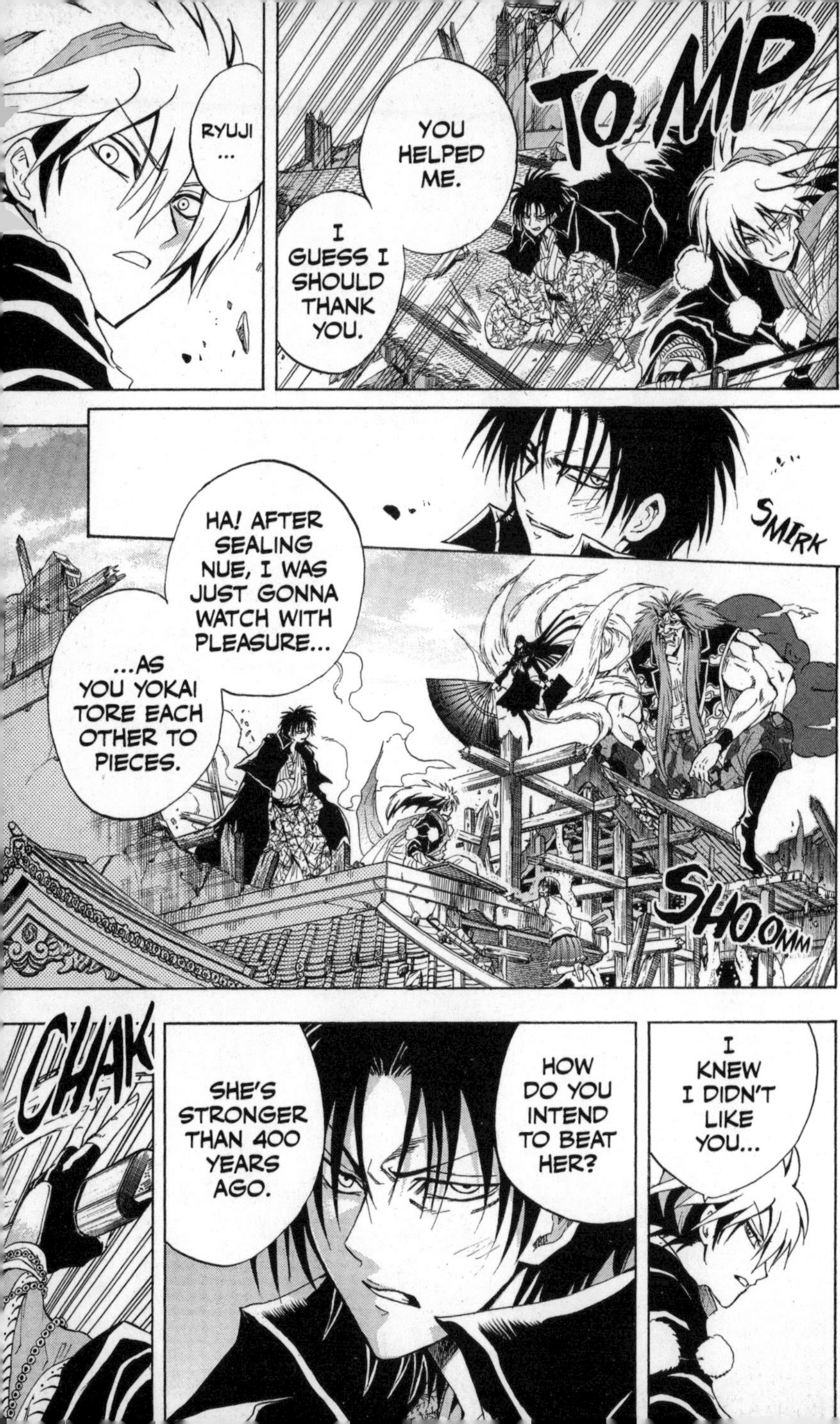

TOMP
YOU HELPED ME.
I GUESS I SHOULD THANK YOU.
RYUJI ...
SMIRK
HA! AFTER SEALING NUE, I WAS JUST GONNA WATCH WITH PLEASURE...
...AS YOU YOKAI TORE EACH OTHER TO PIECES.
SHOOMM
I KNEW I DIDN'T LIKE YOU...
HOW DO YOU INTEND TO BEAT HER?
SHE'S STRONGER THAN 400 YEARS AGO.
CHAK

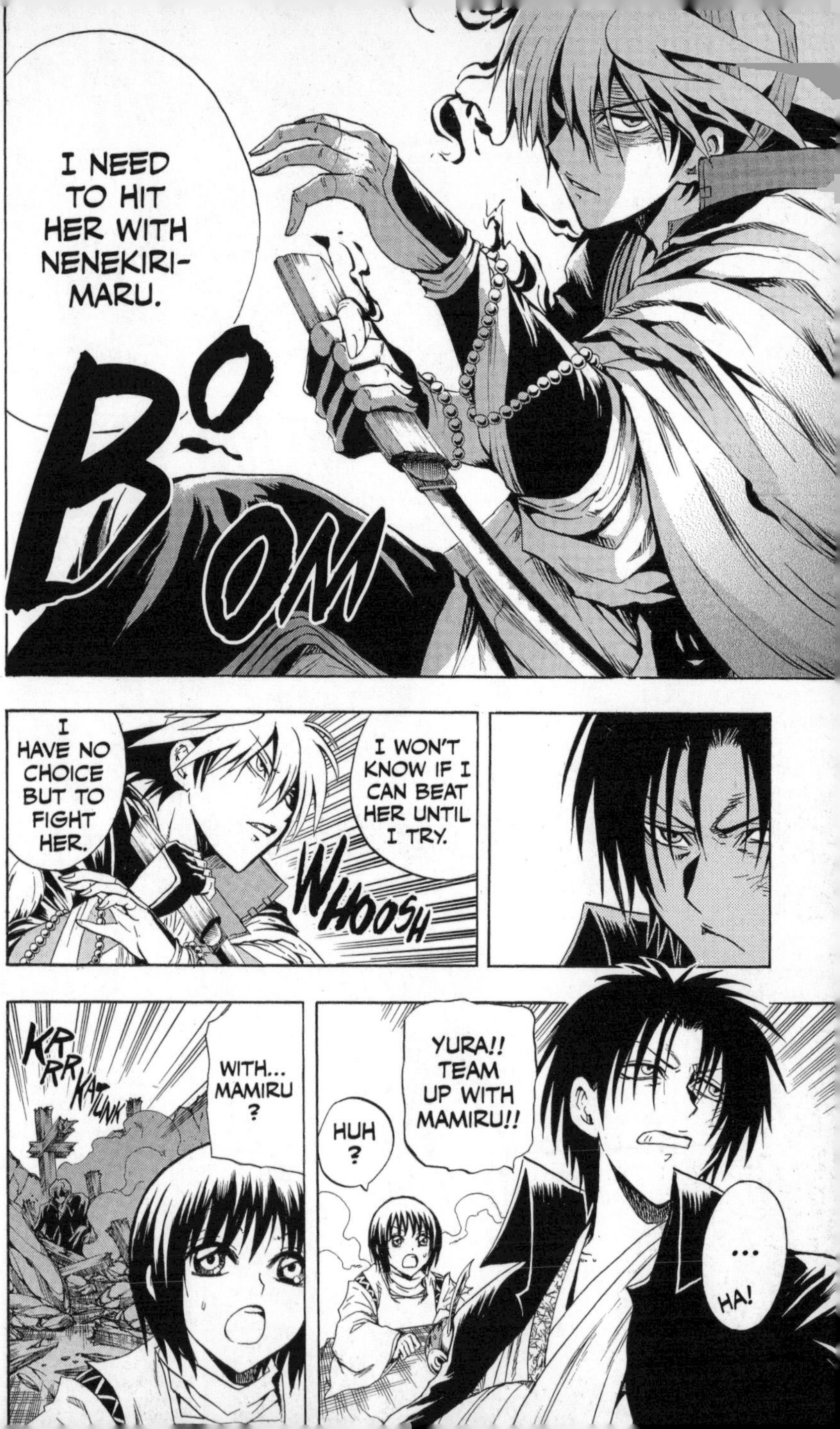
I NEED TO HIT HER WITH NENEKIRI-MARU.
BOOM
I WON'T KNOW IF I CAN BEAT HER UNTIL I TRY.
I HAVE NO CHOICE BUT TO FIGHT HER.
WHOOSH
YURA!! TEAM UP WITH MAMIRU!!
HUH ?
... HA!
WITH... MAMIRU ?
KRRRR KATUNK

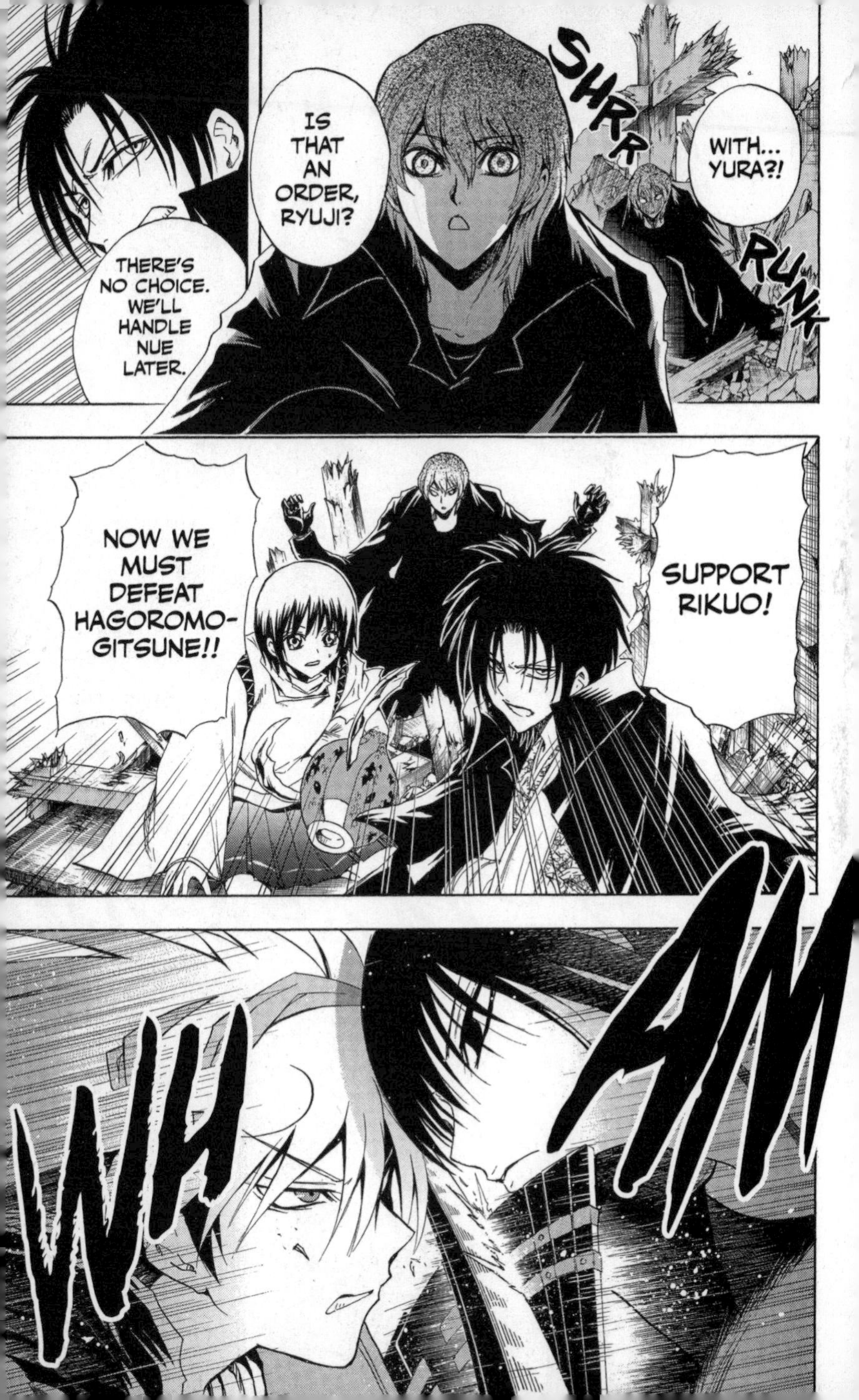
SHRRRUNK
WITH... YURA?!
IS THAT AN ORDER, RYUJI?
THERE'S NO CHOICE. WE'LL HANDLE NUE LATER.
SUPPORT RIKUO!
NOW WE MUST DEFEAT HAGOROMO-GITSUNE!!
WHAM

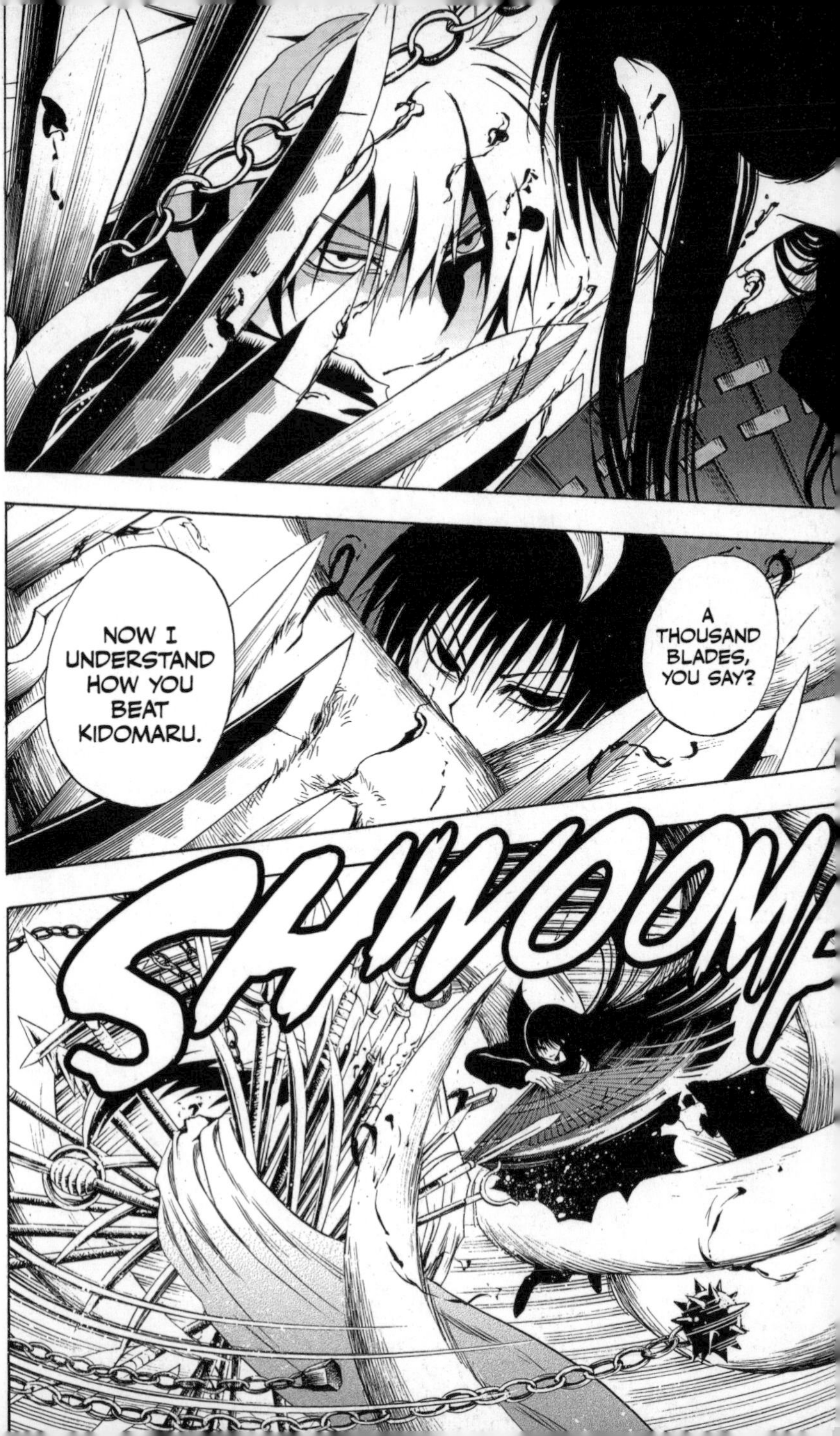
A THOUSAND BLADES, YOU SAY?
NOW I UNDERSTAND HOW YOU BEAT KIDOMARU.
SHWOOM

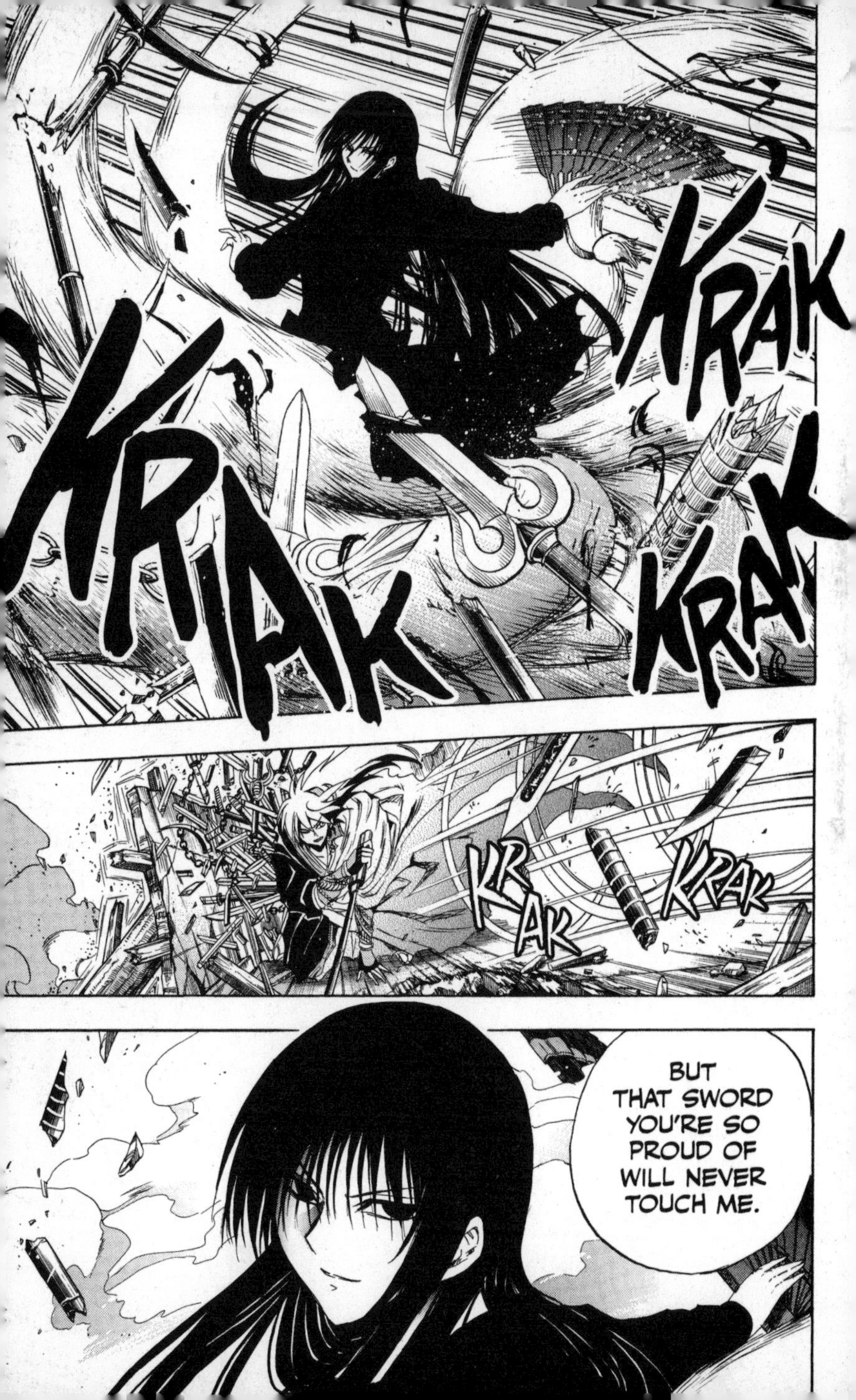
KRAK
KRAK
KRAKAK
KRAK
KRAK
BUT THAT SWORD YOU'RE SO PROUD OF WILL NEVER TOUCH ME.

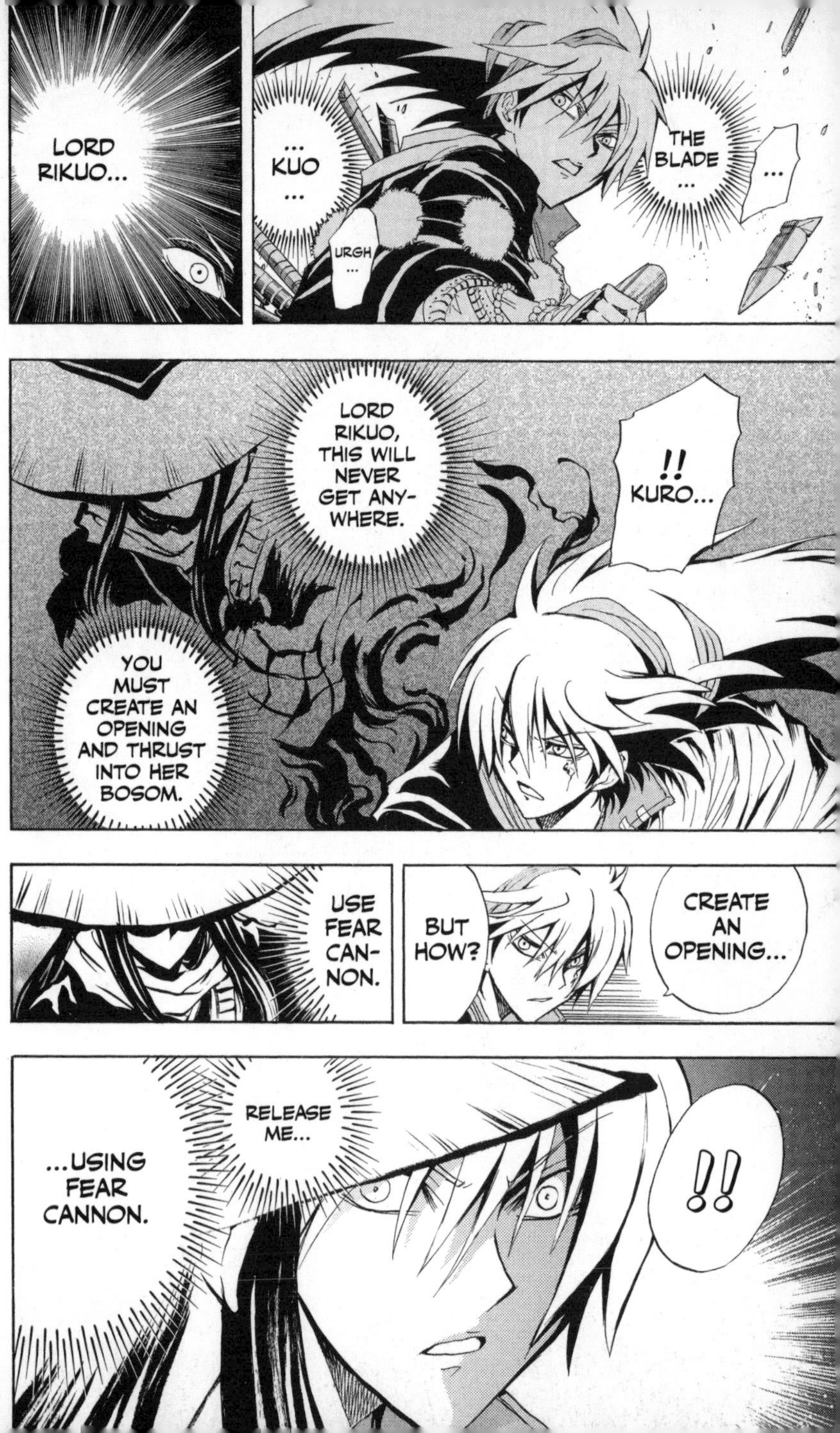
...
THE BLADE ...
... KUO ...
URGH ...
LORD RIKUO...
!! KURO...
LORD RIKUO, THIS WILL NEVER GET ANY-WHERE.
YOU MUST CREATE AN OPENING AND THRUST INTO HER BOSOM.
CREATE AN OPENING...
BUT HOW?
USE FEAR CAN-NON.
!!
RELEASE ME...
...USING FEAR CANNON.

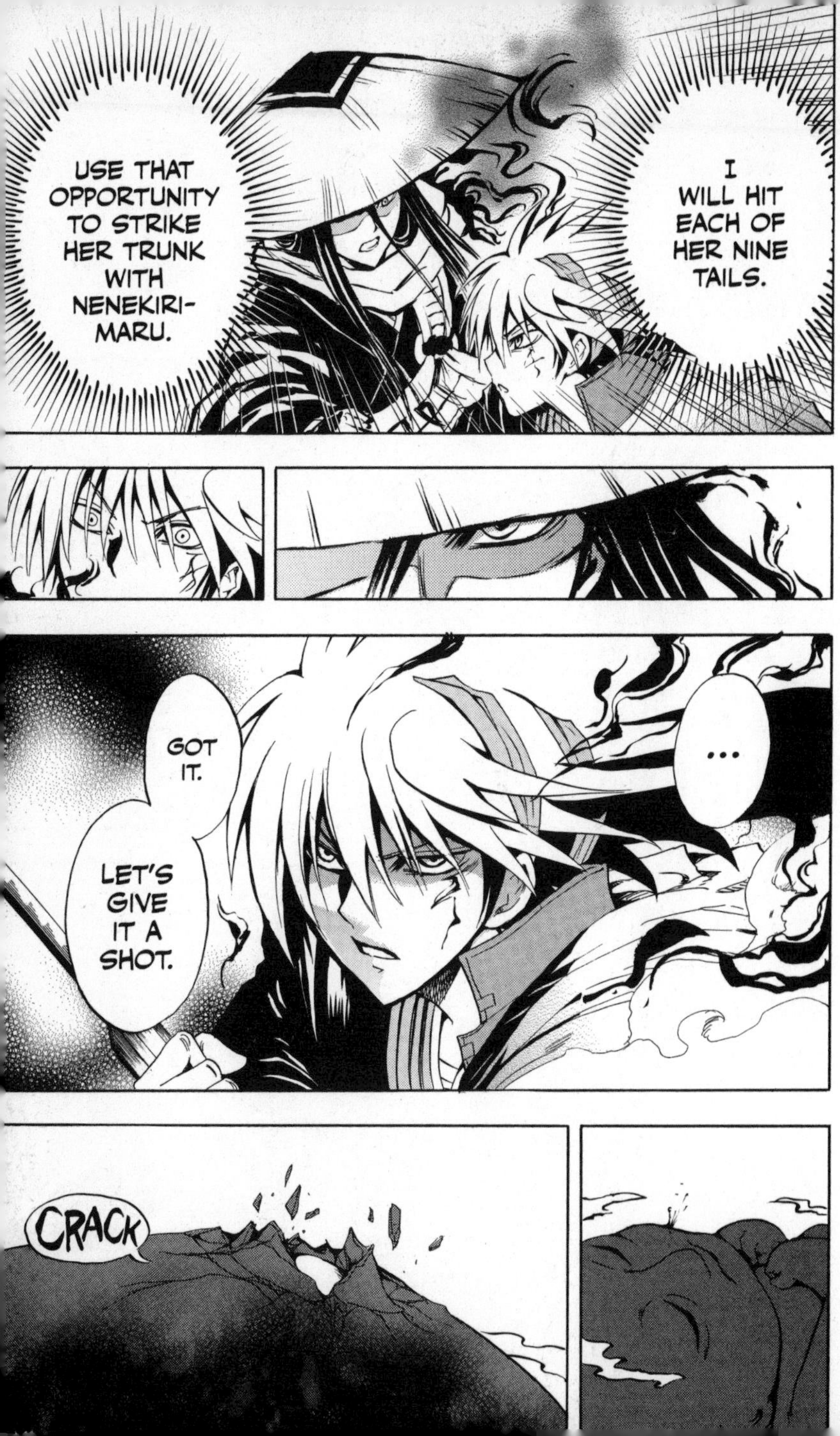
I WILL HIT EACH OF HER NINE TAILS.
USE THAT OPPORTUNITY TO STRIKE HER TRUNK WITH NENEKIRI-MARU.
...
GOT IT.
LET'S GIVE IT A SHOT.
CRACK

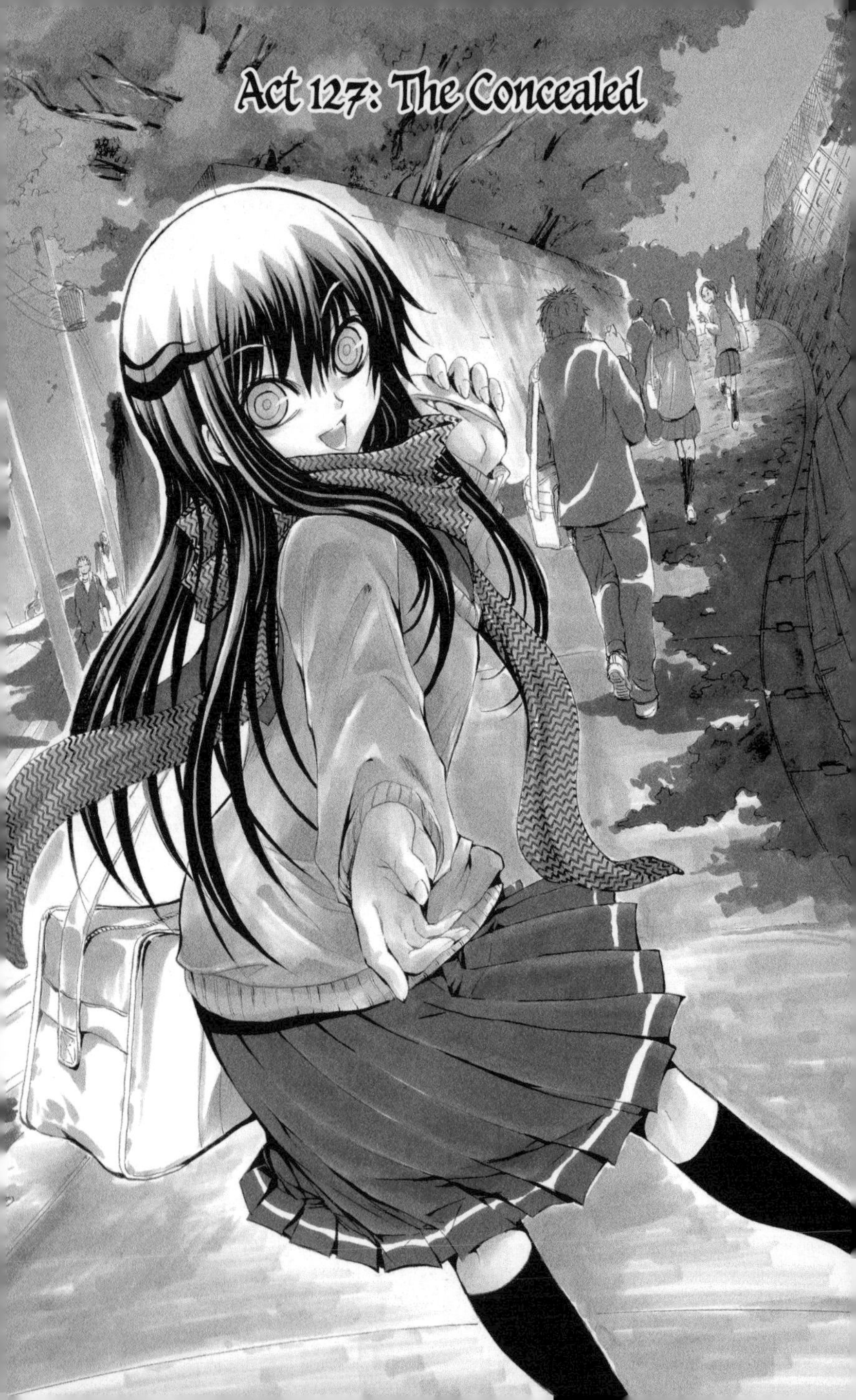
Act 127: The Concealed

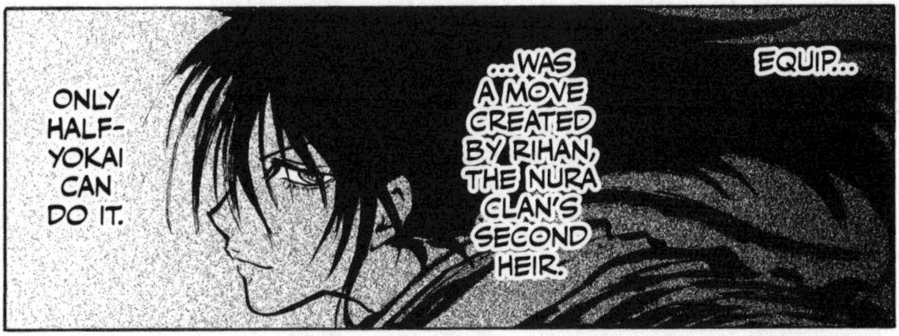
EQUIP...
...WAS A MOVE CREATED BY RIHAN, THE NURA CLAN'S SECOND HEIR.
ONLY HALF-YOKAI CAN DO IT.
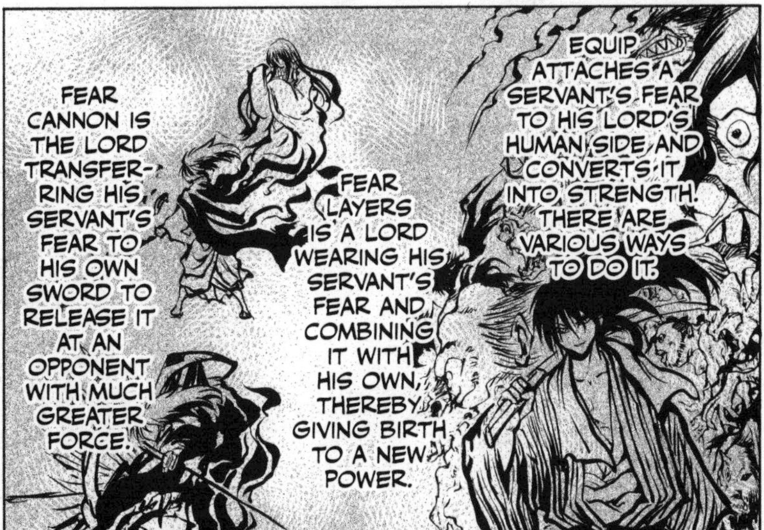
EQUIP ATTACHES A SERVANT'S FEAR TO HIS LORD'S HUMAN SIDE AND CONVERTS IT INTO STRENGTH. THERE ARE VARIOUS WAYS TO DO IT.
FEAR LAYERS IS A LORD WEARING HIS SERVANT'S FEAR AND COMBINING IT WITH HIS OWN, THEREBY GIVING BIRTH TO A NEW POWER.
FEAR CANNON IS THE LORD TRANSFERRING HIS SERVANT'S FEAR TO HIS OWN SWORD TO RELEASE IT AT AN OPPONENT WITH MUCH GREATER FORCE.
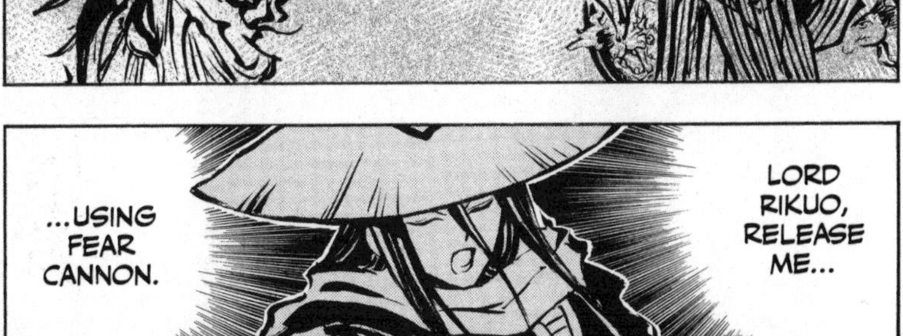
LORD RIKUO, RELEASE ME...
...USING FEAR CANNON.

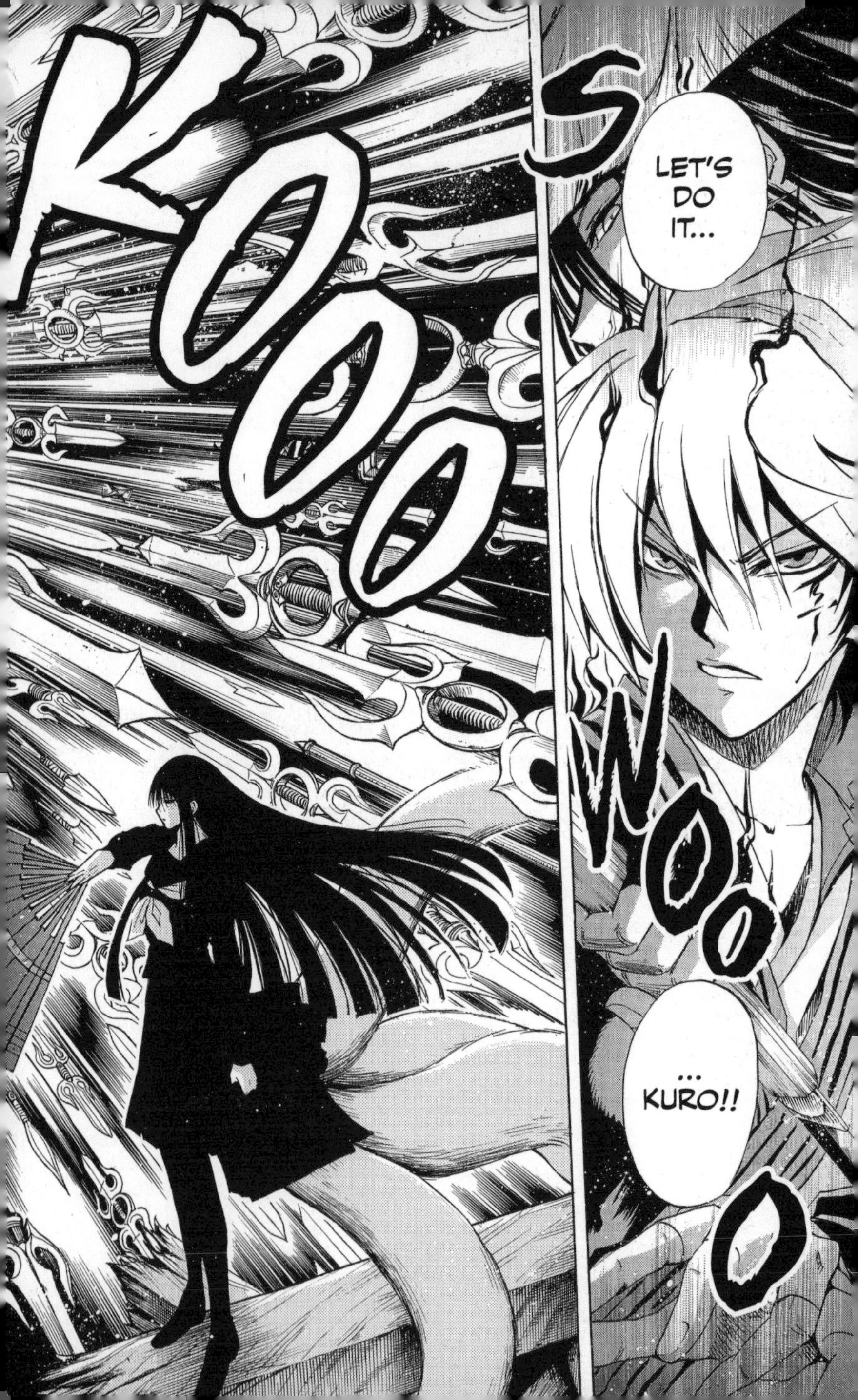
S
LET'S DO IT...
WOOO
... KURO!!
KOOOO

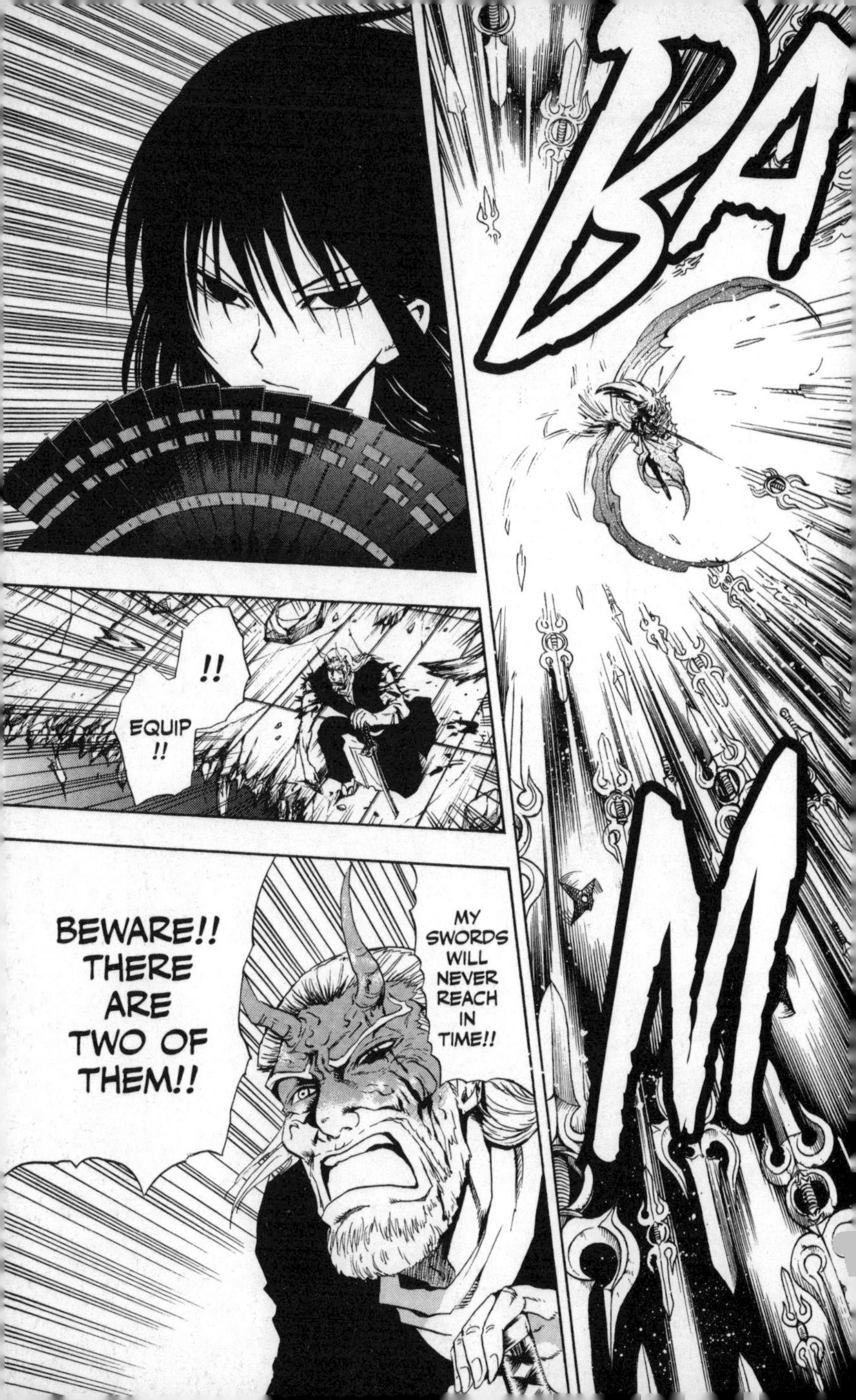
BAM
!!
EQUIP !!
MY SWORDS WILL NEVER REACH IN TIME!!
BEWARE!! THERE ARE TWO OF THEM!!

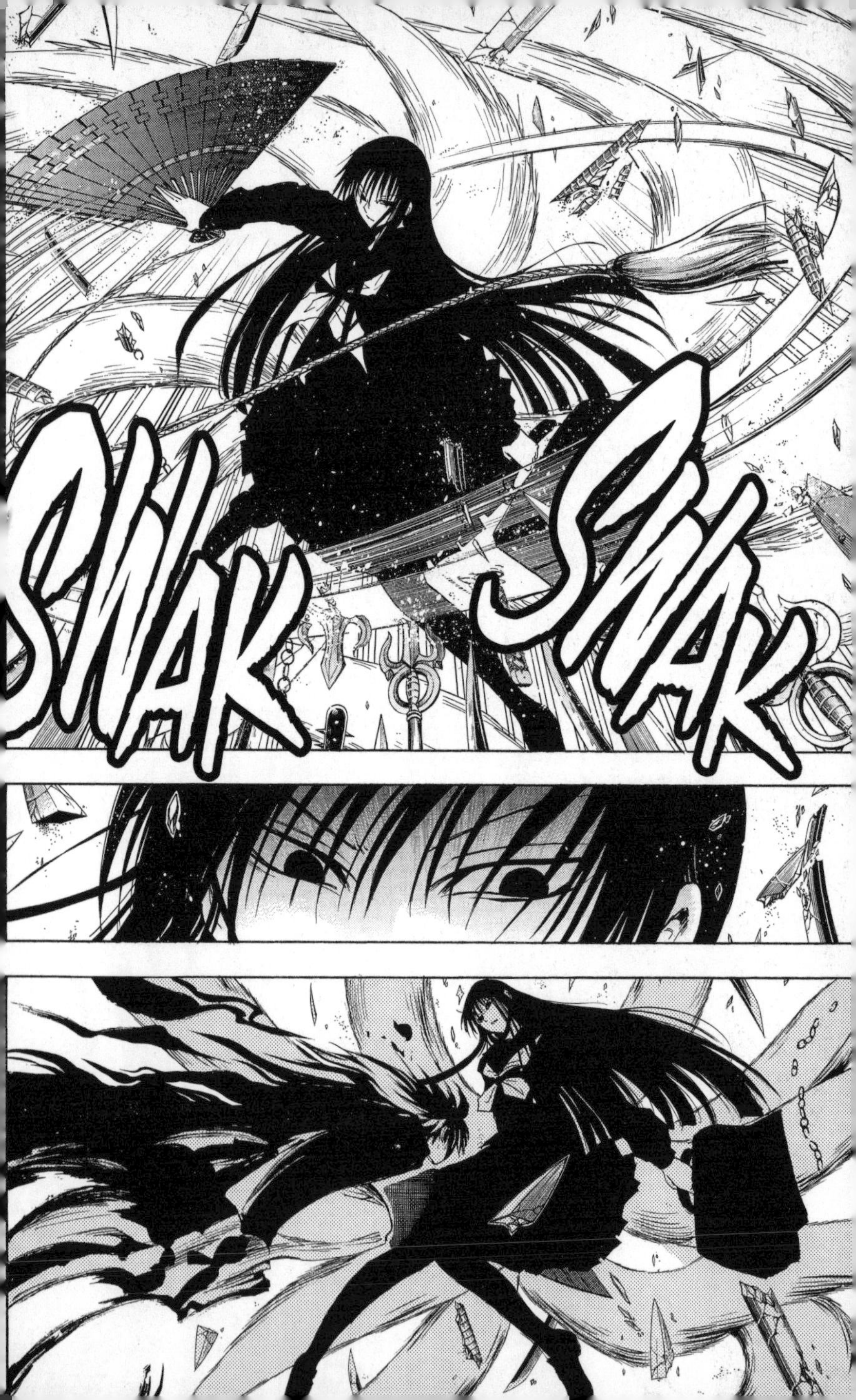
SNAK
SNAK

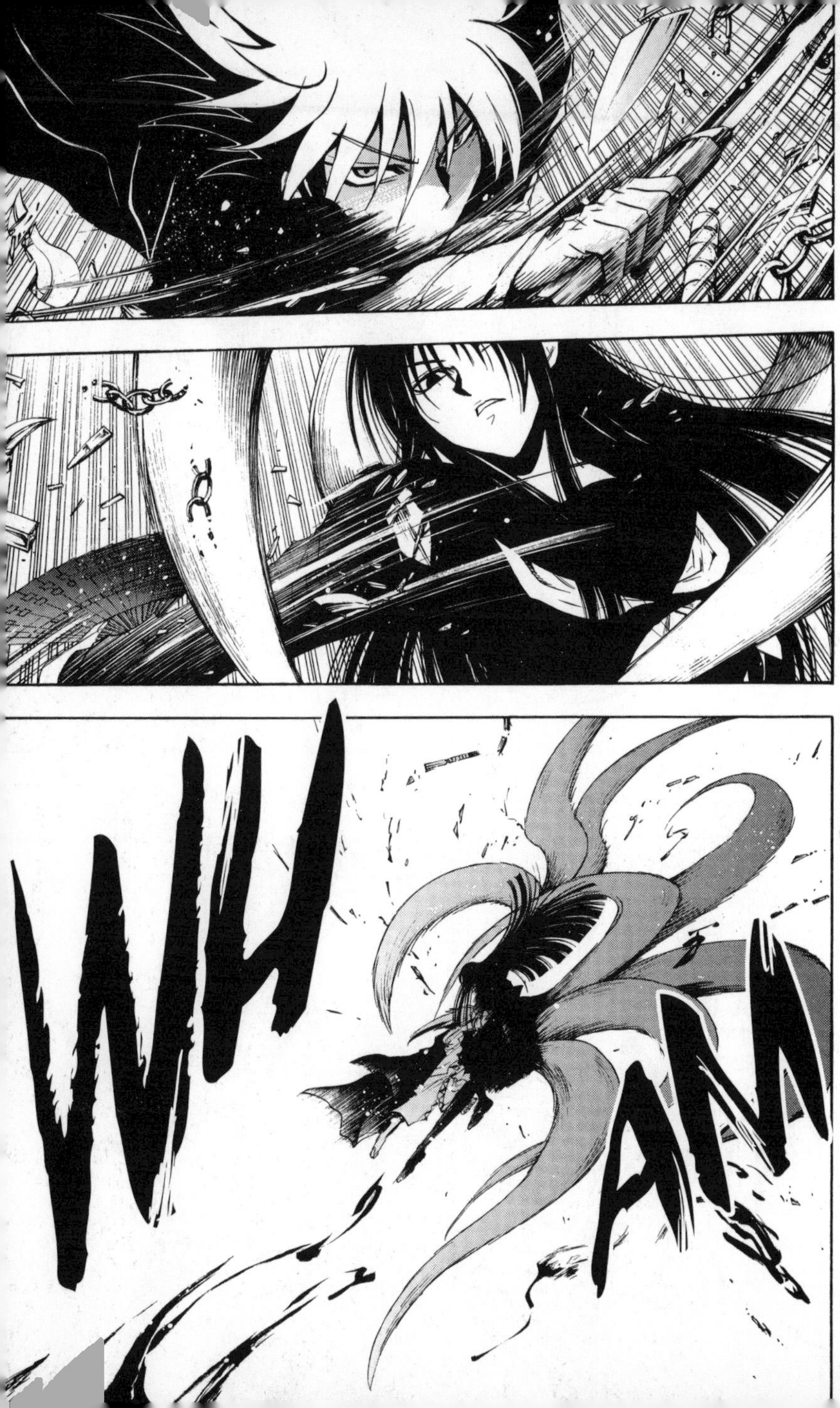
WHAM

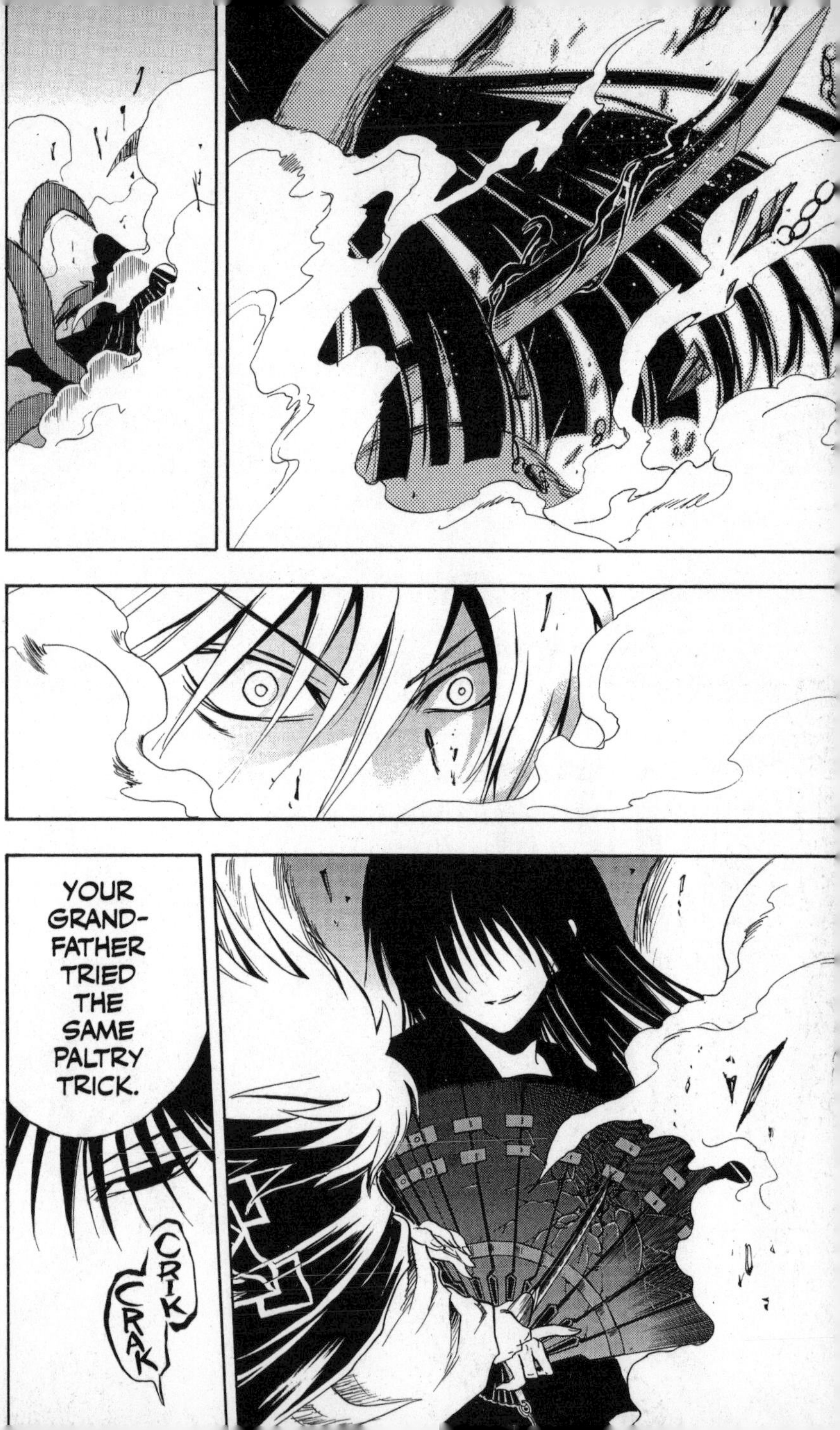
YOUR GRAND-FATHER TRIED THE SAME PALTRY TRICK.
CRIK
CRAK

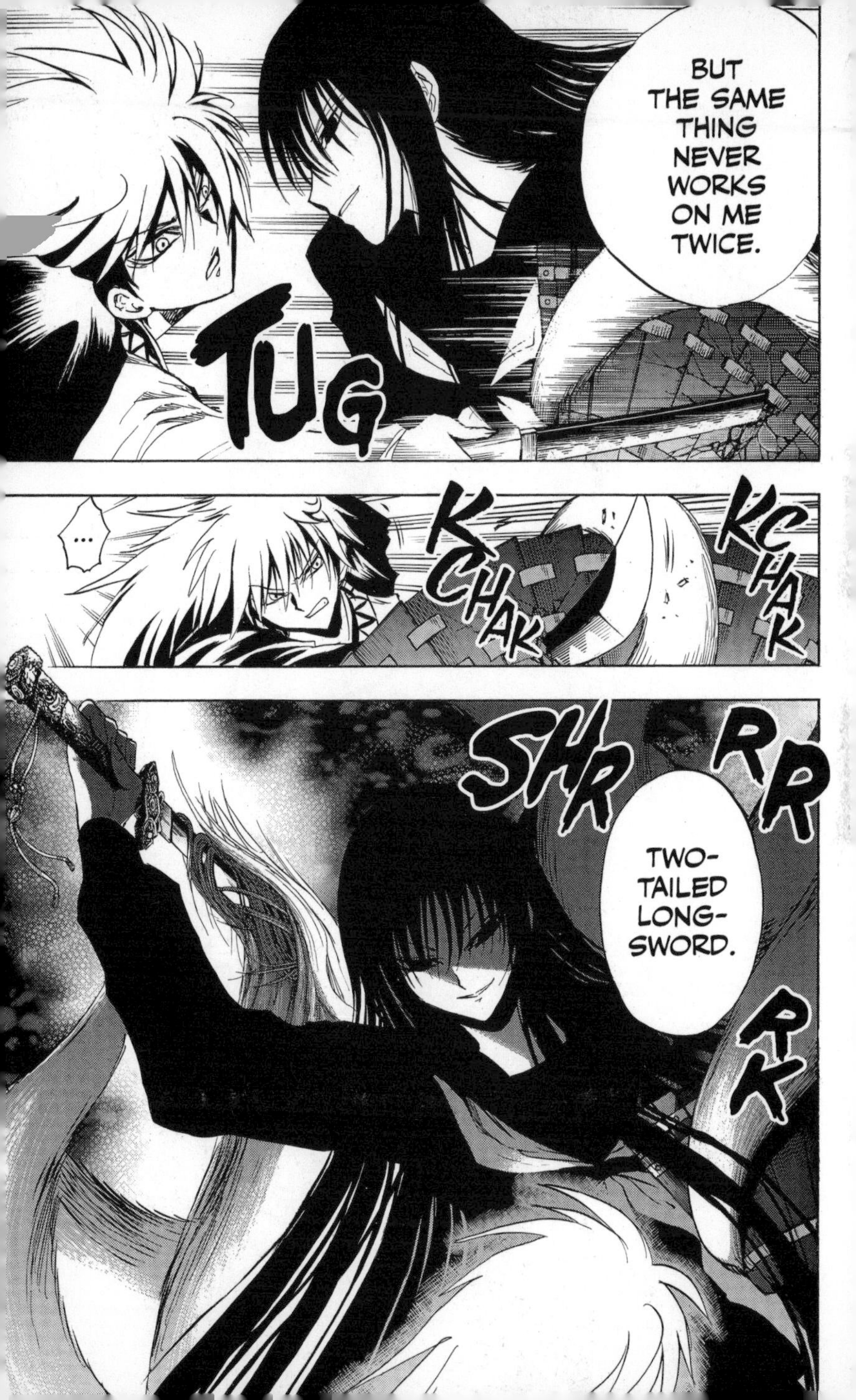
BUT THE SAME THING NEVER WORKS ON ME TWICE.
TUG
KCHAK
KCHAK
...
SHRRRRK
TWO-TAILED LONG-SWORD.

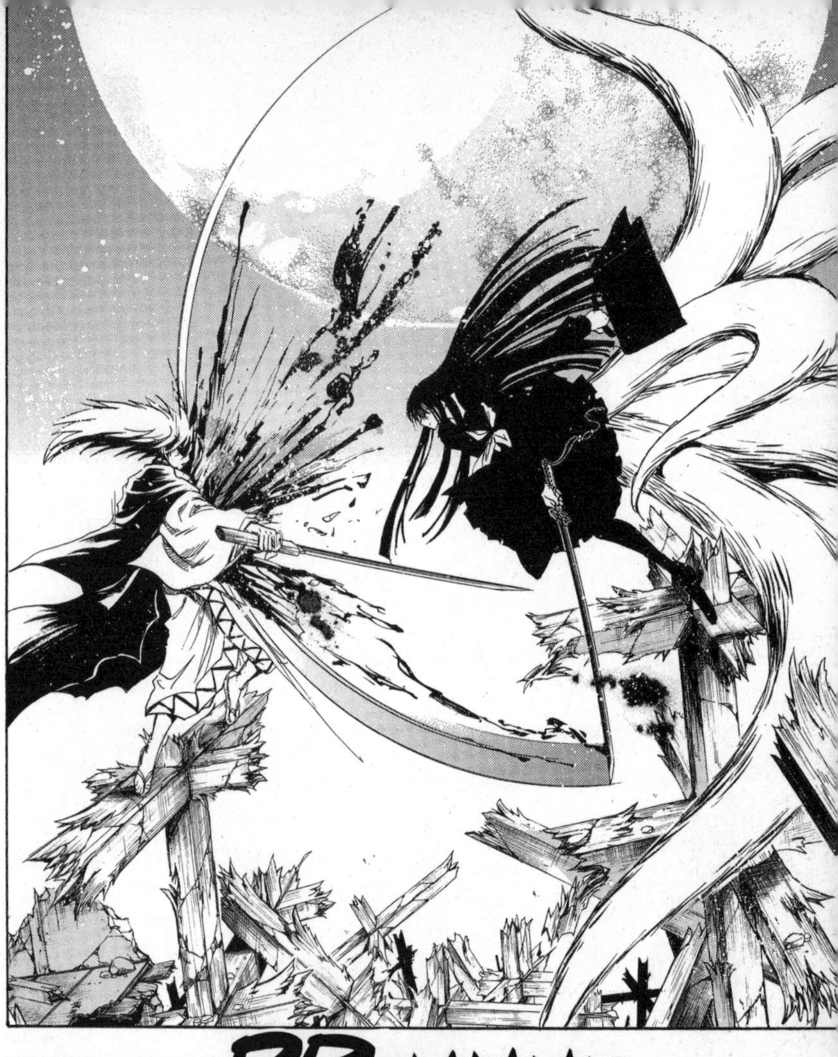

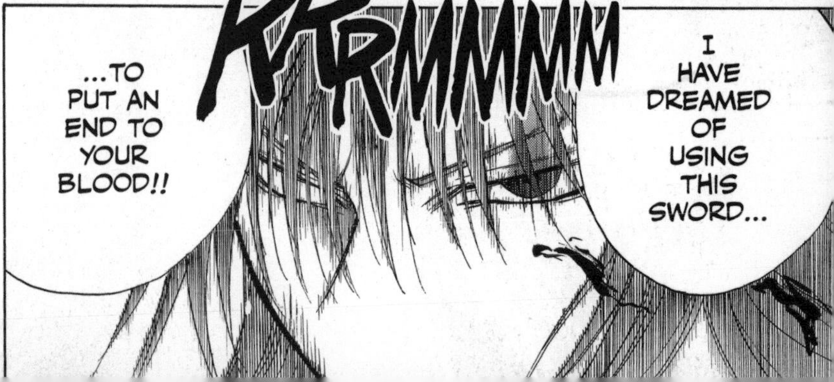
I HAVE DREAMED OF USING THIS SWORD...
RRRMMMMM
...TO PUT AN END TO YOUR BLOOD!!

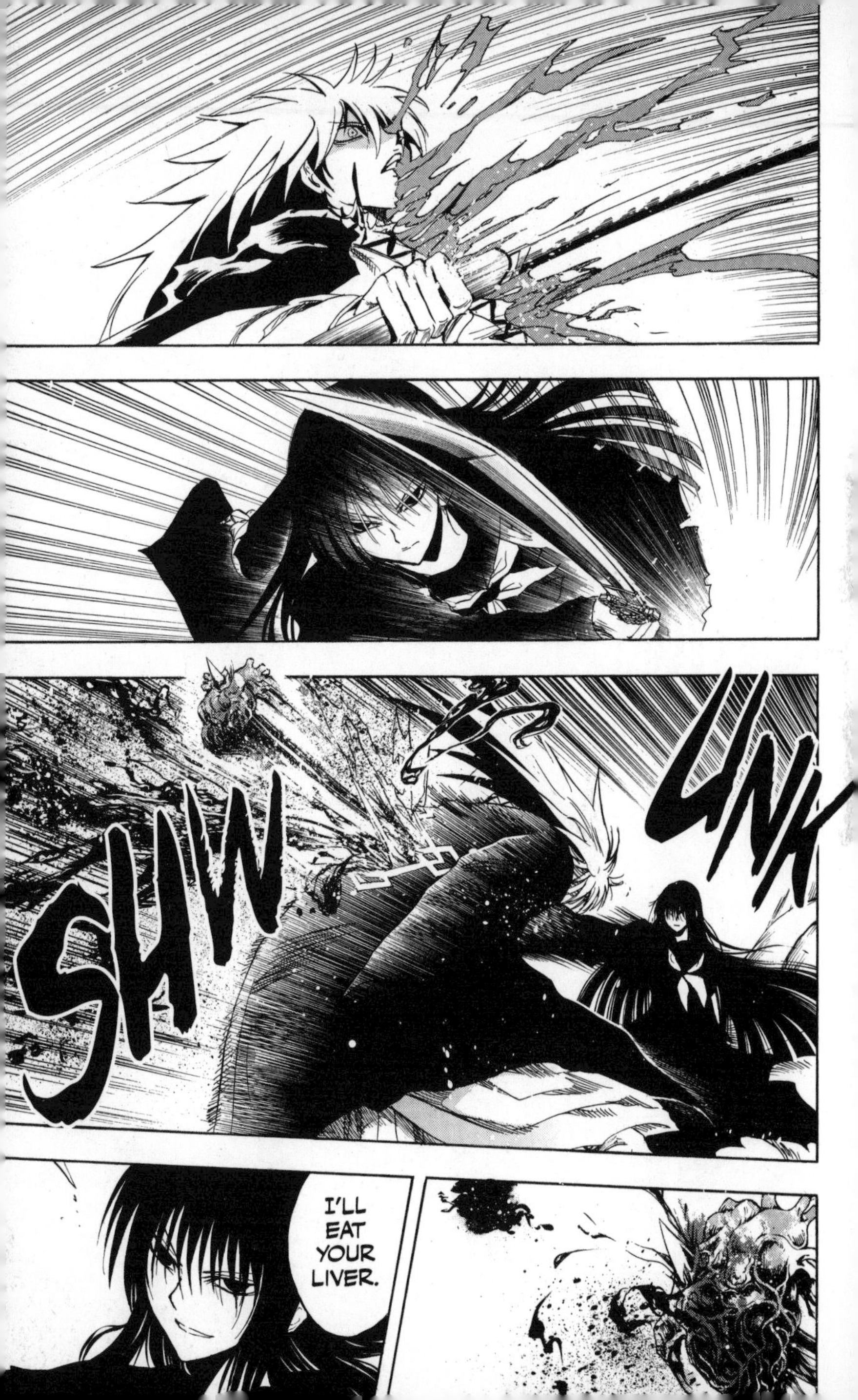
LINK
SHW
I'LL EAT YOUR LIVER.

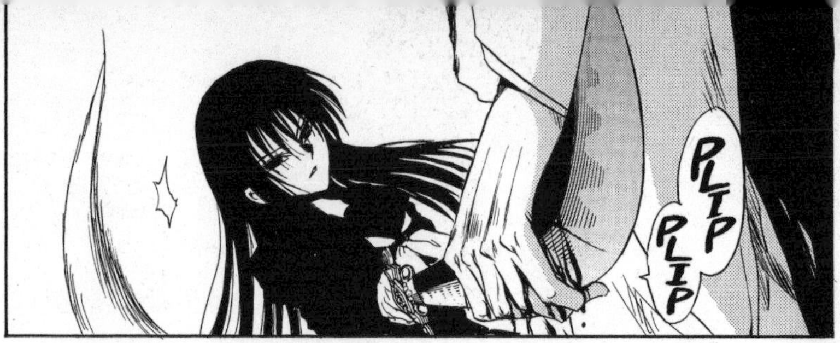
PLIP PLIP PLIP

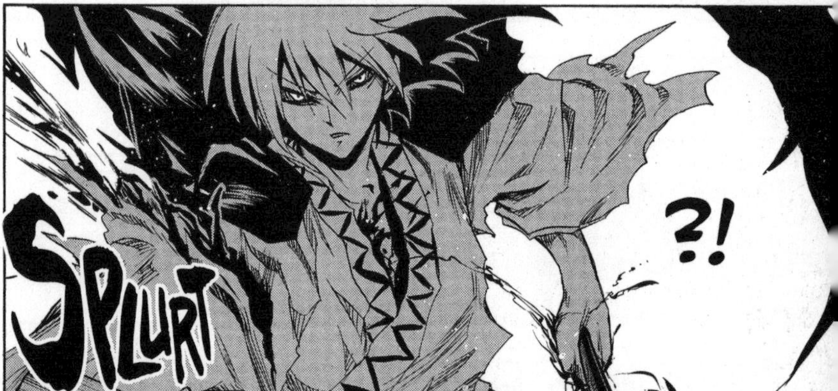
?!
SPLURT

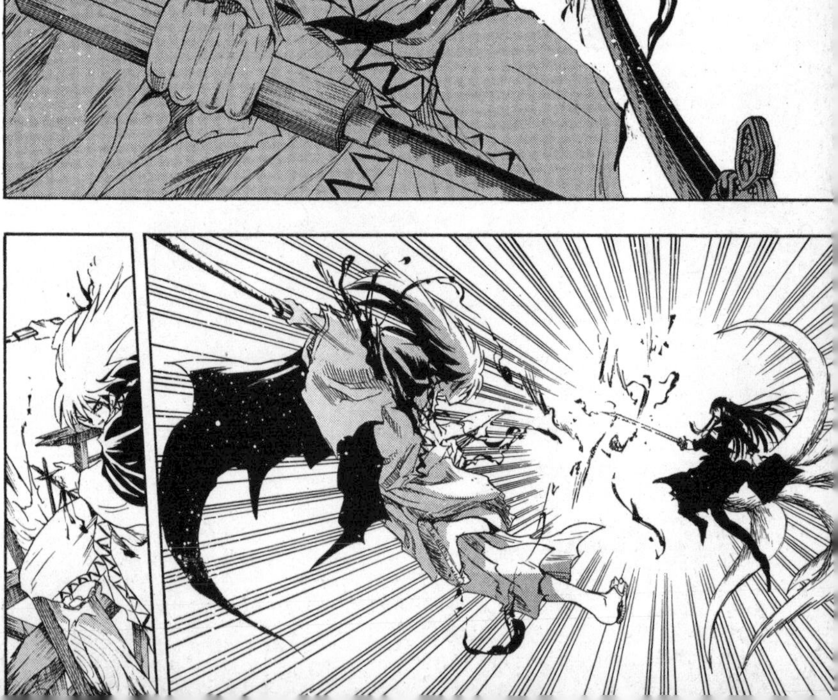

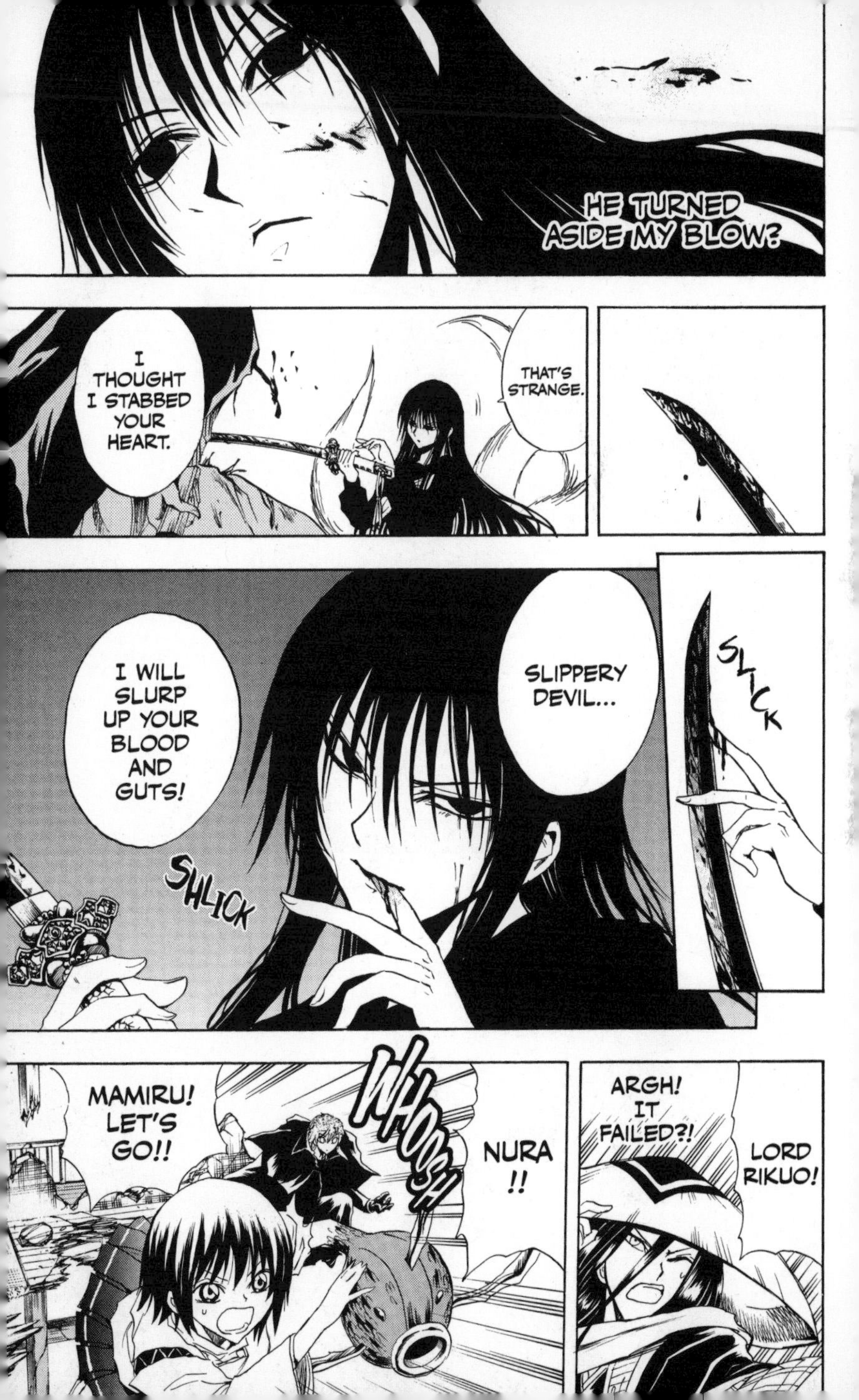
HE TURNED ASIDE MY BLOW?
THAT'S STRANGE.
I THOUGHT I STABBED YOUR HEART.
SLICK
SLIPPERY DEVIL...
I WILL SLURP UP YOUR BLOOD AND GUTS!
SHLICK
LORD RIKUO!
ARGH! IT FAILED?!
NURA!!
WHOOSH
MAMIRU! LET'S GO!!

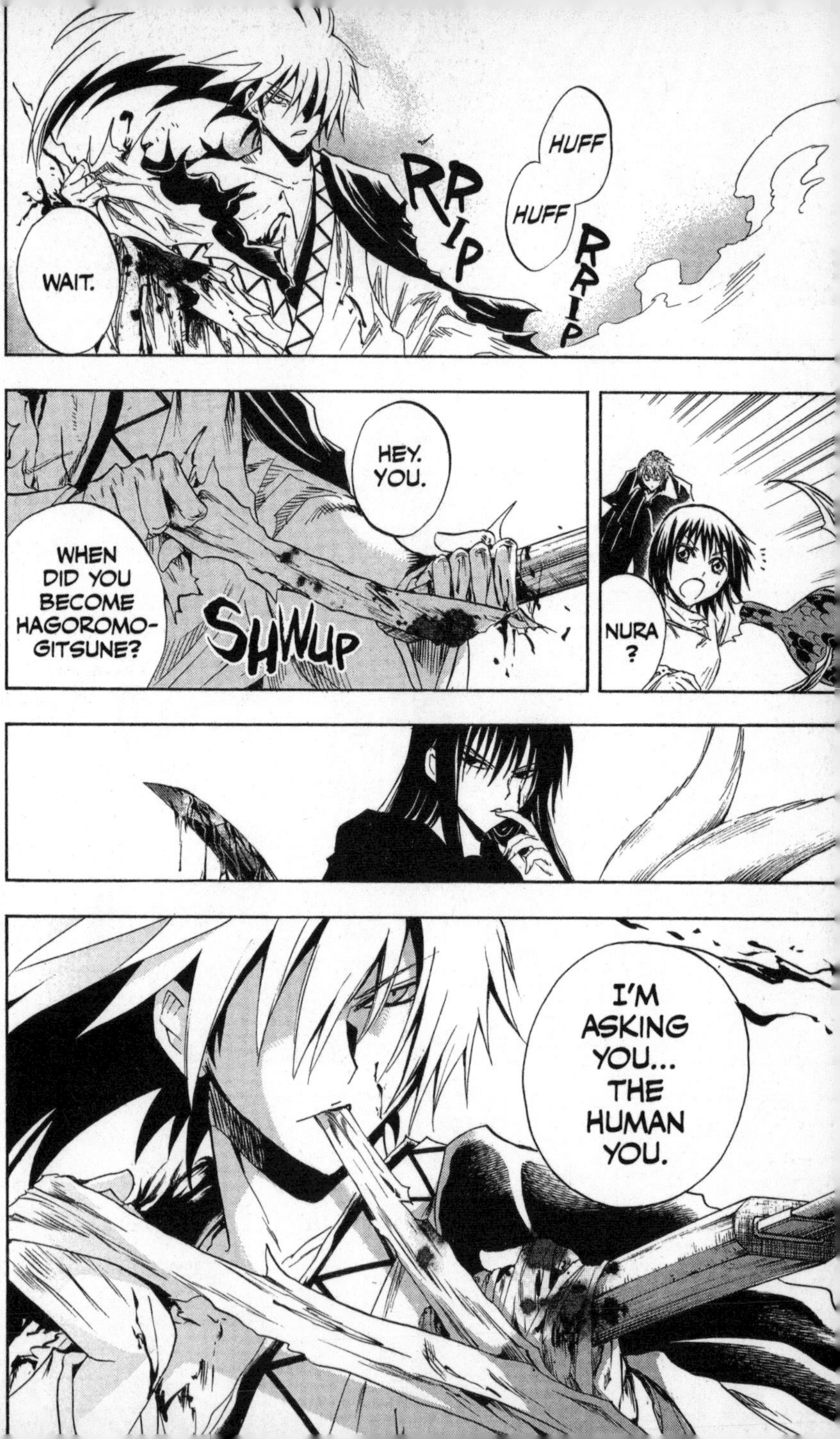
HUFF
HUFF
RRIP
RRIP
WAIT.
NURA?
HEY. YOU.
WHEN DID YOU BECOME HAGOROMO-GITSUNE?
SHWUP
I'M ASKING YOU... THE HUMAN YOU.

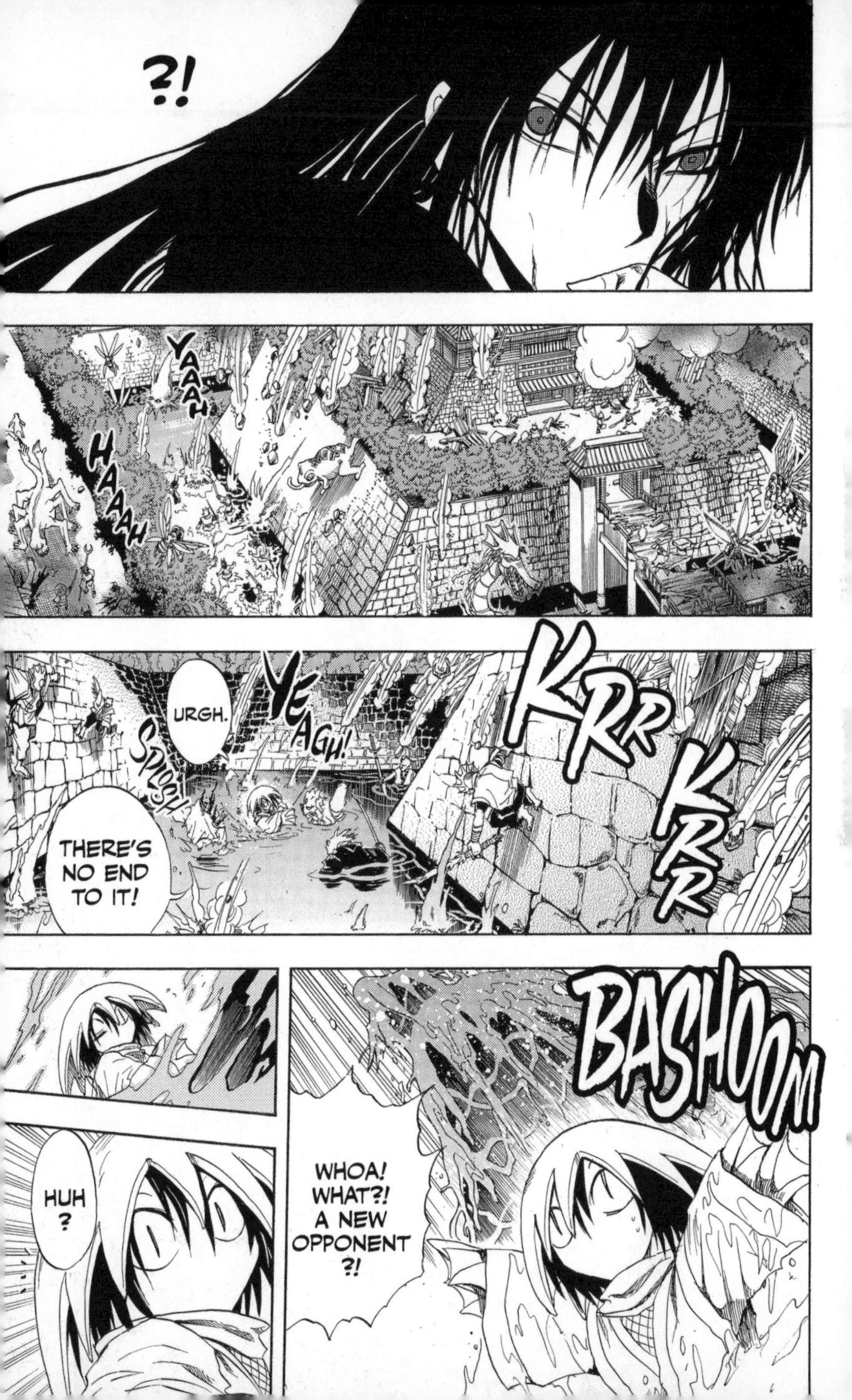
?!
YAAAH
HAAAAH
KRR
KRR
YEAGH!
URGH.
SPLOSH
THERE'S NO END TO IT!
BASHOOM
WHOA! WHAT?! A NEW OPPONENT ?!
HUH ?

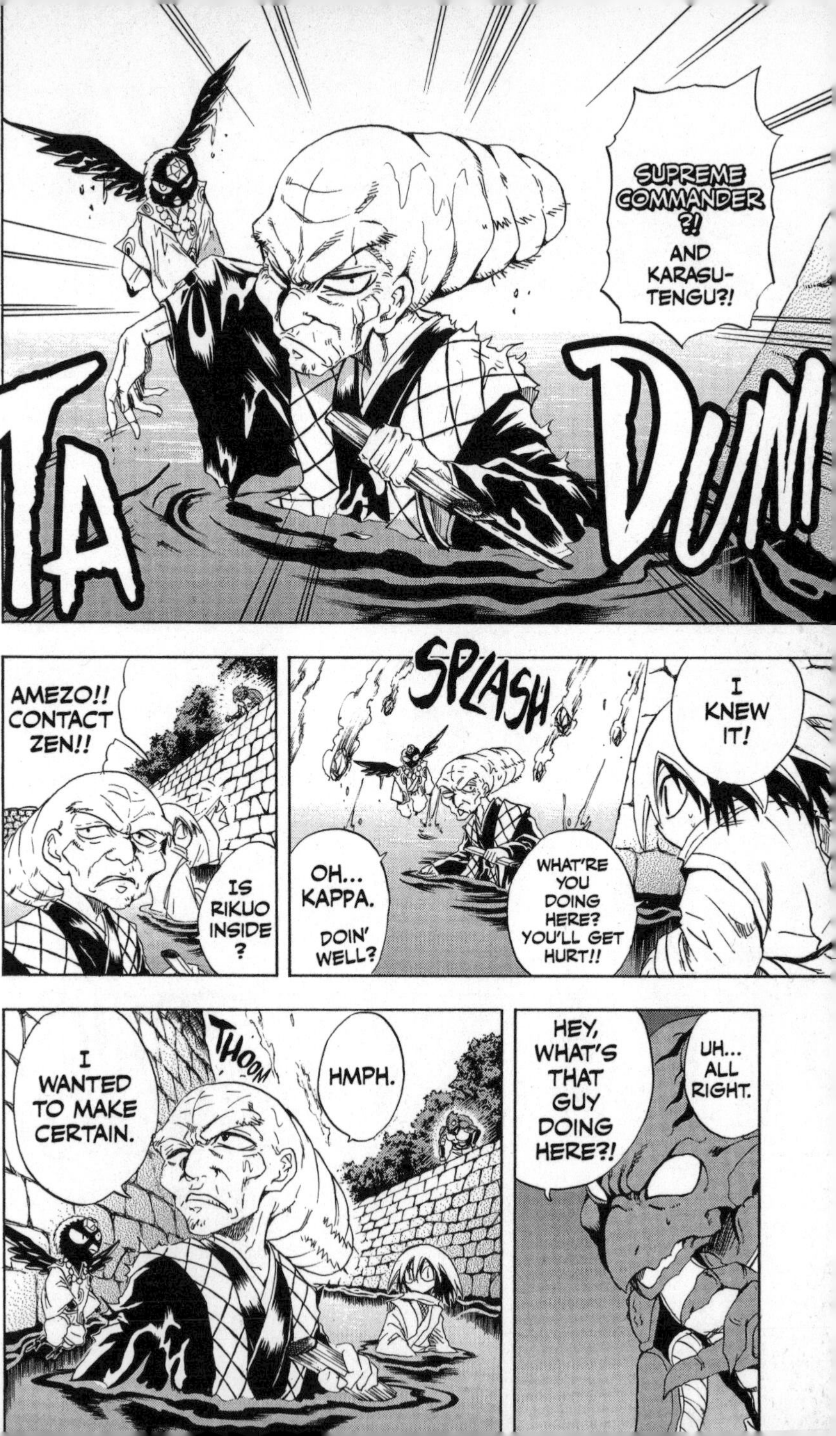
SUPREME COMMANDER?! AND KARASU-TENGU?!
TA
DUM
SPLASH
I KNEW IT!
WHAT'RE YOU DOING HERE? YOU'LL GET HURT!!
OH... KAPPA.
DOIN' WELL?
AMEZO!! CONTACT ZEN!!
IS RIKUO INSIDE?
UH... ALL RIGHT.
HEY, WHAT'S THAT GUY DOING HERE?!
HMPH.
THOOM
I WANTED TO MAKE CERTAIN.

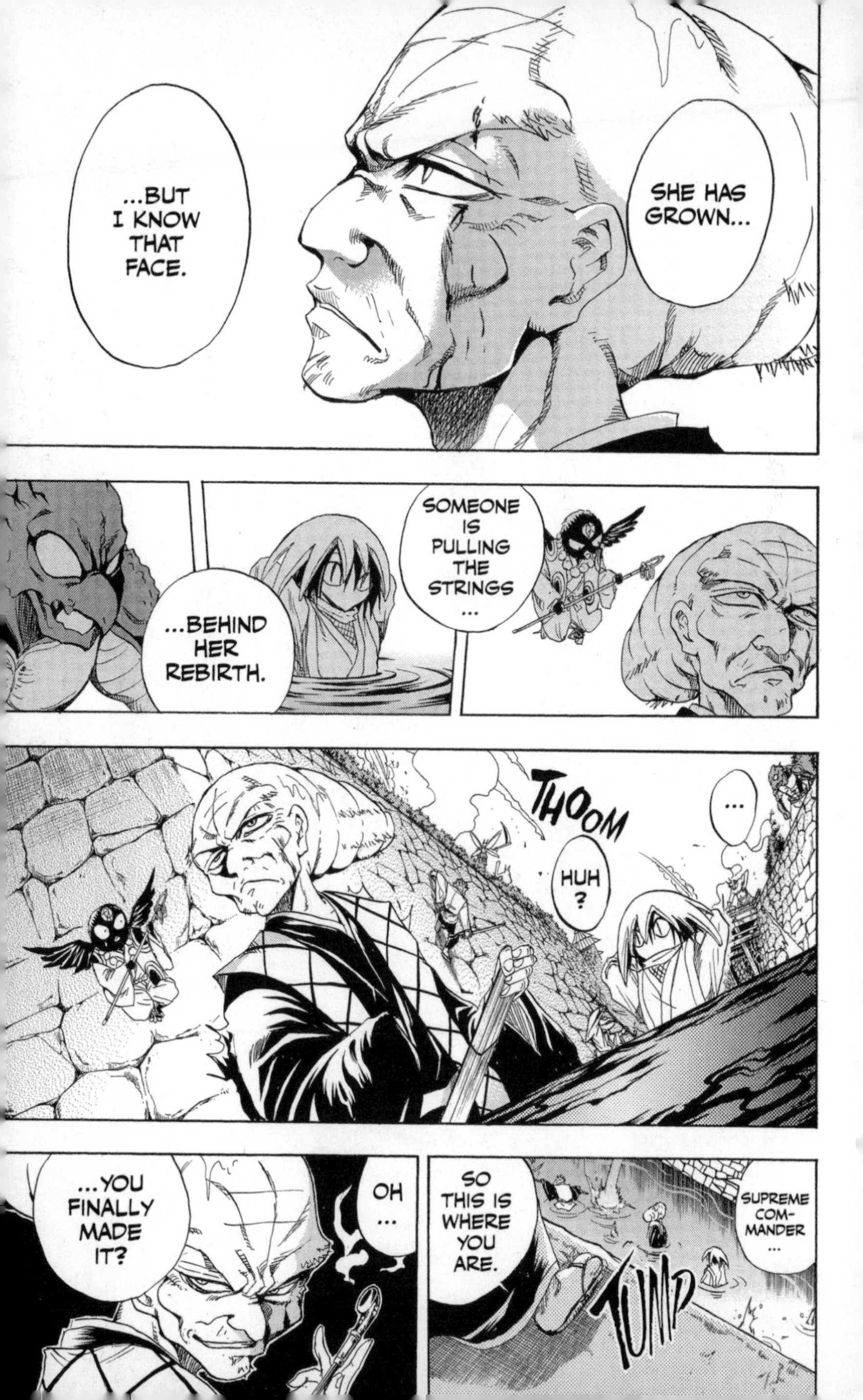
SHE HAS GROWN...
...BUT I KNOW THAT FACE.
SOMEONE IS PULLING THE STRINGS ...
...BEHIND HER REBIRTH.
THOOM
...
HUH ?
SUPREME COMMANDER ...
SO THIS IS WHERE YOU ARE.
TUMP
OH ...
...YOU FINALLY MADE IT?

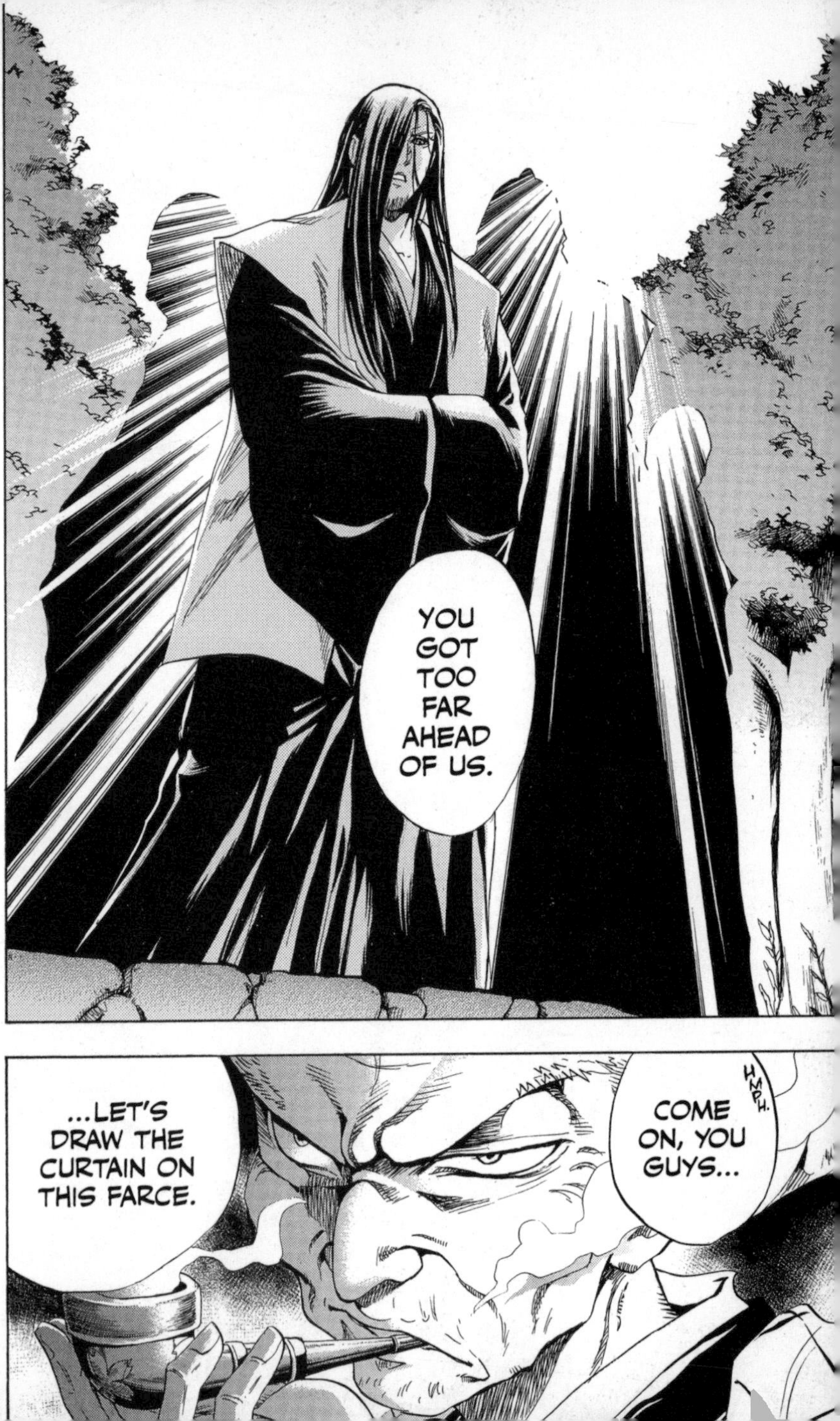
YOU GOT TOO FAR AHEAD OF US.
HMPH.
COME ON, YOU GUYS...
...LET'S DRAW THE CURTAIN ON THIS FARCE.

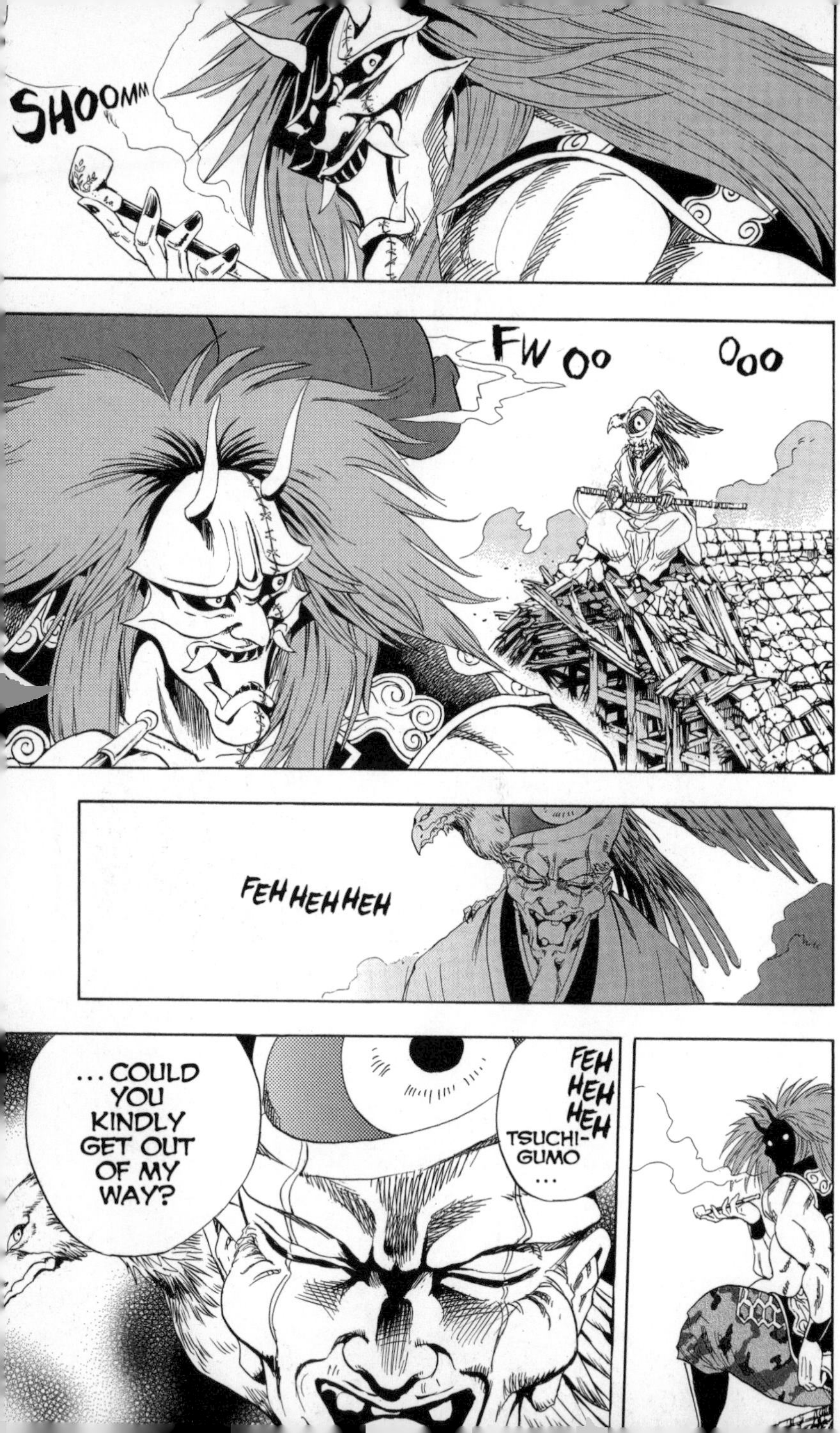
SHOOMM
FW OO OOO
FEH HEH HEH
FEH HEH HEH
TSUCHI-GUMO ...
... COULD YOU KINDLY GET OUT OF MY WAY?

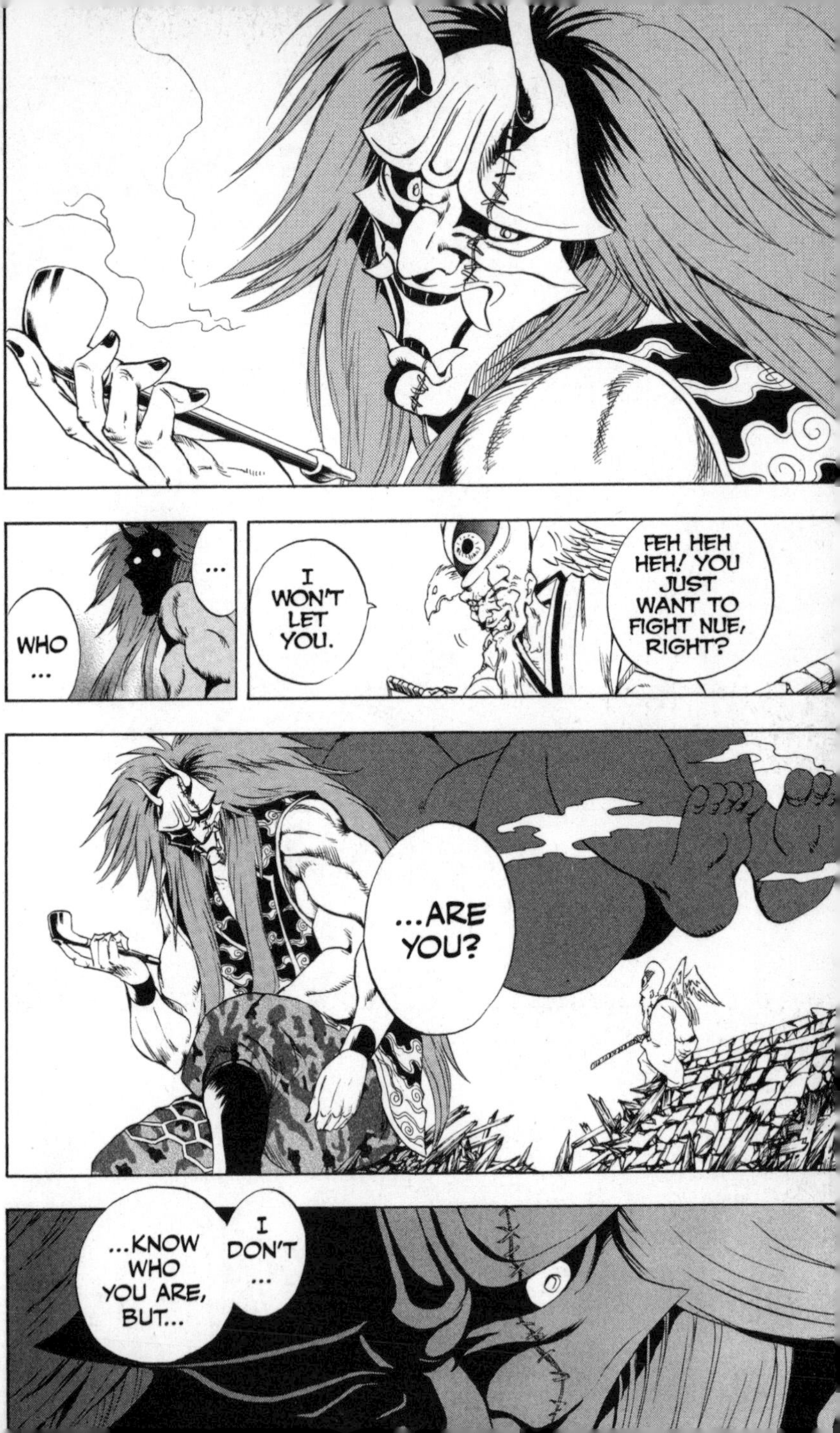
FEH HEH HEH! YOU JUST WANT TO FIGHT NUE, RIGHT?
I WON'T LET YOU.
...
WHO ...
...ARE YOU?
I DON'T ...
...KNOW WHO YOU ARE, BUT...

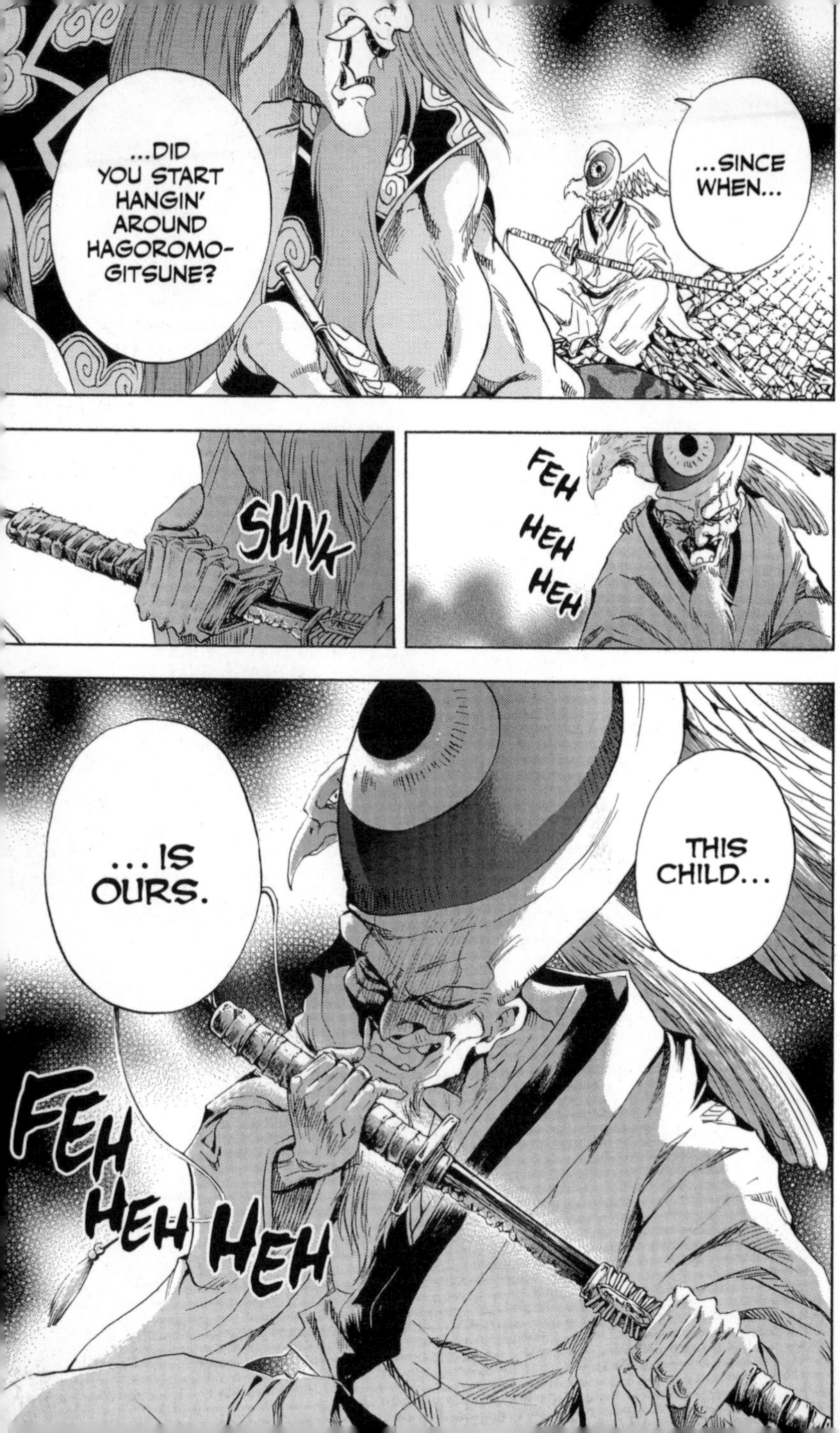
...SINCE WHEN...
...DID YOU START HANGIN' AROUND HAGOROMO-GITSUNE?
FEH HEH HEH
SHNK
THIS CHILD...
...IS OURS.
FEH HEH HEH

KIYOTSUGU'S YOKAI BRAIN #14

Q: THIS IS A QUESTION FOR THE NURA CLAN. IS THERE A YOKAI WITH THE CONFIDENCE TO WATCH A FUNNY TV SHOW WITHOUT BURSTING OUT LAUGHING? *–CHIYO TENGA, MIYAGI PREFECTURE*

KUBINASHI: WHAT KIND OF QUESTION IS THIS?

KEJORO: I KNOW. SHE MUST HAVE THOUGHT OF IT WHILE WATCHING A REALLY FUNNY YEAR-END VARIETY SHOW. I CAN'T DO IT! I PRACTICALLY BUST A GUT WATCHING THOSE!

KUBINASHI: AT PARTIES, THE NURA CLAN MEMBERS USUALLY COLLAPSE WITH LAUGHTER AND TIP BACK SOME SAKE. OH, WAIT... I KNOW WHO!

KEJORO: I THOUGHT OF HIM, TOO. LET'S SAY IT TOGETHER...

KUBINASHI AND KEJORO: GYUKI!!

KEJORO: NO ONE KNOWS WHAT MAKES HIM LAUGH...

Q: THIS IS FOR ZEN. WOULD YOU PRESCRIBE SOME MEDICINE FOR A SICK FRIEND OF MINE? COME VISIT WHEN YOU'RE FEELING GOOD! *–GAREI, KANAGAWA PREFECTURE*

ZEN: YEAH, SOMETIMES I DON'T FEEL SO WELL. HOPEFULLY SOMEDAY WE'LL ALL BE FEELING GOOD AT THE SAME TIME.

Q: DOES ZEN HAVE TUBER-CULOSIS? THAT'S MY GUESS ANYWAY. *–SARAMI, FUKUOKA PREFECTURE*

ZEN: NO, I'M DOWN FROM MY OWN POISON...

Q: DOES AOTABO EAT AS MUCH EACH DAY AS EVERYONE ELSE DOES? *–GIRI, TOYAMA PREFECTURE*

TSURARA: NO, NOT AT ALL!! HE EATS TOO MUCH!!

KEJORO: EACH YOKAI HAS HIS OR HER OWN APPETITE. SOME ONLY EAT LIKE A SINGLE BEAN. PLANNING THE MENU IS A REAL PAIN!

Q: MY BIRTHDAY IS THE SAME AS RIKUO'S. *–HII-KUN, FUKU SHIMA PREFECTURE*

RIKUO: OH...IS THAT SO? COOL! BUT...IS THAT A QUESTION?!

Q: WHEN DO THE YOKAI OF THE NURA CLAN SLEEP? *–USAGI, TOKUSHIMA PREFECTURE*

RIKUO: I WONDER ABOUT THAT MYSELF. YOKAI WHO ARE BUSY DURING THE DAY—LIKE TSURARA AND ME—SLEEP AT NIGHT.

TSURARA: SOME YOKAI CAN'T DO ANYTHING DURING THE DAY, SO THEY MUST TAKE NAPS THEN!

Q: A QUESTION FOR TSURARA!! RIGHT NOW YOU WEAR YOUR HAIR DOWN ALL SMOOTH AND SILKY, BUT IS THERE ANOTHER HAIRSTYLE YOU WOULD LIKE TO TRY? *–MAJIKKU, IWATE PREFECTURE*

TSURARA: TEE-HEE! ACTUALLY, WHEN I FIRST WENT TO SCHOOL, I TRIED MAKING IT WAVY, BUT I DON'T DO THAT ANYMORE. BUT A PONY TAIL MIGHT BE NICE IN THE SUMMER!

Q: RIKUO'S GRANDFATHER AND FATHER BOTH TIE THEIR HAIR, SO WHY DOESN'T RIKUO? *–OIM, NIIGATA PREFECTURE*

TSURARA: LET'S TIE IT RIGHT NOW, LORD RIKUO. COME HERE!

RIKUO: HEY, CUT THAT OUT!!

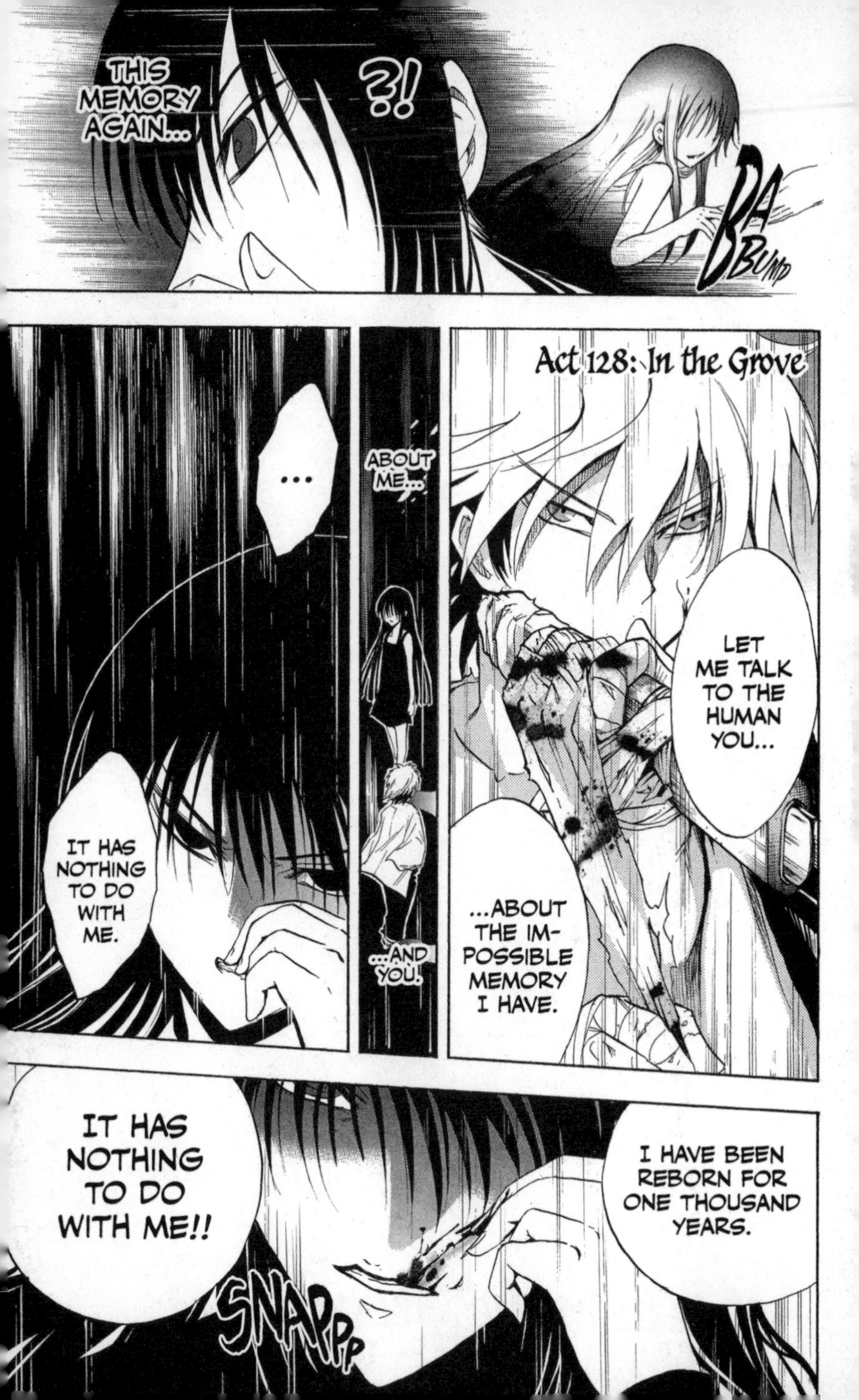
BA-BUMP
?!
THIS MEMORY AGAIN...
Act 128: In the Grove
LET ME TALK TO THE HUMAN YOU...
...ABOUT THE IM-POSSIBLE MEMORY I HAVE.
ABOUT ME...
...AND YOU.
...
IT HAS NOTHING TO DO WITH ME.
I HAVE BEEN REBORN FOR ONE THOUSAND YEARS.
IT HAS NOTHING TO DO WITH ME!!
SNAPPP

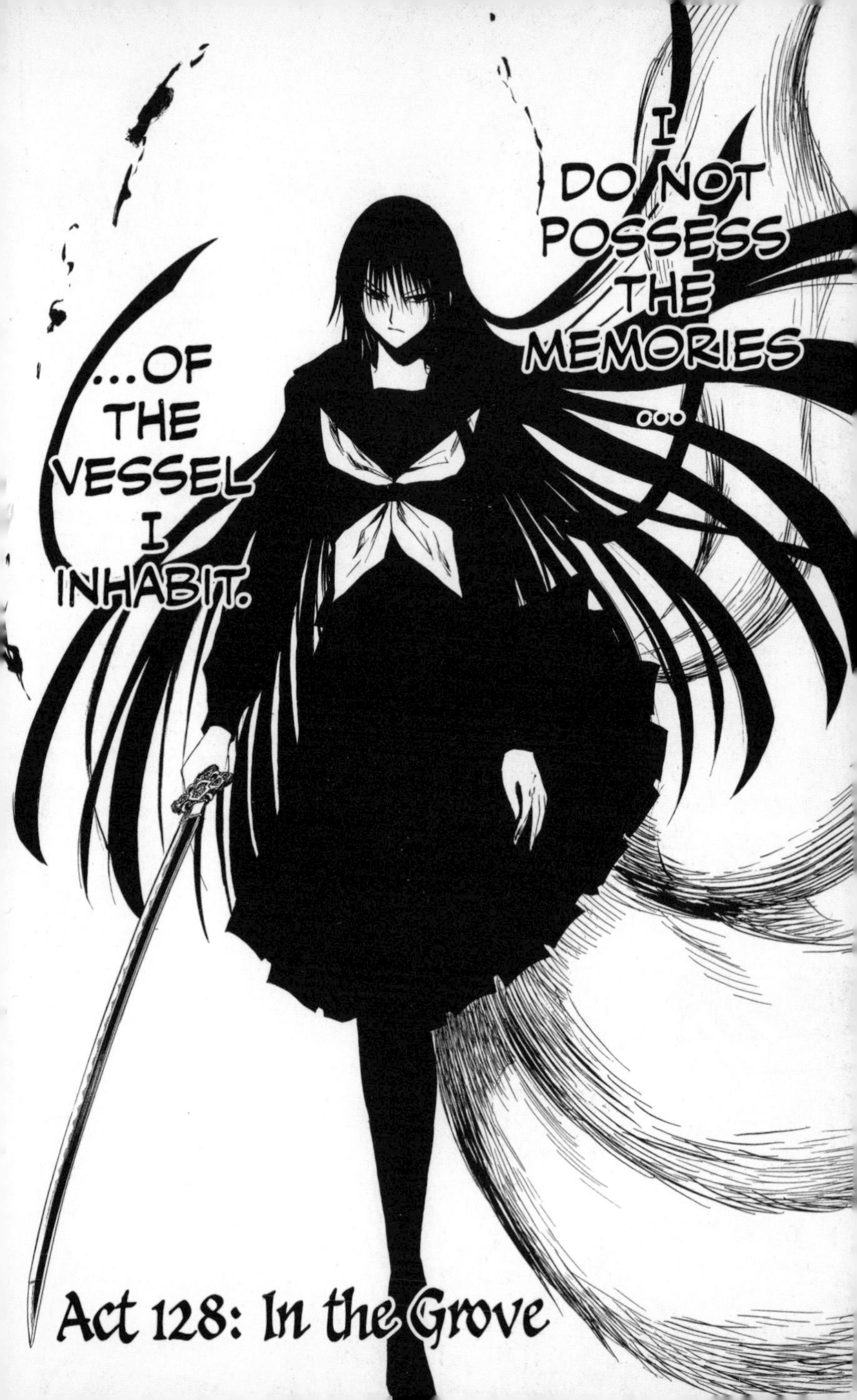
I DO NOT POSSESS THE MEMORIES...
...OF THE VESSEL I INHABIT.

Act 128: In the Grove

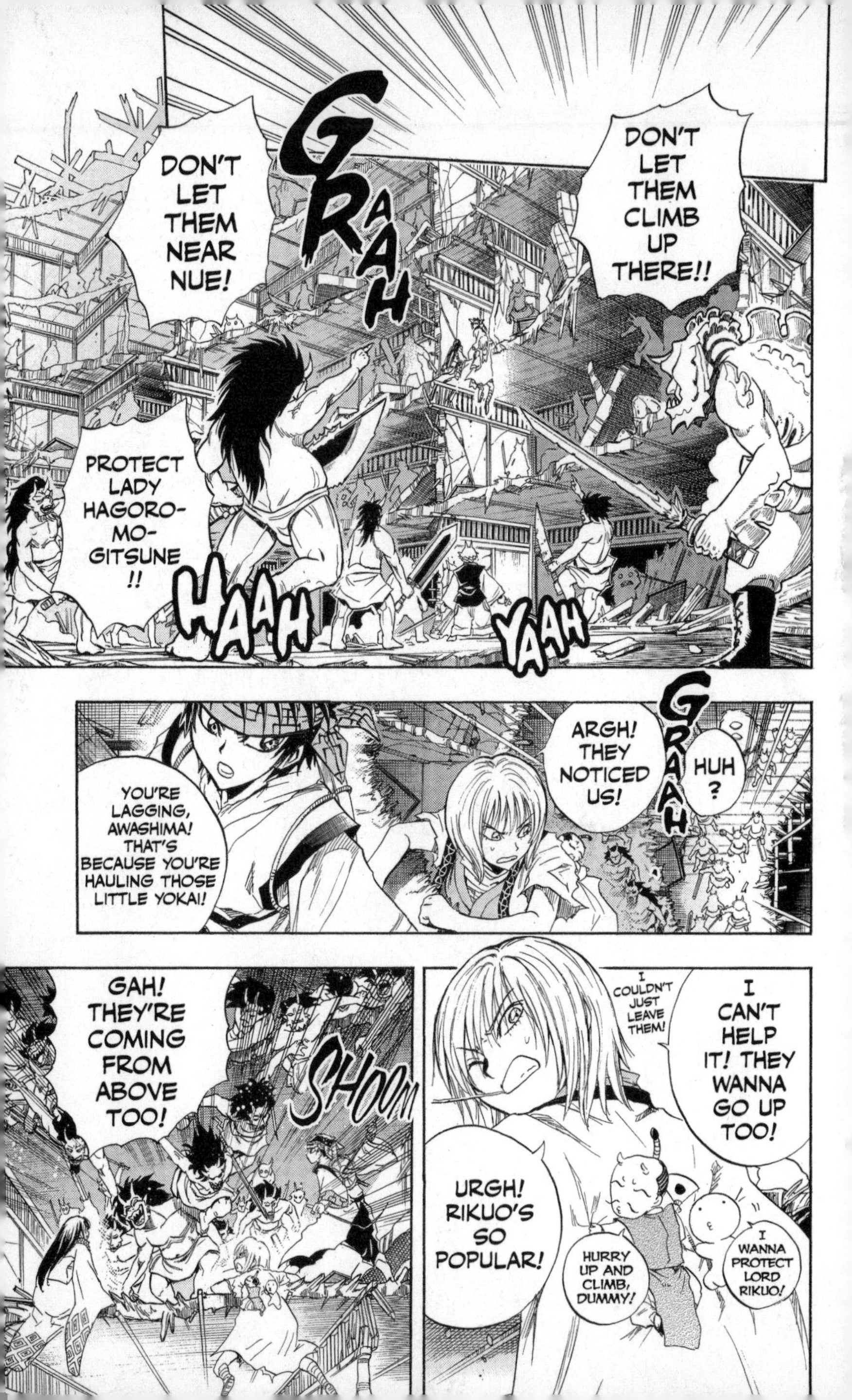
DON'T LET THEM CLIMB UP THERE!!
GRAAH
DON'T LET THEM NEAR NUE!
PROTECT LADY HAGOROMO-GITSUNE!!
YAAH
HAAH
HUH?
GRAAH
ARGH! THEY NOTICED US!
YOU'RE LAGGING, AWASHIMA! THAT'S BECAUSE YOU'RE HAULING THOSE LITTLE YOKAI!
I CAN'T HELP IT! THEY WANNA GO UP TOO!
I COULDN'T JUST LEAVE THEM!
I WANNA PROTECT LORD RIKUO!
HURRY UP AND CLIMB, DUMMY!
URGH! RIKUO'S SO POPULAR!
SHOOM
GAH! THEY'RE COMING FROM ABOVE TOO!

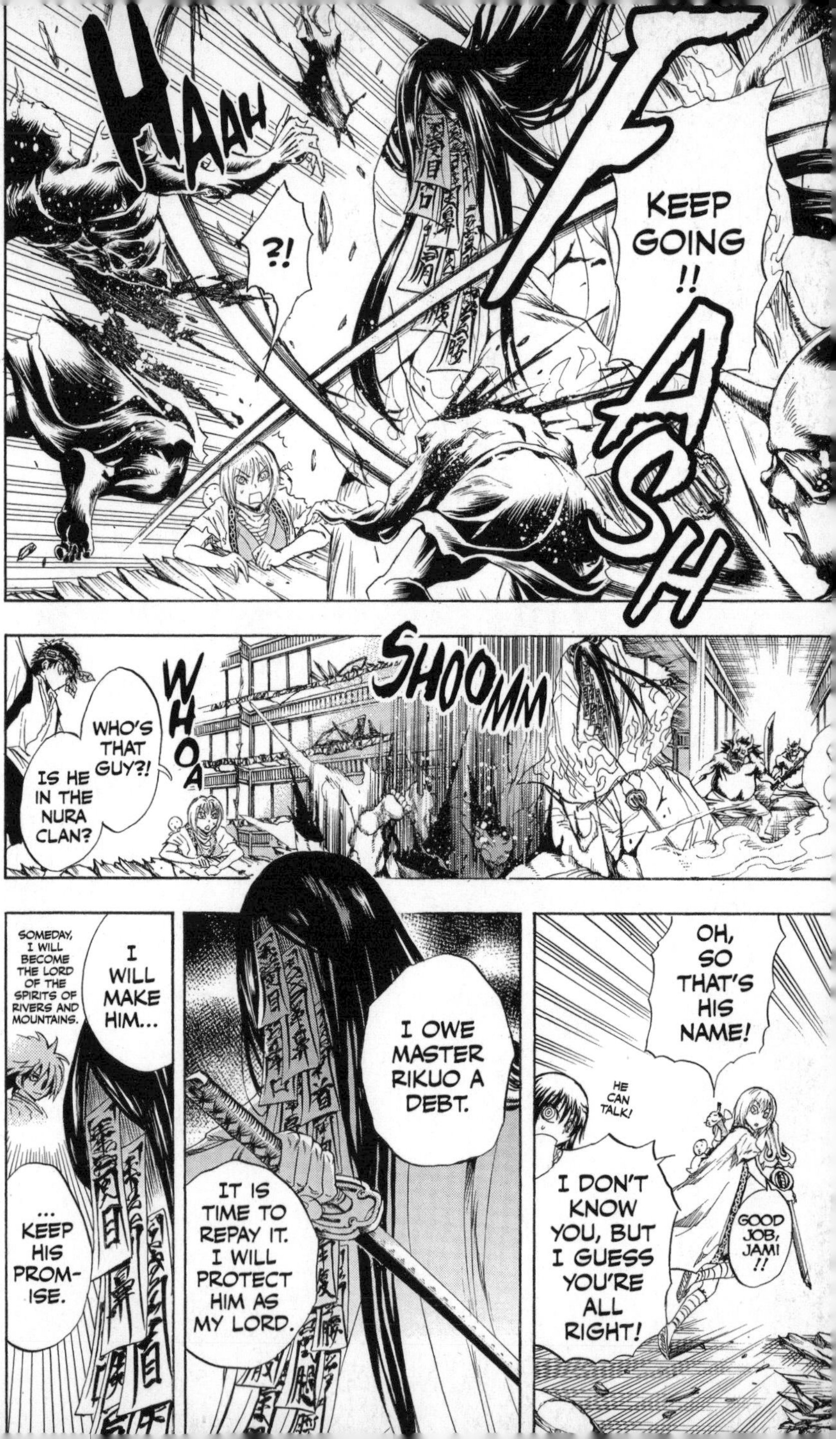
KEEP GOING!!
ASH
?!
HAAH
SHOOMM
WHOA
WHO'S THAT GUY?!
IS HE IN THE NURA CLAN?
OH, SO THAT'S HIS NAME!
HE CAN TALK!
GOOD JOB, JAMI!!
I DON'T KNOW YOU, BUT I GUESS YOU'RE ALL RIGHT!
I OWE MASTER RIKUO A DEBT.
IT IS TIME TO REPAY IT. I WILL PROTECT HIM AS MY LORD.
I WILL MAKE HIM...
SOMEDAY, I WILL BECOME THE LORD OF THE SPIRITS OF RIVERS AND MOUNTAINS.
...KEEP HIS PROMISE.

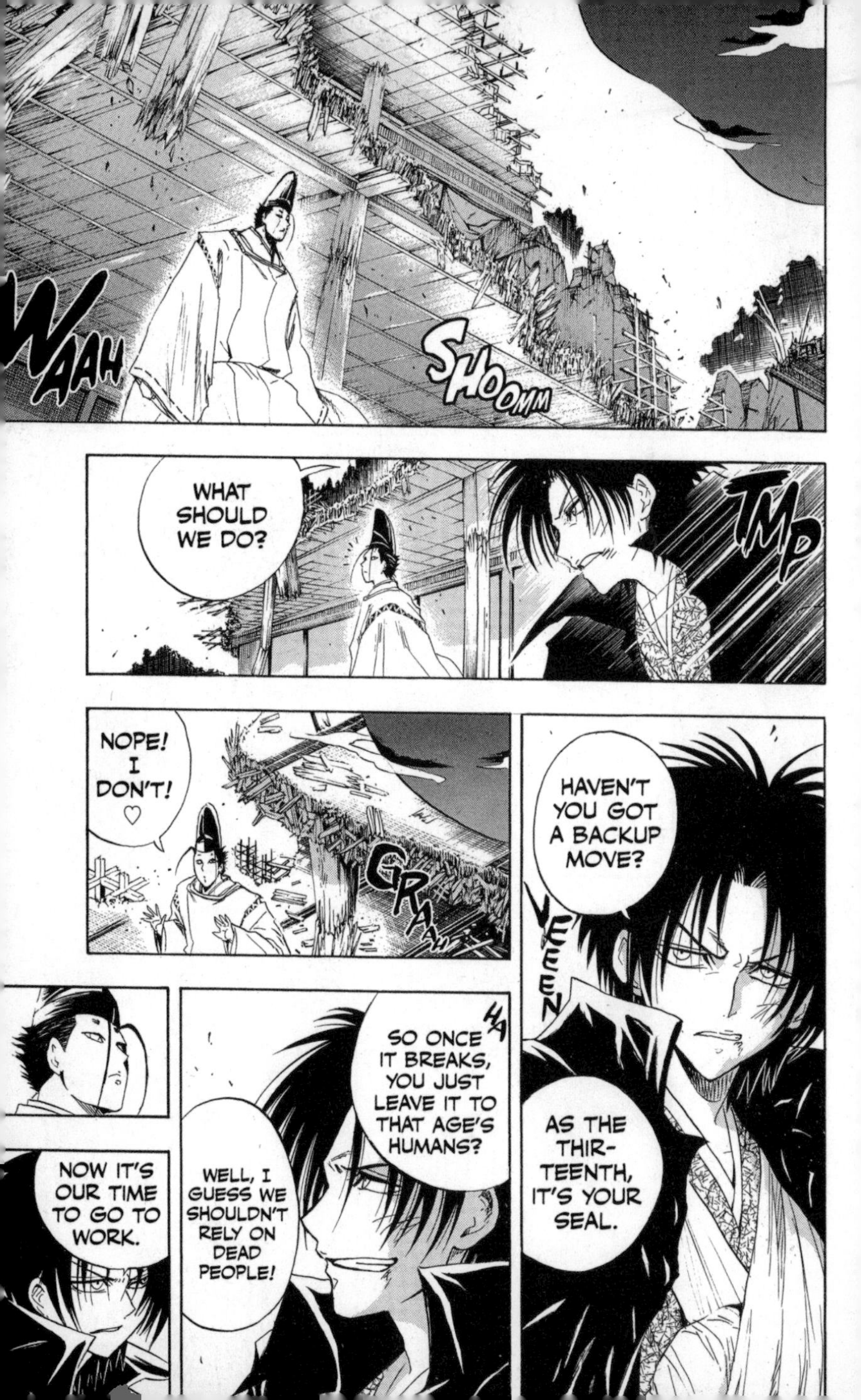
SHOOMM
WAAH
TMP
WHAT SHOULD WE DO?
HAVEN'T YOU GOT A BACKUP MOVE?
VEEEEN
AS THE THIR-TEENTH, IT'S YOUR SEAL.
NOPE! I DON'T! ♡
GRAAH
HA
SO ONCE IT BREAKS, YOU JUST LEAVE IT TO THAT AGE'S HUMANS?
WELL, I GUESS WE SHOULDN'T RELY ON DEAD PEOPLE!
NOW IT'S OUR TIME TO GO TO WORK.

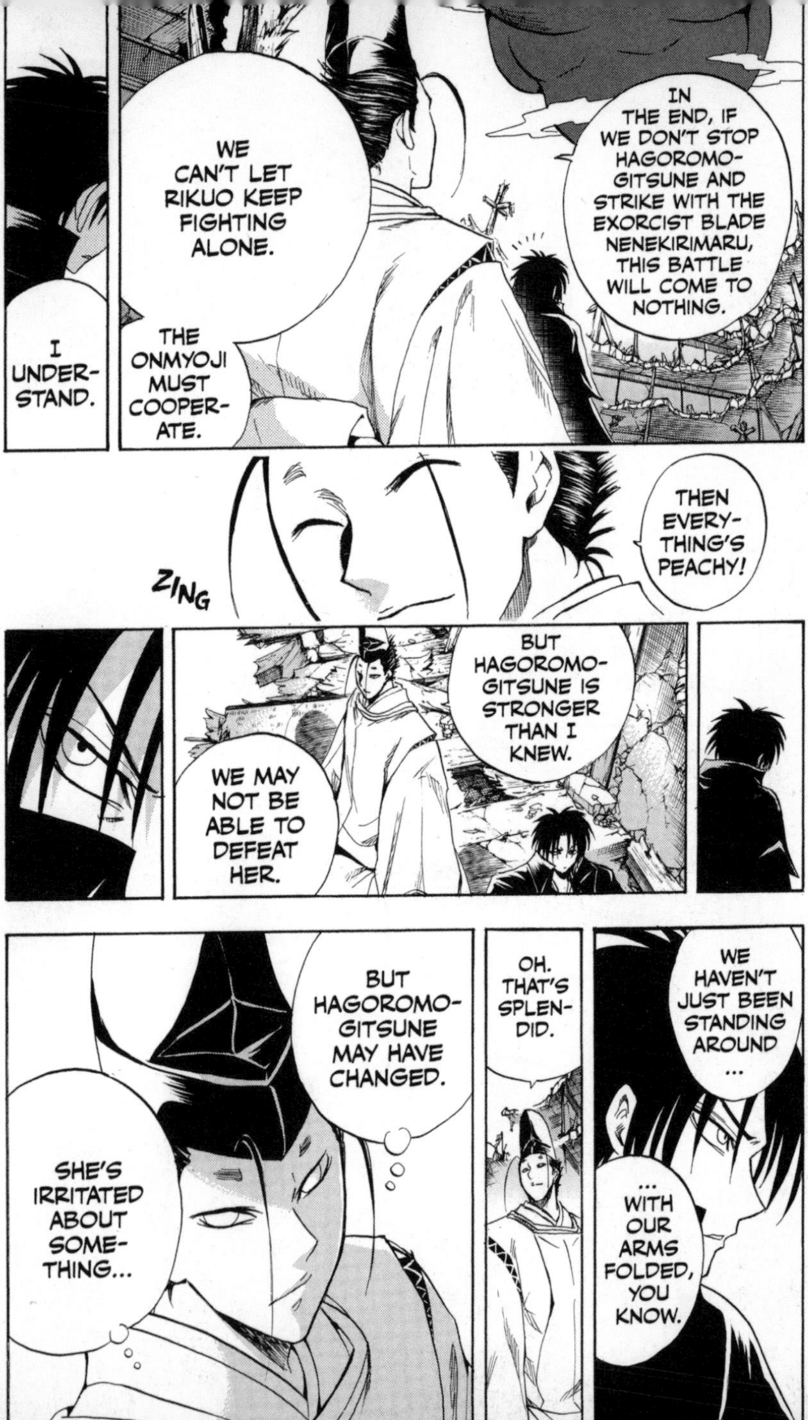
IN THE END, IF WE DON'T STOP HAGOROMO-GITSUNE AND STRIKE WITH THE EXORCIST BLADE NENEKIRIMARU, THIS BATTLE WILL COME TO NOTHING.
WE CAN'T LET RIKUO KEEP FIGHTING ALONE.
THE ONMYOJI MUST COOPER-ATE.
I UNDER-STAND.
THEN EVERY-THING'S PEACHY!
ZING
BUT HAGOROMO-GITSUNE IS STRONGER THAN I KNEW.
WE MAY NOT BE ABLE TO DEFEAT HER.
WE HAVEN'T JUST BEEN STANDING AROUND ...
... WITH OUR ARMS FOLDED, YOU KNOW.
OH. THAT'S SPLEN-DID.
BUT HAGOROMO-GITSUNE MAY HAVE CHANGED.
SHE'S IRRITATED ABOUT SOME-THING...

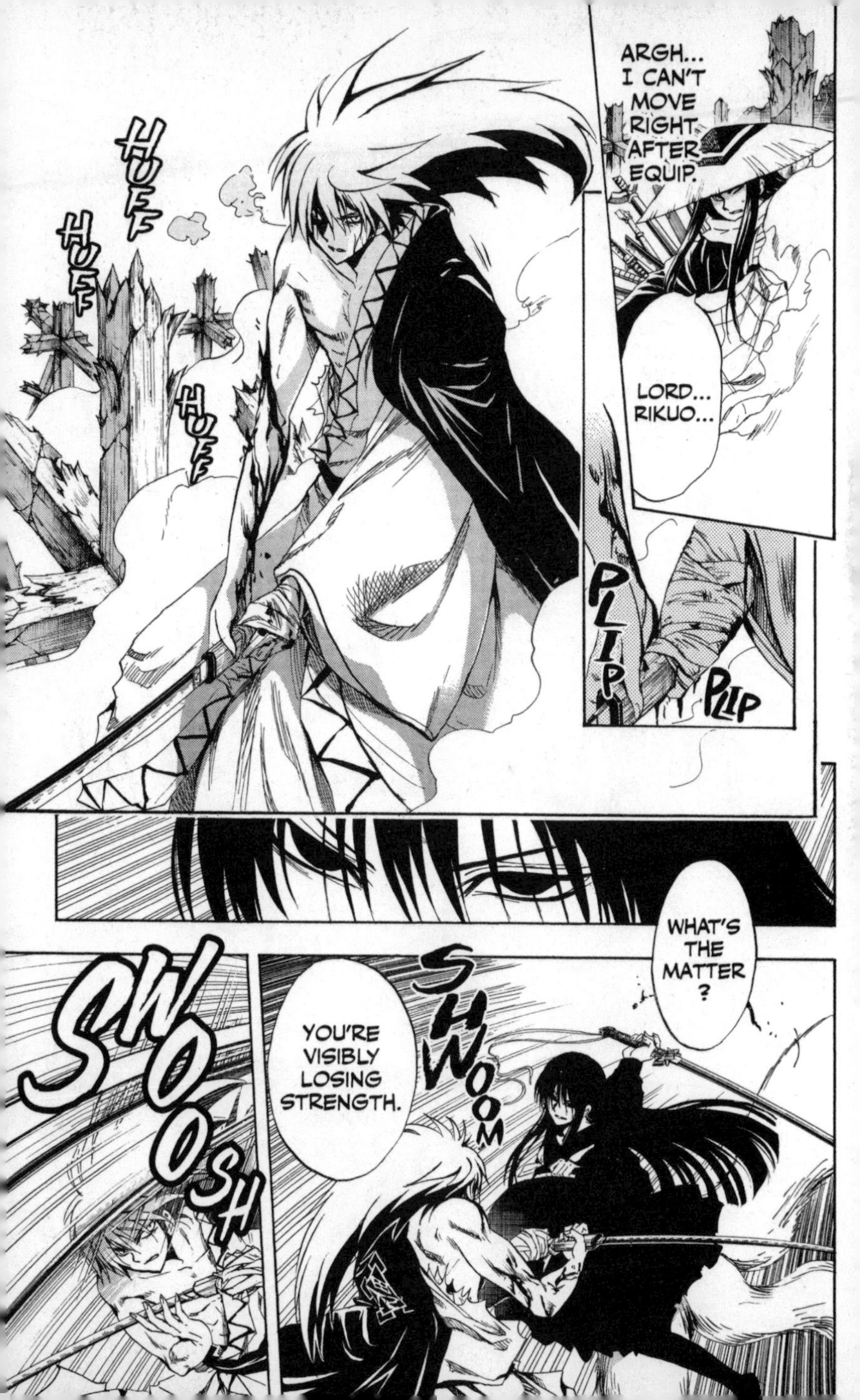
ARGH... I CAN'T MOVE RIGHT AFTER EQUIP.
LORD... RIKUO...
PLIP
PLIP
HUFF
HUFF
HUFF
WHAT'S THE MATTER?
SHWOOM
YOU'RE VISIBLY LOSING STRENGTH.
SWOOSH

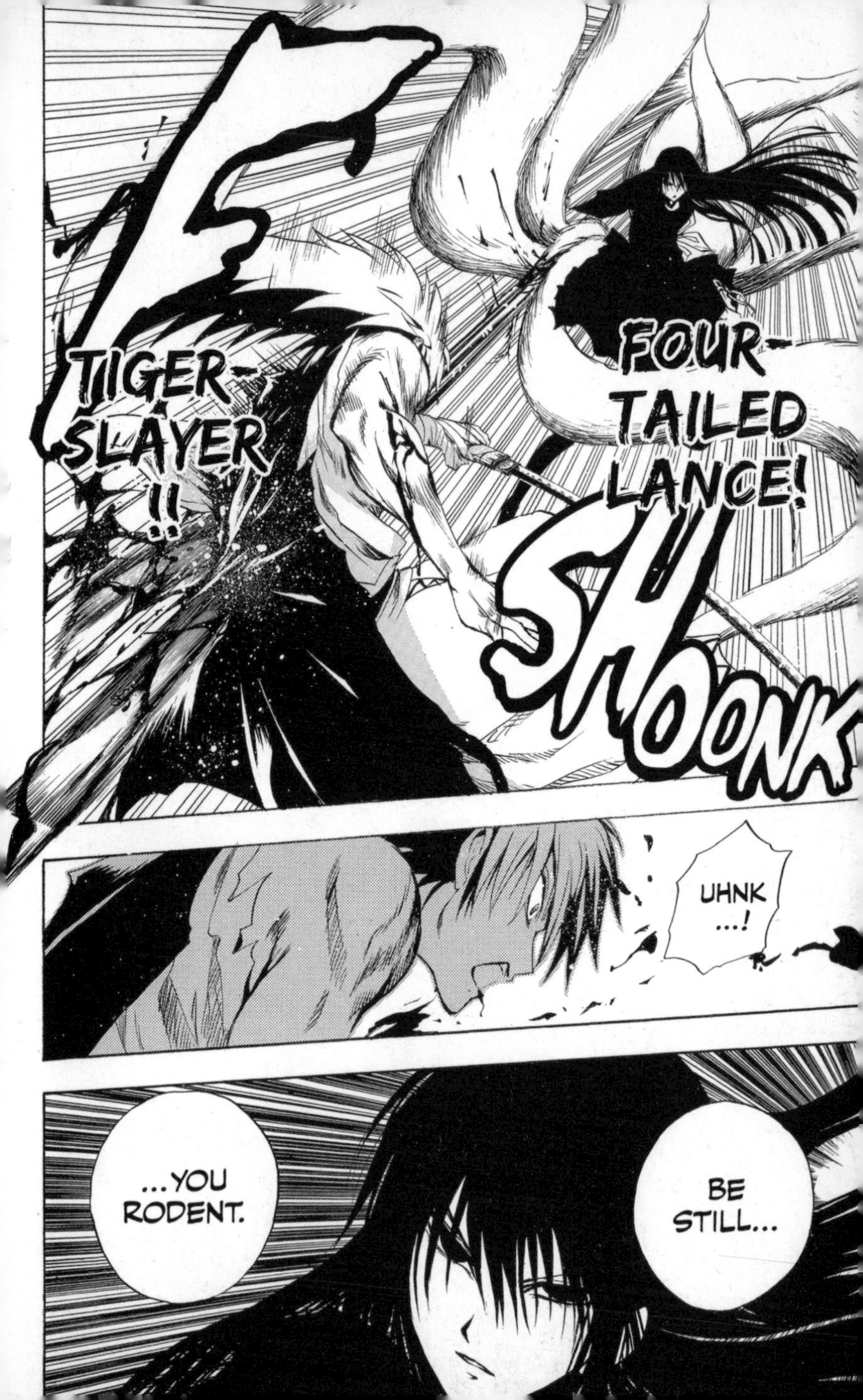
FOUR-TAILED LANCE!
TIGER-SLAYER!!
SHOONK
UHNK ...!
BE STILL...
...YOU RODENT.

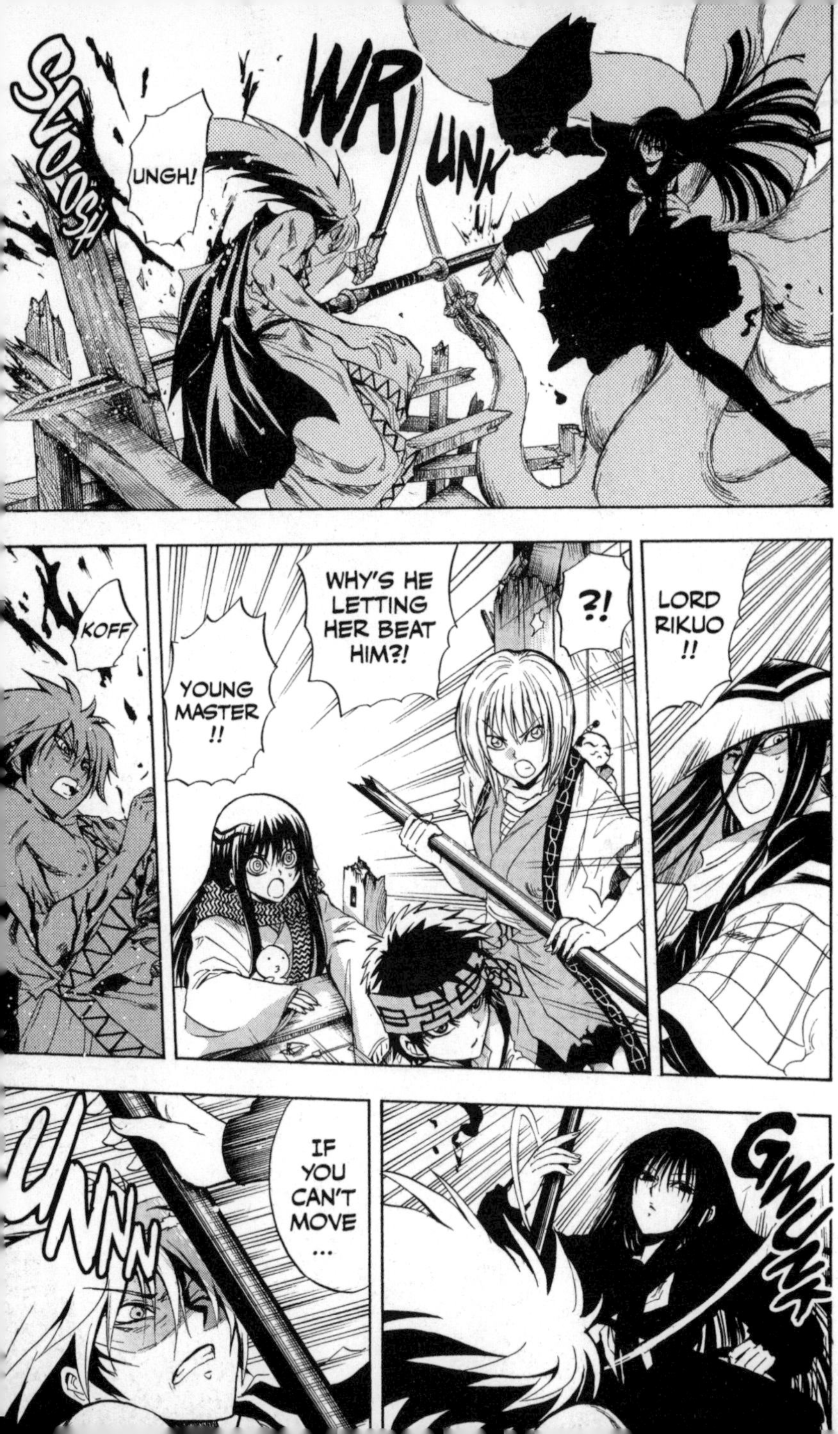
WRUNK
UNGH!
SWOOSH
LORD RIKUO!!
?!
WHY'S HE LETTING HER BEAT HIM?!
YOUNG MASTER!!
KOFF
GWUNK
IF YOU CAN'T MOVE...

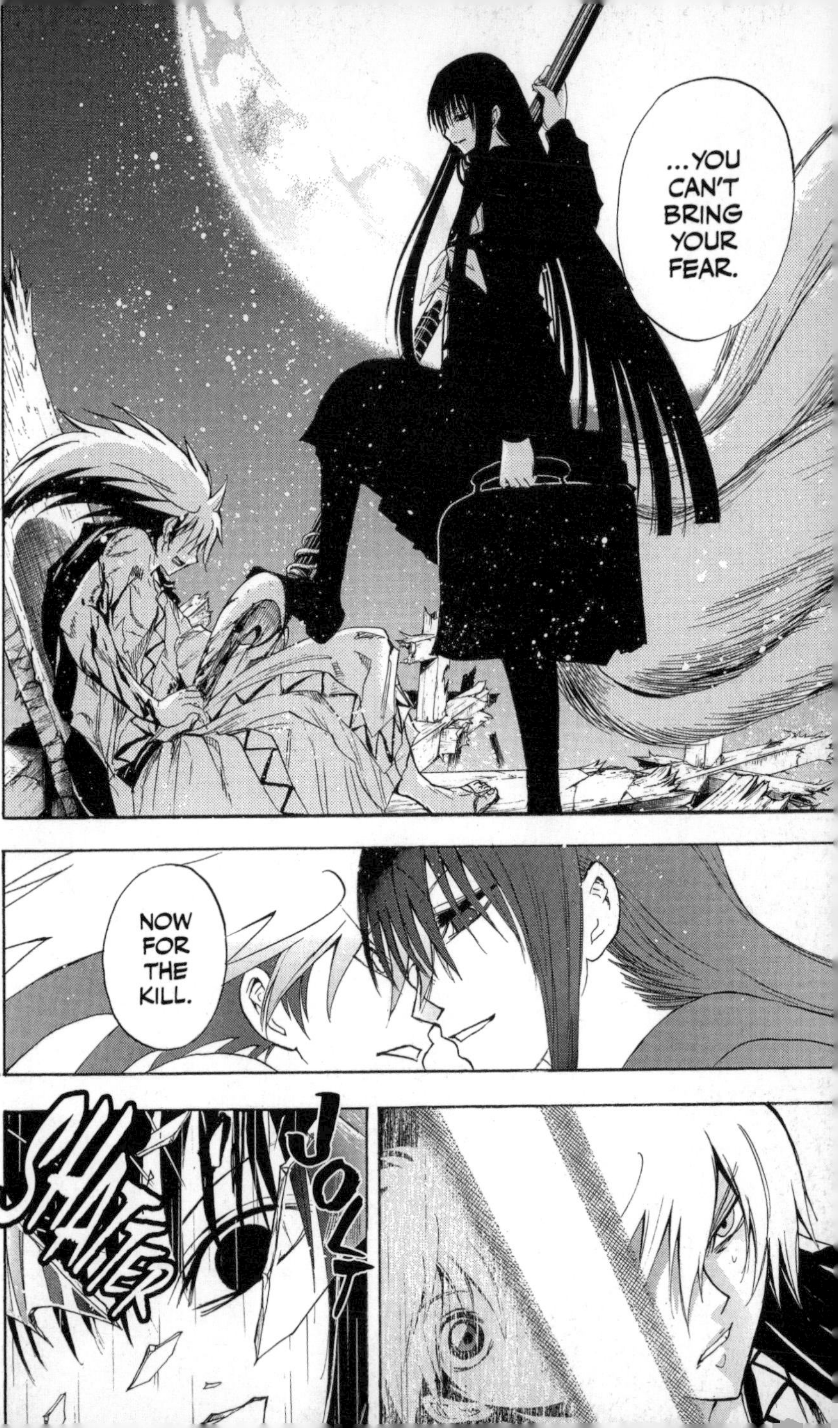
...YOU CAN'T BRING YOUR FEAR.
NOW FOR THE KILL.
JOLT
SHATTER

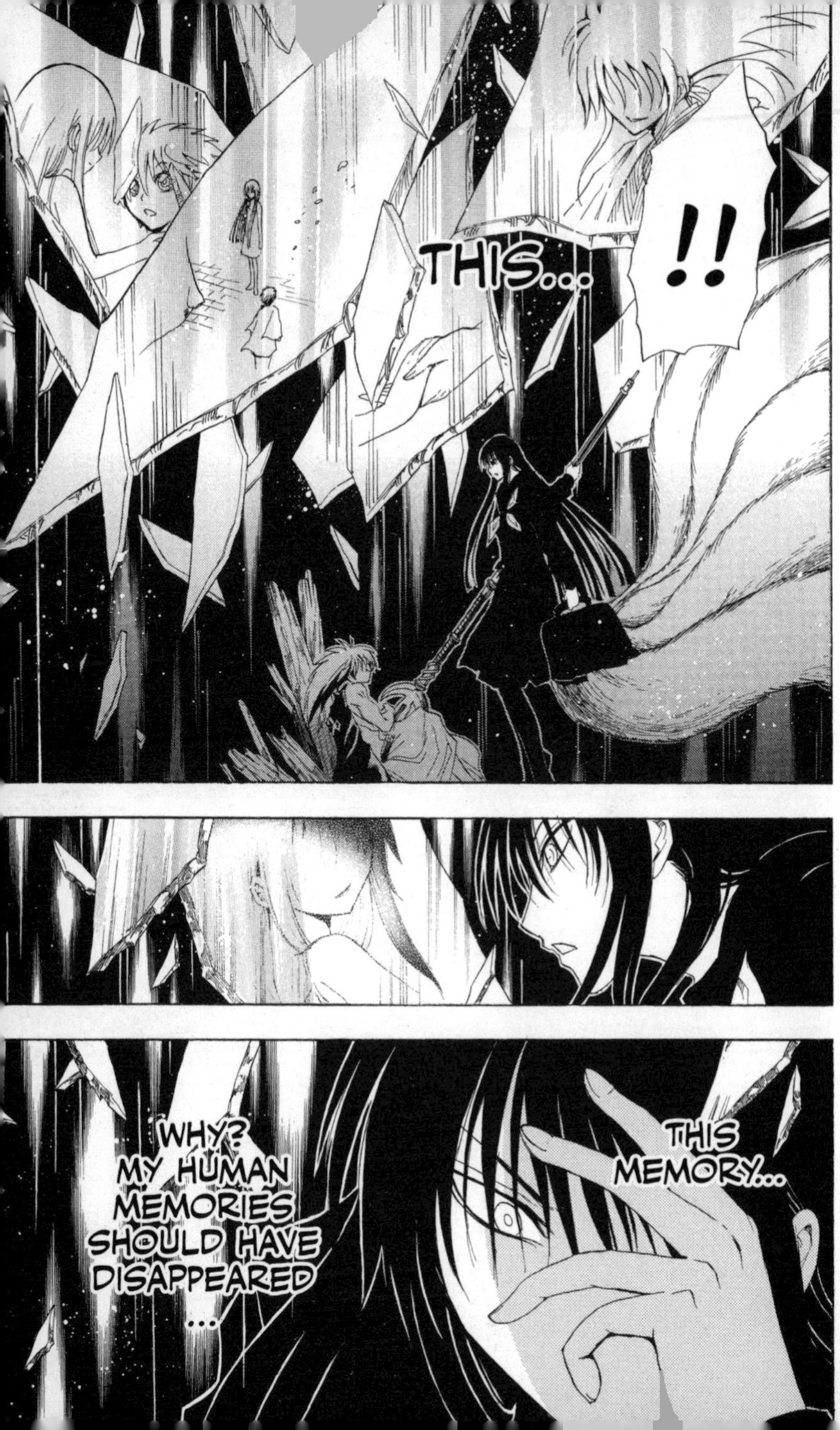
!!
THIS...
THIS MEMORY...
WHY? MY HUMAN MEMORIES SHOULD HAVE DISAPPEARED...

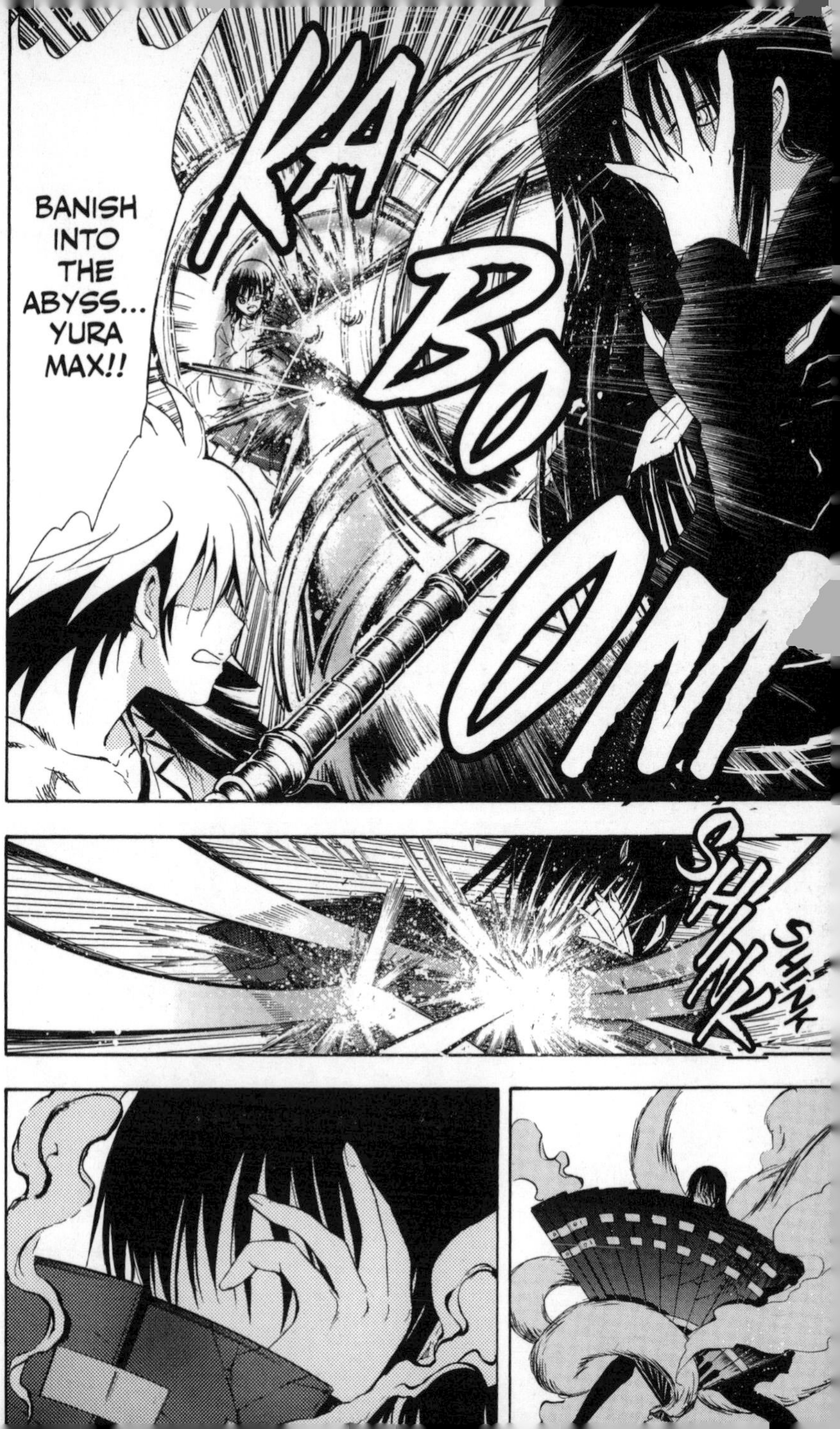
KABOOM
BANISH INTO THE ABYSS... YURA MAX!!
SHINK
SHINK

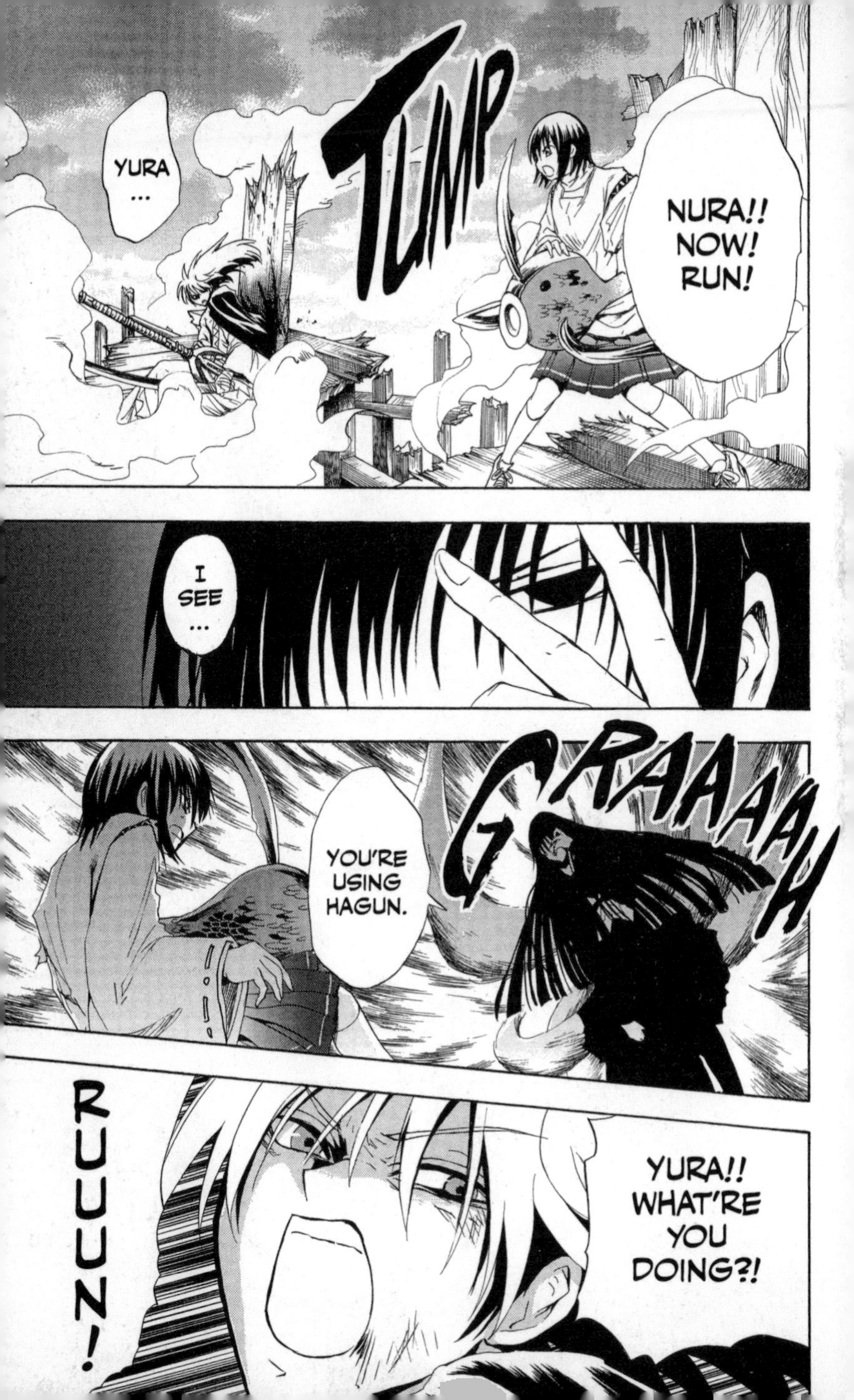
NURA!! NOW! RUN!
TUMP
YURA ...
I SEE ...
GRAAAAAH
YOU'RE USING HAGUN.
YURA!! WHAT'RE YOU DOING?!
RUUUN!

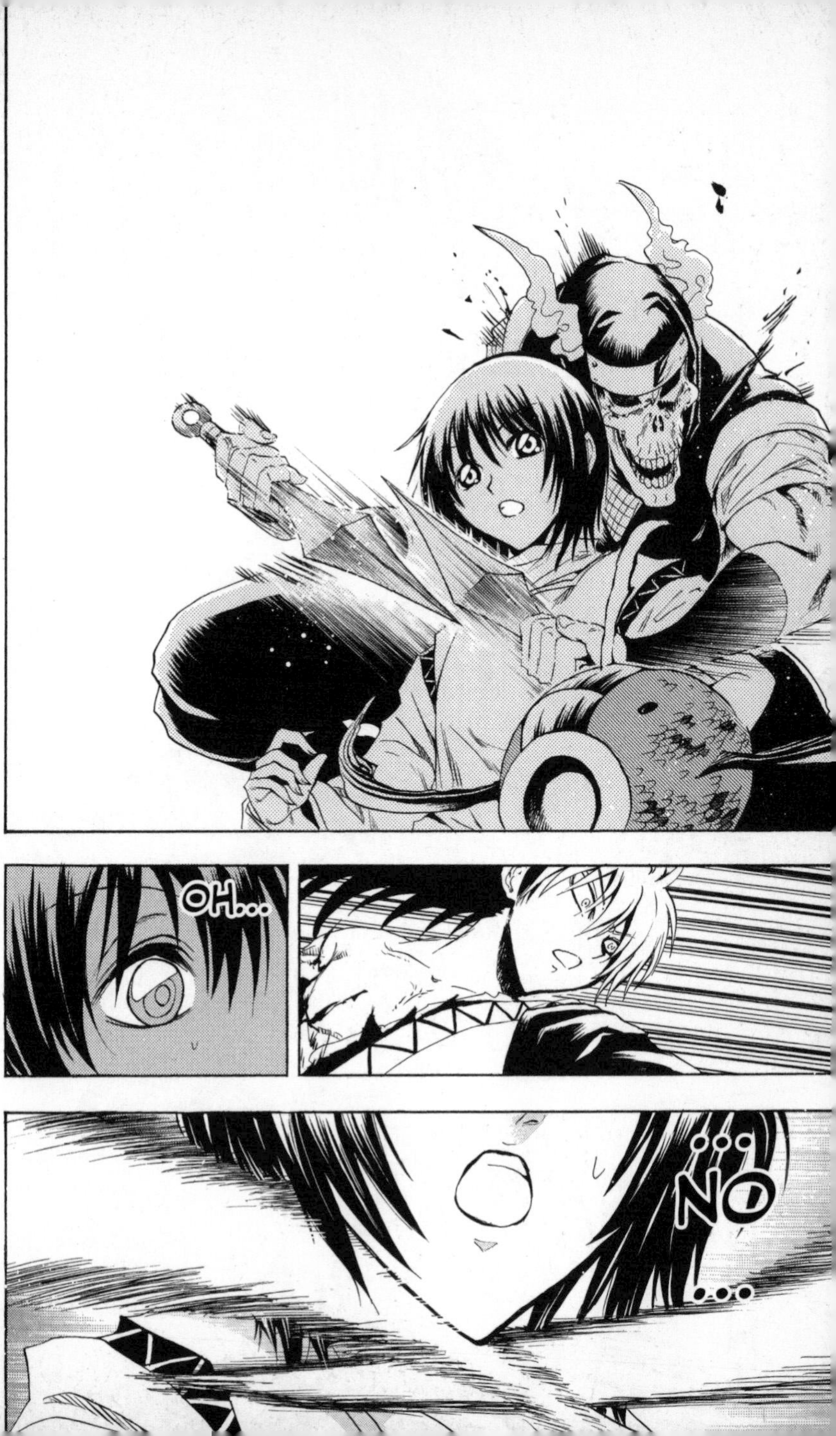
OH...
...NO...

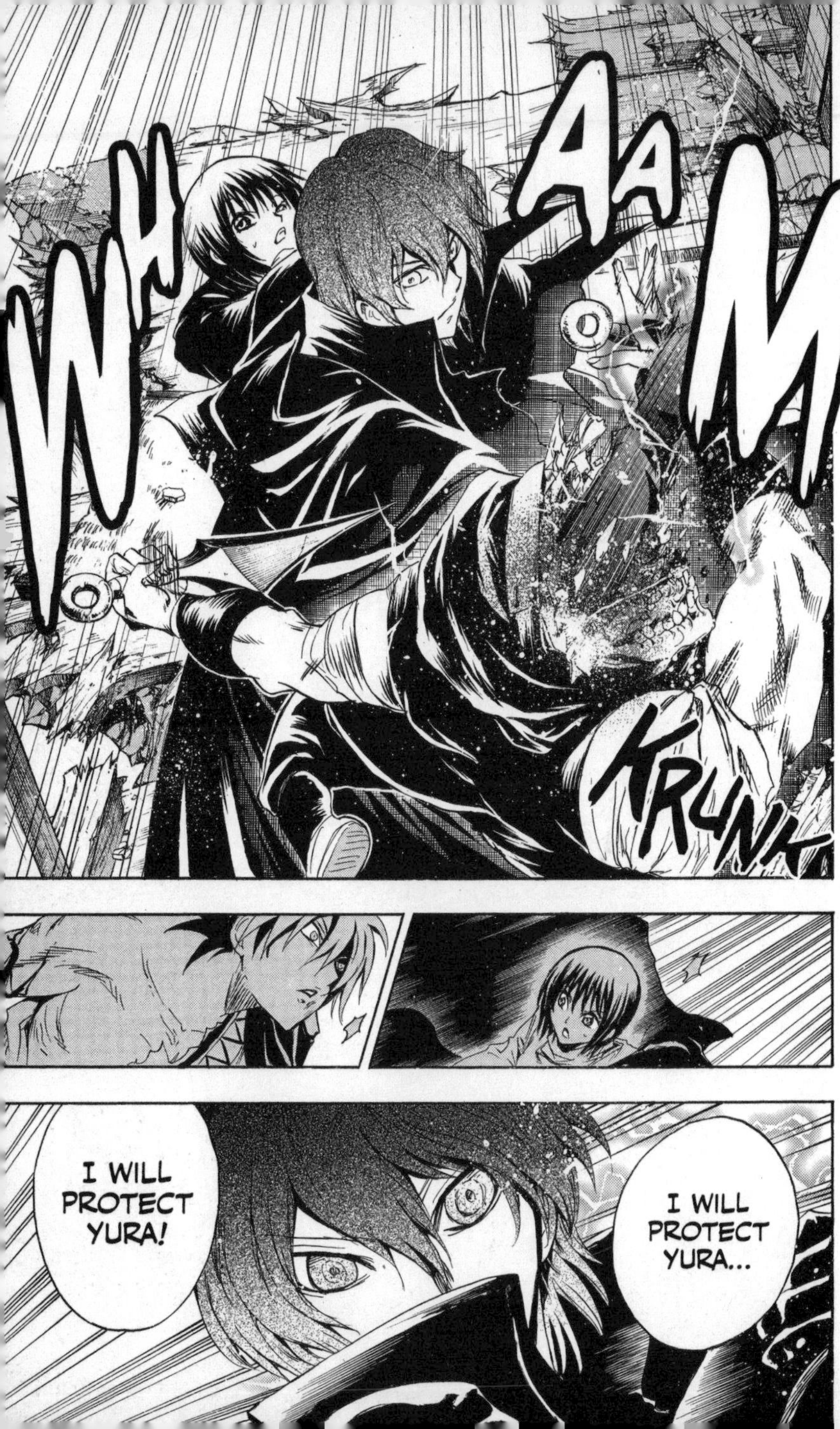
WHAAM
KRUNK
I WILL PROTECT YURA...
I WILL PROTECT YURA!

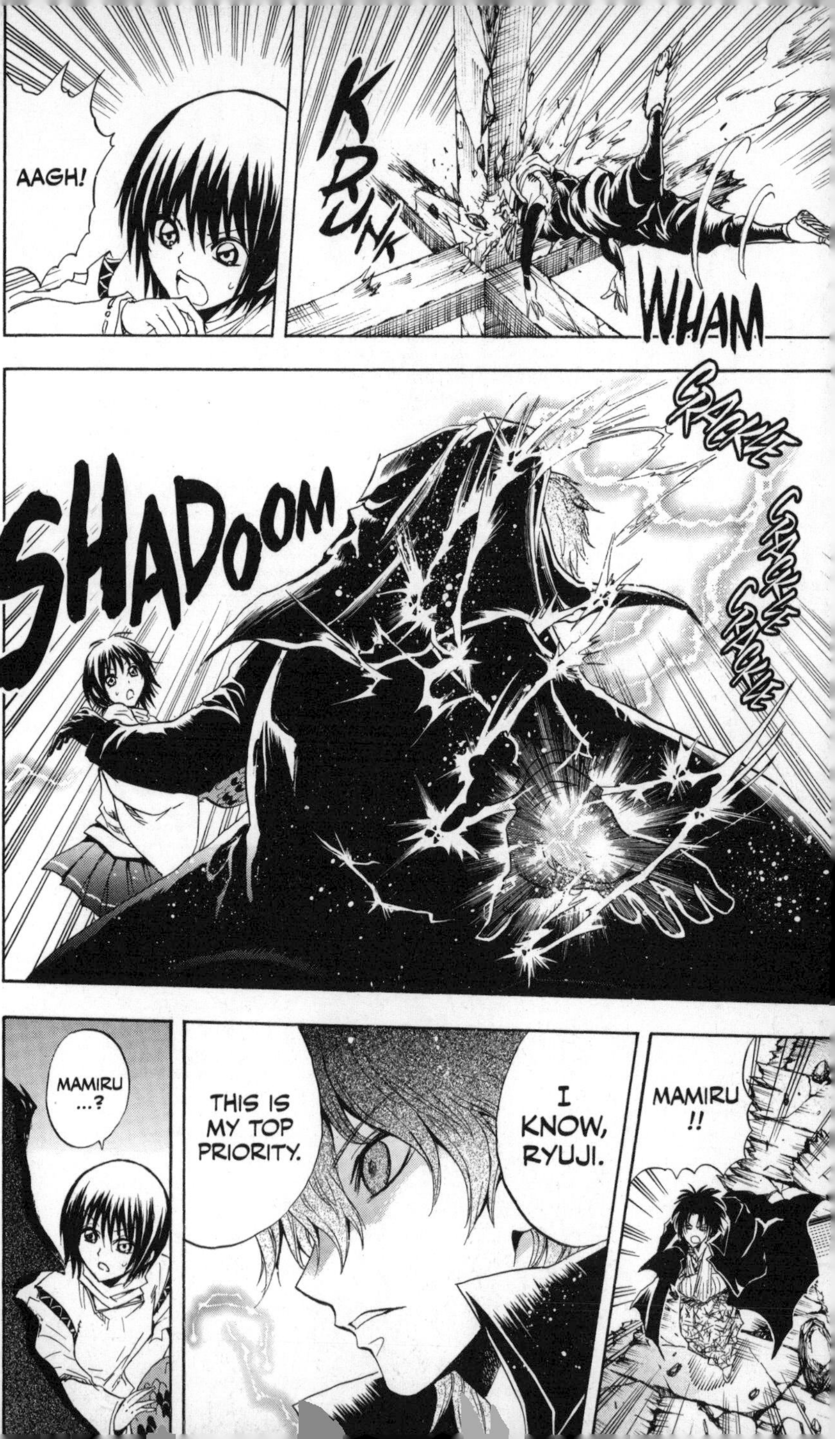
KRUNK
WHAM
AAGH!
CRACKLE
CRACKLE
CRACKLE
SHADOOM
MAMIRU !!
I KNOW, RYUJI.
THIS IS MY TOP PRIORITY.
MAMIRU ...?

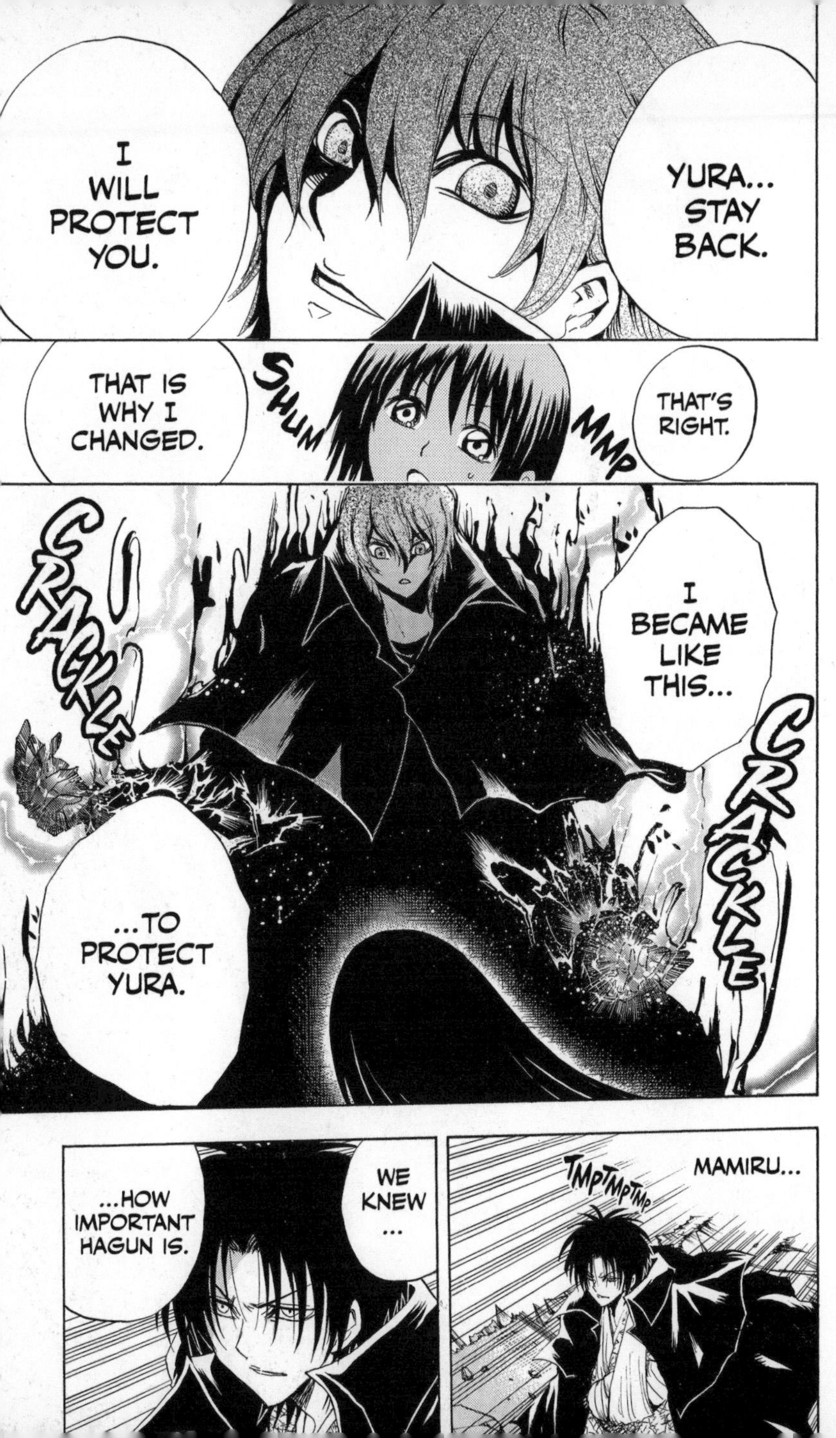
YURA... STAY BACK.
I WILL PROTECT YOU.
THAT'S RIGHT.
MMP
SHUM
THAT IS WHY I CHANGED.
I BECAME LIKE THIS...
CRACKLE
CRACKLE
...TO PROTECT YURA.
MAMIRU...
TMPTMPTMP
WE KNEW ...
...HOW IMPORTANT HAGUN IS.

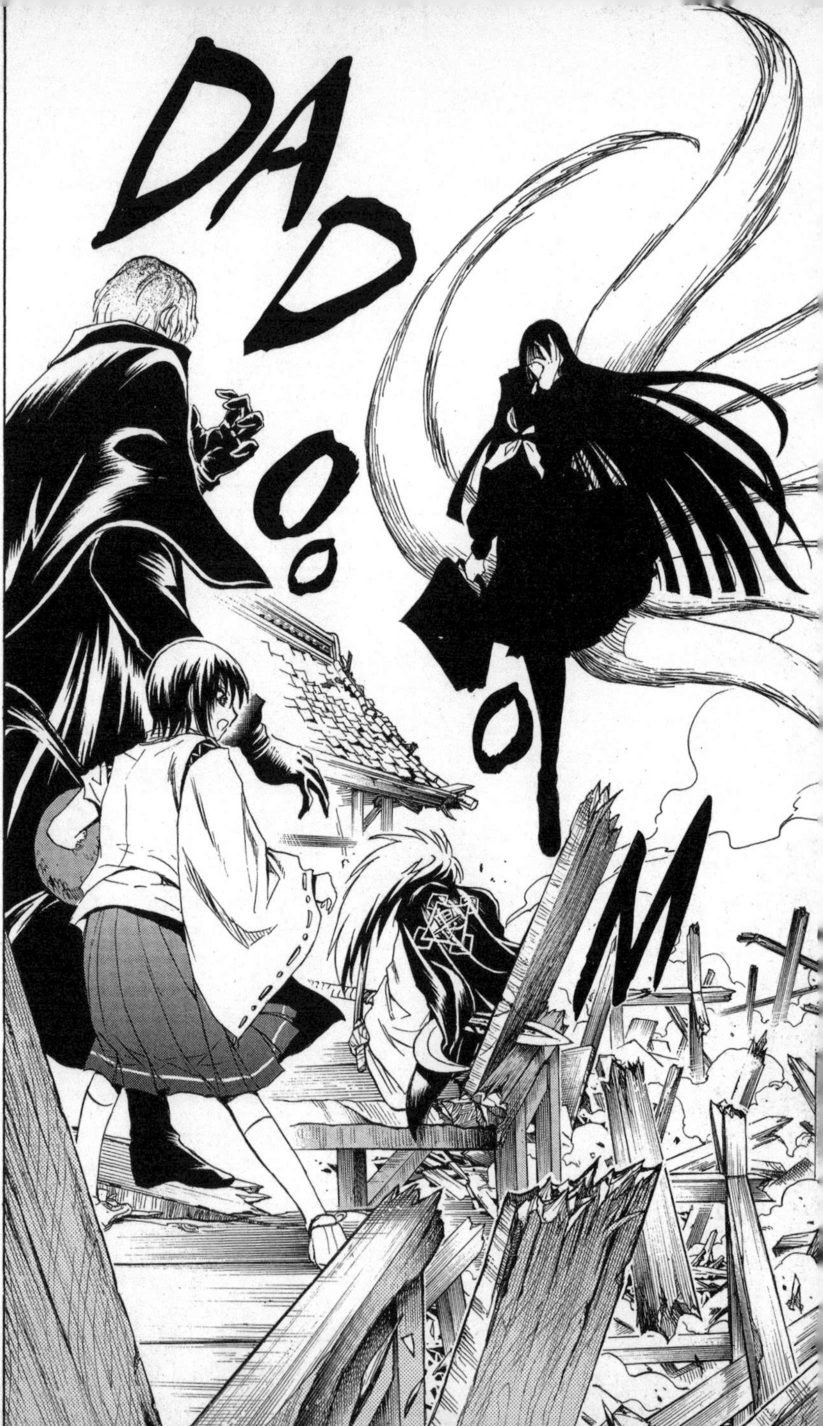
DADOOOOM

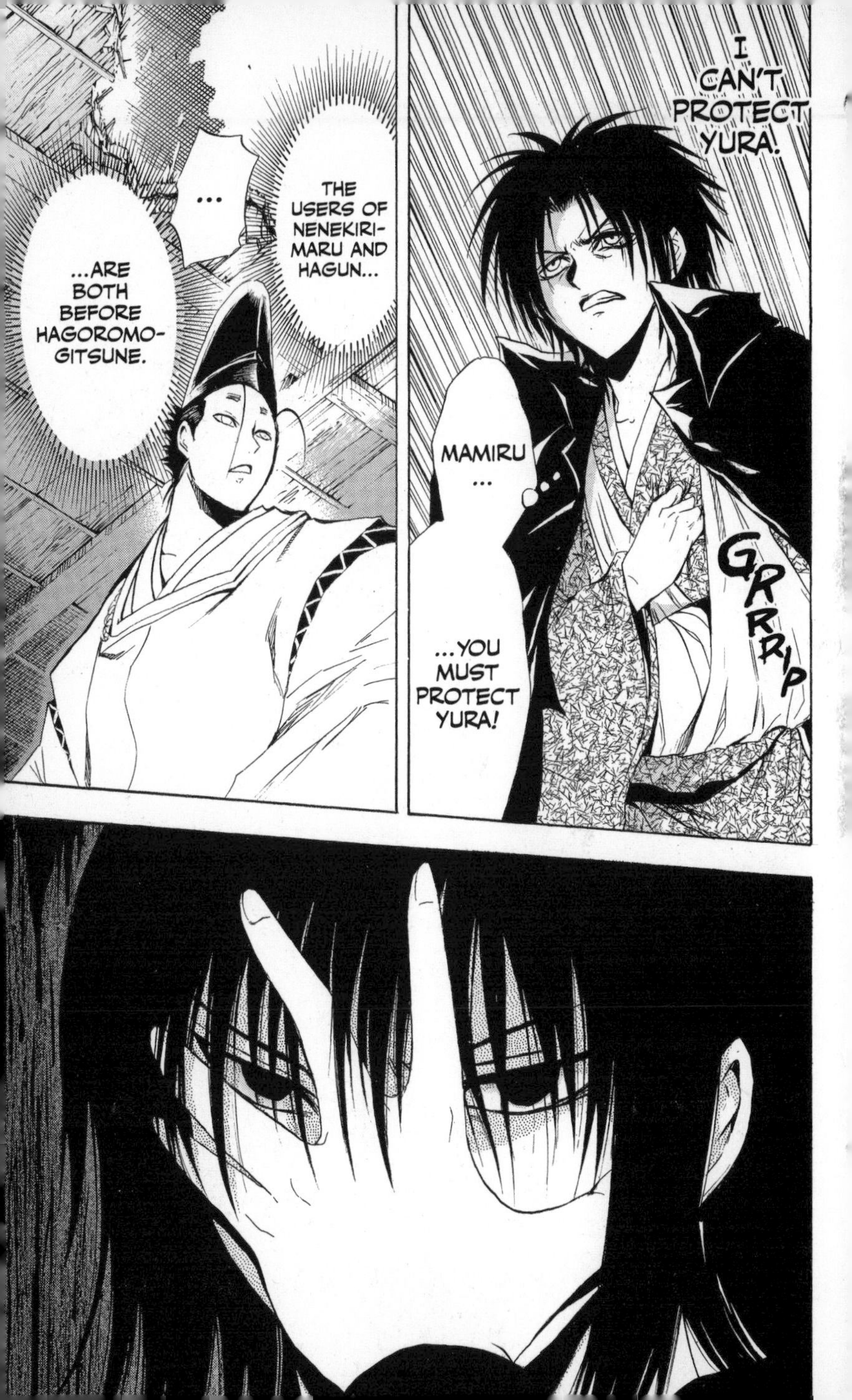
I CAN'T PROTECT YURA!
MAMIRU...
...YOU MUST PROTECT YURA!
GRRRIP
THE USERS OF NENEKIRI-MARU AND HAGUN...
...
...ARE BOTH BEFORE HAGOROMO-GITSUNE.

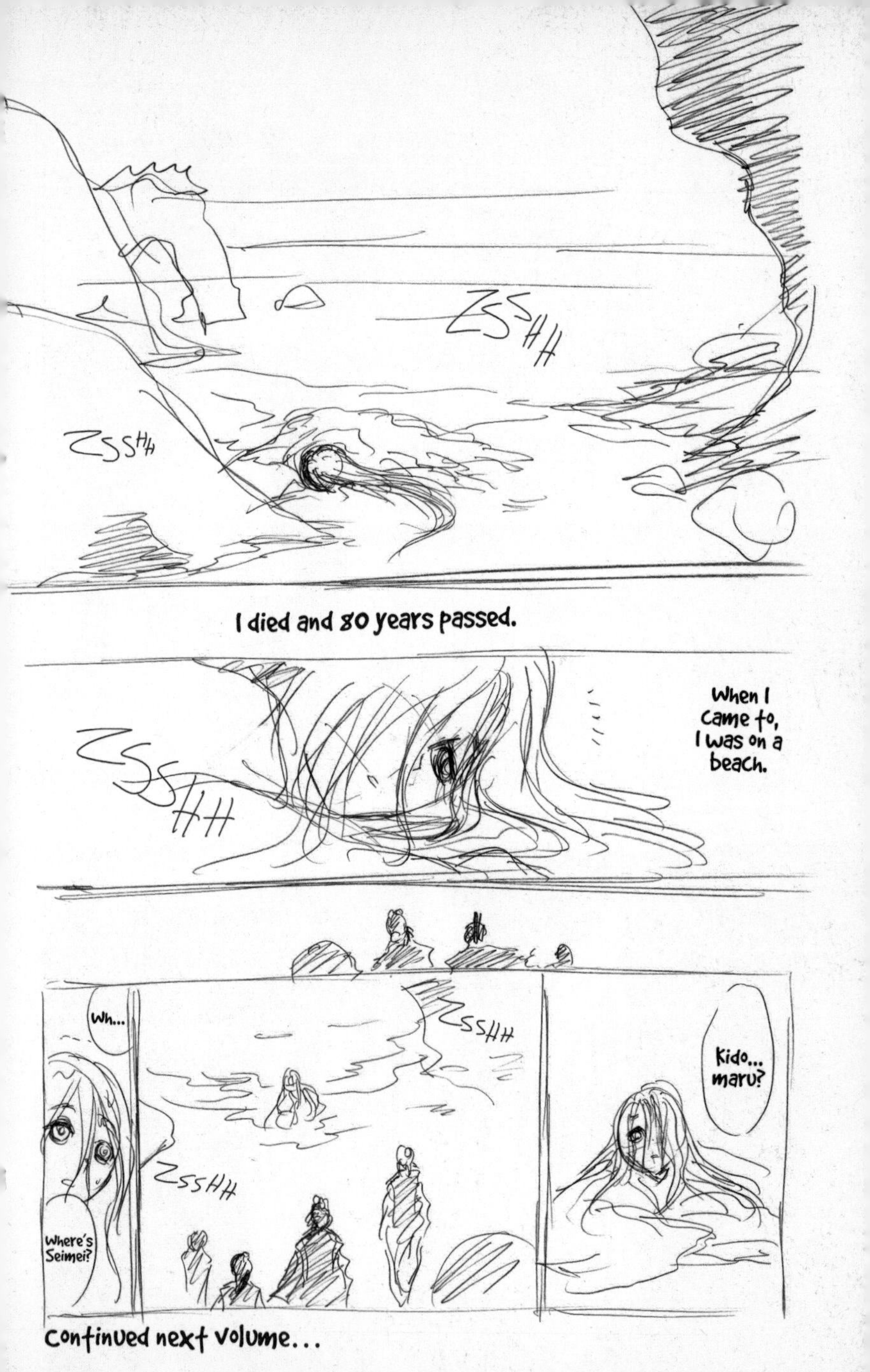
ZSSHH
ZSSHH
I died and 80 years passed.
When I came to, I was on a beach.
ZSSHH
Kido... maru?
ZSSHH
ZSSHH
Wh...
Where's Seimei?

Continued next volume...

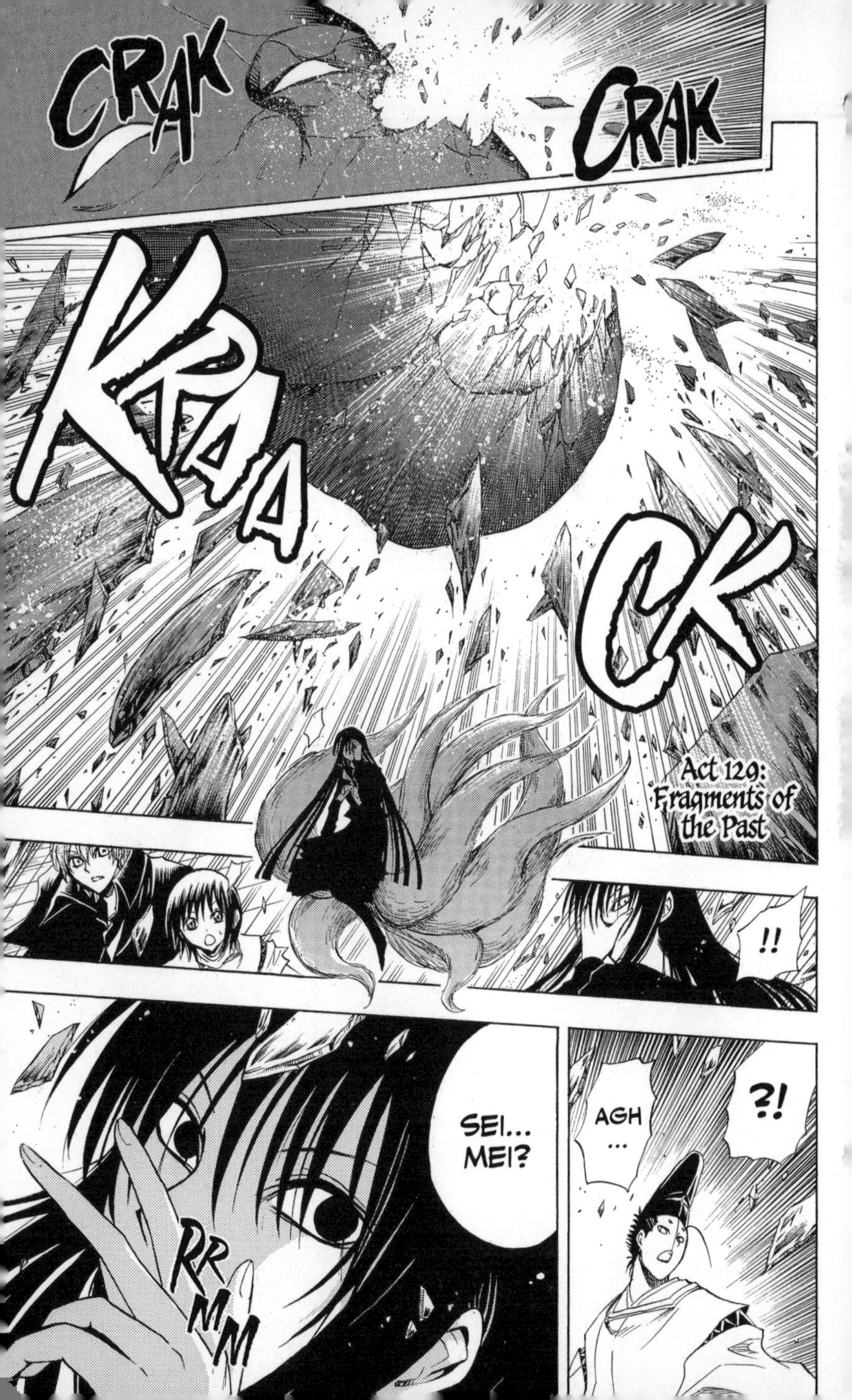
CRAK
CRAK
KRAAACK
Act 129:
Fragments of the Past
!!
?!
AGH
...
SEI...
MEI?
RRMM

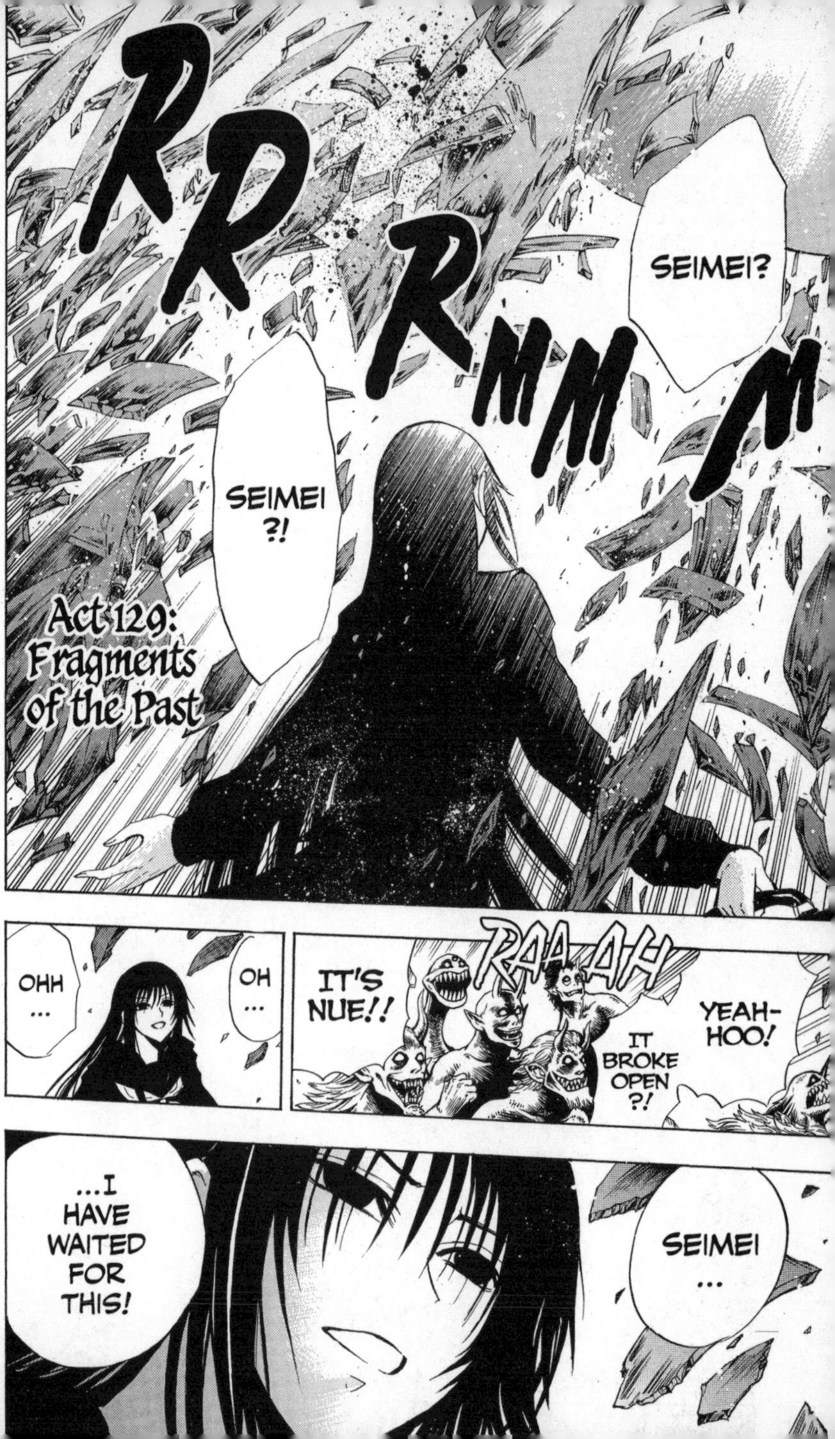
SEIMEI?
RRRMMM
SEIMEI ?!
Act 129: Fragments of the Past
YEAH-HOO!
RAA AH
IT BROKE OPEN ?!
IT'S NUE!!
OH ...
OHH ...
SEIMEI ...
...I HAVE WAITED FOR THIS!

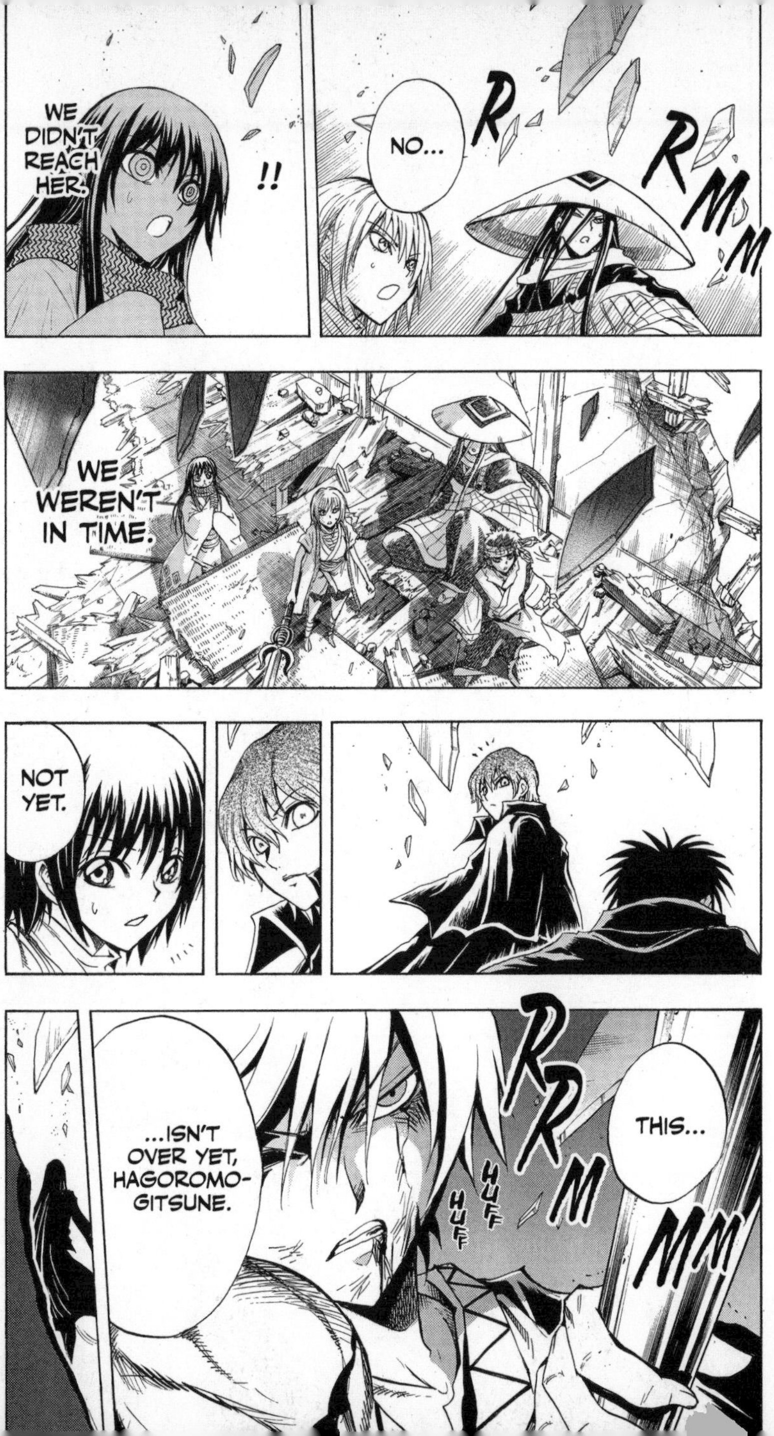
NO...
RRRMMM
WE DIDN'T REACH HER.
!!
WE WEREN'T IN TIME.
NOT YET.
THIS...
RRMMM
HUFF HUFF
...ISN'T OVER YET, HAGOROMO-GITSUNE.

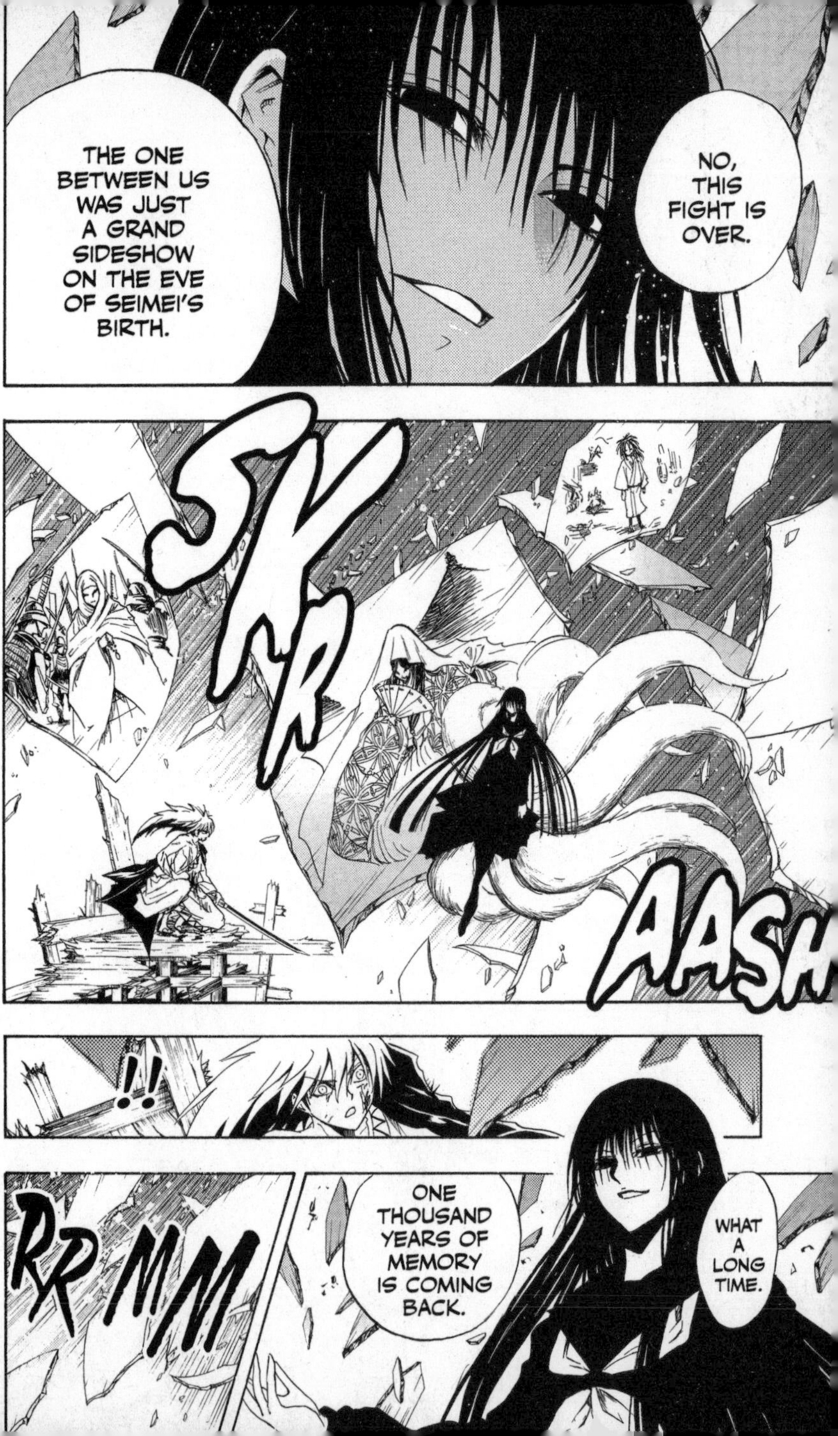
NO, THIS FIGHT IS OVER.
THE ONE BETWEEN US WAS JUST A GRAND SIDESHOW ON THE EVE OF SEIMEI'S BIRTH.
AASH
SNP
!!
WHAT A LONG TIME.
ONE THOUSAND YEARS OF MEMORY IS COMING BACK.
RRMM

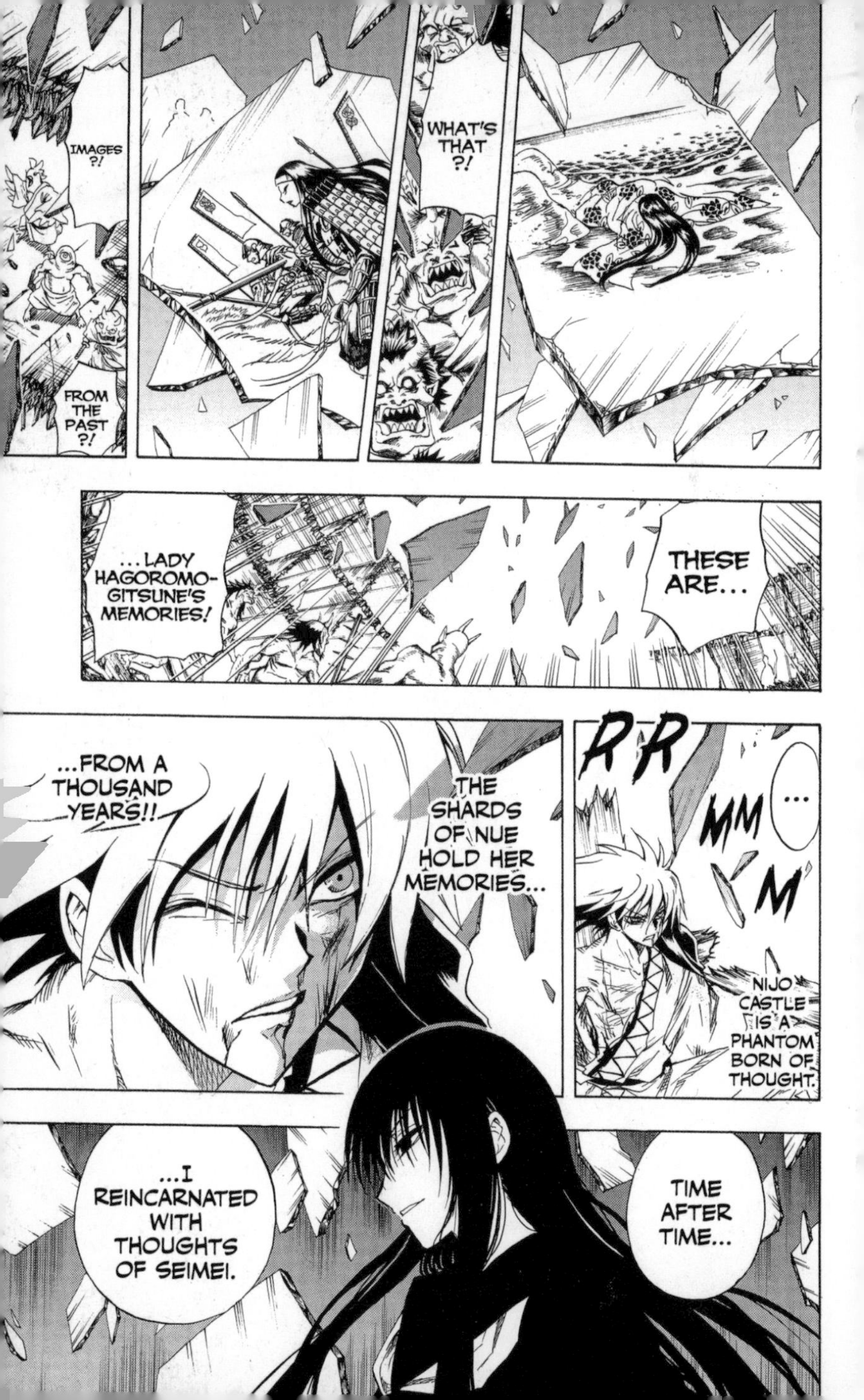
WHAT'S THAT ?!
IMAGES ?!
FROM THE PAST ?!
THESE ARE...
...LADY HAGOROMO-GITSUNE'S MEMORIES!
RRMMM
...
NIJO CASTLE IS A PHANTOM BORN OF THOUGHT.
THE SHARDS OF NUE HOLD HER MEMORIES...
...FROM A THOUSAND YEARS!!
TIME AFTER TIME...
...I REINCARNATED WITH THOUGHTS OF SEIMEI.

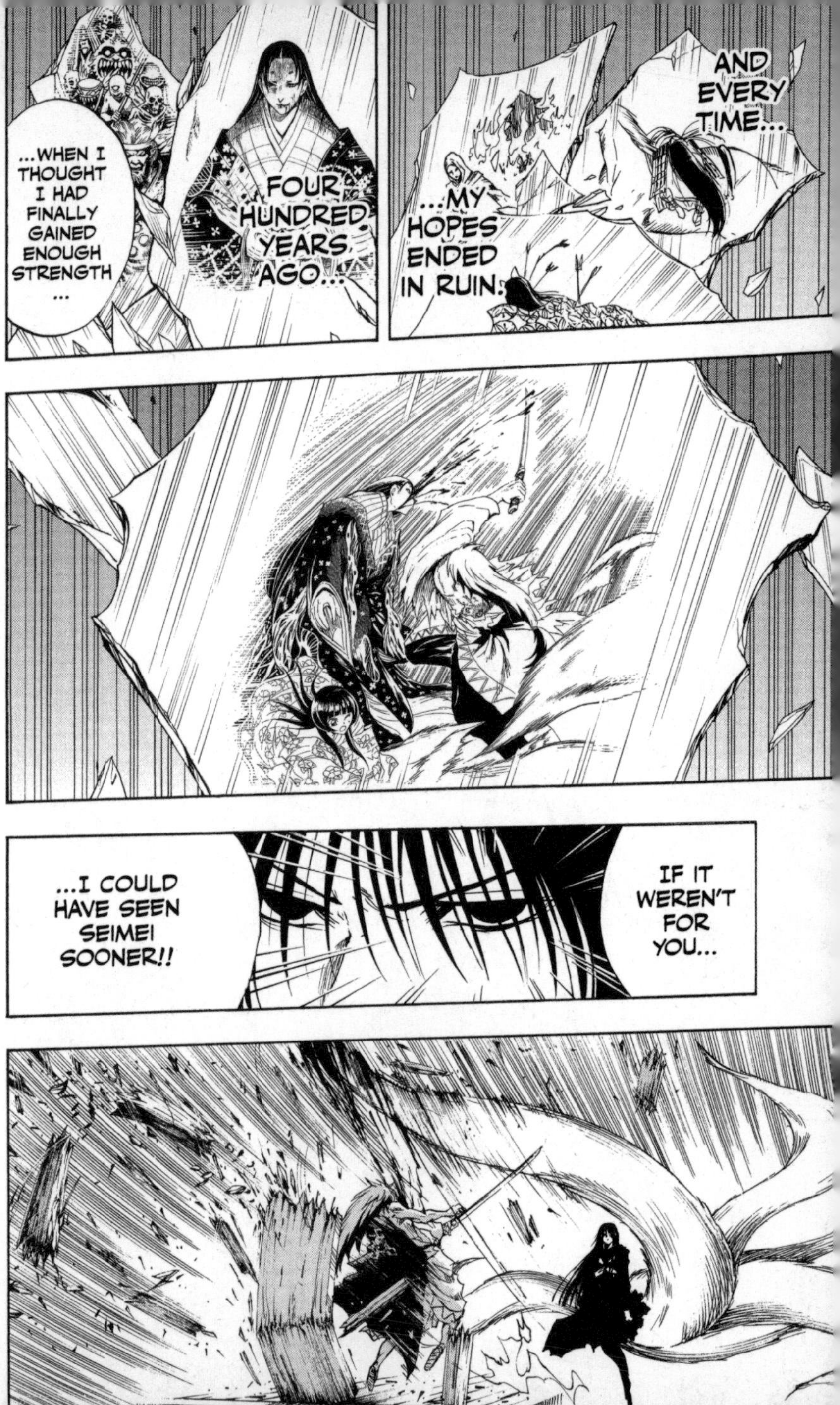
AND EVERY TIME...
...MY HOPES ENDED IN RUIN.
FOUR HUNDRED YEARS AGO...
...WHEN I THOUGHT I HAD FINALLY GAINED ENOUGH STRENGTH ...
IF IT WEREN'T FOR YOU...
...I COULD HAVE SEEN SEIMEI SOONER!!

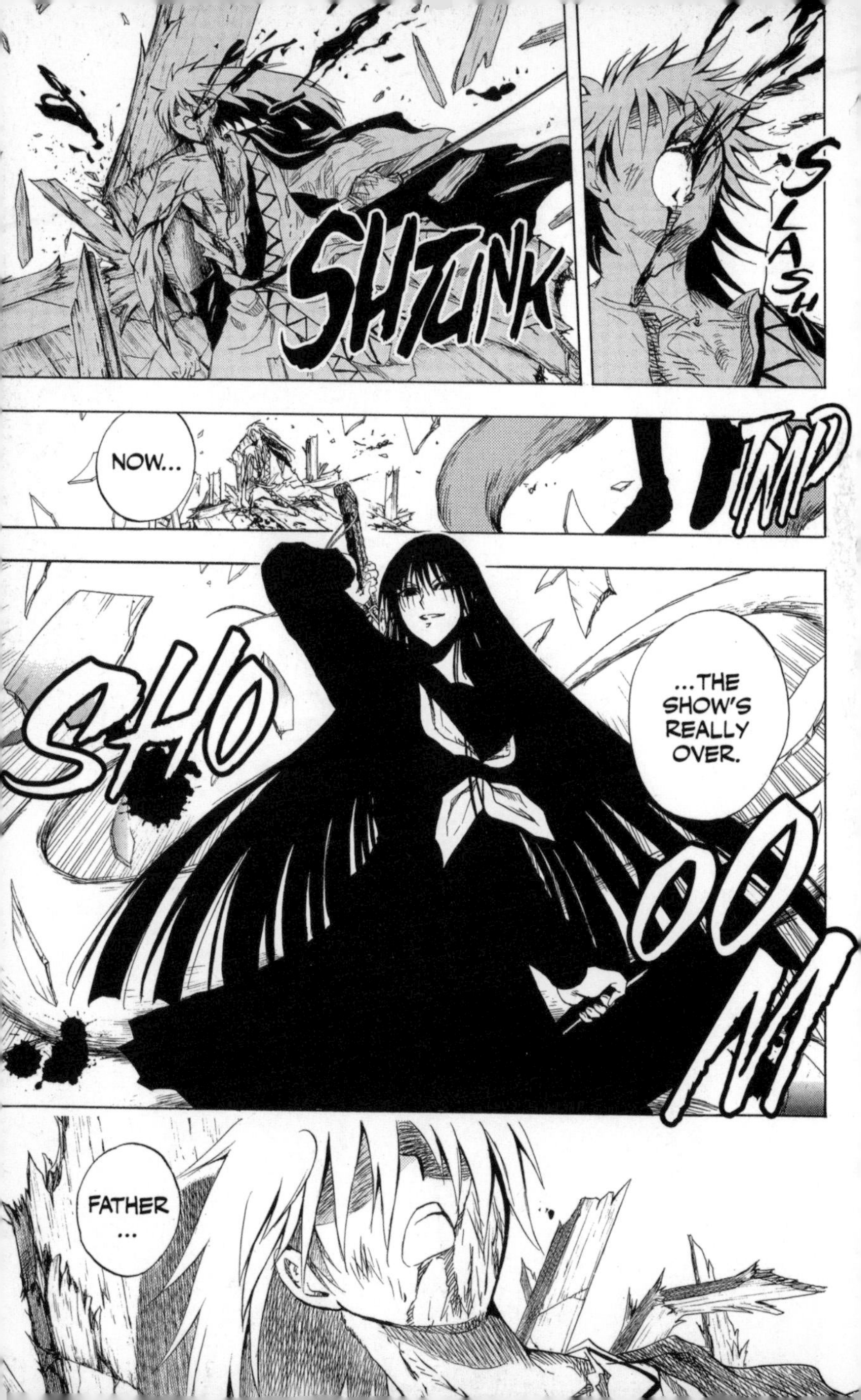
SLASH
SHUNK
TMP
NOW...
...THE SHOW'S REALLY OVER.
SHOOOM
FATHER ...

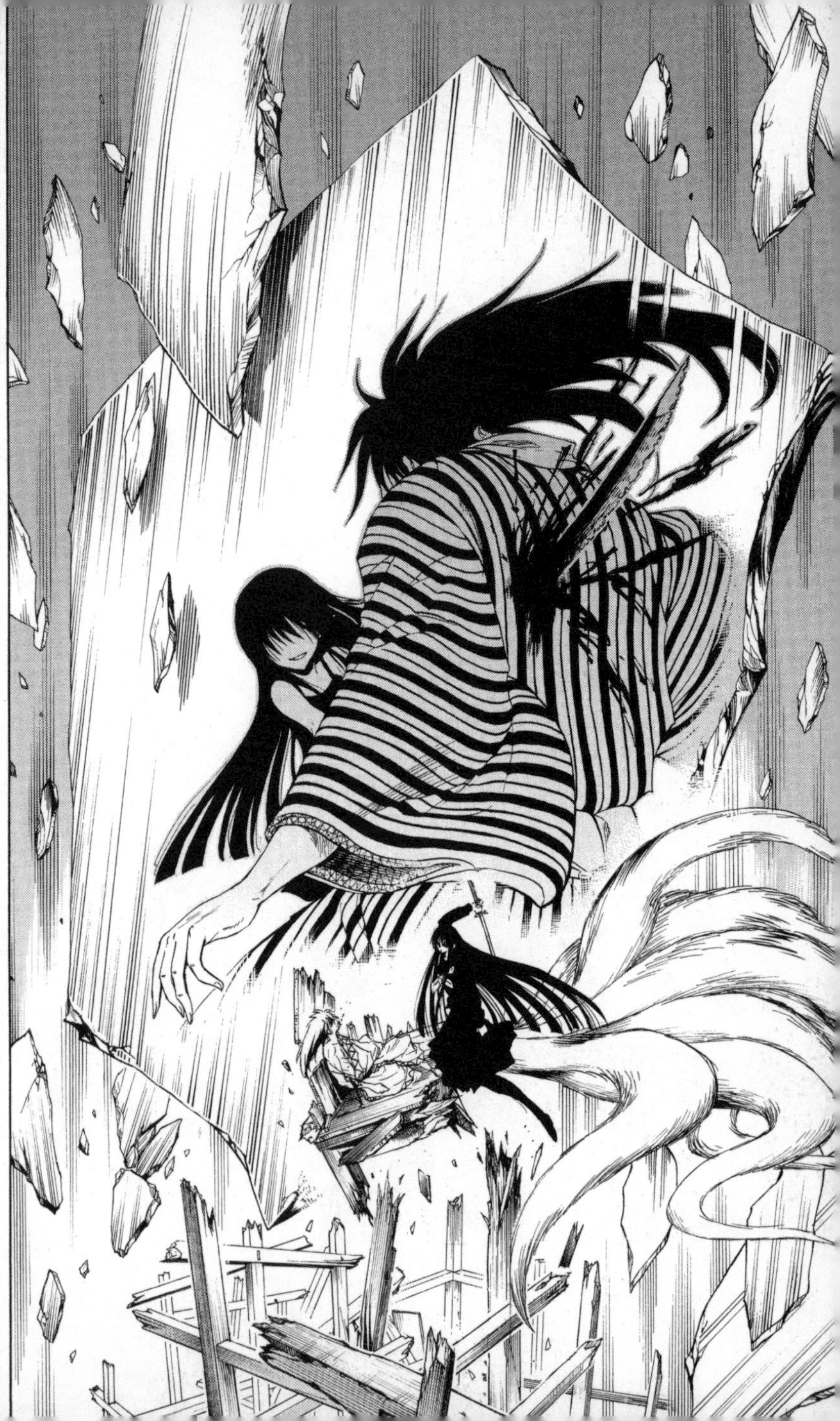

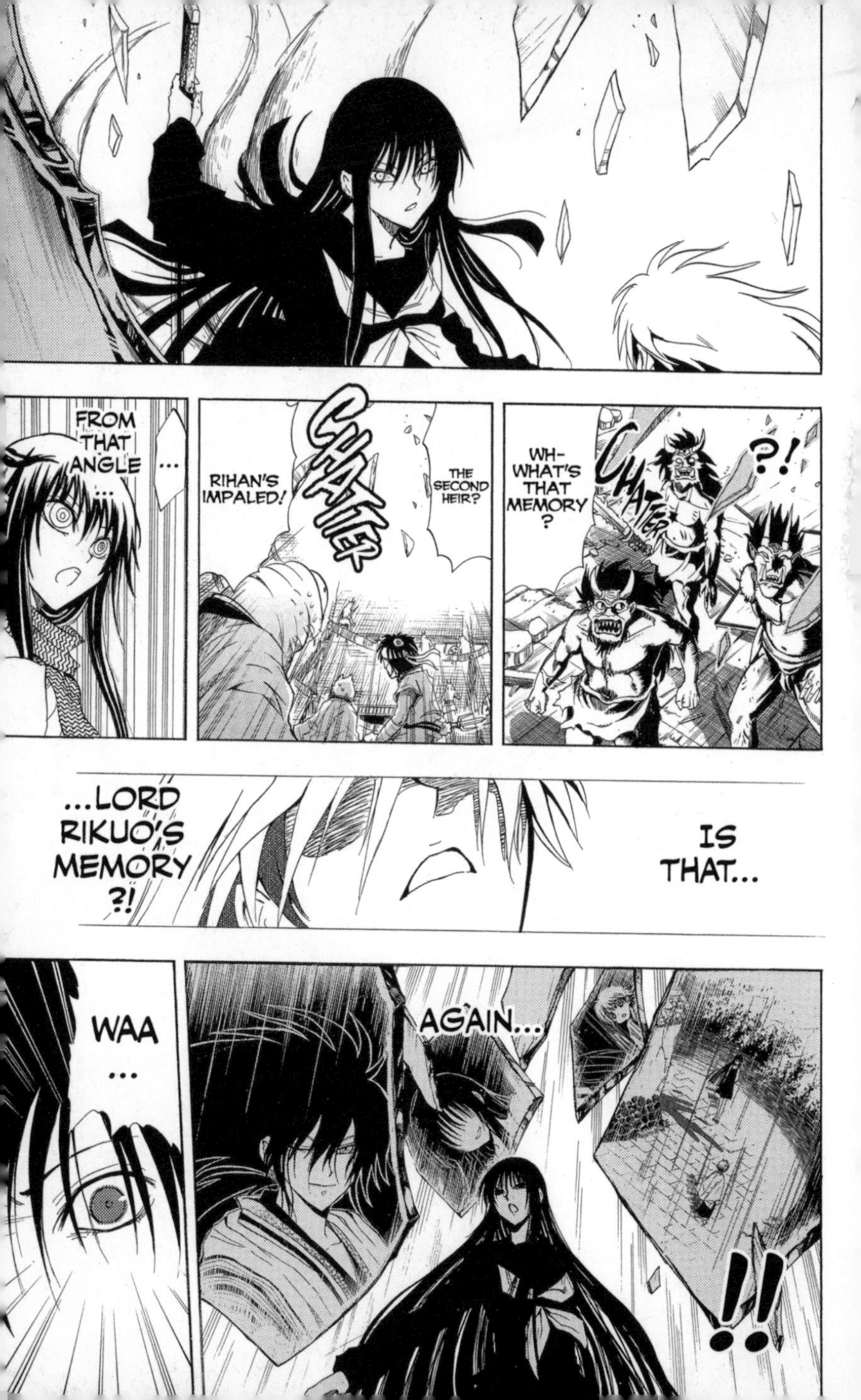
?!
WH- WHAT'S THAT MEMORY?
CHATER
THE SECOND HEIR?
CHATTER
RIHAN'S IMPALED!
...
FROM THAT ANGLE ...
IS THAT...
...LORD RIKUO'S MEMORY ?!
!!
AGAIN...
WAA ...

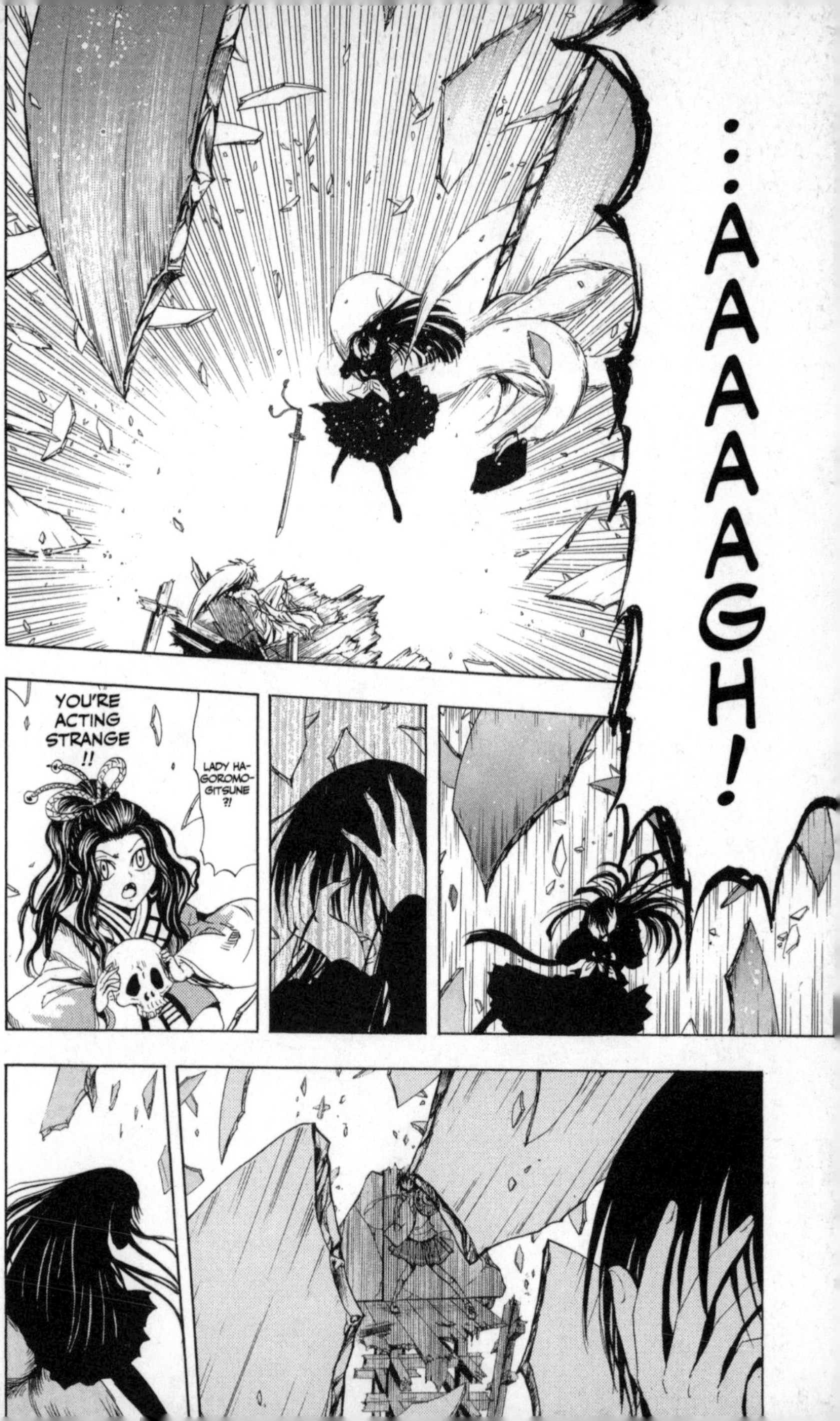
...AAAAAAGH!
LADY HAGOROMO-GITSUNE ?!
YOU'RE ACTING STRANGE !!

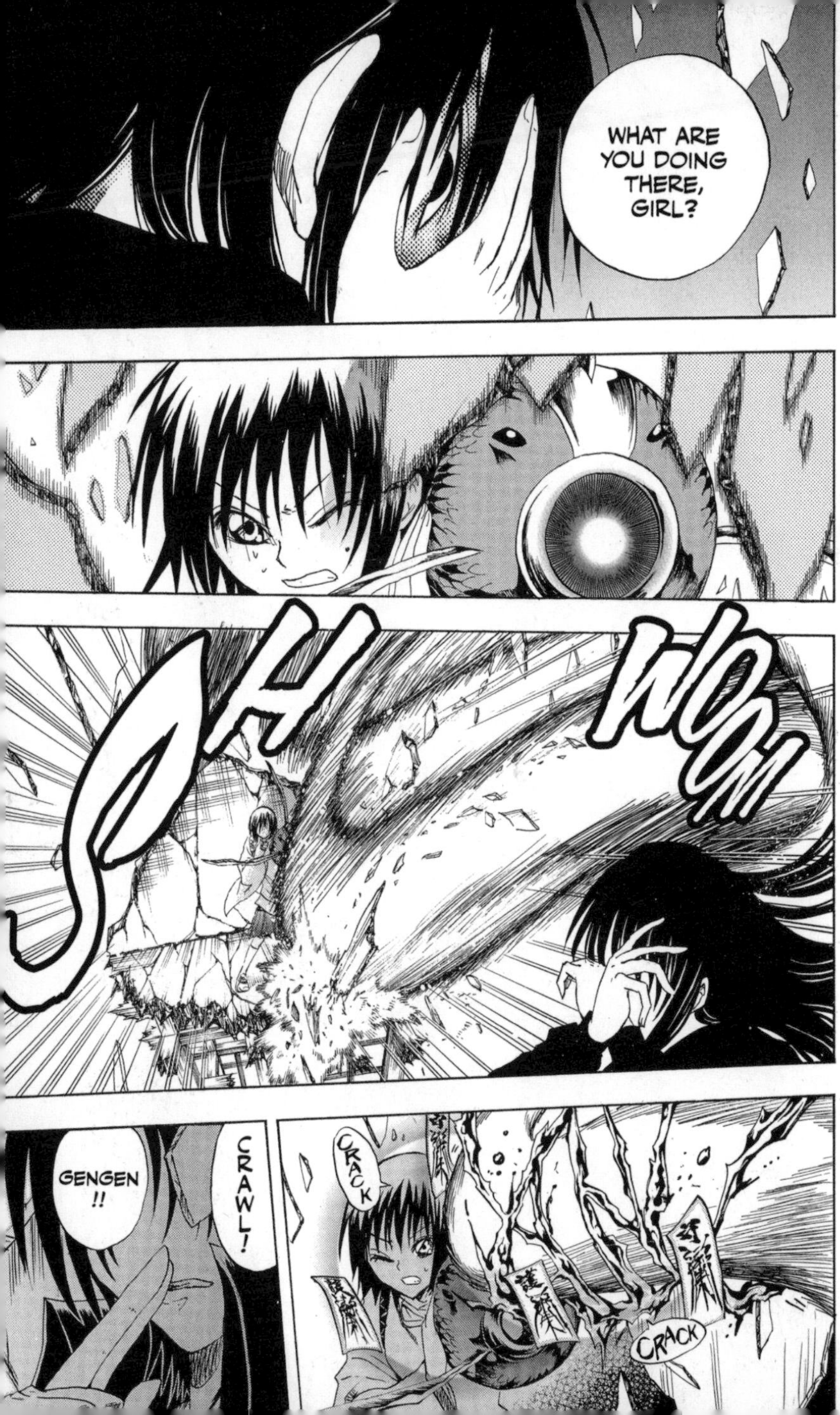
WHAT ARE YOU DOING THERE, GIRL?
SHWOOM
CRACK
CRACK
CRAWL!
GENGEN !!

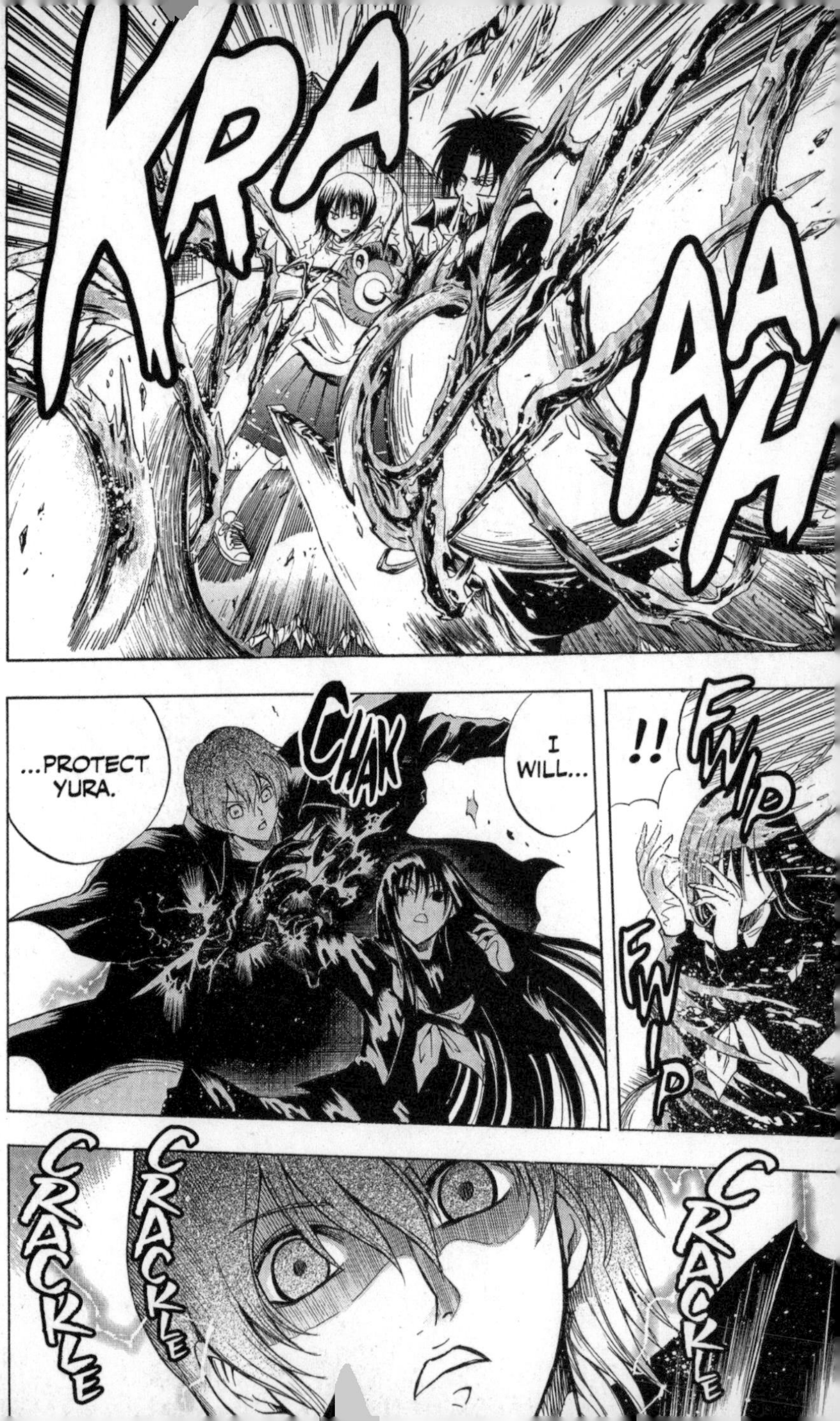
KRAAAAH
!!
FWIP
FWIP
I WILL...
...PROTECT YURA.
CHAK
CRACKLE
CRACKLE
CRACKLE

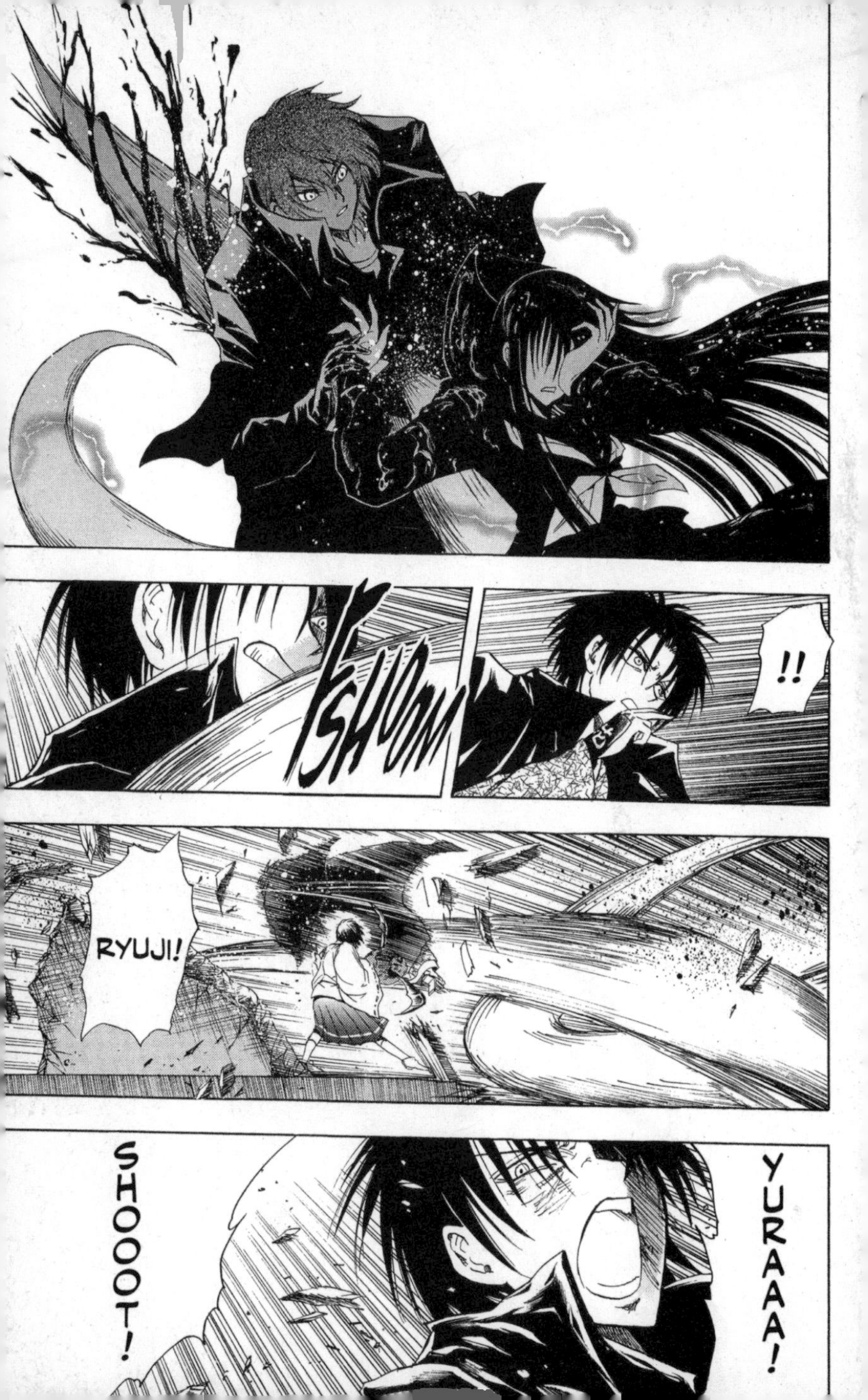
!!
FSHOOM
RYUJI!
YURAAA!
SHOOOOT!

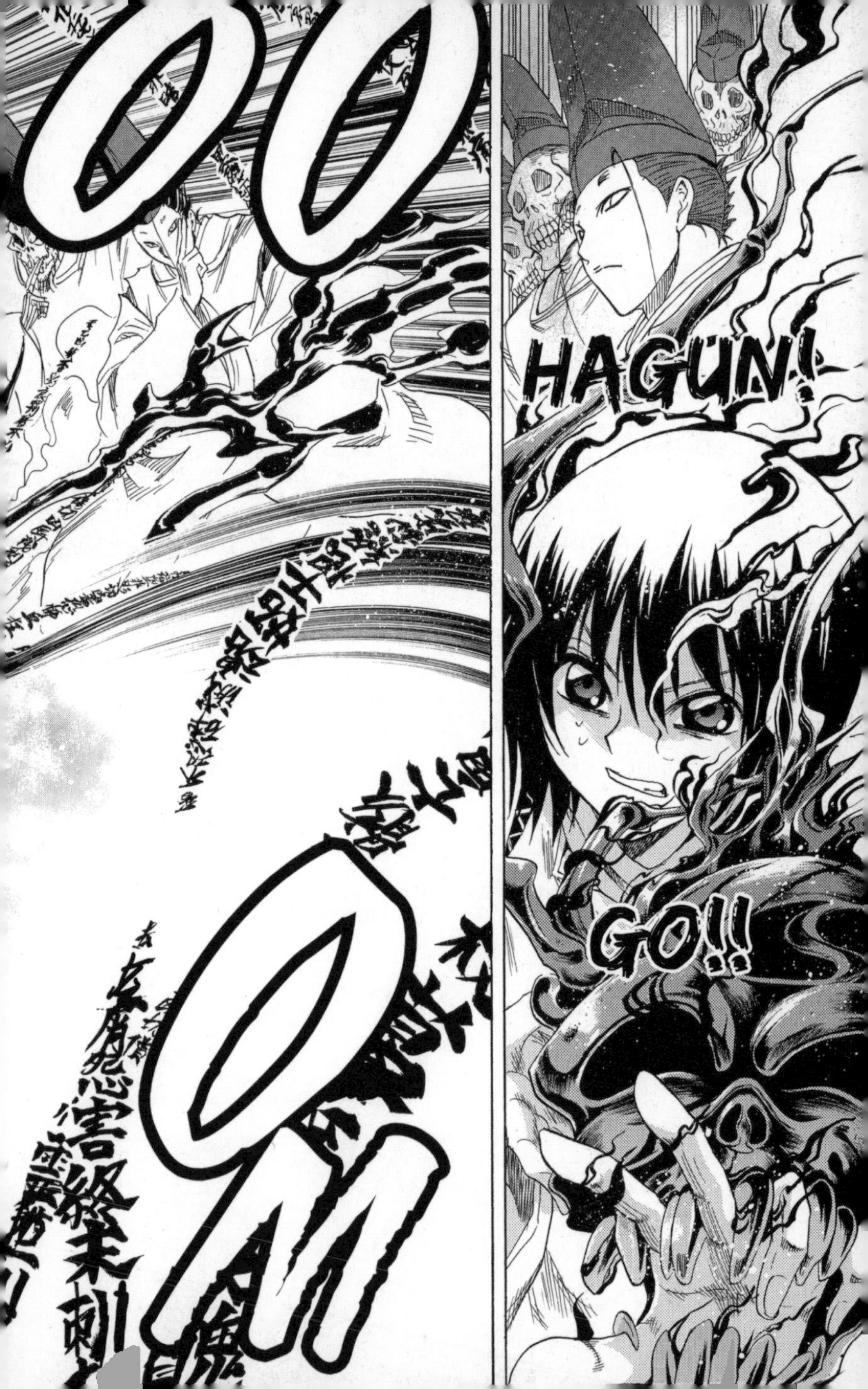
HAGUN!
GO!!
OO
ON

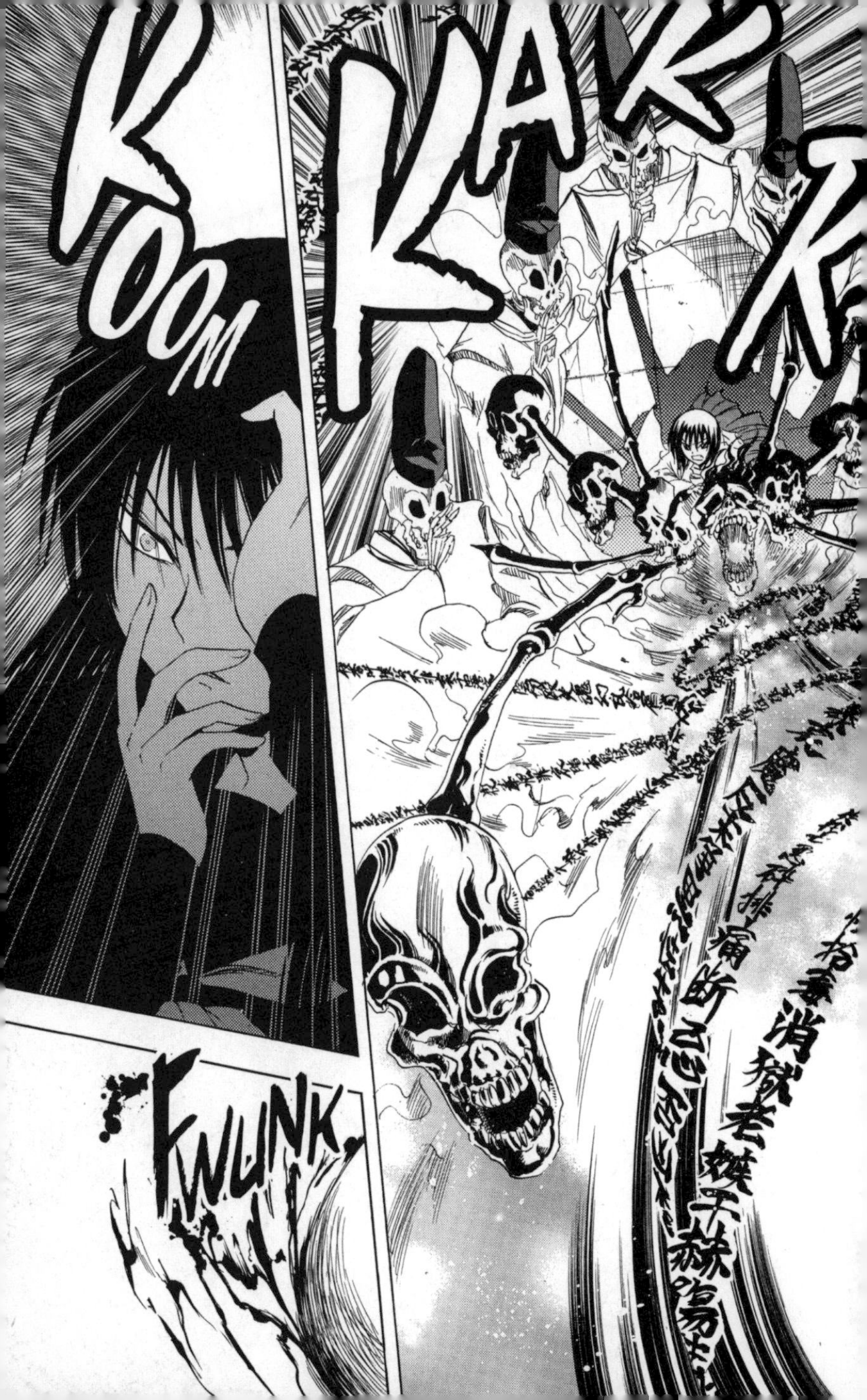
KVOOM
FWUNK

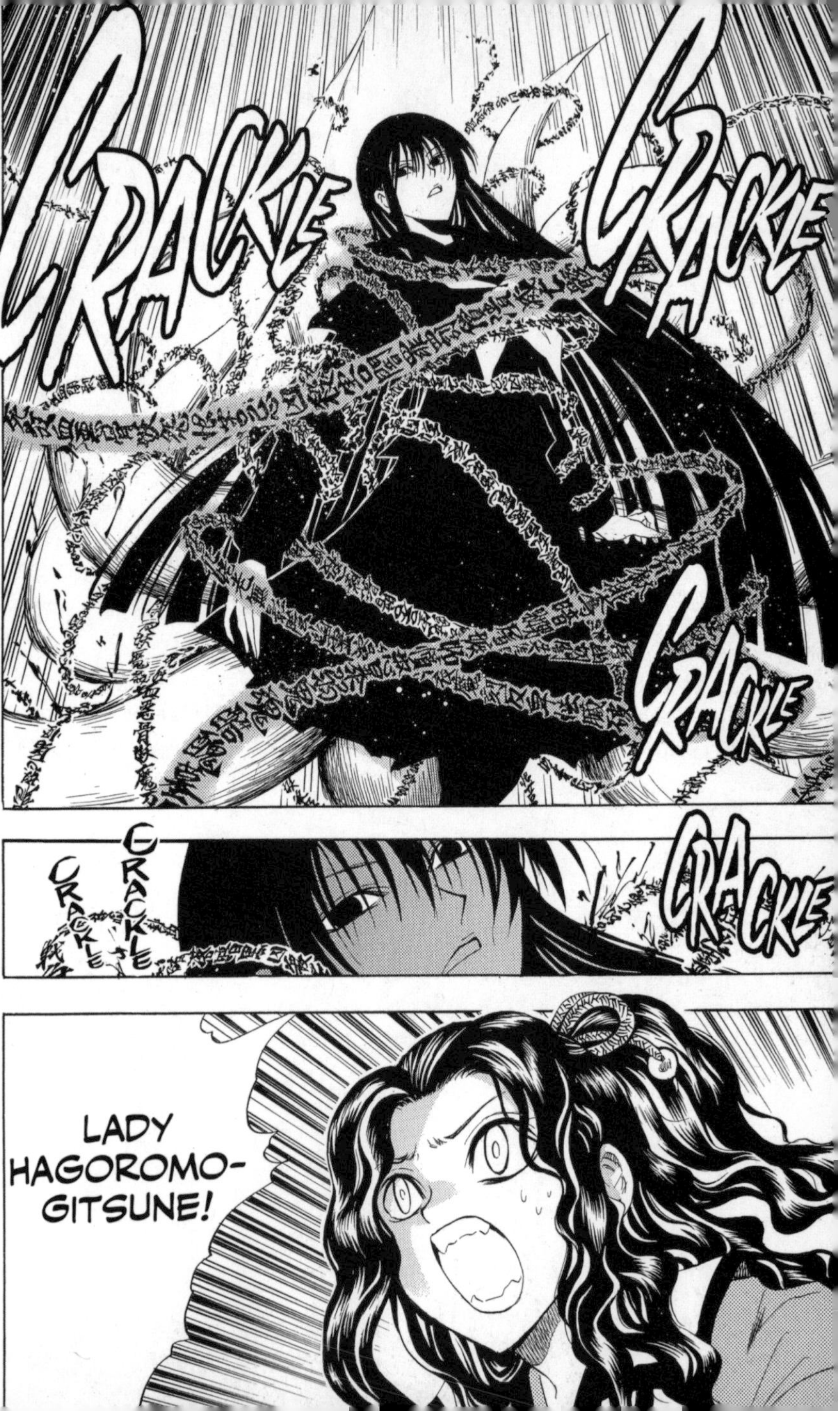
CRACKLE
CRACKLE
CRACKLE
CRACKLE
CRACKLE
CRACKLE
LADY HAGOROMO-GITSUNE!

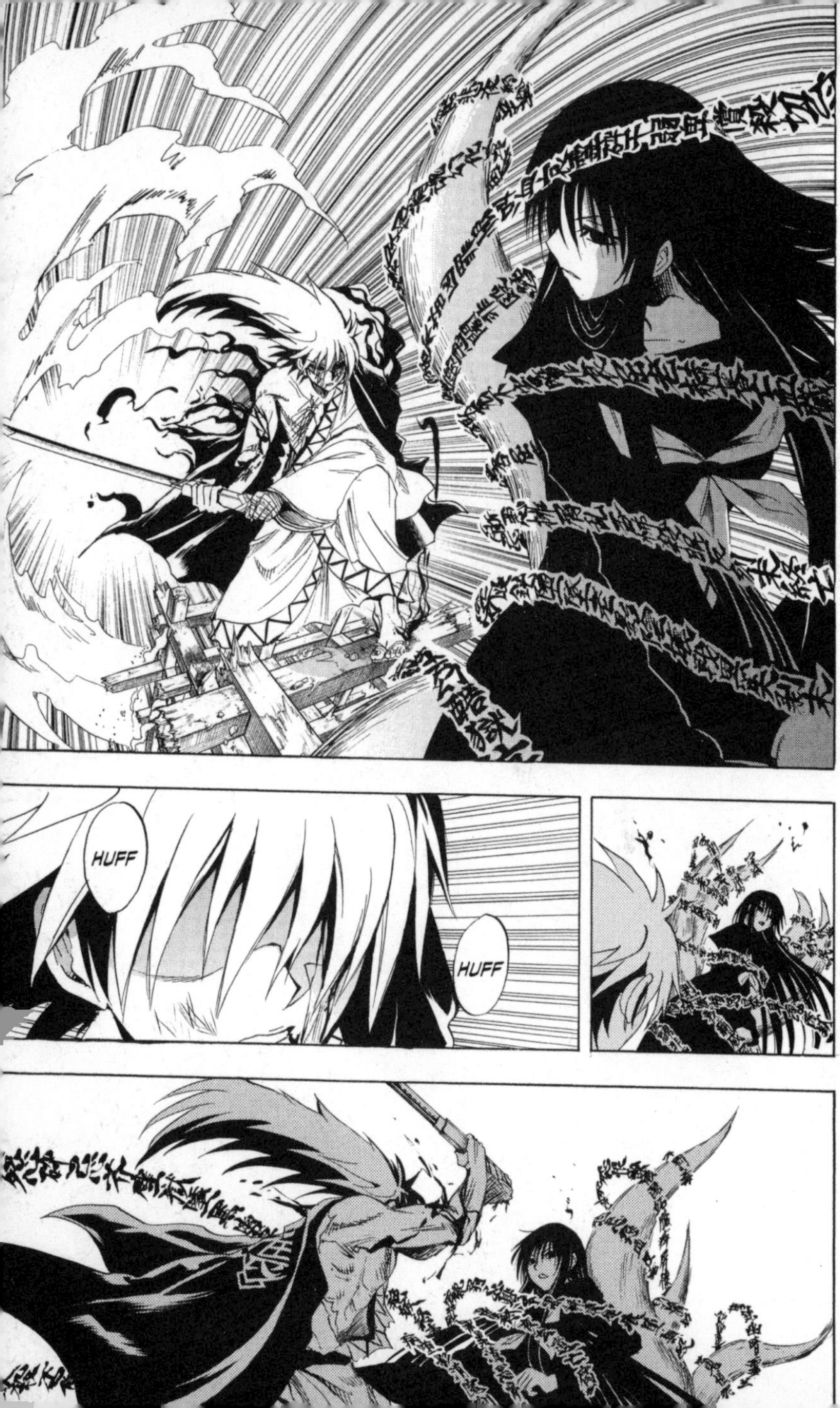
HUFF
HUFF

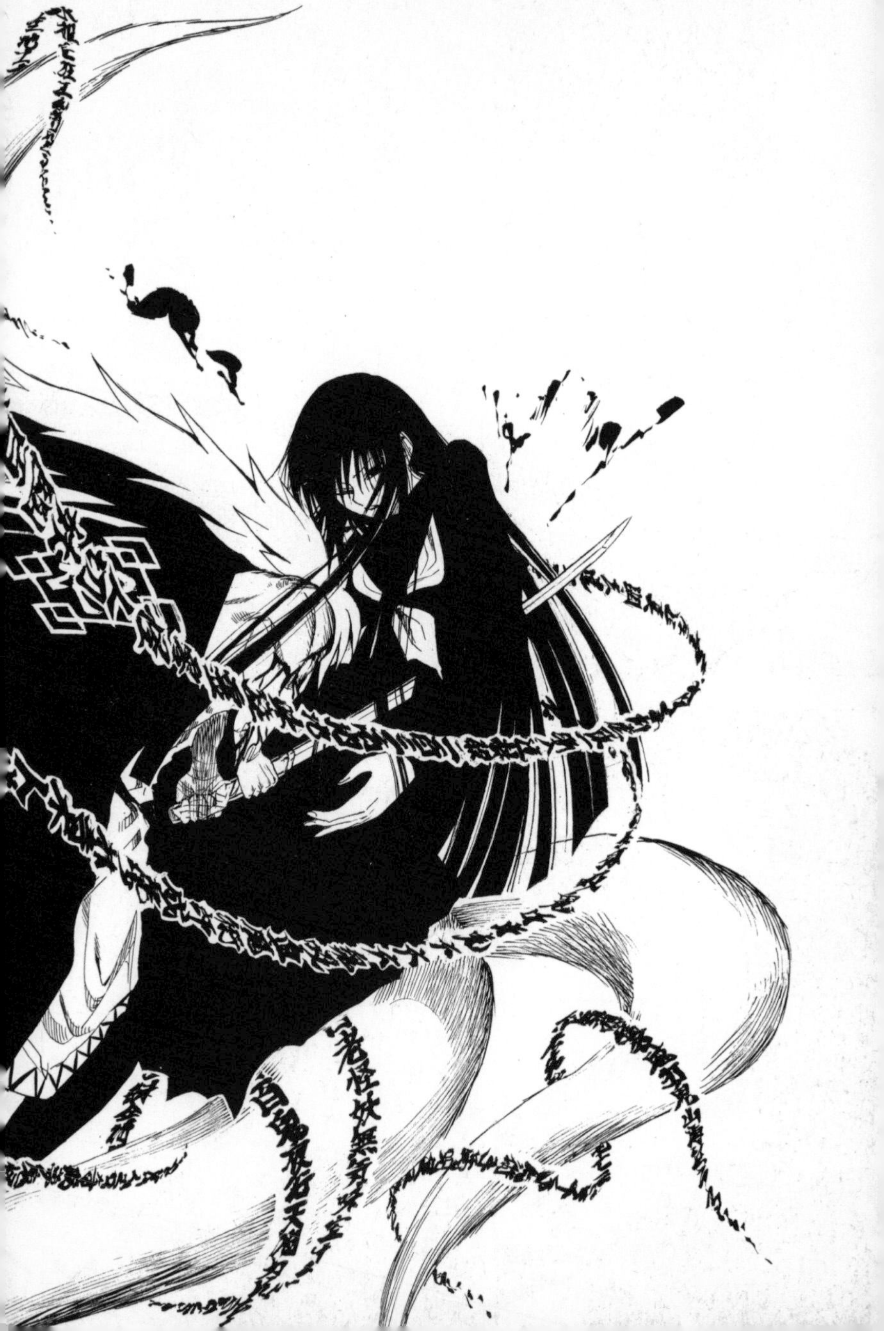

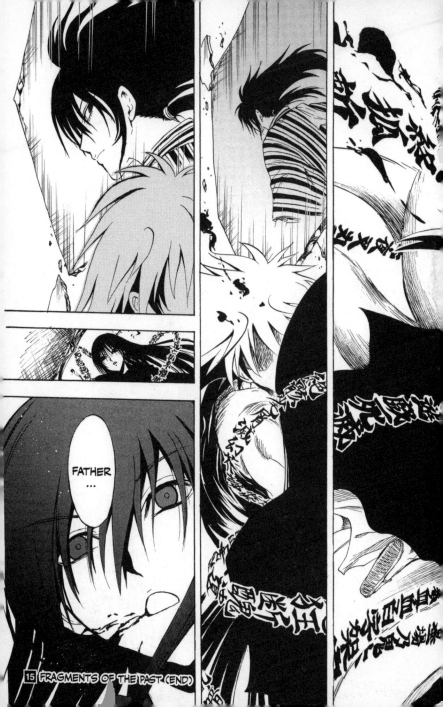

FATHER
...

15 FRAGMENTS OF THE PAST (END)

NURA: RISE OF THE YOKAI CLAN

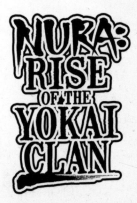

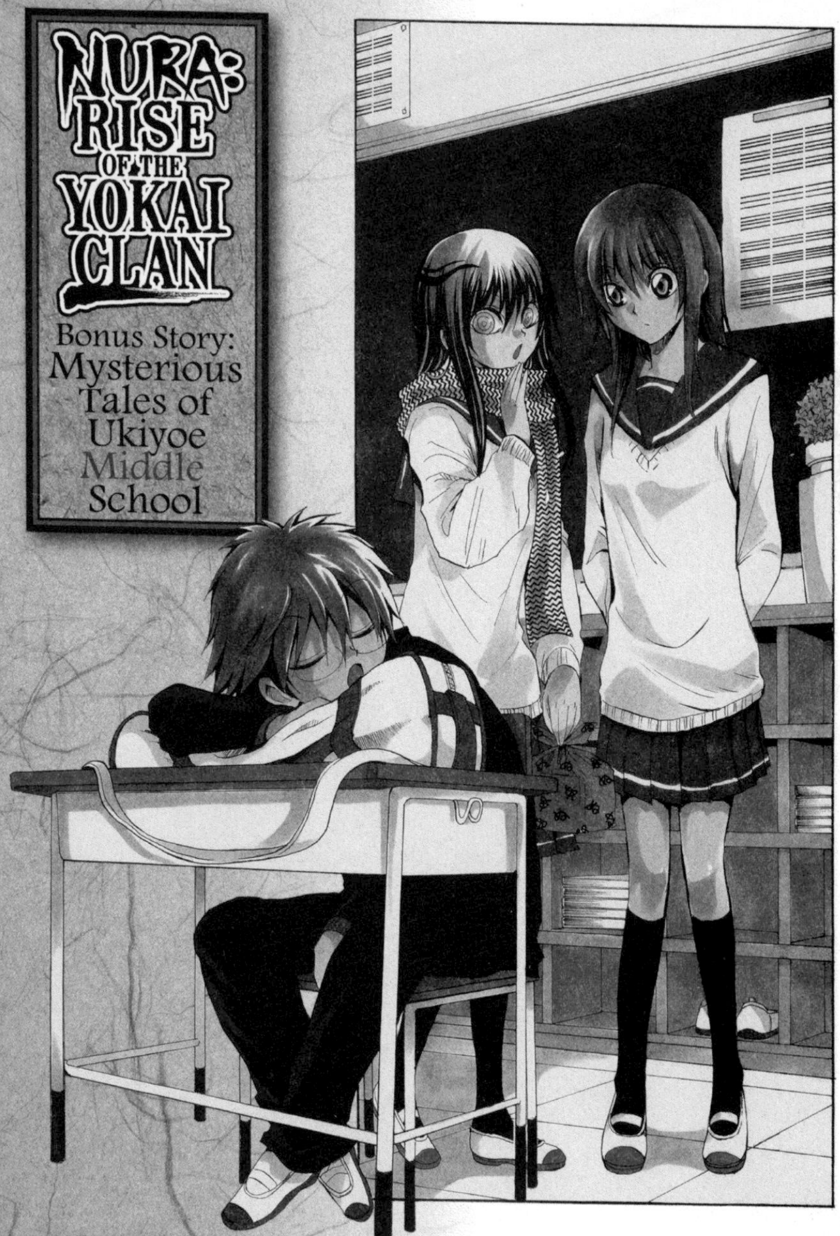
NURA: RISE OF THE YOKAI CLAN
Bonus Story: Mysterious Tales of Ukiyoe Middle School

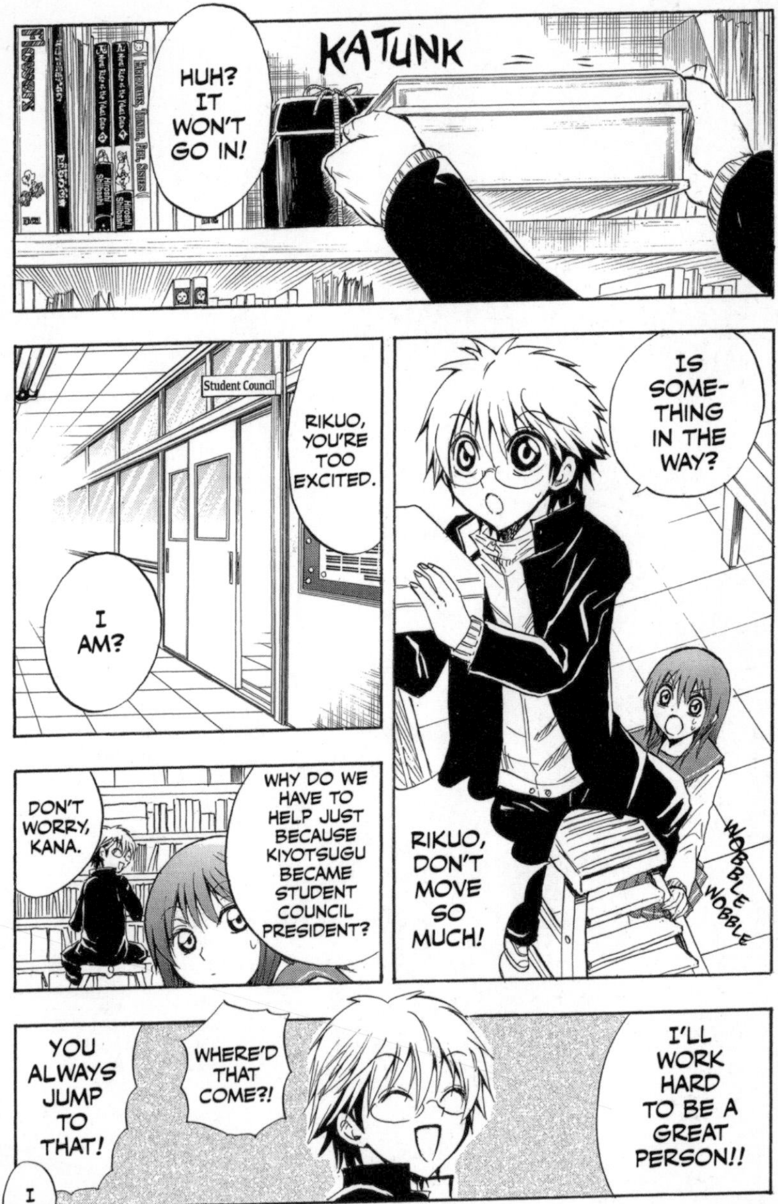
KATUNK
HUH? IT WON'T GO IN!
IS SOMETHING IN THE WAY?
RIKUO, DON'T MOVE SO MUCH!
WOBBLE WOBBLE
Student Council
RIKUO, YOU'RE TOO EXCITED.
I AM?
WHY DO WE HAVE TO HELP JUST BECAUSE KIYOTSUGU BECAME STUDENT COUNCIL PRESIDENT?
DON'T WORRY, KANA.
I'LL WORK HARD TO BE A GREAT PERSON!!
WHERE'D THAT COME?!
YOU ALWAYS JUMP TO THAT!
I DO?

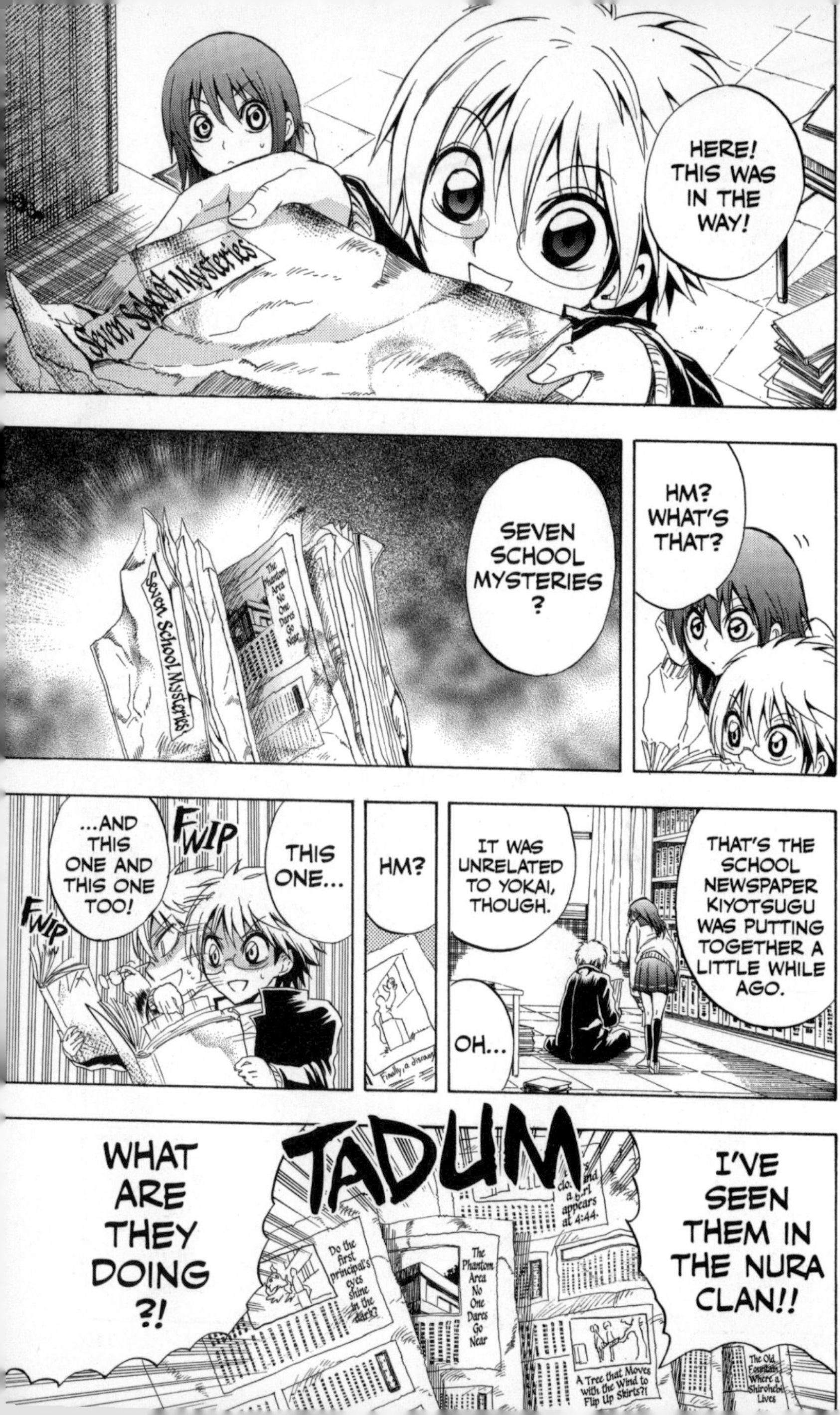
HERE! THIS WAS IN THE WAY!
Seven School Mysteries
HM? WHAT'S THAT?
SEVEN SCHOOL MYSTERIES ?
Seven School Mysteries
The Phantom Area No One Dares Go Near
THAT'S THE SCHOOL NEWSPAPER KIYOTSUGU WAS PUTTING TOGETHER A LITTLE WHILE AGO.
IT WAS UNRELATED TO YOKAI, THOUGH.
OH...
HM?
THIS ONE...
FWIP
...AND THIS ONE AND THIS ONE TOO!
FWIP
I'VE SEEN THEM IN THE NURA CLAN!!
TADUM
Do the first principal's eyes shine in the dark?
The Phantom Area No One Dares Go Near
A Tree that Moves with the Wind to Flip Up Skirts?!
WHAT ARE THEY DOING ?!

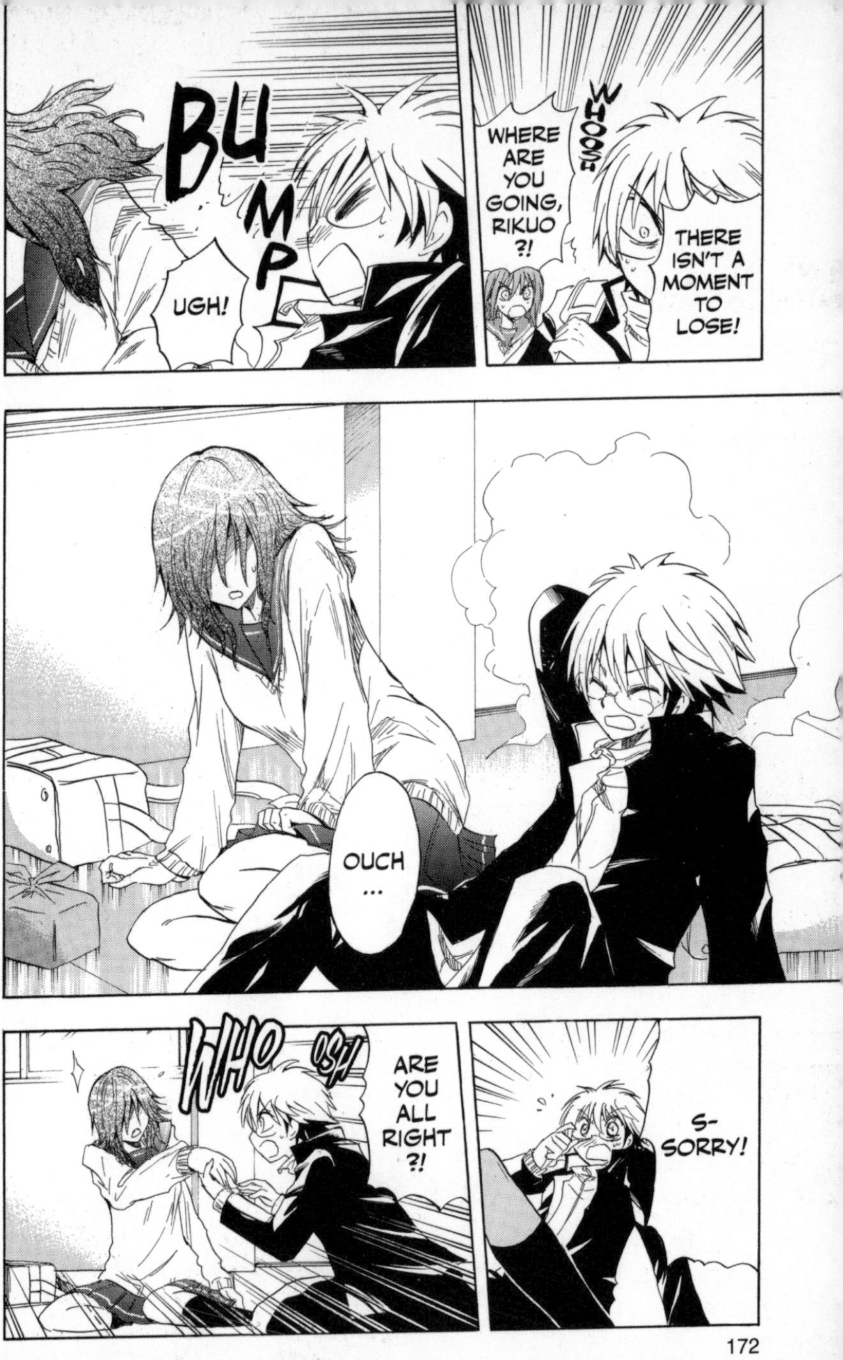
WHOOSH
WHERE ARE YOU GOING, RIKUO ?!
THERE ISN'T A MOMENT TO LOSE!
BUMP
UGH!
OUCH ...
S-SORRY!
WHOOSH
ARE YOU ALL RIGHT ?!

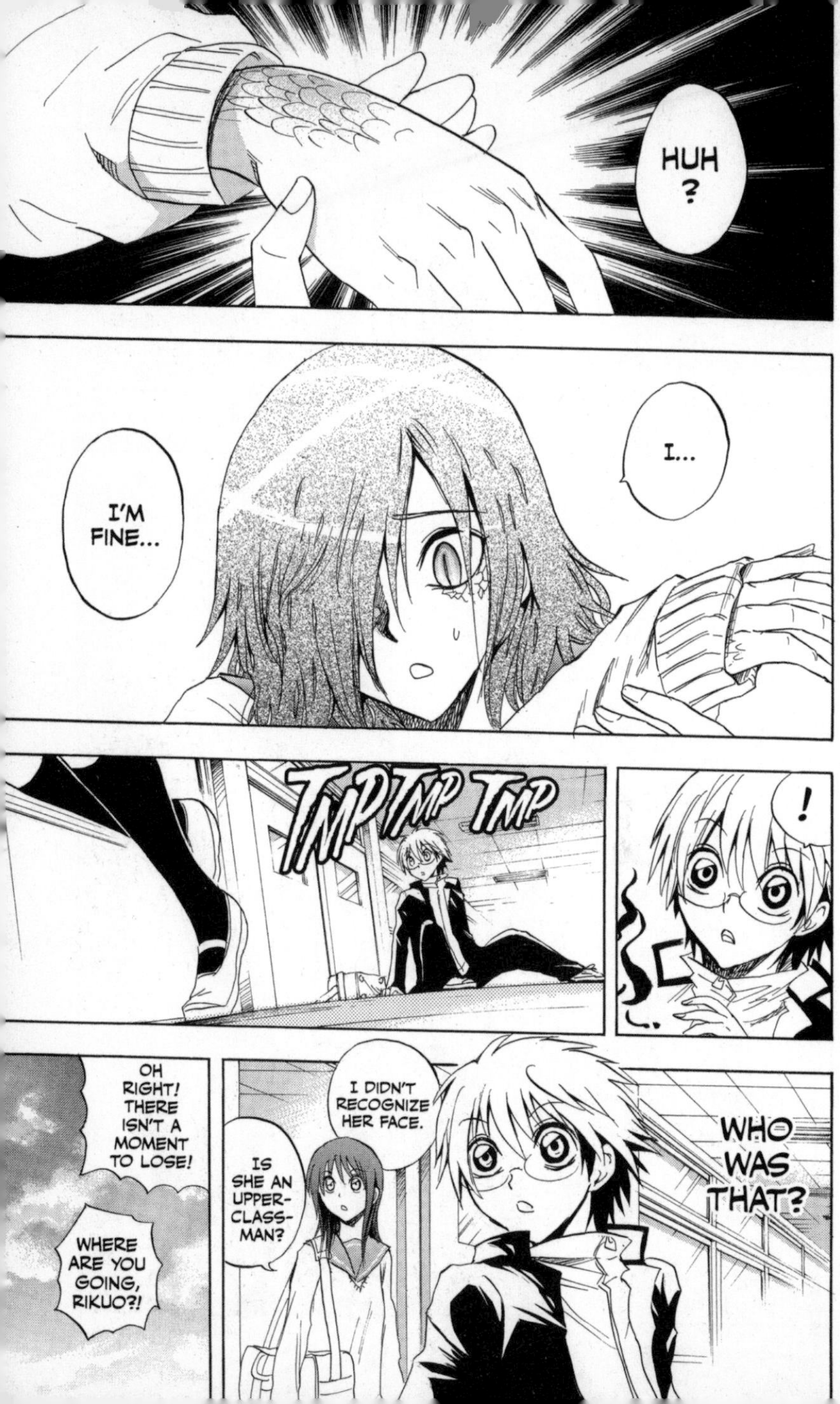
HUH?
I...
I'M FINE...
!
TMP TMP TMP
WHO WAS THAT?
I DIDN'T RECOGNIZE HER FACE.
IS SHE AN UPPER-CLASSMAN?
OH RIGHT! THERE ISN'T A MOMENT TO LOSE!
WHERE ARE YOU GOING, RIKUO?!

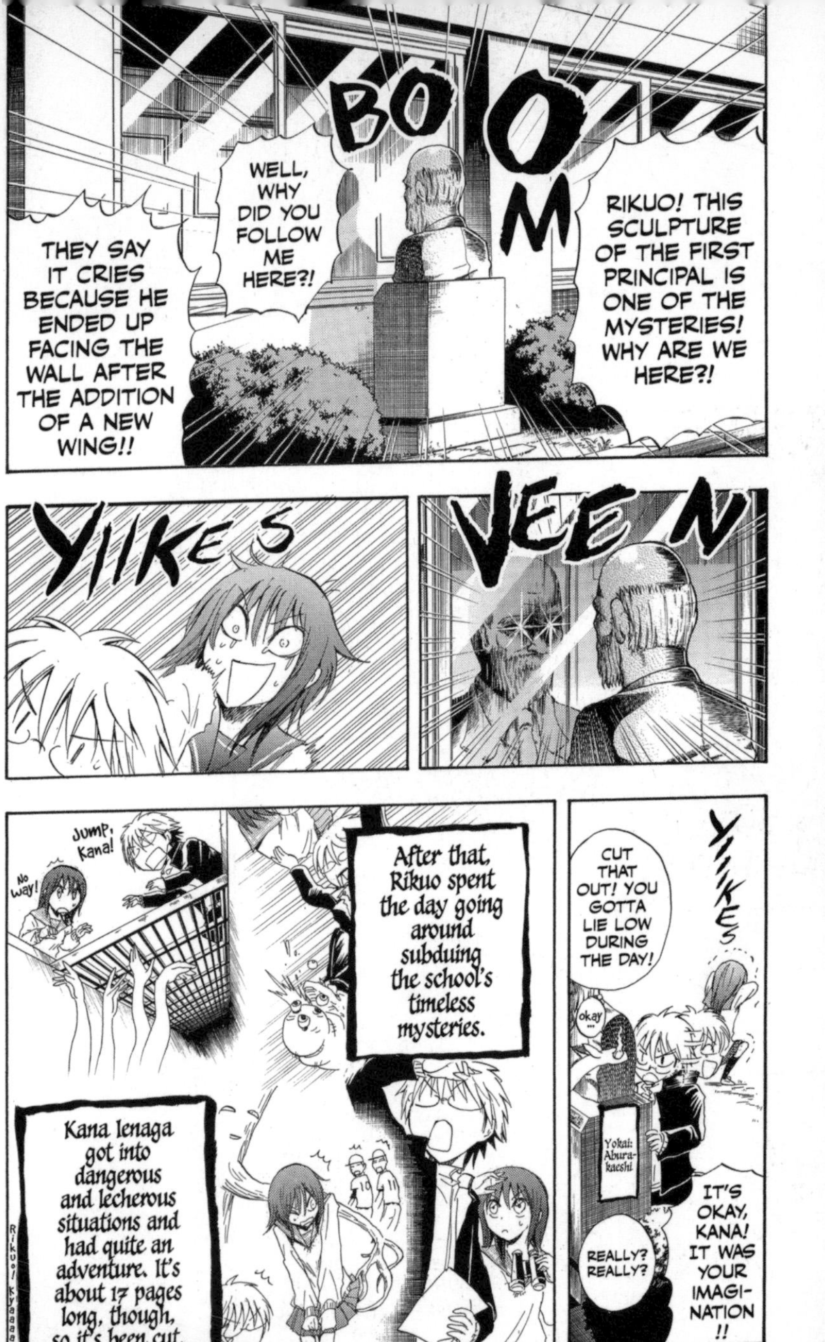
BOOM
RIKUO! THIS SCULPTURE OF THE FIRST PRINCIPAL IS ONE OF THE MYSTERIES! WHY ARE WE HERE?!
WELL, WHY DID YOU FOLLOW ME HERE?!
THEY SAY IT CRIES BECAUSE HE ENDED UP FACING THE WALL AFTER THE ADDITION OF A NEW WING!!
VEEN
YIIKES
YIIKES
CUT THAT OUT! YOU GOTTA LIE LOW DURING THE DAY!
okay...
Yokai: Abura-kaeshi
IT'S OKAY, KANA! IT WAS YOUR IMAGINATION!!
REALLY? REALLY?
After that, Rikuo spent the day going around subduing the school's timeless mysteries.
Jump, Kana!
No way!
Kana Ienaga got into dangerous and lecherous situations and had quite an adventure. It's about 17 pages long, though, so it's been cut.
Rikuo! Kyaaaaah

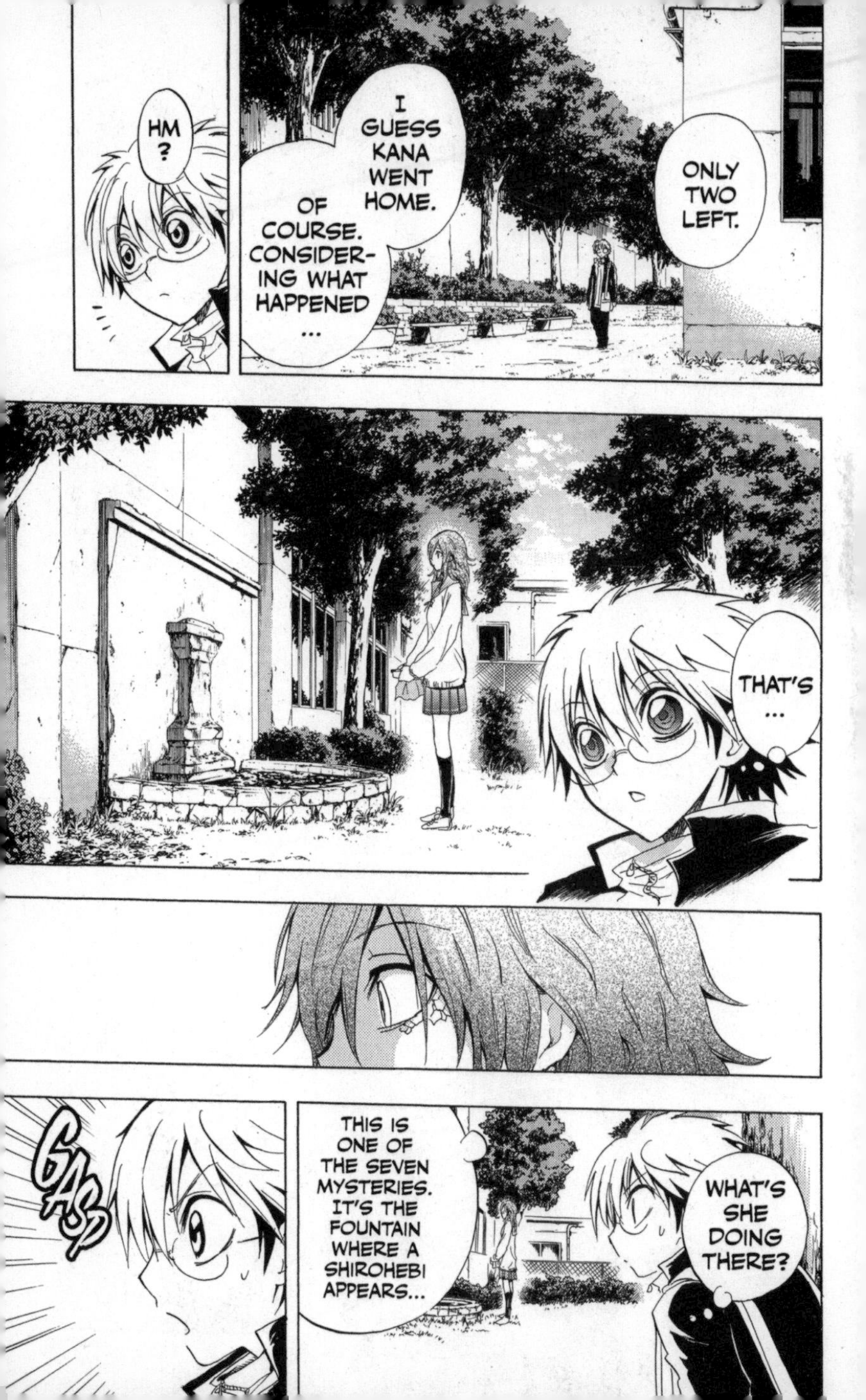
ONLY TWO LEFT.
I GUESS KANA WENT HOME.
OF COURSE. CONSIDERING WHAT HAPPENED ...
HM ?
THAT'S ...
WHAT'S SHE DOING THERE?
THIS IS ONE OF THE SEVEN MYSTERIES. IT'S THE FOUNTAIN WHERE A SHIROHEBI APPEARS...
GASP

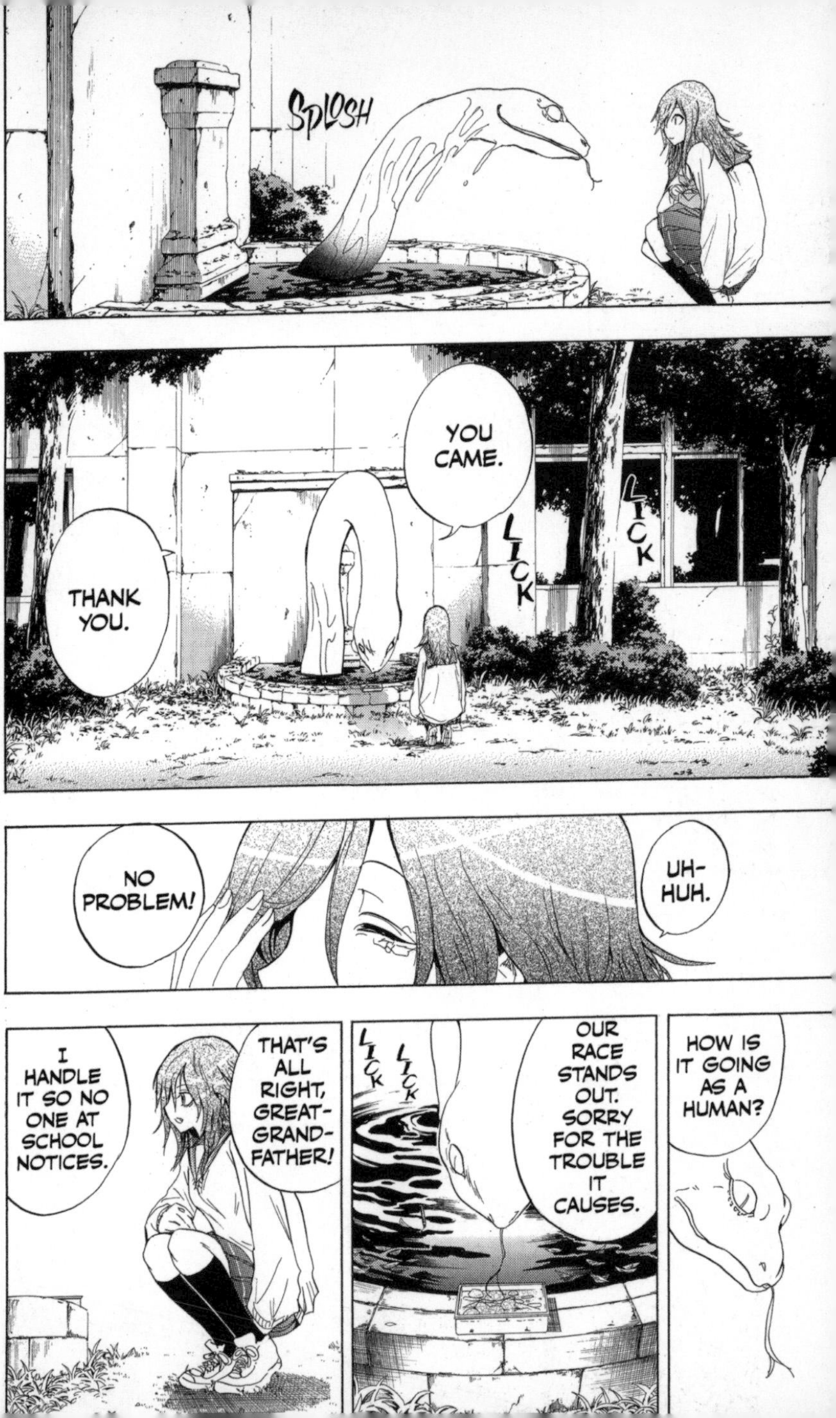
SPLOSH
LICK
LICK
YOU CAME.
THANK YOU.
UH-HUH.
NO PROBLEM!
HOW IS IT GOING AS A HUMAN?
OUR RACE STANDS OUT. SORRY FOR THE TROUBLE IT CAUSES.
LICK
LICK
THAT'S ALL RIGHT, GREAT-GRANDFATHER!
I HANDLE IT SO NO ONE AT SCHOOL NOTICES.

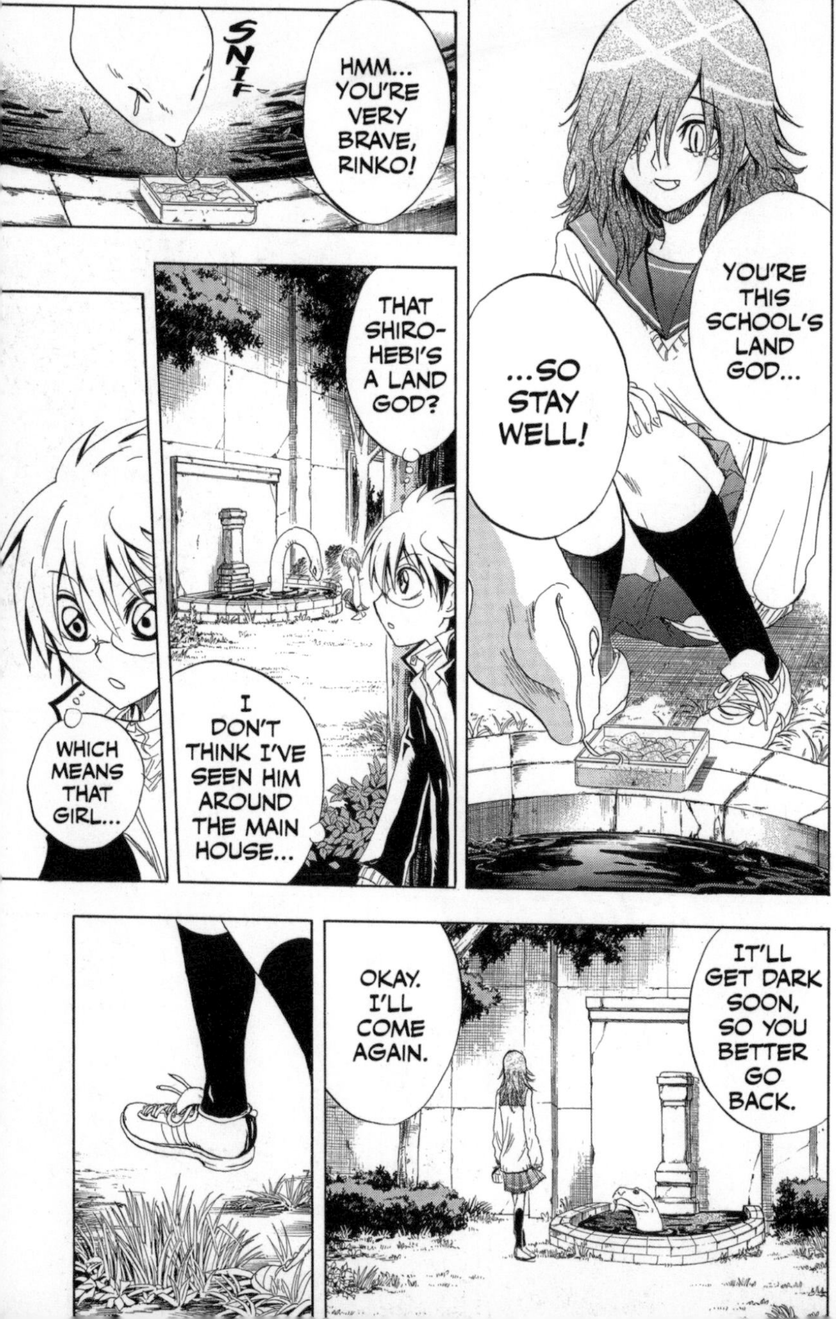
YOU'RE THIS SCHOOL'S LAND GOD...
...SO STAY WELL!
SNIF
HMM... YOU'RE VERY BRAVE, RINKO!
THAT SHIRO-HEBI'S A LAND GOD?
I DON'T THINK I'VE SEEN HIM AROUND THE MAIN HOUSE...
WHICH MEANS THAT GIRL...
IT'LL GET DARK SOON, SO YOU BETTER GO BACK.
OKAY. I'LL COME AGAIN.

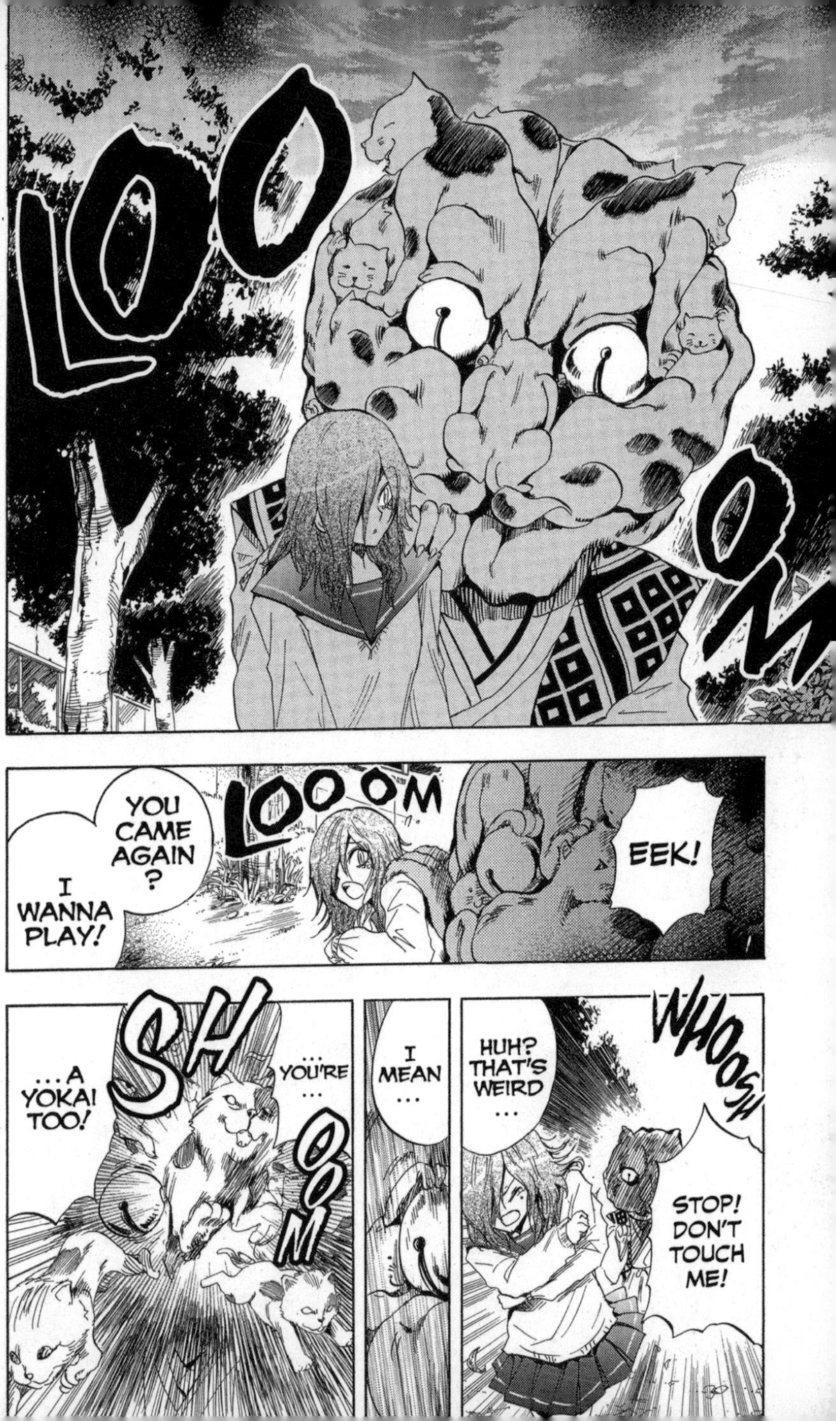
LOO
OM
EEK!
LOOOM
YOU CAME AGAIN?
I WANNA PLAY!
WHOOOSH
HUH? THAT'S WEIRD...
STOP! DON'T TOUCH ME!
I MEAN...
SHOOOM
...YOU'RE...
...A YOKAI TOO!

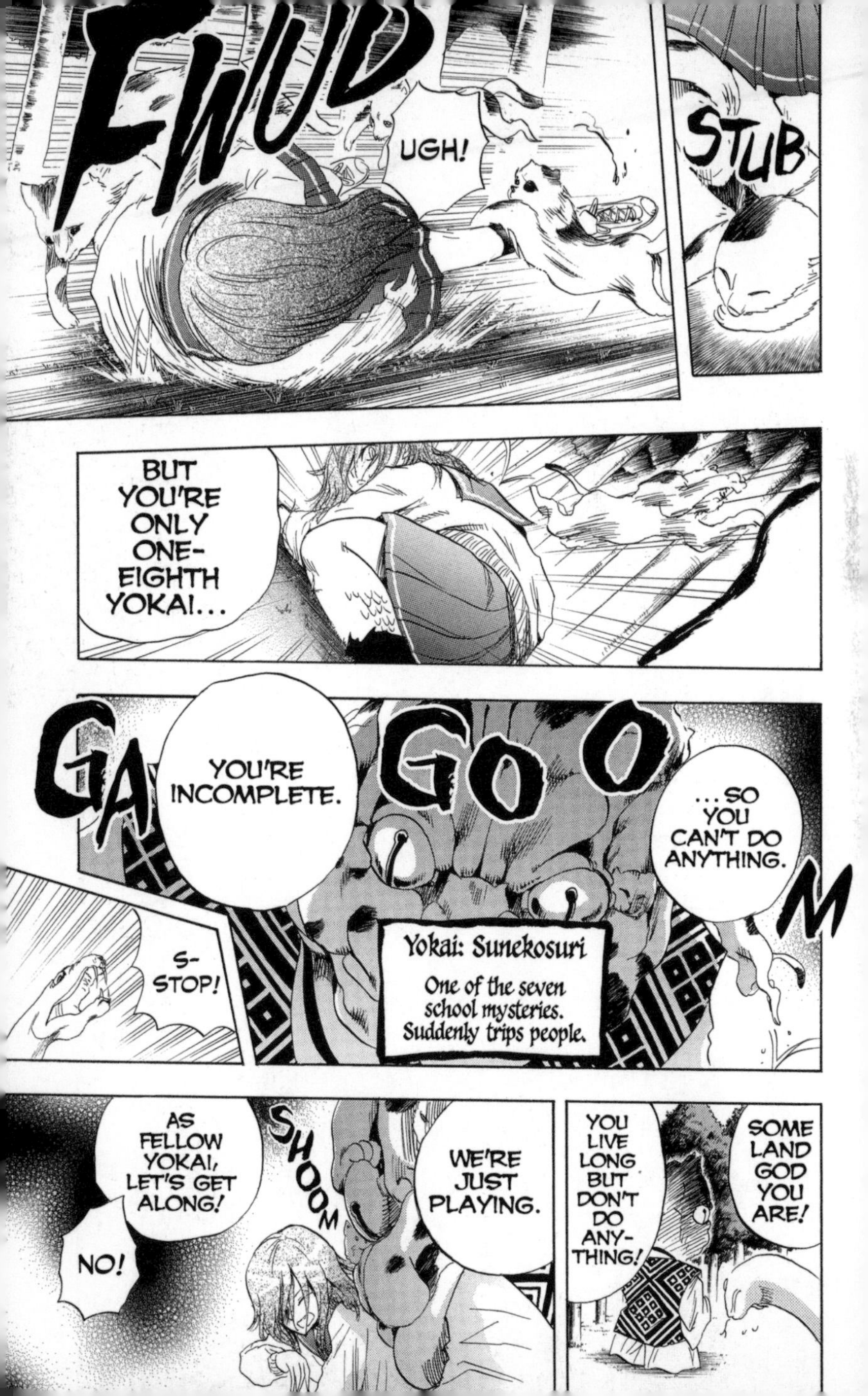
STUB
FWUD
UGH!
BUT YOU'RE ONLY ONE-EIGHTH YOKAI...
GA GO O M
YOU'RE INCOMPLETE.
...SO YOU CAN'T DO ANYTHING.
Yokai: Sunekosuri
One of the seven school mysteries. Suddenly trips people.
S-STOP!
SOME LAND GOD YOU ARE!
YOU LIVE LONG BUT DON'T DO ANY-THING!
WE'RE JUST PLAYING.
SHOOOM
AS FELLOW YOKAI, LET'S GET ALONG!
NO!

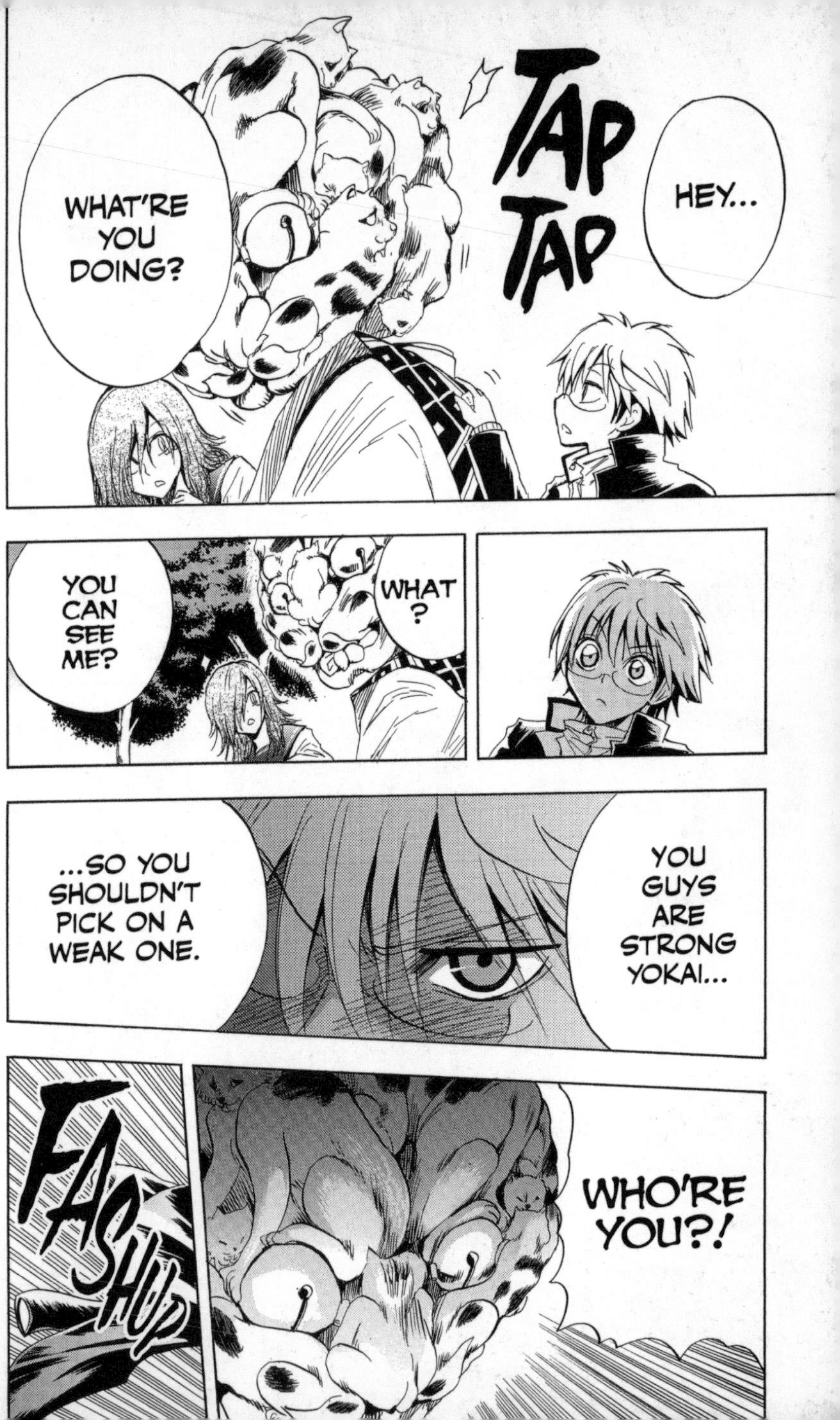
TAP TAP
HEY...
WHAT'RE YOU DOING?
WHAT?
YOU CAN SEE ME?
YOU GUYS ARE STRONG YOKAI...
...SO YOU SHOULDN'T PICK ON A WEAK ONE.
WHO'RE YOU?!
FASHUP

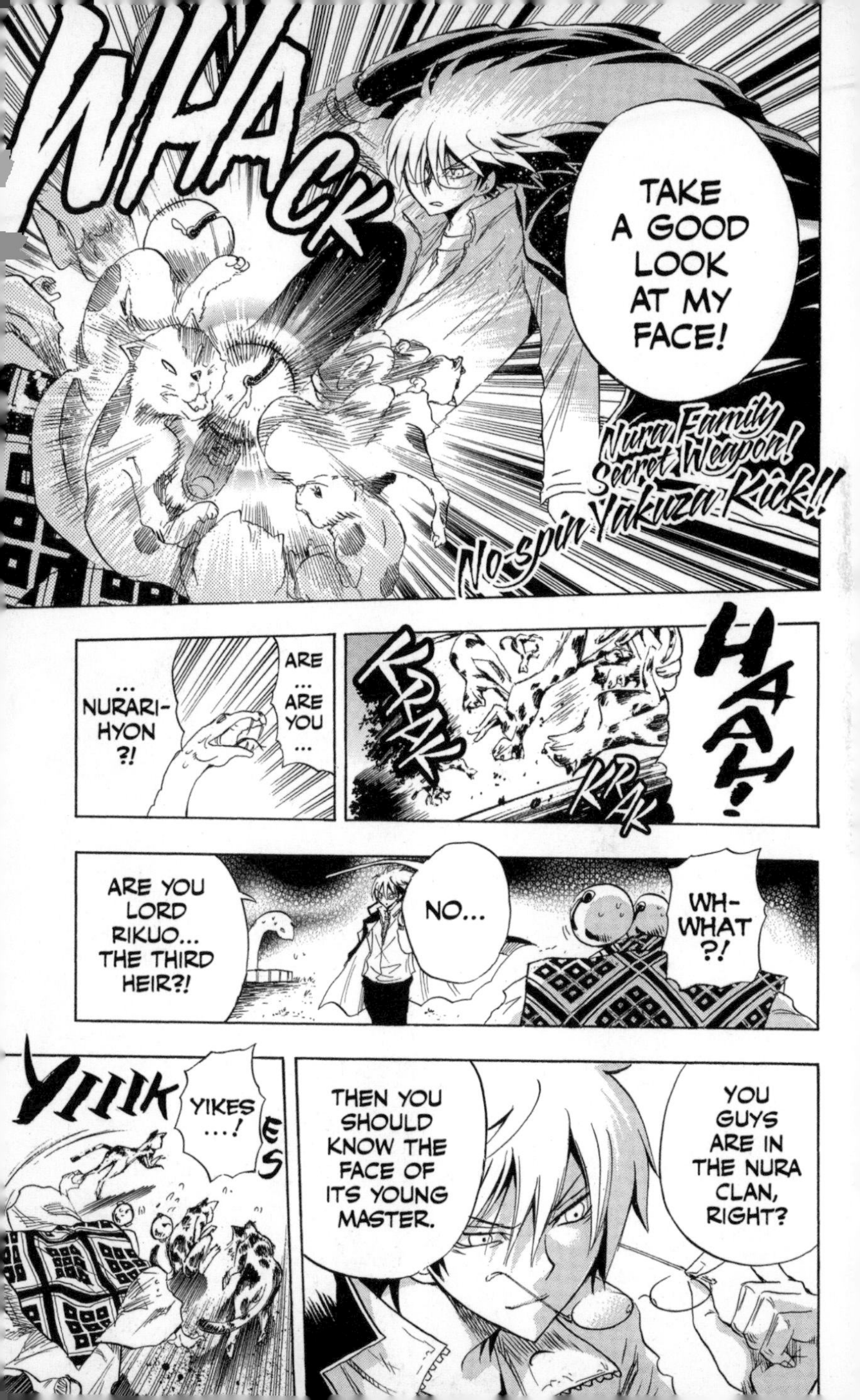
WHACK
TAKE A GOOD LOOK AT MY FACE!
Nura Family Secret Weapon! No-spin Yakuza Kick!!
HAAH!
KRAK KRAK
ARE ... ARE YOU ...
... NURARI-HYON ?!
WH-WHAT ?!
NO...
ARE YOU LORD RIKUO... THE THIRD HEIR?!
YOU GUYS ARE IN THE NURA CLAN, RIGHT?
THEN YOU SHOULD KNOW THE FACE OF ITS YOUNG MASTER.
YIIIKES
YIKES ...!

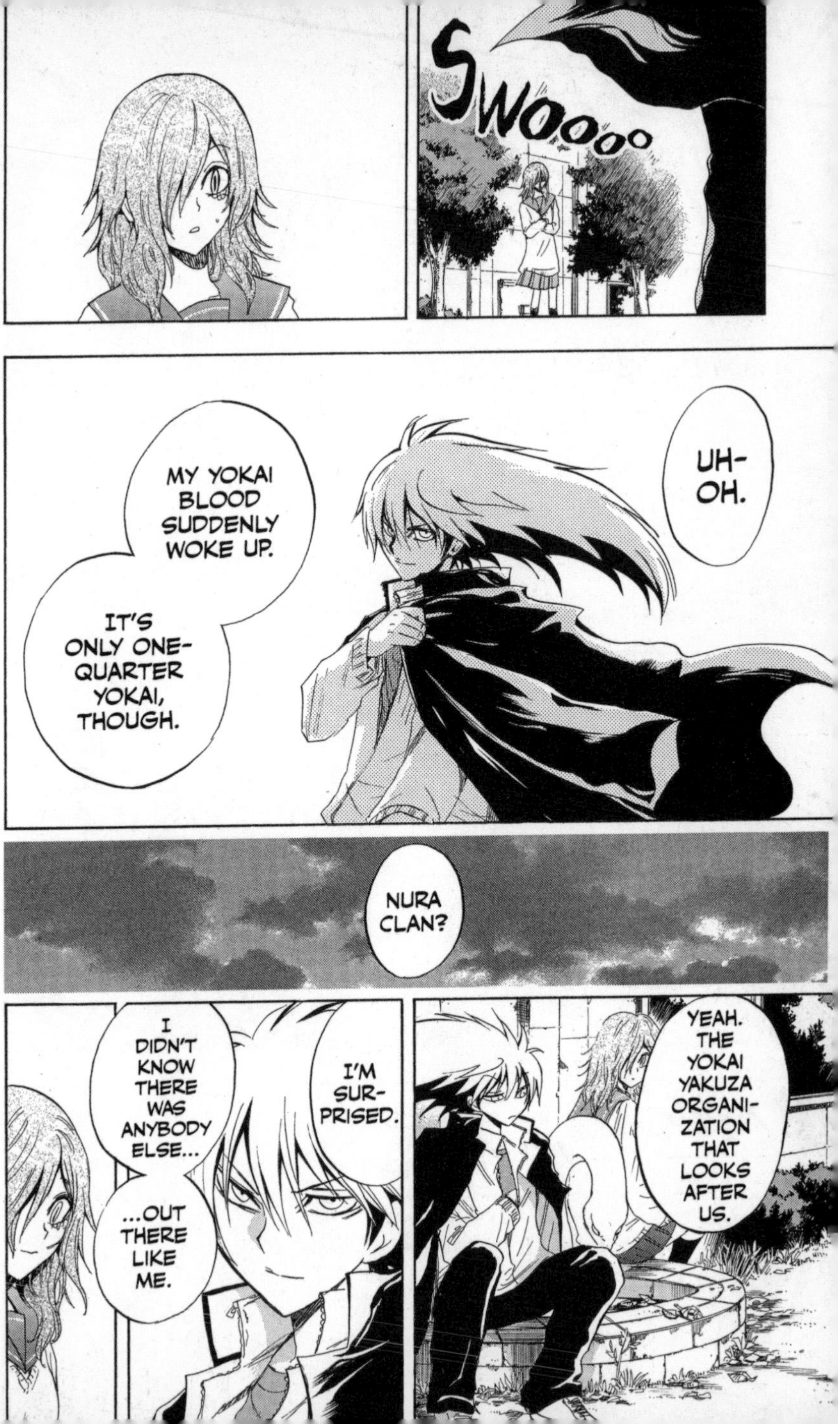
SWOOOO
UH-OH.
MY YOKAI BLOOD SUDDENLY WOKE UP.
IT'S ONLY ONE-QUARTER YOKAI, THOUGH.
NURA CLAN?
YEAH. THE YOKAI YAKUZA ORGANIZATION THAT LOOKS AFTER US.
I'M SURPRISED.
I DIDN'T KNOW THERE WAS ANYBODY ELSE...
...OUT THERE LIKE ME.

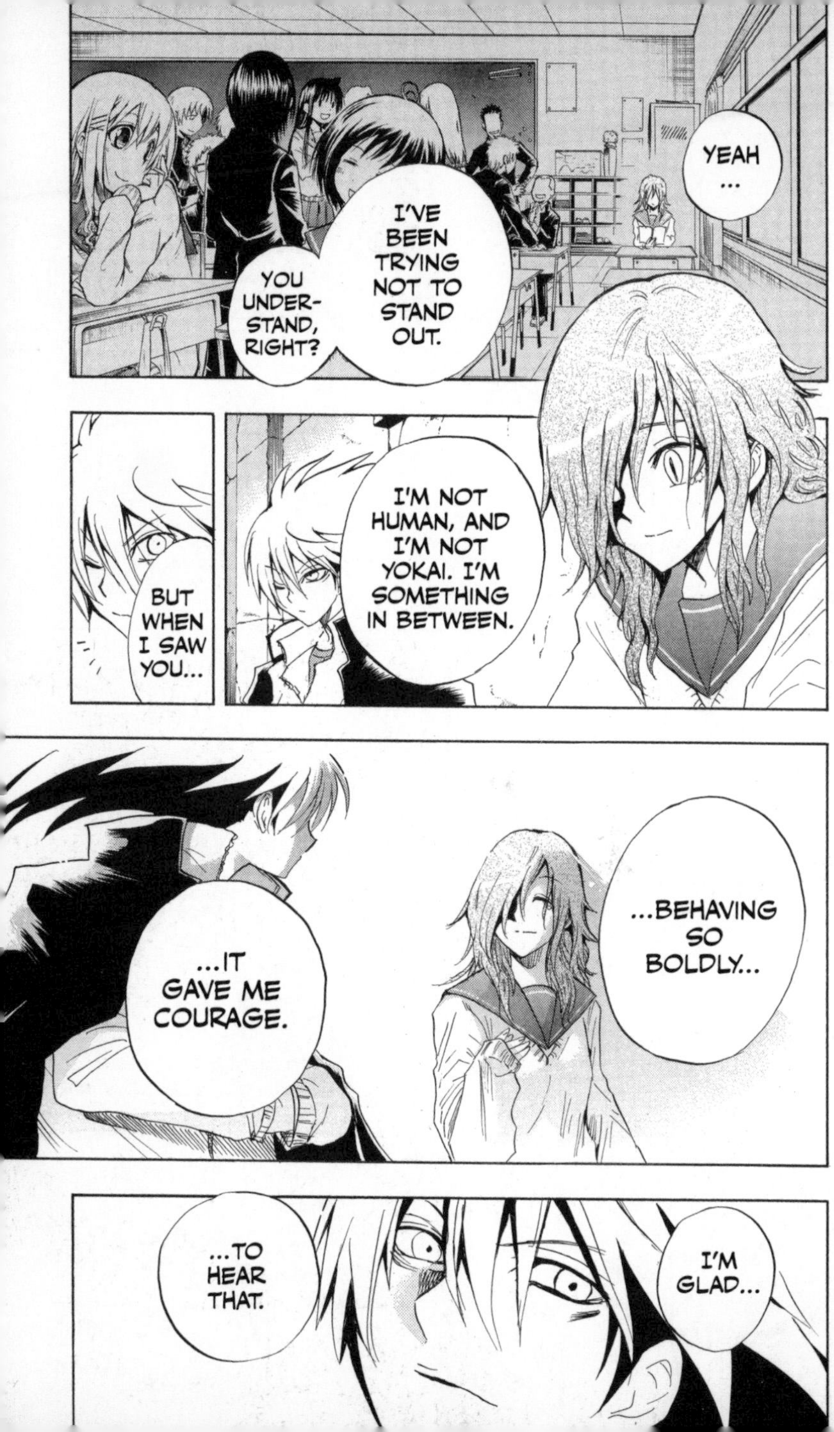
YEAH ...
I'VE BEEN TRYING NOT TO STAND OUT.
YOU UNDER-STAND, RIGHT?
I'M NOT HUMAN, AND I'M NOT YOKAI. I'M SOMETHING IN BETWEEN.
BUT WHEN I SAW YOU...
...BEHAVING SO BOLDLY...
...IT GAVE ME COURAGE.
I'M GLAD...
...TO HEAR THAT.

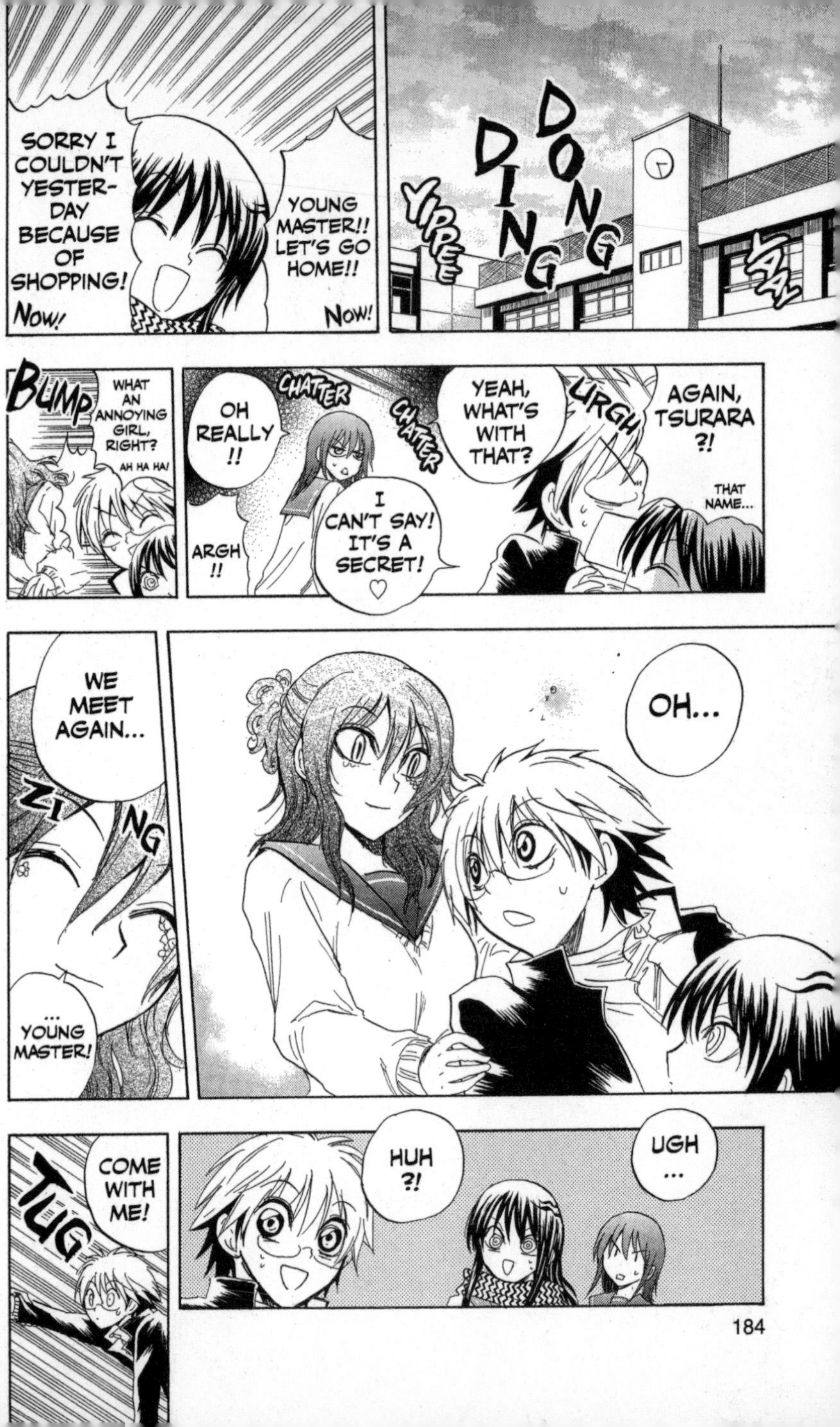
DING DONG
YIPPEE
YAY
YOUNG MASTER!! LET'S GO HOME!!
NOW!
SORRY I COULDN'T YESTER-DAY BECAUSE OF SHOPPING!
NOW!
AGAIN, TSURARA?!
THAT NAME...
URGH
YEAH, WHAT'S WITH THAT?
CHATTER
CHATTER
OH REALLY!!
I CAN'T SAY! IT'S A SECRET! ♡
ARGH!!
BUMP
WHAT AN ANNOYING GIRL, RIGHT?
AH HA HA!
OH...
WE MEET AGAIN...
ZING
...YOUNG MASTER!
UGH...
HUH?!
COME WITH ME!
TUG

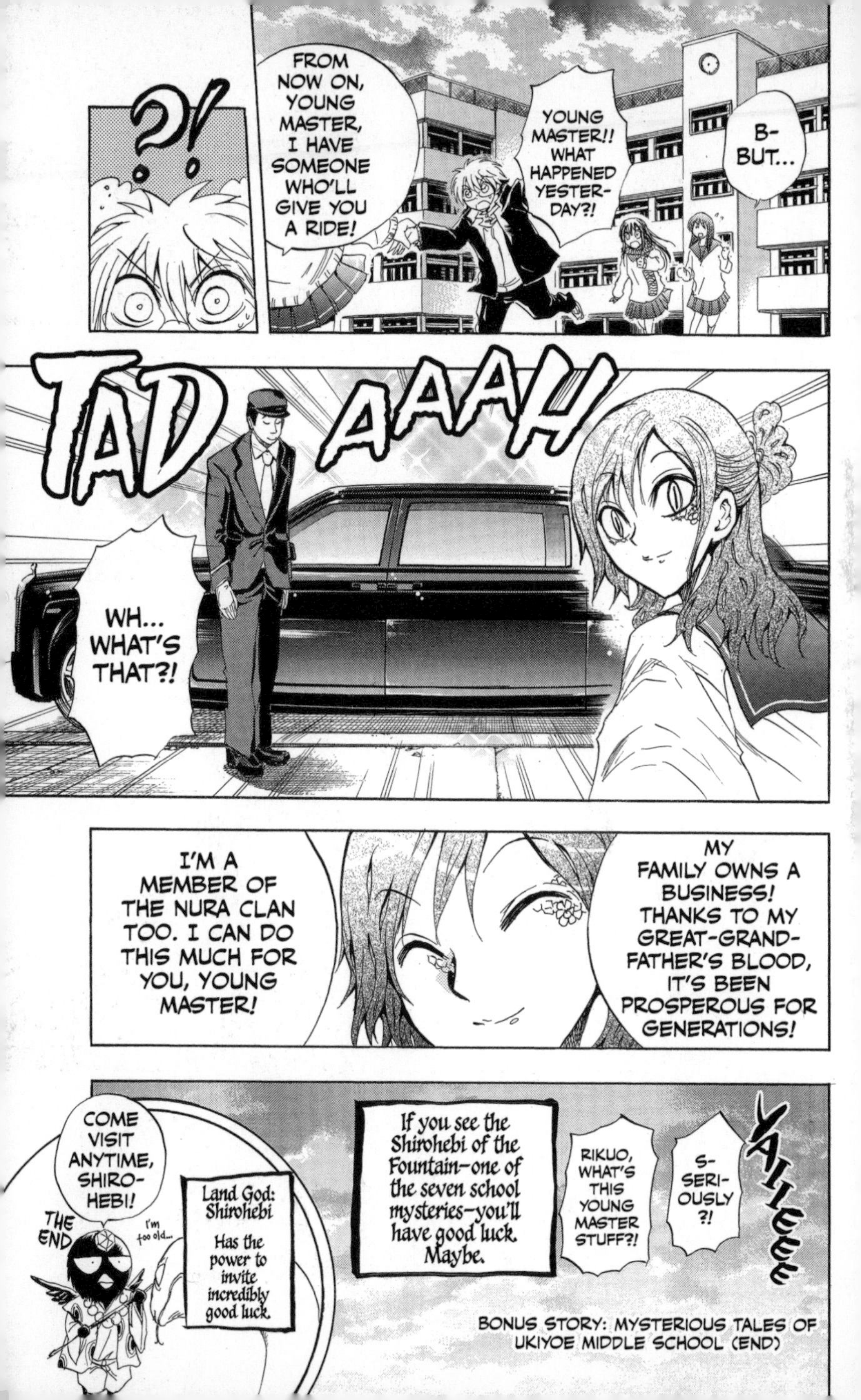
B-BUT...
YOUNG MASTER!! WHAT HAPPENED YESTER-DAY?!
FROM NOW ON, YOUNG MASTER, I HAVE SOMEONE WHO'LL GIVE YOU A RIDE!
?!
TADAAAH
WH... WHAT'S THAT?!
MY FAMILY OWNS A BUSINESS! THANKS TO MY GREAT-GRAND-FATHER'S BLOOD, IT'S BEEN PROSPEROUS FOR GENERATIONS!
I'M A MEMBER OF THE NURA CLAN TOO. I CAN DO THIS MUCH FOR YOU, YOUNG MASTER!
YAIIEEE
S-SERI-OUSLY?!
RIKUO, WHAT'S THIS YOUNG MASTER STUFF?!
If you see the Shirohebi of the Fountain—one of the seven school mysteries—you'll have good luck. Maybe.
Land God: Shirohebi
Has the power to invite incredibly good luck.
COME VISIT ANYTIME, SHIRO-HEBI!
I'm too old...
THE END
BONUS STORY: MYSTERIOUS TALES OF UKIYOE MIDDLE SCHOOL (END)

BONUS STORY: RIKUO HAS THAT ONE DREAM AGAIN

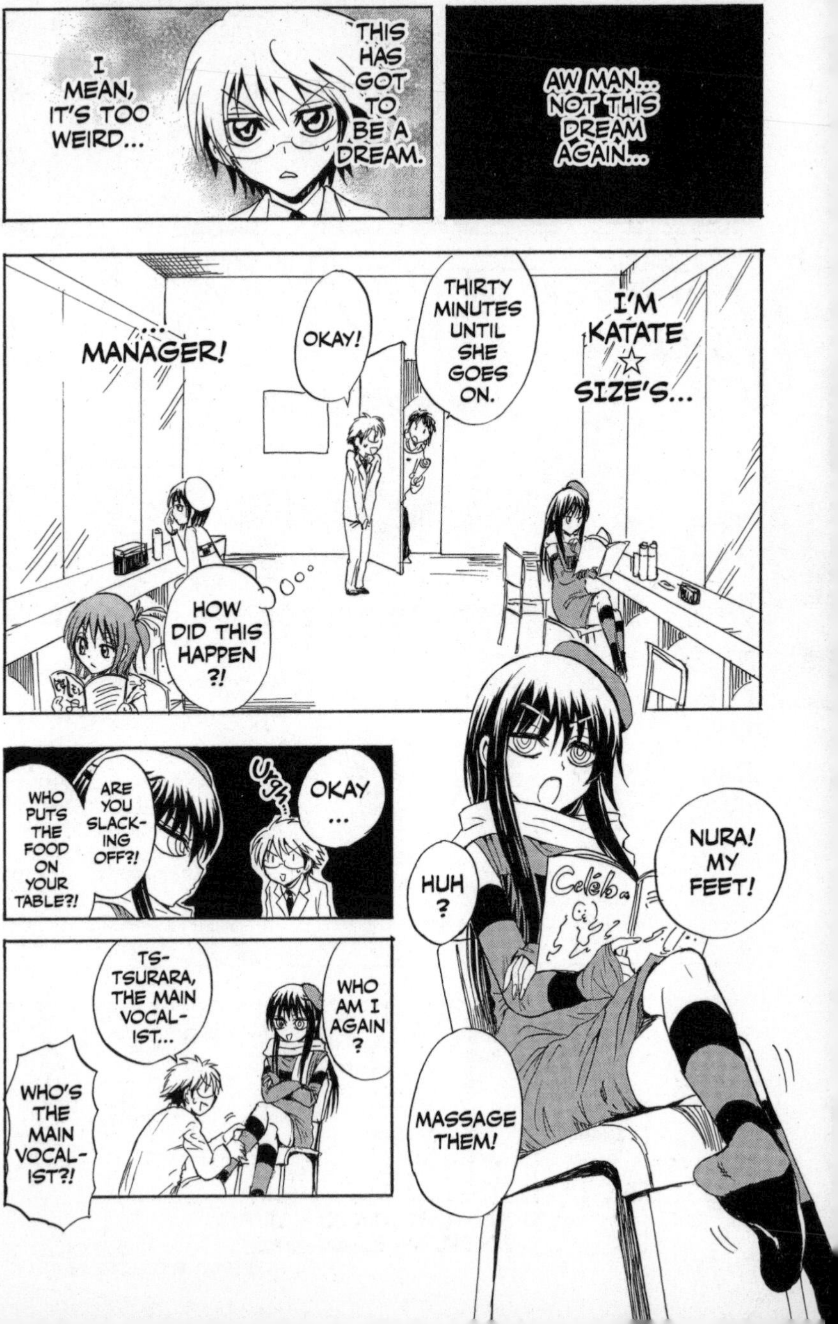
AW MAN... NOT THIS DREAM AGAIN...
THIS HAS GOT TO BE A DREAM.
I MEAN, IT'S TOO WEIRD...
I'M KATATE☆SIZE'S...
...MANAGER!
THIRTY MINUTES UNTIL SHE GOES ON.
OKAY!
HOW DID THIS HAPPEN?!
NURA! MY FEET!
HUH?
MASSAGE THEM!
OKAY...
Urgh...
ARE YOU SLACKING OFF?!
WHO PUTS THE FOOD ON YOUR TABLE?!
WHO AM I AGAIN?
TS-TSURARA, THE MAIN VOCALIST...
WHO'S THE MAIN VOCALIST?!

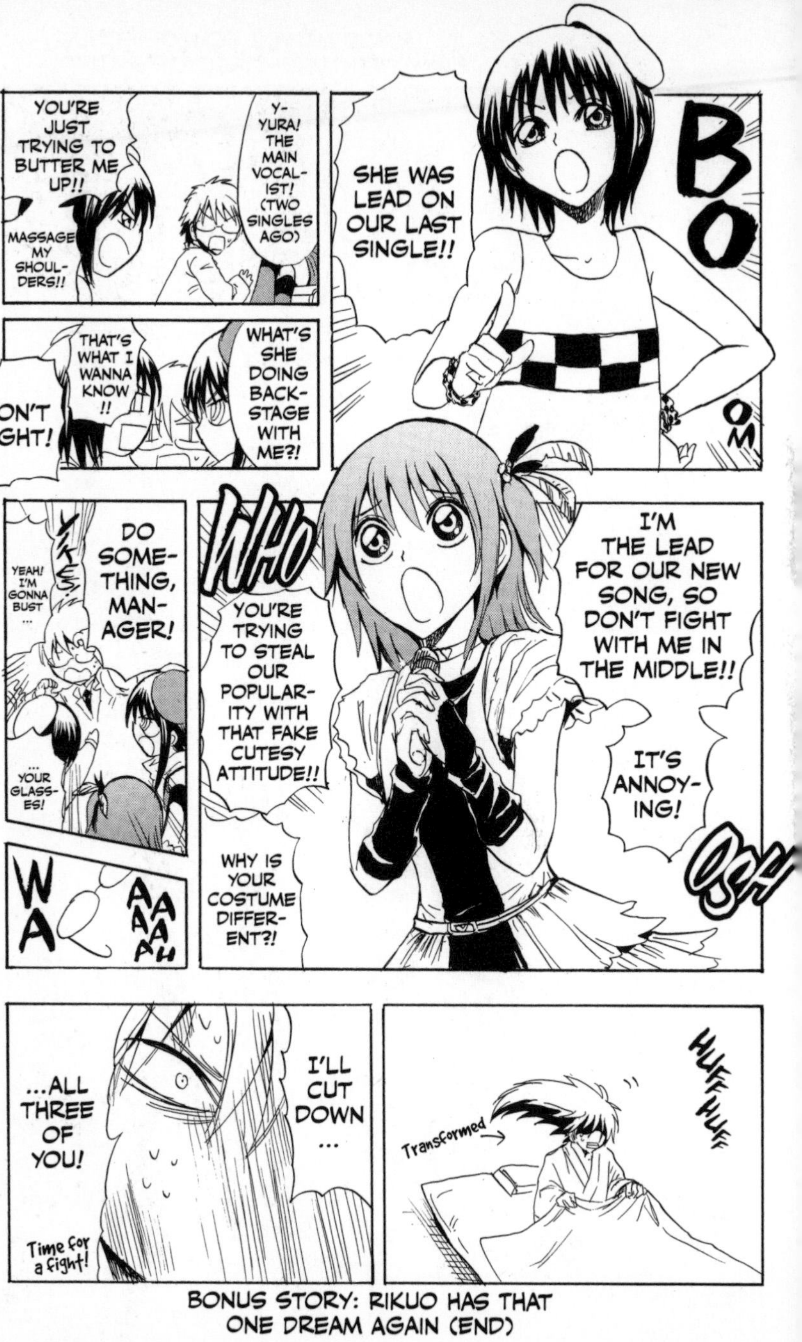
BOOM
SHE WAS LEAD ON OUR LAST SINGLE!!
Y-YURA! THE MAIN VOCALIST! (TWO SINGLES AGO)
YOU'RE JUST TRYING TO BUTTER ME UP!!
MASSAGE MY SHOULDERS!!
WHAT'S SHE DOING BACKSTAGE WITH ME?!
THAT'S WHAT I WANNA KNOW!!
DON'T FIGHT!
I'M THE LEAD FOR OUR NEW SONG, SO DON'T FIGHT WITH ME IN THE MIDDLE!!
WHOOSH
IT'S ANNOYING!
YOU'RE TRYING TO STEAL OUR POPULARITY WITH THAT FAKE CUTESY ATTITUDE!!
WHY IS YOUR COSTUME DIFFERENT?!
DO SOMETHING, MANAGER!
YIKES!
YEAH! I'M GONNA BUST ...
... YOUR GLASSES!
WAAAAAAH
HUFF HUFF
Transformed
I'LL CUT DOWN ...
...ALL THREE OF YOU!
Time for a fight!

BONUS STORY: RIKUO HAS THAT ONE DREAM AGAIN (END)

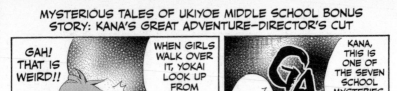

MYSTERIOUS TALES OF UKIYOE MIDDLE SCHOOL BONUS STORY: KANA'S GREAT ADVENTURE—DIRECTOR'S CUT

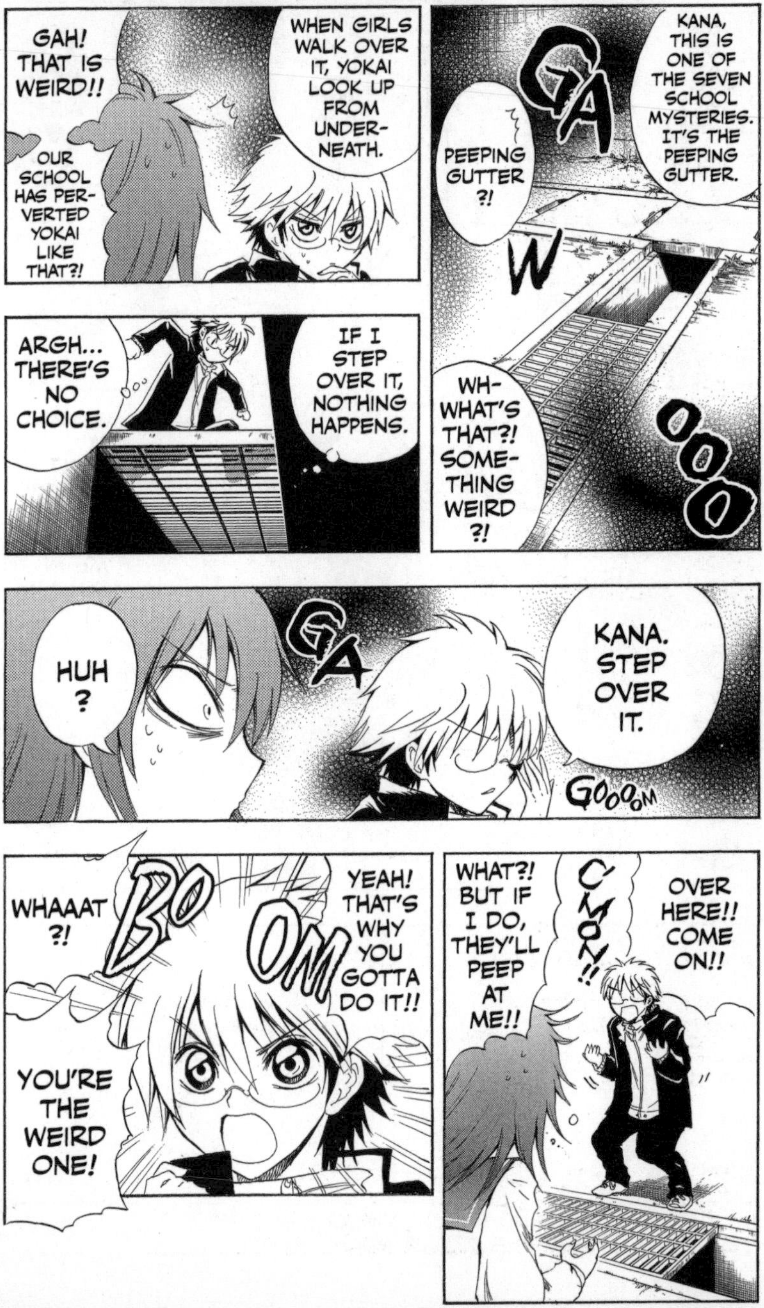
KANA, THIS IS ONE OF THE SEVEN SCHOOL MYSTERIES. IT'S THE PEEPING GUTTER.
GAW
PEEPING GUTTER ?!
OOOO
WH-WHAT'S THAT?! SOME-THING WEIRD ?!
WHEN GIRLS WALK OVER IT, YOKAI LOOK UP FROM UNDER-NEATH.
GAH! THAT IS WEIRD!!
OUR SCHOOL HAS PER-VERTED YOKAI LIKE THAT?!
IF I STEP OVER IT, NOTHING HAPPENS.
ARGH... THERE'S NO CHOICE.
KANA. STEP OVER IT.
GA
HUH ?
GOOOOM
OVER HERE!! COME ON!!
C'MON!!
WHAT?! BUT IF I DO, THEY'LL PEEP AT ME!!
YEAH! THAT'S WHY YOU GOTTA DO IT!!
BOOM
WHAAAT ?!
YOU'RE THE WEIRD ONE!

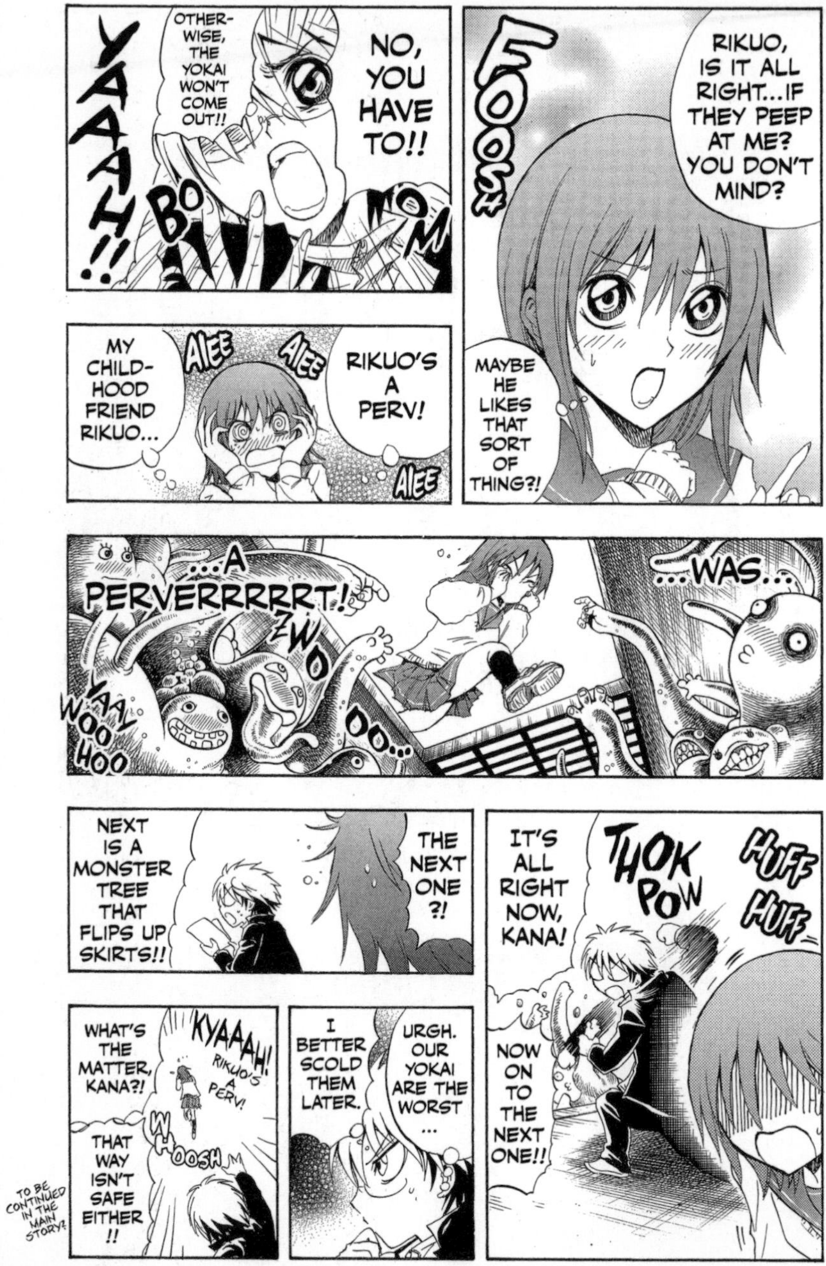
FOOOSH
RIKUO, IS IT ALL RIGHT...IF THEY PEEP AT ME? YOU DON'T MIND?
MAYBE HE LIKES THAT SORT OF THING?!
NO, YOU HAVE TO!!
OTHER-WISE, THE YOKAI WON'T COME OUT!!
BOOM
YAAAH!!
RIKUO'S A PERV!
AIEE
AIEE
AIEE
MY CHILD-HOOD FRIEND RIKUO...
...WAS...
...A PERVERRRRRT!
ZWOOO...
YAAY WOO HOO
THOK POW
HUFF HUFF
IT'S ALL RIGHT NOW, KANA!
NOW ON TO THE NEXT ONE!!
THE NEXT ONE?!
NEXT IS A MONSTER TREE THAT FLIPS UP SKIRTS!!
URGH. OUR YOKAI ARE THE WORST...
I BETTER SCOLD THEM LATER.
KYAAAAH!
RIKUO'S A PERV!
WHAT'S THE MATTER, KANA?!
WHOOSH
THAT WAY ISN'T SAFE EITHER!!
TO BE CONTINUED IN THE MAIN STORY?!

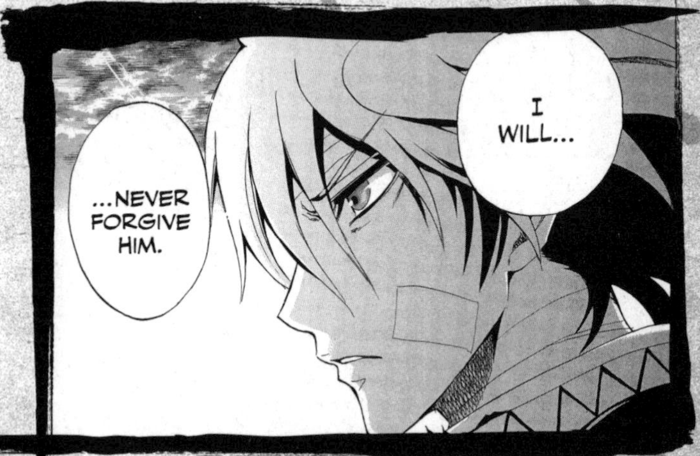
I WILL...
...NEVER FORGIVE HIM.

IN THE NEXT VOLUME...

RIKUO'S DECLARATION

Rikuo takes action to cement himself as the Third Heir to the Nura clan as Nurarihyon prepares to officially hand the mantle of power over to him. The political move will change the landscape of the yokai power structure and could grant Rikuo's friends higher positions than they ever dreamed! But new responsibility brings new problems and breeds new discontent.

AVAILABLE AUGUST 2013!

YOU'RE READING THE WRONG WAY!

Nura: Rise of the Yokai Clan reads from right to left, starting in the upper-right corner. Japanese is read from right to left, meaning that action, sound effects, and word-balloon order are completely reversed from English order.

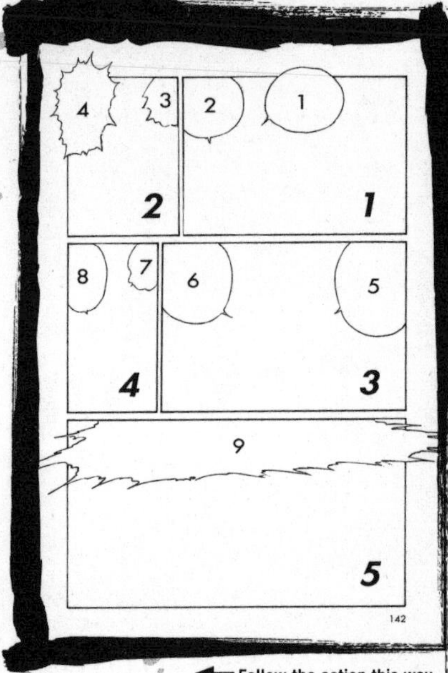

← Follow the action this way.

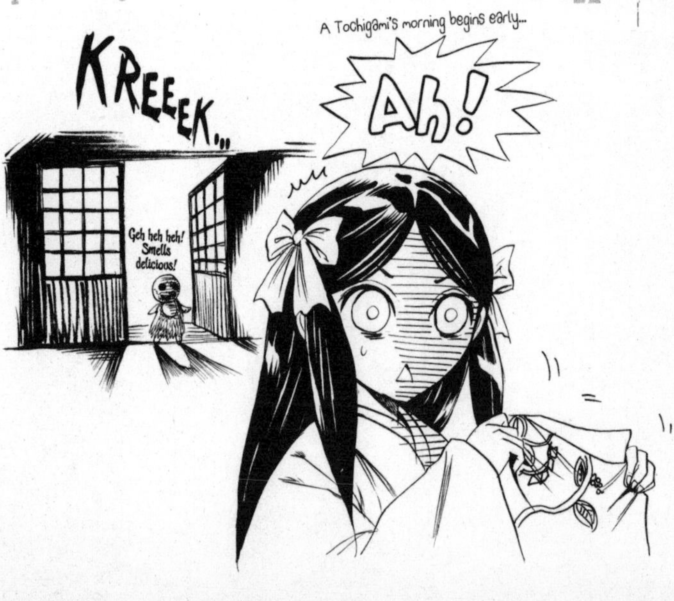
A Tochigami's morning begins early...
Ah!
KREEEK...
Geh heh heh! Smells delicious!